HALVING IT ALL

How Equally Shared Parenting Works

Francine M. Deutsch

Harvard University Press

Cambridge, Massachusetts

London, England

1999

Library of Congress Cataloging-in-Publication Data

Deutsch, Francine, 1948–
Halving it all : how equally shared parenting works / Francine M. Deutsch.
p.   cm.
Includes bibliographical references and index.
ISBN 0-674-36800-2 (alk. paper)
1. Parenting.   2. Sex role.   3. Dual-career families.   4. Child rearing.   I. Title.
HQ755.8.D489   1999
649′.1—dc21   98-30738

To the memory of my father

Samuel Deutsch

who did not share parenting equally,
but was a wonderful father all the same

Contents

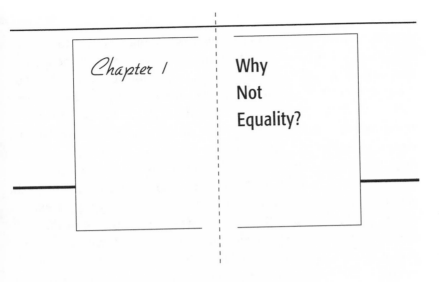

Chapter 1

Why
Not
Equality?

Steve and Beth stood in their kitchen discussing how they were going to manage the afternoon care of their four-year-old. Steve is a Spanish teacher at a community college; Beth is the executive director for the Council on Aging. Like most American dual-earner families today, they lead full and busy lives. But this family differs dramatically from the norm in one important sense. Steve and Beth share parenting equally. Their lives defy what has come to be accepted as the standard scenario in most dual-earner households: the mother and father both work in the paid labor force, but the mother also works a "second shift" at home, a shift that is not shared fully by her husband. Steve and Beth are the exceptions.[1]

I heard their conversation only because I had arrived early for my interview with Steve as part of my study on equally shared parenting. Steve was planning to take their teenage daughter and a friend to a basketball game that afternoon, while Beth needed to go to a meeting for her job. After mutually detailing the intricacies of their afternoons, they arrived at a plan whereby Steve would pick up their four-year-old son, Sean, and deliver him to Beth, who would arrange for him to play with a coworker's child during the meeting. Perhaps my presence influenced them to be on their best behavior, but the conversation I heard couldn't have been faked. The fast-paced coordination and cooperation between the two of them smoothly led to a workable plan. As I watched them good-naturedly discussing how to work things out, it struck me that I was witnessing equality in the making.

As I listened to them go back and forth about who was to do what that afternoon, it was evident that Steve felt every bit as responsible as Beth. There wasn't even the slightest suggestion that caring for children, or even figuring out how to care for them, was solely her job.[2] Steve and Beth have shared a commitment to equal parenting ever since their first child was born. Beth didn't have to fight Steve to get him to share. In fact, they were so equal that when their daughter, Stephanie, was a baby, Beth says, laughing, she seemed to call out for each of them 50 percent of the time. Yet, even when couples don't fight about equality per se, there is a lot to negotiate in working out the details of everyday life. Beth humorously describes how in the early days of parenting they did everything together. Bedtimes were a two-parent affair. One of them would get Stephanie's pajamas, one would run the bath, both were involved in an hour-long ritual each night. Beth muses:

> It hit me that this is ridiculous, we're both using up an hour every night, both of us, two people, two adults, two on one, putting one kid to bed. It doesn't make any sense that we should both feel sort of involved in this. Neither one of us felt free to go read a book because that would be putting too much of a burden on the other one.[3]

So Beth suggested that they take turns. That way, without any guilt, each could have a bit of free time every other night. They worked out alternating responsibility by a process of trial and error. As Beth says: "That was something we learned by doing it wrong . . . It wasn't so much that we changed the proportion of how much he did or how much I did, but rather we realized we were both doing it and it didn't take two people." Turn-taking was an easy, readily agreed-upon solution to the inefficiency of doubling up on the bedtime routine. But other problems of modern family life are not so easy to solve.

Consider the dilemma they face when one of their children gets sick at school or daycare. Someone will have to leave work. With humor again, Beth describes what happens:

> Whoever gets the call, we have a quick conference to see who's got the most important appointments. Of course (suddenly), all our appointments become much more important. "(I've got a) really important meeting with five important people." "Well I've got one

with six important people." We manage. People understand. You may just cancel your appointments.

Just as in unequal couples, a conflict emerges when an unexpected illness interrupts workdays. Yet, in this family there is no assumption that the mother will be the one to leave work.[4] On any given occasion, Beth and Steve decide who goes by sparring over whose meeting is more important. Their infusion of humor in these discussions guarantees that even when there is conflict, it's resolved with good feeling. Their commitment to equality ensures that each is willing to cancel appointments, and overall, Beth reports, they "do it half and half."[5]

Equality in parenting is achieved in the details of everyday life. It derives from explicit mundane decisions like those I witnessed Beth and Steve making: decisions about who is going to pick the child up from daycare and who's going to take the day off from work when the baby suddenly comes down with the flu. But it also results from the ad hoc acts of parenting that occur every day as when a parent notices and wipes a child's runny nose, or steps in to mediate a dispute between siblings. It is these myriad details, some consciously negotiated, some fought over, some just unconsciously lived, that add up to equality or inequality between mothers and fathers. Steve and Beth make equality look easy. But we know from decades of research, and many of us from personal experience, that it isn't easy.

Over the past twenty-five years social scientists have been telling a grim story of inequality. Literally hundreds of studies have examined women's and men's roles at home.[6] Initially, when women started to flood into the paid workforce, some researchers assumed that roles at home would change dramatically. Women and men would become equal partners in marriage, sharing the responsibilities of both bread-winning and domestic labor.[7]

The bad news for proponents of equality started to emerge almost immediately. Although women were taking on paid employment in record numbers, their husbands weren't returning the favor. Changes at home were minimal or nonexistent. Studies of domestic life in the 1970s and 1980s showed that men whose wives worked outside the home didn't seem to be doing any more at home than men whose wives were still full-time homemakers.[8] A few studies did show that the *percentage* of men's contribution to domestic labor increased,[9] but closer examination often revealed that this was not because men were doing more, but because their wives were doing less.[10]

Even if the news from most households wasn't very good for those waiting to welcome an age of gender equality, perhaps at least some families were approaching participation in this new world of role-sharing. Researchers turned to studying the forces that caused variations among couples. A glut of studies, starting in the 1970s, attempted to identify the factors that were associated with an increase in men's participation in domestic labor. Using the findings of these studies, researchers argued that men did more of the work at home if their wives, compared to other women, earned relatively more of the family income[11] or worked more hours per week in the paid workforce,[12] or if they or their wives had relatively liberal ideas about gender.[13]

But doing more of the work doesn't mean doing an equal share. What most of these studies ignored was that even when these variables successfully accounted for variations among men in different households, they didn't come close to explaining the inequality between men and women that persisted in almost all of them. Even in the households in which men did more than their male peers, they usually did a lot less than their wives. Inequality persists even in the face of liberal sex-role ideology, equal work hours, and equal pay.[14]

Not all are content in the face of this persistent inequality. Arlie Hochschild, in a brilliant study of the modern dual-earner household, reports that women doing the "second shift" are tired and not very happy about it. Marriages suffer from the unspoken and spoken resentments of a highly unequal workload. Households in which men aren't frying the bacon are highly problematic in an age in which women are working harder and harder to bring it home.[15]

Equality does exist in some households. I set out to understand a group of couples who share parenting equally, and this book grew out of that study. In contrast to most previous research, which has relentlessly documented, described, and reiterated the persistence of inequality, my study focuses on couples who have transformed roles at home to create truly equal families.[16]

Equal sharers constitute an unusual group of people.[17] They are exceptional not just in the United States, but throughout the world. Currently, there is no known society in which women do not do the majority of childcare.[18] Until now the equal sharers who *are* out there have been virtually invisible. It is important to bring this revolution in parenting to light because the gender roles of "mother" and "father" can seem so intractable.[19] Typically, even among the most egalitarian of couples, after the birth of a first child husbands and wives revert to more traditional roles.[20] Couples are often shocked at the extent to which they look and act like their own mothers and fathers once they have children. When they look around at their friends they see the same thing happening to them. It is easy to mistakenly conclude that no other kind of family is possible. Equal sharers show us, however, that this trajectory toward traditionalism is not inevitable.[21]

Parenting is the key issue in the gendered division of labor at home because the drastic asymmetry in workloads and the divergence in life courses between husbands and wives develop when children enter the picture. When dual-earner childless couples who work full time divide up household labor, women may do a bit more than their husbands. Children, however, create an inequality of crisis proportions.[22] Hochschild estimated that compared to their husbands women work an extra month per year, a workload that leaves them sleep deprived and without a moment for leisure.[23] In families in which two full-time incomes aren't a necessity, women can opt out of the paid full-time workforce, relieving themselves of the relentless burden of demands by following a path different from their husbands'.[24] However, for women socialized to believe they could have it all, that is a compromise laden with costs.[25]

The existence of equally shared parenting shows that there *is* an alternative to each of these scenarios. Equality is achievable. Although equality may still be the exception in American households, men and women today increasingly believe in gender equality. When my students surveyed dual-earner couples at a local shopping mall, over 70 percent of them thought that if both parents were employed full time, they should split the care of their children 50-50. Despite the ubiquity and persistence of gender inequality, and the forces and dynamics that sustain it, couples *can* thwart those forces, and produce a revolution at home. Equal sharers, though rare today, are our models for tomorrow.

The definition of equality I used for my study was a simple one. Families were classified as equal sharers if husband and wife agreed that, overall, when everything that went into the care of children in a typical week was taken into account, the work was split 50-50. Equality takes many forms. This definition included parents who split each task down the middle, alternating who cooked the kids' dinners, who took them to daycare, and who got them dressed in the morning, as well as families who split the work into separate but equal spheres. By and large, in these equally sharing couples, fathers spent as much time with children, and were as involved in the less glamorous aspects of parenting as were mothers.[26] Equality meant that fathers were more than playmates, more than helpers, and more than substitutes for mothers. Just like their wives, they were primary in their children's lives.[27]

My definition of equality is bound to raise two questions. First, "What about housework?" Although I did not specifically ask about the division of housework, many of the tasks associated with taking care of children could also be classified as household chores—preparing meals for children, washing and buying their clothes, and picking up their toys. Housework was spontaneously mentioned in virtually all the interviews. Given these comments, I estimate that approximately two thirds of the equally sharing parents split all the housework that did not involve childcare equally. A quarter of the equally sharing families solved at least part of the housework problem by paying someone else to do it.

The second question is, "Can't families be equal if men work more hours for pay while their wives put more time in at home?"[28] In approximately three fourths of the "unequal" couples I interviewed, when paid work and household work were considered together, women worked more hours than their husbands. Although in a fourth of the "unequal" couples, the overall amount of time spouses spent working was equal, I am reluctant to call equal time working true gender equality. In this "separate but equal" model of equality women have less say in the family, are less valued outside the family, have worse mental health,[29] and are more economically vulnerable than their husbands in the case of divorce.[30] Even if we do consider those families "equal" in some sense, I hope to show that both men and women lose by splitting parenthood and paid work unequally by gender.

In my study I interviewed a wide range of dual-earner couples, who had children ranging in age from babies to teenagers. My research assistants and I recruited them from daycare centers, schools, and through word of mouth. We asked everyone we contacted to recommend couples who equally shared childcare. We then called all those who had volunteered or had been recommended and asked their overall estimates of the division of childcare in their families. Many of those reputed to be equal were not. However, a surprisingly high number of couples we talked to by phone initially claimed to divide the care of children 50-50. When we investigated further with questions about specific tasks their estimates changed. "How do you divide picking up after children? diapering them? getting up at night with them? feeding them? taking them to birthday parties?" Reminded of the myriad tasks associated with childcare, many of the couples revised their estimates to more realistically reflect the disproportionate share shouldered by mothers.

Equal sharers, of course, were the stars of the study, but I also interviewed their unequal counterparts to highlight what made equal sharers special, as well as what made them ordinary. The unequal couples I interviewed were not all the same. Among them were some in which mothers did the vast majority of childcare (75-25 split) and some in which mothers did only a bit more than half of it (60-40 split).[31] Participants included doctors, lawyers, dentists, teachers, artists, social workers, college professors, business people, administrators, and therapists. Although the majority of these equal sharers and their counterparts were affluent, highly educated men and women who worked in high-status professions, I also interviewed fire fighters, mail carriers, and secretaries. Almost all of the participants were white.[32] (See "How I Did the Study" for detailed information about the sample and my methods.)

Finally, I interviewed another group of couples whose lives were very different from the lives of the rest. In these "alternating-shift" couples, blue-collar husbands shared the care of their children by working different shifts than did their wives. While the men worked at their paid jobs, the women were home with the kids and vice versa, eliminating most of the need for paid childcare. That meant that even when they weren't equal sharers, the working-class fathers in these couples were extensively involved in childcare. I included them because their involvement debunks middle-class stereotypes that hard hats wouldn't be caught dead changing diapers. They make eminently clear that the "revolution at home" is not simply an upper-middle-class phenomenon.[33]

To understand how equally shared parenting works, I spent over a year talking to equal sharers and other dual-earner couples. In all, I interviewed husbands and wives in 150 dual-earner couples (a total of 300 interviews). These tape-recorded interviews were conducted separately with husbands and wives at a place of their choice, usually their homes. Occasionally, however, an interviewee preferred to meet with me at my office, my home, or at his or her workplace. The interviews lasted an average of two hours each, but some were as long as four hours, and a few were as short as an hour. Transcripts of the tapes, as well as the notes I recorded after each interview, provided me with rich information about the couples.

These men and women told me the history of their lives as parents, shared their conflicts, and explained why they had made the choices they had. The questions I asked all participants are included in "How I Did the Study" at the back of the book, but I also elaborated on those questions to pursue issues in more depth when it seemed appropriate to do so. For example, occasionally couples claimed to be completely satisfied with the division of domestic labor when asked about it directly, but at some point later in the interview hinted at conflict over roles at home. When the issue reemerged, I would probe to allow the participant to expand on it.

The description of the uniform procedures I followed, however, gives nothing of the flavor and diversity of these interviews. For me, each interview was an uncharted voyage into a world created by each family, and my role was to discover as much as I could about this world. Because the families' incomes varied widely, each setting was a bit different, from cramped walk-up apartments to luxurious designer homes. But what struck me more than the economic disparities among the families were the attitudes toward life that they conveyed. Some couples imbued their family life with love and joy that were almost palpable. One particularly memorable mother laughed as she described how she and her husband would drop everything to take their kids for a surprise trip to an ice-cream stand, and enthusiastically told me how much she enjoyed the challenge of shopping with coupons when I questioned her about recent financial difficulties in her family. In a few families, however, sadness or tension seemed to prevail. Although equality was neither a prerequisite nor an assurance of happiness, in homes where both parents worked full time and women did most of the work at home, free and easy happiness never emerged.

To a person, the interviewees were extremely generous with their time and their willingness to share their lives. Some initially appeared to be worried about how they appeared to me, or nervous about talking on tape, but in the course of conversation, virtually all seemed to relax and welcome the opportunity to tell their stories.

I undertook this study partly for personal reasons. In the late 1970s and early 1980s, as a young female academic just beginning my career, I was worried. I wanted to have children some day, but reports from the homefront sounded ominous. The troublesome tale being told by social scientists was coming across loud and clear; whether women worked outside the home or not, they were responsible for the work at home. This problem began to loom large in my future. Two images in particular, both promoted in the popular media, haunted me: superwoman and former superwoman.

Superwoman, able to spend fifty hours a week pursuing success in the profession of her choice, who, disguised as traditional woman, returns home to juggle a never-ending onslaught of meals, baths, bedtimes, and household responsibilities. I just knew I didn't have it in me to do that. The glamour of the media image seemed ludicrous. I remember one particularly infuriating TV ad in which a woman, alternately dressed for success, housework, and seduction, sang, "I can bring home the bacon. Fry it up in a pan. And never let you forget you're a man."[34] How could any woman achieve that? Who would want to?

The image of former superwoman was even more disturbing to me. This was the woman who had tried to do it all, had failed, and had now happily retreated to domestic bliss in her immaculate house, spending her days building Legos, baking cookies, and thoroughly enjoying life as a full-time mom.[35] Although I am certainly in favor of parents of any gender spending time with their children, and I would be the last to advocate a seventy-hour workweek, several aspects of this former superwoman picture troubled me.

I doubted that I would be content as a stay-at-home mother. After six years of graduate school pursuing a Ph.D., and five more years on the job market until I obtained a position on the faculty at Mount Holyoke College, I couldn't imagine throwing my job over so lightly. I wondered how many women could really be so sanguine about relinquishing their professional lives.

I couldn't know then how intensely I would love my child when I did actually become a mother, and how silly the rewards of career would sometimes seem compared to the joy of listening to my child laugh, watching him play the violin, or hearing "I love you, Mommy," after I had managed to assuage one of his worries. Nevertheless, I know that full-time childcare has its downside. Your patience can wear thin after you clean up the umpteenth spill, whining can grate on your nerves, the lack of adult company can make you lonely, and playing with Legos can quickly lose its thrill. No matter how intensely you love them, caring for small children full time is incredibly hard work, much of it stressful, boring, and isolating. Even though I feel a bit guilty as I write this, I know I'm not the only mother who feels this way.

In fact, there is mounting evidence that regardless of educational background, mothers in America today are happier when they work outside the home. Women whose jobs might be viewed as dead-end by more privileged women also derive satisfaction from bringing home a paycheck, and from the accomplishment of paid work well done, no matter how poorly it is remunerated.[36] The image of the blissful full-time mom belies the depression, low self-esteem, and stress that women often experience when motherhood is their only job.[37]

And for those women who would enjoy a chance to be home full time, what about the money? The unstated message about the former superwoman is that, married to a high-earning husband, she is unfettered by financial concerns; the decision to stay home is entirely her choice. This image blatantly ignores the real economic constraints faced by most American families today. For the average family, two incomes are simply necessary for survival, or at least to achieve middle-class status.[38] In more affluent dual-career families, the sacrifice of the mother's income would mean a substantial decline in the family's standard of living. The economic forces that have driven women into the marketplace operate to keep them there. For most women, dropping out entirely is not a viable option.

As solutions to the dilemmas of modern family life, the superwoman and the former superwoman are both illusions. It is not glamorous to "do it all"; it's stressful and exhausting. It is not blissful to revert to traditional roles; it's depressing or financially unfeasible.

As I pondered my future, another solution kept coming to mind: equality—men and women equally sharing the care of their children. Coming of age in a feminist era, I thought equality was simple and sensible. If parents could be peers, not only would women escape from the no-win bind of superwoman or former superwoman, but men would be liberated from the burdens of solitary breadwinning and freed to develop meaningful relationships with their children. The question I asked myself then seemed as relevant a decade later when I began interviewing: "Why not equality?" Out of that question my study was born.

I found that families come to equality through many paths. Steve and Beth are exactly the kind of people that you might expect to be equal sharers. Sixties activists, profoundly influenced by the women's movement, they are nontraditional, liberal people who believe in equality between the sexes. Yet they are not typical of equal sharers. Many of the couples I interviewed don't seem the least bit radical. For example, unlike Steve and Beth, only a minority of them began parenthood sharing equally. An ideological commitment to gender equality is neither a necessary nor a sufficient condition for the creation of an equally sharing family. Couples who share parenting are more likely to become equal to deal with the overwhelming labor demands of a two-job household than to fulfill an ideological agenda. Equal sharing is not simply an end; it is a by-product of the negotiations over all the details of everyday life in a family. Like Steve and Beth, all couples who share parenting equally are on their own journey, which they continue to improvise and revise as they go along.

When I began listening to the stories of the people I interviewed, I was looking for the magic key to equality. What was it that made equal sharers different from other couples? Yet what I discovered was that the paths that eventually took equal sharers and their traditional counterparts on different journeys initially diverged only slightly. The real scoop about equal sharing is that it is not primarily a story of who but a story about how—how equality is created.

Equality exists without magic. Husbands and wives become equal sharers together, fighting, negotiating, and building as they go. The big news is that despite its rarity, equal sharing is not the province of a special elite. Avoiding the pitfalls of a home life built around superwoman or former superwoman, equal sharers are ordinary people simply inventing and reinventing solutions to the dilemmas of modern family life.

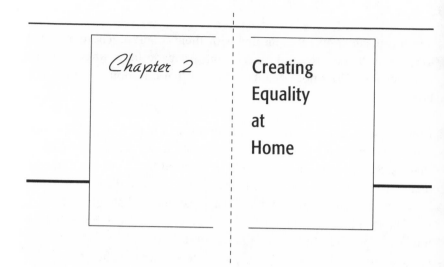

Chapter 2

Creating
Equality
at
Home

No couple is ever really prepared for the upheavals that accompany the birth of a first child. Although expectant parents probably attended childbirth classes together, chances are little was said about what each would do when they arrived home with their new infant.[1] The humorist Nora Ephron confided what new parents soon find out: the baby is "a grenade" that sets off an "explosion" in the marriage.[2] Sociologists concur, describing the birth of a new infant as a crisis in the family.[3] Certainly it was a crisis in the days when it was taken for granted that women (at least in middle-class families) would leave their jobs to care for their infants and men would shoulder the breadwinning responsibilities, and today that crisis has deepened with the breakdown of consensus over roles in the family. Now, more than ever, family life must be created day by day.

"Create" is the key word here because there is nothing automatic about equally shared parenting. Equal sharers must work out all the details. Will husband and wife divide all tasks 50-50 so that their roles are interchangeable, or will they create separate but equal roles? Will one of them stay home with the new infant? Who will do what, with and for children? Who's going to buy their clothes, take responsibility for doctor's appointments, research the best preschools, change the sheets on children's beds, teach them to tie their shoelaces? Who will respond to a child's cry from bed, "I'm thirsty"?

Surprisingly, many of the parents I interviewed more or less fell into equal sharing, not because of their initial intentions or a particularly passionate egalitarian ideology, but because it was a practical solution to the problems of modern family life. But even when equality *is* intended, putting egalitarian principles into practice is a shaky and messy business. There are no guarantees. Some factors, like comparable jobs, liberal friends, and a belief in nontraditional sex roles, can help. These factors, however, do not predetermine the choices couples make, but simply provide the milieu in which couples negotiate, struggle, and cooperate to create an equally sharing family.

The milieu of family life changes continually. Intentionally or unintentionally, jobs change, friends change, interests change. Most important, children and their perceived needs change. This means that the division of labor at home is never settled once and for all, but must be continually recreated. Although the equal sharers in my study were dividing domestic labor 50-50 at the time of the interviews, sixteen of the twenty-six had not always done so.[4] In fact, thirteen of the mothers had taken more than a year off from paid labor while their husbands continued to work, and thus they had a rather traditional division of labor in the early months of their parenting. Equality today does not ensure it tomorrow, nor does inequality in the present preclude it in the future.[5]

Creating equality is fraught with potential pitfalls as husbands and wives struggle with the anger, guilt, frustration, and ambivalence produced by the conflicts between them and within each of them, and by the sometimes impossible demands of paid work. In their struggles, couples differ among themselves in three important ways: in how they define and divide family work (the "who does what" of equality), in how they explain it (the "why" of equality), and in how they negotiate equality.

To examine how these families fashion equal sharing, let's look inside a few homes. These forays will reveal the creative process at work in all the families, as well as a bit of the diversity among them. First, let's visit Janet and Daniel, two untenured professors in the same political science department at a small liberal arts college in Vermont.

Janet and Daniel: Just a Rational Choice

Janet and Daniel are the proud parents of a twenty-three-month-old baby boy named Noah. Daniel chuckles when he recounts how Noah announces every move he is about to make: "I'm going to pick up this book." "I'm going to read it now." "I'm going to come over to see Daddy." Janet beams when she reports Noah's "fantastic memory." Not even two years old yet, Noah knows his ABCs, he counts, he sings songs. Describing him as "the baby who didn't cry," Janet is as enchanted with his good-natured temperament as with his intelligence.

Janet herself grew up in a large affectionate family of Polish Jews. Her American-born mother, an "earth mother" in Janet's mind because of her loving and knowledgeable ways with children, was also a shrewd businessperson who invested the family's money with great success. Her father was born in Poland. After emigrating to the United States, he became a successful international lawyer and encouraged all his children to achieve as much as they could through education. Janet was more outstanding academically than her three brothers, and her father was very proud of her. Although in his humorous way her father was more likely to question her about the one B on her report card than praise her for all the A's, there was no mistaking his joy in her accomplishments.

Hugs and kisses were plentiful in her family and she, in turn, is a very affectionate mother. When I asked Daniel whether motherhood had changed Janet he replied: "Janet has always been a sensitive, insightful, and caring person. Maybe it's a lot more intense with Noah . . . but it's just an extension of things that I'd seen in her before."

"Intense" is a word that fits Janet's approach to motherhood. Like most of the mothers I interviewed, equal sharers or not, Janet cares deeply about being a good mother. She's a worrier. She worries about all the details in Noah's life, big and small. Is he dressed warmly enough? Is he getting the right nutrition? Is it safe for him to play on the climber? Is the car seat secure? Why is he eating dirt? When Noah wakes up at night, she worries about whether he has an ear infection. But when she rocked him for hours to get him to go back to sleep, she worried that she was being too indulgent. Like many employed mothers, at first she worried about the effects of daycare. Sometimes it seems that mothers can't win, worrying if their children are unhappy at daycare, but also worrying if they seem too content. Janet confided an often secret worry of many mothers who use paid childcare:

Maybe he (Noah) wouldn't be so attached to me, or he'll like the babysitters more than he likes me . . . I remember once when he was in the infant room . . . I had (to go back into the room) to give the teacher something I'd forgotten . . . He paid no attention to me when I went in. I remember going back to my office and just crying and thinking this is what you've done. He doesn't see you as different from anyone else. I was just heartbroken.

But, she told me, "It didn't last." Although she still worries about Noah, her early insecurity about her role in Noah's life has disappeared. She's looking forward to getting tenure so that some of the pressures at work will diminish and allow her to spend more time with her son. Yet even now she seems comfortable with her own mothering: "I think he's a great kid and I feel I've done a good job. I feel he's really attached to me . . . He's developing just as he should be. I don't see any kind of problems as a result of my working or being in a daycare center. I think we're doing fine."

Janet also appreciates Daniel as a father and pooh-poohs the naysayers who asked her, "What are you going to do if the baby becomes really attached to Daniel?" She is touched by Noah's attachment to Daniel, and despite all her other worries she quickly learned to discount the people who warned that the baby might "bond" with the father rather than the mother:

> I think it's wonderful if he loves his father. It doesn't bother me. He seems to go through Mommy and Daddy phases. For a couple of weeks it's my Mommy everything and a couple of weeks it's Daddy, Daddy everything. I realize that it goes back and forth. He's not more permanently attached to one than the other.

She sees Noah benefiting from Daniel's kind of fatherhood: "I think he has two parents that are really involved and they're always trying to show him a good time and always trying to be very close with him. I'm very happy. I think he's a great father."

Daniel came to fatherhood from a background that was quite different from Janet's. His father, an auto worker in Detroit, was a taciturn man who did his best to keep the family together, while Daniel's mother went in and out of psychiatric hospitals for recurring bouts of depression. Daniel knew his mother was sick throughout his childhood, but the nature of her illness was a taboo topic in the family. Well-intentioned, but uncommunicative and unaffectionate with his son, Daniel's father is an anti-model for him. In our interview, Daniel recounted a childhood incident that left a mark on him that seems still painful over twenty-five years later. Just after Daniel's seventh birthday, he and his two sisters came downstairs in their pajamas to kiss their parents goodnight, as they had routinely done every night. His father took him aside and told him that he was seven years old and it was time for him to stop kissing his dad. "It's OK to kiss your mother, but you shouldn't be kissing your dad." His father was beginning to teach him a model of manhood that he has since rejected in no uncertain terms. With feeling in his voice, he underlined the difference, "Until Noah is fifty and I'm dead, he can always hug me and kiss me goodnight."

Noah feels his father's nurturing presence. He also knows Daniel as a father who doesn't shirk any of the everyday tasks that his mother does. Daniel cooks Noah's dinner, gives him baths, feeds him, gets him ready to go in the mornings, and picks up his toys just as often as Janet does.

Janet reports a complicated scheme for how they divide the family work. Because Daniel is on sabbatical this year while she is teaching, they trade off time with Noah depending on her teaching schedule. When asked what share of the work she is doing, Janet replies emphatically:

> I'd say 50 percent. When it comes to chores, we're very much aware of the fact that, "Well, I missed work last time 'cause I had the doctor's appointment; you do this doctor's appointment." We split the days of the week so I know we both transport equally. We take different nights on and off with him so I know we spend the same amount of time with him, so I couldn't imagine where a big difference would be.

Janet describes the equality in their relationship as the only possible rational choice given their identical work lives:

> We both take very active roles. From the beginning, there's no reason for us not to do exactly the same thing in terms of childcare. My husband and I do the same job; we work in the same department at the same college with the same teaching schedule. We do everything the same, so it just seems completely irrational that one of us would have to do more with the baby . . . We both believe that pretty strongly and we divide things equally.

Although she describes the choice as the only rational one, it is certainly not the only one that couples make. At the same college where they teach, another academic couple, two astronomers, have a 60-40 arrangement, with the mother taking a greater role at home. Furthermore, a husband and wife I interviewed who share a law practice have a much more traditional division of labor: she leaves the practice early each day to fulfill the primary role at home, while he stays and takes the more interesting cases at work. Janet and Daniel's arrangements, although justified by their equal work arrangements, are not simply explained by them. How then did Daniel and Janet create equality at home?

Before Noah was born there wasn't a lot of talk between them about how they would divide family work, but by both of their accounts, they shared the expectation that Daniel would be an equal partner. Janet's decision not to breastfeed facilitated the mechanics of equal sharing, and underscored her claim that this was the rational way to do things: "I didn't breastfeed so from the beginning there just seemed like no reason why he couldn't wake up as often as I did and feed the baby as often as I did. He could make a bottle as well as I could."[6]

But there were still obstacles to overcome. When Noah was a newborn Janet had time off from classes, while Daniel had to teach. Although this difference in their responsibilities at work could have led to Janet's taking a larger role at home, Daniel describes how she prevented that from happening: "She knew I taught until three-fifty. My phone would ring at four: 'Well, when are you coming home?' . . . I would come home at four-fifteen and she'd put on her coat and say, 'I'm out of here.'" As much as Janet loved her new son, by late afternoon cabin fever would strike. She just needed to get out of the house. Although initially Daniel told me that was fine with him, on reflection he revealed: "There were times when I'd come home and I'd had my own sort of bad day and . . . I wasn't really in the mood. (However,) *I really couldn't argue with her.* He (Noah) was very scary in the beginning. I was very unprepared for this, how helpless (he was)." But even if Daniel was scared about dealing with a helpless new infant, as many parents are, or not in the mood after a day of work, he didn't opt out. Janet simply expected him to take over, and he "couldn't argue with her." He accepted her claim that equal work outside the home entitled her to equal consideration at home: "We have the same job and there is no basis on which either of us can claim that what we are doing outside the home is more important than what the other one is doing."

Daniel and Janet believed in equality. They shared the belief that her career was just as important as his. Moreover, Daniel wanted to be the kind of father that his father wasn't. He hoped instead to emulate one of his own college professors who was an involved father. But principles, even shared ones, don't ensure equality. Principles have to be put into practice. Daniel talks about how easy it would be for things to slide in an unequal direction. "I could even see it happening to us."

He paints a perceptive portrait of what typically occurs to push families toward inequality:

> Mom says, "I'm exhausted. I'm going to go take a shower, you take care of him." He (Dad) comes in and says, "He's pooped." Wife says, "Change the diaper." "Well, I don't know how." "Well, they're underneath there. You open it up. You clean him off."

If the father hesitates, the moment is ripe for the mother to give up:

> She gets out of the shower dripping wet and says, "Here, I'll do it." And it's very easy for the dad to disappear if he's so inclined . . . If the father is scared of the kid or ambivalent . . . I can imagine situations where mothers can make it very easy for dads to disappear.

This scenario did not occur in Daniel and Janet's house. Daniel might have been scared, but he did diaper the baby just as much as Janet did. However, when Daniel says, "I could even see it happening to us," perhaps he is obliquely referring to a major conflict between them in their early days of parenting. The conflict centered on Daniel's frustration over Janet's checking up on him: "If I made the baby's lunch she would come down and open the lunch box and check it. [Sarcastically] I'm going to put strychnine in my boy's lunch?" When Janet corrected him, Daniel exploded:

> I'm changing the diaper . . . I put the tapes on his Pampers and she would be there, come in, and while I'm going to put his clothes on, she'll like come over and just reach over and adjust the tapes on the Pamper. At first I used to just go nuts. "Well, it looks like it's too tight." "If it's too loose it leaks." "Well, the thing is it's going to cut him here." "Have you ever seen a cut on him?" "No."

Rather than giving up and disappearing as some men might have, Daniel fought back. He was willing to admit how her checking up affected him: "You're making me feel very inadequate and it's important to me to feel like I'm doing a good job and when somebody's checking up on me I'm not feeling like I'm doing a good job."

Janet concedes that she is a "worrier" who found it difficult to trust her husband because he is "looser" than she is. But perhaps more than the difference in their styles was at the core of their struggle to find a comfortable way to parent together. Control was at the heart of the issue. Janet confesses: "I'm the type of person (who likes) to do things myself. I've always been like that and it was very hard for me to trust my husband enough." Daniel perceptively notes: "What she needed to feel adequate and what I needed to do to feel adequate were just in direct conflict."

Because mothers in the past have been in charge of the care of their children, equally sharing mothers potentially face a loss of control and authority at home. If wives try to maintain their authority, husbands who do half of the childcare are likely to balk, or to cede control at the cost of their equal participation. But Daniel and Janet persevered. Daniel didn't use Janet's desire for control as an opportunity to escape parenting. Janet needed Daniel's involvement to enable her to continue her level of commitment at work, and to feel that their arrangements were fair. She needed and wanted it enough to change, enough to back off and stop checking up.

Despite the routine flow of everyday life that now prevails in this equally sharing household, changing circumstances bring new issues that must be resolved. During Daniel's sabbatical, for example, their work lives were not exactly parallel. Although Janet described a very structured division of time in which each of them was responsible for Noah on different nights, Daniel gave a slightly different picture of their arrangements. He described structured mornings when he took responsibility for dressing and feeding Noah, but less structured nights than she reported: "If it's a night before she has to teach it's understood that I'm going to take care of him that night. If it's not a night when she has to teach we sort of touch base at dinner . . . the morning routine is pretty structured, but after that it's pretty much on a rolling needs basis." Because he was on sabbatical and she wasn't, "rolling needs" meant that he took more responsibility at night when she needed to work. At times the lack of structure caused conflicts, however, especially when Daniel and Janet didn't discuss how to divide the work on a specific evening. He calls it a communication conflict: "I will assume like I took care of him last night and so when we get home from work tonight it's her turn . . . She has something she needs to do and sort of thinking maybe I'll take care of him. That's where the conflict arises, because I didn't communicate my expectations and she didn't communicate hers."

Communication is critical in working out an equally sharing relationship. In traditional families it was clear who was going to attend to a crying baby in the middle of the night, but today's couples must negotiate that as well as the other exigencies of everyday life. Talking allows couples to sort through various ways to manage things. In considering how to deal with those nightly wake-ups, equal sharers might take turns; or they might decide it is more efficient for a nursing mother to wake up; or as Daniel and Janet do, they might delegate responsibility for nighttime duty to a father who can fall asleep more easily than his insomniac wife. Negotiation is an ongoing process and when agreed-upon arrangements don't work, they have to be renegotiated. So, for instance, when Noah's ear infections meant all-night duty, Janet agreed to take her turn at getting up despite her insomnia.

This is not to say that all the equal sharers sit down and rationally discuss how to organize the myriad details of their lives. As all parents do, they muddle through, adjusting as they go. Parenthood is an overwhelming, exciting, frightening, and constantly changing experience. It has the capacity to change a person's deeply held beliefs, relation to work, relationships with other people, and even one's identity. The magnitude of the changes parenthood entails almost always comes as a shock to new parents.

Most modern parents say that they simply had no idea how much work was involved in childcare. When fathers agree to share the work at home, they are often unaware that the work at home is in conflict with other things they want to do. Daniel says his assumptions about what life was going to be like went completely by the board after Noah was born: "I had a complete mental image of parenthood and fatherhood that didn't last twenty-four hours after Noah came home." Daniel says that the most important trait he's developed as a parent is "flexibility." For example, he describes how he coped with the discovery that watching a two-month-old baby is not compatible with working:

He'd go down for a nap. Maybe I'd make a cup of coffee, sit down, just get organized at the table, maybe work for ten minutes, and he'd wake up . . . I found that the only way to cope with it, because then I got very angry . . . The only way to get around that was just to say, "Okay, for these eight hours he's mine to watch and that's what I'm going to do. I'm going to watch him. I'm not going to try to work."

In this example, it is not a struggle or even a discussion with Janet that enabled Daniel to continue to share the care of his baby, but a change within himself. This change gave him new appreciation for the wonder of the moment, for dropping everything just "to enjoy something else that is going on."

By letting go of the necessity of carefully controlling his work life, Daniel has opened himself to the rewards of a relationship with his child. It hasn't always been easy: "There were times I thought during the first year when I didn't even want to be here." But Daniel was there, and by being there he developed a relationship with his son that has provided the impetus for continuing to share. When Noah wants comfort he is equally likely to go to either his mother or his father. When he wants someone to read him a book, Daniel reports, Noah will chase either parent with "equal fervor." Noah's insistence that Dad is as important as Mom provides some of the momentum that keeps equal sharing on track. The rewards Daniel now reaps from life with his two-year-old son are so gratifying that he can't understand how men would want it otherwise: "I don't understand why they don't want to be in on this . . . from eighteen months on they're a gas . . . it's not that he's easy; he's exhausting, but he's really a blast!"

Why has this couple been able to overcome the obstacles that might have derailed equal sharing? When asked what makes them different from less equal couples, Daniel says: "I couldn't get away with it with Janet. She would hand me the baby and head out the door. I guess I'm kind of amazed that wives let their husbands get away with it." Janet shies away from taking credit and refers instead to her husband's unconventional masculinity. When other teenage boys were playing football and delivering newspapers after school, Daniel had a regular babysitting job. But when I questioned her further about her influence in creating equality, she insisted that she simply could not be in another kind of relationship:

How can I be in a relationship with someone that says, "Yes, you can work all day long and then do all those things for the rest of the family"? It's just not fair. It doesn't show any respect for the other person.

Daniel and Janet had identical jobs, they earned similar incomes, they believed in equality. The stage was set for equal sharing. Nonetheless, equality was not a foregone conclusion; even they had some rocky moments. For equality to prevail in their home, Daniel had to come home after his classes so that Janet could have time off, Janet had to trust Daniel to do things his own way, and both had to readjust their work lives. Their belief that equity at home should reflect equality at work, Daniel's desire to differ from his own father, and Janet's insistence on and Daniel's acceptance of equal sharing as the only rational way to do things, provided the justification for what they were doing even when they didn't want to do it.

Janet and Daniel talk as though equal sharing was the only kind of life that made sense to them. In contrast, a majority of the equally sharing families did not explicitly set out to become equal sharers, but discovered that they had in the process of working out family life.[7] Mary and Paul are just such a couple. Let's look in at them.

Mary and Paul: We Work Better Together

Mary and Paul do not live far from Janet and Daniel. Chances are they don't know each other, and at least on the surface they have a very different kind of family. For one thing they have five children. Mary is a medical secretary for a pediatrics practice, and Paul is a fire inspector for the local municipality. Neither graduated from college and they make a lot less money than Janet and Daniel. But like Janet and Daniel, Mary and Paul are an equally sharing couple. In this respect, their lives are every bit as nontraditional. The two couples also express an optimism and energy for life and its challenges that seem similar.

Mary and Paul are avid fans of their children's sports teams. It took months for me to schedule interviews into their busy lives because with five kids they go to a lot of evening games. The night I finally did meet with them, I drove around for a long time trying to figure out which of the small, similar 1960s-style ranches in their housing development was theirs. Although their house was barely distinguishable from their neighbors' houses on the outside, the inside was quite a different matter. The jumble of sights and sounds that greeted me when I opened the door advertised one of the most child-centered houses I had visited. Pictures of their children were everywhere—on the walls, on the window sills, on the refrigerator. Sports trophies were prominently displayed. A noisy hubbub seemed to emanate from every corner of the house. Their two teenage children were sprawled on the living room floor arguing about whether a word one had used was legitimate in a Scrabble game. In another room an unemployed cousin staying with them was teaching the three-year-old to sing "Take Me Out to the Ball Game." Mary and Paul greeted me warmly at the door and then introduced me to their two other children. As soon as I got out my tape recorder, those two came close to me. "Do you want to hear your voices?" I asked them. "Yes!" they answered eagerly.

I was amazed and impressed with the sense of fun in this family. It almost seemed too good to be true. The mother of one child myself, I have often felt sorry for parents in bigger families. Imagining that they were weighted down with all the work more children entailed, I had assumed that less of their parenting would be fun. Not so in this equally sharing household. A conspicuous sense of enjoyment pervades the way Mary and Paul talk about their experiences as parents, despite the work. When I asked Mary how parenthood had changed her, she said it had made her more relaxed. Like Daniel, she no longer expected everything to be organized perfectly, but had learned how to "go with the flow": "It's made me a real happy person. My kids are an awful lot to me."

Each parent in this family is the softie on some issues. The kids have figured out that Dad can't say "no" to a game of catch, whereas Mom is the pushover when the ice-cream truck rolls around. Mary and Paul tease each other good-naturedly about "spoiling" the kids.

Like all families, of course, they have their share of conflicts and crises. They are not strangers to either tragedy or challenge. Several years ago their oldest daughter was in a very serious car accident in which she suffered brain injuries that required months of intensive rehabilitation. Currently, their "difficult" son is having problems in school. Paul occasionally loses his temper when trying to manage him, and Mary can get irritated by Paul's lack of patience. In their hectic mornings sometimes Mary loses patience herself trying to get her large brood out the door. She regrets it if she's gotten "up-tight" and yelled at the kids, but she also doesn't hold herself to superhuman standards: "I hate to have the kids go off to school like that. So sometimes when that happens I go to work thinking, 'Oh, I wish I hadn't done that this morning.' But then I just realize that I'm human and that I'll try not to do it again." It might sound a bit corny, but love sustains this family through all the challenges, large and small, including how to divide the work at home.

There is certainly a lot of domestic labor to be done in a family of five children who range in age from seventeen to three. Unlike their more affluent counterparts who often hire outside help, Mary and Paul do all the work themselves.[8] Paul is no shirker. He outlines his typical day:

> I get up at four, make lunches for the four oldest kids, get to work at five, work until one-thirty, come home, basically, pick up from what's left from breakfast, (finish the) dishes, do a load of wash, pick up Crystal at the babysitter at quarter of three . . . help Chuck (the seven-year-old) with his paper route, usually (give) Derek a ride home from basketball at three-thirty, (put) clothes in the dryer, (do) another load of wash . . . I do the suppers, cook supper.

Mary, whose job is from eight-thirty to five, gets the children on their way in the morning, and often comes home during her lunch hour to straighten up, put in a load of laundry, or get dinner started. She continues the description of their evening:

> We eat supper, and I usually do some laundry. Paul usually does the dishes or we'll do them together and by then, seven at night, he's had it so he just collapses. I get the kids to get into the tub and one of us will go upstairs or read them a story. Often nights we're just so busy that we're all in bed by nine or nine-thirty.

Paul contributes the bulk of his share of the work from the time he gets home from his job in the early afternoon until evening, whereas Mary takes over the daily chores at night. She also spends Saturday with the kids, while Paul goes to his job.

Although he is often tired and not entirely happy with his current work duties, he recently passed up a tempting opportunity for a different job with more inspections and less paperwork because the later hours of that job would interfere with his afternoon family responsibilities. Mary is concerned about his job conditions, but Paul hesitates to change because, as Mary puts it, a switch in his job schedule would "create total chaos with our babysitting situation."

Although Mary and Paul share equally the work of parenting, which is a heavy load in their family, in their direct interactions with their children, much of their parenting divides along gender lines. Both agree that Mary is more involved in their children's emotional lives. She says:

> I think sometimes I'm more in tune to what the kids are going through . . . I like to do that kind of stuff. I like trying to figure out what's making my kids tick, what's going on in their lives . . . I think sometimes I listen to the kids a little bit more or can see a problem there easier than Paul can. He's more apt to go outside and play with the kids than I am. He'll go out, especially in the spring and summer, and play whiffle ball with the kids for an hour, an hour and a half every night.

As in many traditional families, she's the confidant, he's the playmate. They seem comfortable with these roles and not out to create gender-less parenting. Neither seems overburdened, and although they spend time differently with their children, they devote an equal amount of time to them and overall their involvement seems equal.

Mary and Paul took on more traditional gender roles when their children were younger. Mary worked at a series of part-time jobs that she fit around primary parenting responsibilities. Why was she the one to stay home? At first she attributes her staying home to his job: "He has always had a more stable job, a better-paying job, a job we could count on day in and day out." But she admits the question of who was to stay home was never discussed; it was assumed that she, the mother, would: "I really enjoyed my children when they were babies . . . I don't think I would want to give that up."

How then did they come to share parenting equally? Although it didn't become entirely equal until Mary went back to work full time, Paul pitched in early on. Mary recounts: "To me, being a mother was just the most natural thing. I don't know if I was surprised that Paul took to being a dad so easily, or wanted to be so involved, but I just can't ever remember him not being involved." Paul recalls "helping out" in the early days of parenting:

> I think I always helped out. Mary never breastfed so we had bottles and (I) got up and helped feed and I didn't mind at all. It was actually kind of neat, it really was . . . I think I volunteered more than anything. It was like, "Geez, can I help you do something?" and she said, "Sure," and it was a matter of doing it. We had a

diaper pail with diapers and stuff like that, wash them and dry them and fold them, feed the baby and ourselves, do our own laundry and make dinners and lunch and whatnot. It's just something. You don't enjoy doing it, but the time's there, you do it . . . I'll do it. It's no big deal. That's the way it kind of evolved.

When Mary took a night job, Paul took over the care of the children. There's a matter-of-factness about their descriptions of sharing that reminded me of Janet and Daniel. Mary, like Janet, talks about their equality as the only sensible way to do things: "When you decide to have so many kids you have to know that that's going to happen because one person simply can't do it all themselves. You have to know you are going to work together."

As Janet and Daniel invoke their work lives to explain equality at home, Mary and Paul invoke the amount of work that five children entail. But it is not at all clear that fathers do more of the work at home as the number of children increase, and even among those who do, few share equally as Paul does.[9] In this family equality has developed not out of a self-conscious attempt to create a feminist household, not because of Mary or Paul's unconventional orientation to parenting or work, but because of the kind of marriage Mary and Paul have. There was work to do, so Paul wasn't going to just stand by and watch Mary do it. He offered his help and she accepted. He says, "We love each other very much and I think it just goes from there. I mean there's just so much work to do . . . You have to help out. How can you not help out? . . . I don't know, it just happened, no complaints I'll tell you, it's great."

Clearly, Mary and Paul are not stuck in gender roles. But they did not specifically set out to change those roles. In fact, the only indirect mention of this issue was when Mary said:

I think a lot of times I don't tell people (about how we divide domestic responsibilities). I guess they just assume that I do so much because I'm a woman . . . I hesitate to tell people what Paul does because they think, "Oh my God, what are you doing, lady?"

Even if there is a gender revolution going on inside this household, these parents don't think of themselves or particularly want to be known as revolutionaries. Paul didn't even seem to realize that his behavior was unusual.

Neither Paul nor Mary has an exceptional work life for people of their respective genders. Mary takes pride in the work that she does as a medical secretary, likes the people she works with, and enjoys a challenge. Nonetheless, her job has always been the secondary one in the family. She earns about half of what Paul does. As is typical of women who have tried to fit in jobs around parenting, she's had a checkered work history. Like most of the more traditional men in the study, Paul's job has been the stable one in the family, the job they've depended on. Although it might seem unusual that he recently passed up a more desirable job, that job would not have meant a promotion or more money. Mary and Paul did not become equal sharers to sustain nontraditional identities as either parents or workers; they did it out of their commitment to each other and their marriage. Mary says: "It's funny. As important as the kids are to us, I think that (to) each other we are number one . . . I think he's my only ally in there. If I don't talk to him, I'll be in trouble." When asked why their family was different from other families in that the two of them shared, Mary replied, "The best thing for us is to share. We always have. I don't know if it was just a deeper commitment to each other that was made after our daughter's accident, because I mean we got through that together."

Paul has given up a lot of male prerogatives in his willingness to share the work of parenting with his wife. He does so graciously, minimizing the extraordinariness of his role, and with no thought of being paid back with excessive appreciation. When asked what he personally gained by sharing the work, he replied:

> Time with my wife. I mean it's not much time, but whatever time there is in the evening. If one of us had to do everything, then we wouldn't have the time together . . . I enjoy spending time with my wife too (as well as with the kids). It's crazy sometimes, crazy most days, (but) I love my life. I love the way it is and I can't see living any other way.

Mary explains their family life simply: "We work better together."

Donna and Kevin: Gentle and Tough-nosed

Donna and Kevin are attractive, vivacious parents of a ten-year-old son and a six-year-old daughter. Donna is a highly committed ESL (English as a second language) teacher. Kevin is a media director for a small

advertising company. Donna is one of the few mothers I spoke with
who allow themselves a passion outside the family and paid work—
in Donna's case, gymnastics. Kevin is a very "maternal" father, even
among the equal sharers. He is one of the few who truly share the
mental work of parenting. He worries about how his children's lives are
organized and oversees the details—making sure permission slips are in
their backpacks when they go to school, calling at three-fifteen to make
sure they got off the bus all right. As Kevin puts it, he and Donna have
"blurred" some old gender lines:

> It's okay for a father to be gentle and caring and nurturing as much
> as a mother and for a mother to be an aggressive tough-nosed son
> of a bitch when it has to be done . . . Donna can be comfortable
> taking her son to the wrestling match and pounding on the floor
> and I can feel comfortable giving my little girl a bath and watching
> her play with her dolls and having fun. I hope we're blurring some
> of those lines. I would like to think we're blurring some of those.

Donna leaves for work earlier than Kevin so he gets the children off
to school in the morning, taking most of the responsibility for making
sure they are dressed, fed, and equipped with everything they need for
school that day. She pitches in when he needs help, making a hot breakfast if she has the time, choosing "acceptable" clothing for her daughter,
or giving children lunch money. Donna returns from her job before
Kevin, shortly after the children get home from school. After giving the
children a snack, she indulges her passion for gymnastics by spending
an hour in the small gym they built on to their house. Then she usually
prepares dinner, sometimes with Kevin's help when he gets home.
Donna reports that he cleans up after dinner, sometimes alone and
sometimes with her help. In the evenings Kevin bathes the children and
helps them with their homework, while Donna does more of the household chores, such as laundry, and more of the "keeping after them."
They both spend time hanging out and watching TV with their children,
although Kevin is more likely to actively play with them in the evenings. According to Donna, both parents put children to bed, but Kevin
reports that he has a more elaborate bedtime routine with them, reading and singing songs. Both agree that overall the division of childcare
between them is 50-50.

  Their early years as parents were quite different. When their first
child was born, Donna and Kevin had comparable jobs with compara-

ble salaries, but when the time came to decide who would stay home with a small child there was no contest. Both believed that "a parent" should be home when children were small, but neither relished the idea of putting aside career to tend the home fires. Liberal people, they didn't just assume that "the mother" would stay home; it was discussed. Yet the discussion had a foregone conclusion. Donna reports: "Oh, it was discussed . . . but I felt . . . that there wasn't really a question." Why was it so obvious that Donna would be the one to stay home? Donna answers: "I think partly because I was breastfeeding, but mainly because of the way things have been." According to Kevin, both felt compelled to adhere to traditional roles:

> Donna decided that it was appropriate to stay home with your kids and she wanted to do that . . . Donna really felt and I supported her because I thought it was important to have a parent home with the children. At that point I think Donna was making more money than I was or we were making an equal amount of money. Why the mother stayed home? I probably wasn't strong enough to say that I could do it and Donna, on the other hand, was traditional enough to think she should. I wouldn't have volunteered; the kids would have gone to childcare. I would have compromised my values to keep working.

Kevin muses on the contradictions:

> Despite the fact, if you had asked me at the time I would have said that Donna and I are equal . . . I truly believe in my mind that I thought that we were equal. I couldn't have done it, I couldn't have given up my traditional male role as the supporter and the person who would go out . . . I felt I had to be the provider.

Although both parents agreed that rather than relying on childcare, a parent should stay at home with young children, only Donna was willing to make the sacrifice.

She did do it, but she reports, "Those were difficult years: I don't regret it. I'm glad I did it, but it was hard, self-worth and all of that. I get little satisfaction out of a clean kitchen, that kind of mindless stuff." She found ways to get out of the house at night, completing a master's degree and even waitressing. When her younger child started kindergarten, Donna began tutoring, "just . . . to build up my confidence, my self-esteem, my self-worth . . . just to feel if I was marketable."

Before she felt ready for it, a full-time teaching position became available. It was an extremely attractive job, teaching in a special transitional program for immigrant children, some of whom had escaped war-torn countries. Donna describes her panic at the thought of managing it all: "I was really . . . so afraid I wouldn't be able to juggle it, just panic-stricken, that either my career would be a flop or my home life and my children would just fall apart. I was just horrified." Anticipating all the new demands propelled Donna into negotiations with Kevin over their division of labor:

> I talked to Kevin about it over and over and over again. He reassured me that he'd help out. "You've got to help me. You've got to do more." Because he didn't back then, I didn't expect him to. My job was being with the kids . . . He promised (to change) and that's when it (equal sharing) started. He just promised and it was a big deal.

His willingness to change at home gave her the courage to take on the full-time teaching job and has helped her succeed at work. She talks about her accomplishments at her job with great pride:

> I love it. I feel I'm very good at what I do . . . My room is very unique. It's the only type in this district . . . I work very closely with other teachers and the school psychologist. My prime concern is to provide a warm, loving, caring environment. Academics are secondary . . . I feel the kids do real well in my room. I do. I feel I'm the best person for this job, I really do.

When Donna insisted that their family arrangements change, Kevin made up a chart with all the tasks that needed to be done in a week, with the idea that they would alternate. The chart was a way of committing himself to equality:

> I said that unless we make it a hard and fast rule, if I find myself not having to do it, I probably won't . . . "If you make a supper one night when it's my turn I'm going to be greatly relieved and then likely to let you do it again and again," so I thought the chart was a way of establishing rules and it gave her something to complain about . . . We could hold ourselves to something.

In principle, Kevin was not resistant to doing more. In fact, he reports that he "looked forward to it," because it would give him "something to strut" about, a way to show people he was a good parent.

Reality, however, does not always go as smoothly as planned. Kevin admits that they've "fallen off the chart." Each of them has a tendency to avoid particular household and parenting chores, creating different roles for the two of them. Hence Donna does more child-related housework, while Kevin does more of the helping with homework and organizing of the children's recreational activities. Donna reports: "When we used the list everything worked out very well. I don't know why we stopped . . . We just do more what comes naturally."

Kevin doesn't like the idea that the two of them operate in separate spheres. When asked how he would like to change their family arrangements, he answers: "I would like to see Donna become more involved in the actual teaching part of the home activities, the schooling . . . I think if that happened . . . I would want Donna . . . to put more pressure on me to do more in the house."

"Doing things naturally" leads to a separate and uneasy equality, leaving both parents feeling a bit disgruntled about areas in which their spouse's contribution falls short of theirs, and a bit guilty about the areas in which their contribution falls short of their spouse's. Kevin complains that Donna isn't active enough in helping the kids with their homework. Donna complains that Kevin doesn't do enough housework.

Kevin admits to resisting a bit. He'll do more housework, he says, but he might have to be asked twice, despite feeling somewhat guilty: "I'm doing more of the stuff that's fun. I feel a little guilty about that." Kevin relies on Donna to be the enforcer of the chart. He describes how they go back and forth on the division of responsibilities:

> I am just waiting for Donna . . . for her to say, "Come on Kevin, . . . back to the chart." If she was willing to hold me to that I would probably stay on the chart all the time, but she lets me not do it. We'll probably last three months and then we'll start slipping . . . then we'll reach a point where we have to go back on to the chart and then slip off again. It's just the nature of the way we go.

Although he feels guilty, he also defends his lack by citing hers: "I don't feel as inclined to help out when I'm sitting there with the kids sweating buckets because they're not getting their math program."

Donna may complain to Kevin about wanting him to pitch in more, but it is clear that she doesn't feel entirely justified in complaining. For example, although she gets "a little annoyed" when he reads the newspaper while she is "hustling" to make dinner, she says she usually "likes to let him just hang out," and will only ask for help if she is "feeling weak." In general, Donna feels more guilty than Kevin does. She berates herself for wanting to work out when she gets home from her job and for not living up to an idealized image of motherhood: "I feel I'm not the typical Susie Homemaker. I don't sit there baking cookies all day or making arts and crafts things. Some mothers do . . . Maybe I should be making brownies with them (after school) or something, but . . . I need to work out . . . I just need that."

Despite having spent all day patiently helping her students with their schoolwork, Donna is very hard on herself for not having as much patience as Kevin does in helping their own children with homework at night. She even worried about being interviewed, because her equally sharing role would be exposed: "Maybe I would feel less of a person . . . because I'm not doing 90 percent."

Both Donna and Kevin are ambivalent about discarding old identities that are traditional for their sex. Some aspects of nontraditional identities suit them well. Donna, a gifted teacher, is gratified by her career success; Kevin, a nurturing father, is fulfilled by his relationship with his children. Yet they struggle over the issues of identity that are posed by the equality they have created. Despite Kevin's attraction to less traditional identities for men and women, he repeatedly stated that he could not give up the role of provider. Why? "The importance of work to my male identity would be to be the supporter . . . the money and the prestige. There's something that goes along with being a successful person in a job. I wasn't prepared to say I could be as successful as a mother or father who stayed home . . . I wasn't prepared to say those were equal things."

Likewise, mothers are not immune to experiencing a loss of self-esteem when they relinquish paid work to take care of children.[10] Donna, in particular, talked about the loss of self-worth she experienced during her years at home. Yet for her and other women, the desire or felt obligation to adopt a traditional maternal identity can keep them from pressing their husbands about who should cut back on paid work to stay home with children. Donna's work life was as remunerative and rewarding as her husband's before children, yet she never really argued strongly that he should be the one to stay home. Even if traditionally defined motherhood didn't and doesn't suit Donna very well, it shaped her choices and continues to affect how she feels about their division of labor. Although now their parenting is equal, she feels guilty for not living up to traditional maternal ideals, for not doing 90 percent.

Kevin doesn't like to do housework; Donna doesn't like to help with homework. Those personal preferences shape what they do on a day-to-day basis. Homework and housework are more than personal preferences, however. They continue to be sources of conflict and struggle between Donna and Kevin and within each of them because homework and housework are also symbols.[11] Kevin's ideal of a genderless world is in conflict with his aversion to housework; Donna's standard of motherhood is violated by her impatience with homework at the end of a day teaching. Their family arrangements reflect not only what each has to do, but the kind of parent and person each will be.

Janet and Daniel, Mary and Paul, and Donna and Kevin, illustrate the differences I found among the equally sharing couples: differences in defining and dividing the work of parenting, in explaining equality, and in negotiating equality.[12]

Defining and Dividing Family Work

The three families' daily lives have been organized in dissimilar ways. Most strikingly, the degree to which the parents' roles are gendered differs among these equally sharing couples. Mary and Paul, the parents of five children, represent one end of a gendered continuum, whereas Daniel and Janet, the two college professors, represent the other end of that continuum with their relatively genderless parenting. Donna and Kevin illustrate a more mixed pattern. But these differences should not be overdrawn. When asked if the nature of a good father is different from that of a good mother, both Mary and Paul demur. All equally sharing parents have by definition transformed old gender roles, yet none of them are entirely free of the influence of those roles. Paul's degree of involvement in parenting necessitates that he take a maternal role at times. Conversely, despite divvying up tasks without respect to gender, Janet finds herself worrying more than her husband, and both Janet and Daniel agree that they may take different roles in the future depending on Noah's interests.

Parenting among the three couples also differs in two all-important areas: time and tasks. Equally sharing couples vary in the amount of time they spend with their children. Fifty-fifty parenting still leaves open questions about the size of the parenting pie to be divided and how much should be delegated to substitute caregivers.[13] Moreover, parents vary in how time with children is organized. For example, Janet and Daniel engage in what one of the equally sharing parents described as "tag-team parenting," in which they divide up time with Noah, whereas the other two couples spend more of their parenting time together as a family.[14]

The three couples differed in their use of nonparental care. Daniel and Janet used daycare early on; Mary and Paul used babysitters more for their later children than for their first-born; and Kevin and Donna completely avoided paid childcare. Although these three couples reported few conflicts over how much childcare to delegate outside the family, that issue loomed large for other families, and in some, it was *the* insurmountable obstacle that kept them from equality. Sometimes fathers who were "theoretically" willing to share really meant that they wanted to use more daycare than their wives wanted, and then they would equally share the smaller leftover parental pie. I found few mothers willing to make that deal. When faced with this resistance, women either capitulated to inequality or fought hard to convince their husbands that their children needed more parental time.

None of the three couples described here wrestled over the way their time is organized, but one equally sharing mother I interviewed yearned for more time alone with her children. Her husband, a charming and entertaining father, dominated the children's attention when the family was together. Conversely, another academic dad like Daniel lived with tag-team parenting, but was nostalgic for the days when families went on Sunday outings together.

Tasks to be divided by equal sharers vary widely, depending partly on the age of the child. A toddler like Noah needs a lot of basic care: to be dressed, diapered, fed, and so on. School-aged children need to be chauffeured between activities, disciplined, and helped with homework. However, parents also vary in how they conceptualize their children's needs and how they decide to meet those needs. Kevin, for example, believes that parents should be on the front lines helping children with homework, sitting with them as they do it to answer their questions or keep them company. So their family time in the evenings is spent doing just that. For Mary and Paul, who barely mention children's homework, homework help is not a major parental task.[15] To create equality parents must decide what is to be divided as well as how it will be divided.

Conflicts over the tasks that constituted good parenting also undermined some couples' efforts to share equally. For example, one highly feminist mother settled for a 60-40 relationship because she could not persuade her husband that watching TV with their four-year-old did not constitute quality time. She stepped in to fill the gap in what she saw as her child's need. Interestingly, he argued strongly and convincingly that she was too intrusive, that their son didn't need constant interaction but was happy just hanging out with his dad. They couldn't agree, so by default she ended up doing more.

In most cases of conflicts over tasks, mothers wanted more than their husbands thought was necessary: more protectiveness, more attention, more interaction. But the most painful conflicts occurred in the few instances among the equal sharers when fathers wanted their wives to do more. Kevin's criticism of Donna for not helping with homework when the kids got home from school was hard for her to bear. The idealized images of motherhood that live in women's minds leave them easily prone to guilt. Even though Donna thought that homework time after school wasn't necessary because her children should have some time to relax, she felt very guilty that she used the time to work out instead of acting like "Susie Homemaker."

Explaining Equality

Although the three couples have all worked out some version of equally shared parenting, the meaning of those arrangements differs dramatically among them. The contrast between Janet and Daniel and Mary and Paul is the most clear-cut. When Janet and Daniel talk about working out parenting arrangements, they speak of individual rights; because they have essentially the same jobs, each is entitled to the same rights. When Mary and Paul talk about their arrangements, they use their relationship with each other to justify and explain their equality. Janet and Daniel are proud of the equality they have created at home; Mary and Paul are a bit embarrassed about theirs. Janet and Daniel consciously set out to create an equally sharing family and have been successful; Mary and Paul decided to have five children and discovered that to protect their time together and avoid Mary's being totally overwhelmed, equality was a solution that worked. If the underlying principle in Janet and Daniel's family is that equal roles at work deserve equal roles at home, the corresponding principle in Mary and Paul's house is that fairness dictates that no one shoulder a disproportionate burden of work in the family. Mary and Paul don't talk about principles, however; they talk about love.

For Donna and Kevin, family arrangements reflect not rights or love, but their individual identities—identities that are fraught with ambivalence. The traditional division of labor they adopted in the early part of their parenting allowed Kevin to conceive of himself as a breadwinner and Donna to see herself as a responsible mother. These identities, although compelling, were not particularly comfortable. Today, Kevin is proud of the equality in their household, but is a bit embarrassed by his lapses over housework. Donna needs equality at home in order to juggle the two parts of her life, but criticizes herself for needing it. When she complains about Kevin's lapses, she invokes her own weakness rather than her right to equality. Moreover, Donna worries about departing from the "maternal" role. She is not always happy with the identity equality confers on her. Both Kevin and Donna seem torn between the benefits of equality and the benefits conferred by traditional roles. In part, Donna wishes she could think of herself as "Susie Homemaker" and Kevin wishes he could have the prerogative to get out of housework. Yet Donna's self-conception as a successful teacher and Kevin's as a special kind of father do provide them with alternate rewards that give meaning to their nontraditional lives.

Negotiating Equality

Janet and Daniel, Mary and Paul, and Donna and Kevin took different routes to equality. Mary and Paul, highly unusual among the equal sharers, never fought over this issue. Paul's offers to "help out" were matched by Mary's encouragement of his efforts, and equality was established quite easily once Mary was working full time. Daniel and Janet committed themselves to equality, but vied over control. Donna and Kevin struggled and continue to struggle to find a balance. They argue and even snipe when the division gets uneven, but they also problem-solve constructively. The chart they agreed on is a back-up that keeps their conflicts from escalating. As a last resort they can always "go back to the chart," which both think is fair.

Kevin waits for Donna to hold him to equality, because in their family, as in many other equally sharing families, the woman is the driving force behind nontraditional arrangements. The conflicts in these three families were neither bitter nor threatening to their marriages. In a few of the families, however, establishing equality came at the cost of a severe struggle that brought the couple to the brink of divorce. Men who resisted or were simply oblivious learned the hard lesson that their wives wouldn't put up with inequality. They changed.

Although conflicts were sometimes painful, when couples successfully worked through the resentments, anger, and frustration born of inequality, they often emerged with stronger relationships. Janet, like other equal sharers, invoked the importance of respect. Anything less than equality, she argued, would not show respect for her. Equally sharing men sometimes also talked about the respect they had for their wives, which sustained their commitment to share. The women who struggled to establish equality were also conveying a deep respect for their husbands, though they rarely mentioned it. To fight for equality means you believe your husband is fair-minded and you believe that he is capable of being as good a parent as you are. Avoidance of conflict by couples may reflect a lack of mutual respect or the secret worry that their marriages are not strong enough to withstand confronting these issues head-on. But buried conflicts can live on in unresolved resentments, lost intimacy, and compromised affection.

Nothing at home is set in stone. As Mary and Donna illustrate, all of the women who were sharing equally at the time of the interview had not always done so. Changes occurred when traditional roles simply did not work anymore. For example, a few mothers who worked full time and did a majority of the childcare when they had one child balked after a second child made their disproportionate share too heavy. In other families, like Donna's, things changed when women went back to full-time paid work. These women, who took time off from paid work or cut back to part time, assumed the primary role of parenthood early on and did not object to the inequality. But after the women went back into the paid workforce full time, the couples negotiated a 50-50 sharing of parenting responsibilities. Even in families that intend to share equally from the start, things do not always go as planned. One equally sharing father reported that despite his wife's insistence on their equal time commitment to parenting, they really only became equal partners in parenting after their son's infancy, when she seemed more willing to share her son's affection. Parents who start off equally sometimes get derailed because of changing circumstances. One mother reported that her family's equal arrangements fell apart when a series of professional opportunities for her husband left her holding the parenting bag until she took stock of what was happening and renegotiated the division of labor.

In all three of the couples described in this chapter, we can see how changing circumstances lead parents to continually recreate their family arrangements. The serendipitous opportunity for Donna to work full time was the spark that ignited the dramatic change in her family. In a smaller way, the everyday ups and downs of Donna and Kevin's satisfactions with their family arrangements can propel them to "go back to the chart" or "fall off the chart." In Janet and Daniel's case, there is always the question of which one of them will do professional work instead of childcare. A sabbatical for one of them creates a dilemma because the demands of their jobs become asymmetrical. With that change, they have to reassess what is fair. Is it fair to simply divide up the time with Noah, or is it fair that Janet, who still has the everyday demands of teaching, be granted more time to work? Because each one has goals that conflict with spending time with the family, occasionally Daniel and Janet clash. As for Paul and Mary, who certainly seem to have the most stable set-up of the three couples, recall Mary's remark that a job change for Paul would throw their babysitting arrangements into "chaos" and presumably precipitate a shake-up in the division of labor at home.

Just as changes in the family's circumstances affect the division of labor at home, the creation of family arrangements transforms those circumstances. Paul's commitment to involvement at home has led him to turn down a job change that could produce problems with the family arrangements. Donna's ability to negotiate a more equal division of labor at home made it possible for her to commit to a full-time teaching job. Family arrangements also change parents' identities, ideologies, friends, and beliefs.

Janet and Daniel, Mary and Paul, and Donna and Kevin illustrate some, but not all, of the dilemmas faced by equal sharers. What all share is the struggle to work out family life in an age that lacks consensus about how that should be done.

It's not just equal sharers who face this dilemma: all dual earners do. Women's work outside the home calls into question traditional roles at home even in families in which mothers are still doing three fourths of the work at home. Those families must also grapple with the issues of who is going to do what and with the meaning of those choices. They are, however, working out very different solutions.

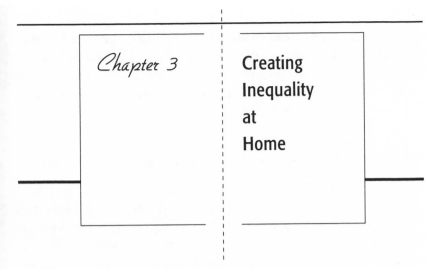

Chapter 3 | Creating
Inequality
at
Home

Everyone negotiates. Although inequality still prevails in the homes of most dual-earner couples, unequal roles are no longer adopted without question or controversy. Like equality, inequality develops in the day-to-day struggles in families over how to manage. Inequality is not simply an outgrowth of the individual personalities of husbands and wives or a predetermined response to their jobs or upbringing. Inequality emerges out of the ongoing pressures, decisions, negotiations, and conflict that occur inside and outside their families. Unequal couples, like their equally sharing counterparts, vary in what they do and in how they explain why they do it. Today, couples feel as much need to justify inequality at home as they do to make sense of equality. If some couples are becoming more equal, unequal couples need to explain why they are not.[1]

In this chapter we will visit two couples who represent two common patterns I saw among the unequal families. In the first pattern, women modified their work lives while their children were young, cutting back substantially on the number of hours they worked outside the home. In the second, women continued to work full time while juggling the majority of family responsibilities. Both strategies create no-win situations for many women, because either they must sacrifice the rewards of their jobs, or, alternatively, they must try to manage the unmanageable burdens of the supermom.

Cutting back on their jobs often meant a step down for women. In a few families, women seemed to welcome this traditional division of labor, in which they retained an anchor in paid work, but turned most of their attention to parenting. But for those who had previously believed in the new feminist dreams of women's equality, these compromises seemed particularly painful. Denise and Eric's story illustrates the dilemmas these families face.

Denise and Eric: We Were Coming from a Political Place as Feminists

Denise and Eric live in a ramshackle Victorian house in a revitalized neighborhood of an old mill town in the Northeast. They have two young children, five-year-old Mark and eighteen-month-old Lisa. Denise, a nurse-midwife, has a part-time job near home; Eric is trying to establish a business developing electronic equipment for hearing impaired and visually impaired people. By some standards Eric could be considered a modern father. He gets up at night to tend his children, bathes them occasionally, takes them to daycare, and even makes their lunches. He is obviously very emotionally attached to the two children, and both readily go to him for comfort. When Mark was their only child, Eric used to take him on outings on Saturday mornings so that Denise could have some time to herself. Although he works at paid labor more hours a week than Denise, his work is "flexible" and he can occasionally respond to children's needs when she can't. Yet according to both his and Denise's reports, she is definitely the primary parent in the family. The bottom line is that Eric fits parenting around his work life, and Denise fits her work life around parenting.

Denise and Eric had struggled for a long time over whether or not to have children. Denise explains:

> Eric and I have been together for years and years and years, since college, and neither of us were going to have kids but when I was about twenty-five I changed my mind. When I was about thirty-five I had my first child, and that ten years we struggled a lot and broke up. I really wanted to have a child and he just didn't see how he could fit it into his busy life. It took a really long time to convince him.

She finally convinced him to have children by offering to shoulder most of the burdens of parenting herself, thus compromising her idea that parenting should be a shared enterprise:

While we were coming from a political place as feminists that believed in co-parenting and alternative roles, the only way that we would have children is . . . (that) our agreement before the kids was that having kids was my project and if he wanted to help he would. I mean we verbalized that . . . I desperately wanted kids and I wanted to be with Eric.

Denise underestimated what she was agreeing to undertake. The overwhelming demands of the first year of parenting put a great deal of stress on her, Eric, and on their marriage: "For the first year of both of our kids' lives Eric was pretty miserable actually with how much work it takes . . . can't believe how overwhelming this is, the tasks, how unavailable, how much I needed him to help me. The first year was just awful." She was home for the first three months of Mark's life. Denise reported that when Eric came home from his job, he was critical: "wondering why the house was such a mess and why I hadn't cooked dinner, and why there was so much left to do."

Denise had planned to go back to her job after three months of maternity leave:

When Mark was born I was working with a group of midwives at a job that was wonderful. I mean I loved the people that I worked with. I loved my job. It was my dream job. It was really perfect. I loved it and I was planning on coming back full time.

She changed her mind. Although she attributes her decision to work part time to her desire to spend more time with her child, perhaps it would not have been so difficult had Eric been as involved in parenting as she. She said near the end of the interview: "When one of us (Eric) is working hard—lots and lots of hours—that made us realize I had to work less. We wouldn't survive." Denise tried unsuccessfully to negotiate a part-time position. When she couldn't, she quit: "I wasn't allowed to work part time so I ended up leaving. I cried and I cried and I cried because I loved my job so much."

Denise found a part-time job closer to home. When she describes her current job as a midwife, the emphasis is on its flexibility with respect to parenting, which compensates for the loss of fulfillment in the work itself:

It wasn't this dream job . . . I was really making some significant compromises . . . They've just been really really accommodating and made it very very clear that whenever I need my schedule to be able to do what I needed to do for my kids . . . basically I was able to make my schedule so that I could do those things.

Denise says that she is happy with her work life for now. When the children are older, she explains, there will be time for her professional development. She has made a partial peace with those compromises by focusing on the shift of identity she has experienced: "My profession is being a parent at this point."[2] Denise talks about parenting with passion:

> This is the one thing that really mattered to me to do my best at. I find parenting tremendously satisfying and while I know it fits right into Eric's needs for me to do so much, I really want to do it too. Like the question is who's going to take Mark to swimming lessons. I don't want to miss out on doing it.

In contrast, parenting and the work at home for Eric has an optional quality. Denise says: "His priority is to get his business off the ground. What's changed over the years is that I've become more supportive of him doing that . . . that's his project, like children are my project, his project is to do his business." Eric concurs: "Denise has been very willing to let me do whatever I can do (at home). She's willing to do whatever has to get done and if I can help and do things that's great."

But Denise is not quite as sanguine about Eric's approach to parenting as he maintains or as she tries to maintain. She struggles within herself to accept a definition of family roles that will bring peace. Her talk of becoming more supportive alludes to the rocky road they have traveled. Denise reports struggles between them over his work. On weekends and nights when he wants to work, conflict erupts. Denise explains:

> I really like to spend some time, all of us together because that's what I think weekends are for, a time for us to be together as a family. Eric would say, "But I've got all this work that's got to get done. I've got a deadline coming up."

Some compromise is reached. Eric doesn't work the whole weekend, but devotes part of it to the family. Denise seems torn between accepting the principle that work comes first for him and her desire to have him share more in family life. The situation is exacerbated by the ongoing demands of house renovation. If he doesn't spend time with the kids on the weekend, she cannot get the work done, leaving the house in a "depressing" state.

Although Denise focuses on the conflict over the amount of togetherness she and Eric will share, a second issue is the burden on Denise that is created by her putting home responsibilities first in the absence of a husband who does so as well. There's a lot of work to do with two small children and an old house. Interestingly, although she always frames her decision to work part time with reference to the needs of her children, when she actually describes her weekly routine, a lot of the additional time she spends at home is devoted to household chores other than childcare.[3] In fact, she says: "I think part of the reason that we're doing as well as we are right now is I spend a lot of time doing housework." Her criticisms of her husband focus on his absence from the emotional life of the family, but I wondered whether there was also conflict over his absence from the drudgery of family work. Denise does the bulk of childcare and almost all of the housework: "In our household he (Eric) doesn't do any cleaning unless I say, 'All right, tonight we're going to clean the house because we have company tomorrow.'"

The other disadvantage for Denise is the loss of freedom to pursue her individual goals: "(I want) Eric to be more willing to be home with the kids on nights that I need to go out to do more of the things that I need to do to be more of a professional person, or more of my own person, as opposed to just being a mother."

Eric recounted a story that reveals how they manage conflicts over this issue. Denise wanted to go on a trip to New York City with friends the same weekend that Eric wanted to go to an out-of-town marketing conference. Eric thought they could both go and hire outside help; Denise thought the children needed one of them to stay home. Denise pressures Eric to give her more support by taking over childcare when she wants to pursue other things; Eric's response is to argue for substitute care. The inevitable resolution is that Denise stays home and Eric goes, but feels a bit guilty. Because of her greater commitment to the children, she is in a weak bargaining position when it's time to decide who gets time off. In the end she will put what she perceives as the children's needs first.

Eric deflects the demands on him to parent more by arguing that individual needs should not always be sacrificed for children. He reports, "We have conflicts around the degree to which the kids totally determine our lives." Rather than making more "sacrifices" himself, he tries to get Denise to make fewer: "I'm sometimes pushing that we should have more childcare so that she can have some time to herself."

Eric feels uncomfortable and embarrassed when he acknowledges their inequality. When asked if he ever gets criticized, Eric answers: "Just from myself. I don't think we're all that nontraditional. I wish we were a lot more equal . . . We're pretty traditional. It's really amazing. Who ever thought we would have been this way?" However, his description of a nontraditional alternative again shifts the focus away from his contribution relative to Denise's: "We're even living in this little nuclear family which I hate . . . I think it's a really dumb way to bring up kids with two adults." His allusion to communal life conjures up an image of a much better adult-to-child ratio in which he would not have to increase his contribution to childcare. The burden would be relieved for Denise, but at no cost to him.

Denise has made peace, at least for now, with the losses in her work life, but seems troubled when her life diverges too much from Eric's. Denise seems happiest when she recounts the moments of shared parenting between them, for instance when Eric investigated their daycare options, and helped decide which would be the best for Lisa. But Denise's pleasure in those moments is marred by Eric's reluctance to get involved. When asked what she would like to change about the division of responsibilities in the family, Denise replied: "For Eric to take more initiative and be more excited, to take more of the overseeing, to share the excitement a bit more."

When Eric reflects on their life at home he feels bad, but also admits that he doesn't expect much to change soon:

> I wish it were more 50-50, but I don't think it's going to be, just because of where we are in our lives. I'm trying to start a company . . . I work full time at least and tend to just need more time or take more time for things that I need to do, want to do . . . I feel badly sometimes that I don't do more. Sometimes I try to do more but I can't.

Despite these conflicts, Denise and Eric were happy at the time I interviewed them. Eric had recently worked on renovations of the house with Denise, which she loved, both because house-building feels like nest-building to her and because she enjoyed the time spent working together on a project. Perhaps their optimism reflects the transition they are undergoing. Eric had quit a steady paid job recently to work exclusively on establishing his own business. The success of that business could influence his flexibility and availability to relieve Denise. In any case, as children get older their family circumstances are likely to change. The needs of children diminish, and even if a father does not increase his involvement, his percentage of involvement is likely to increase because the mother cuts back on hers. Denise's professional aspirations will wait for a future time.

Denise and Eric's story illustrates some of the dilemmas faced by the unequal families. What kind of role will fathers assume? How can inequality be justified? How much involvement from fathers is enough? Eric's role as a helper, Denise's rationalization that their family arrangements reflect differences in ambition between her and Eric, and the couple's struggle over the extent of Eric's involvement, reflect common patterns seen among some, but not all, of the unequal couples. Unequal couples vary in how they divide family work, in how they explain inequality, and in how they negotiate.

Dividing Family Work

Fathers in the unequal families play one of three roles: helpers, sharers, or slackers. Eric is a helper, the most common role for the unequal fathers.[4] As Denise puts it: "Eric will do stuff but he wants to be asked. He wants to put it on his list . . . It's not something that he's thinking about unless I get him thinking, although he's really helpful." Eric helps with his assigned jobs when he has the time, while Denise orchestrates and manages it all, and does the lion's (or really the lioness's) share herself.[5] Eric is a pretty good helper compared with many of the fathers in couples who split the work 75-25. He willingly assumes a wide variety of tasks in the household when he has the time, but like all helpers, he does not carry the responsibility for making sure the job is done. Denise is the parent of final resort; she makes sure the job is done, whether or not she has the time.

In contrast to the helpers, sharers are the men who are fully involved in parenting when they are not doing paid work. The only difference between them and the fathers who split work 50-50 with their wives is that they have a greater time commitment to paid work than their wives. Yet like the equal sharers, when they are available they are every bit as involved as their wives.

A number of the fathers in couples who split work 60-40 fall into this category. Take John, a casework manager at the same social service agency where his wife, Marilyn, is employed as a caseworker. Although they began as equals at their jobs, he was offered more professional opportunities, and consequently works longer hours than she. Nevertheless, when he is at home, which is quite a bit, he is right there: making lunches for his children, helping them with their homework, chauffeuring them from one activity to another, participating in the myriad tasks that fall to parents of school-aged children.

Finally, there are the slackers, the men who relax while their wives work a second shift. As a divorced woman recently described it to me, "My husband knew how to sit." Often these men have wives who work as many hours as they, and in some cases even more than they. For example, Beverly is a highly paid executive at an insurance company who works a sixty-hour week, while her husband, Dennis, works forty hours a week, in a nine-to-five job as a podiatrist. Dennis picks up his two young children from daycare at the end of the day, but, typically, when Beverly arrives home at six-thirty, he is relaxing with the newspaper and a drink, the children are unfed, and none of the routine nightly tasks has even been begun. When Beverly arrives, she runs around frantically trying to do everything. With this kind of division of work at home, you would think only one parent is in the paid labor force. When husbands in such families do little to lessen their wives' workloads, their wives are left with a grueling double day of work.

I don't mean to suggest that sharers, helpers, and slackers are three different types of men. These are three different roles that are created in dual-earner households through implicit and explicit negotiation. Sometimes men try to pitch in and their wives make room and encourage them to become sharers. To men in other families, the work of the home is invisible and they have to be prodded to become helpers. In some, even prodding doesn't help. In a few cases wives avoid ceding control over family life by discouraging helpers from becoming sharers, or sharers from becoming equal sharers. The ongoing negotiation of work splits is rife with conflict, as competing desires and needs of husbands and wives clash within the constraints of their lives.

Explaining Inequality

When Denise and Eric explain their current parenting arrangements, they use the language of individual needs and goals. Denise emphasizes the difference between her needs and Eric's: "I have greater needs as a nurturer . . . I don't think he (Eric) has such a need to nurture." Eric also stresses the differences between them, but his focus is on his desire to pursue his own goals: "I'm either more selfish or I just don't have the patience . . . and really wanting to do things for me more . . . At some point I begin to feel it was a sacrifice before she does."

Unlike Janet and Daniel, the equally sharing couple who believed equality was the only rational and fair way to divide the work, Denise and Eric do not invoke notions of fairness to explain the division of responsibility in their household. In fact the word "fair" never comes up with respect to the division of responsibility in either of their interviews. I sensed, however, that when Denise says that children are her project and work is his, she is trying to create an equivalency that seems fair at least to herself.[6] It is an equivalency that is strained, however, because she does have professional aspirations beyond motherhood. Notwithstanding the deep satisfactions that motherhood holds for her, Denise, like her husband, does have individual needs, however much she tries to minimize them in talking about their arrangements.

Denise promotes a myth that Eric is the one with the ambition. True, Eric is vigorously pursuing big plans for getting his business off the ground. It is also true that she has been willing to put her professional aspirations on the back burner because of her desire for children. However, Denise is a professionally ambitious woman. She criticizes herself for getting by at her current job: "I could be a lot more creative on my job than I am . . . If I read a couple of articles a week I'm doing well and I probably would be better if I read a couple of articles a night."

Moreover, she has some exciting ideas for new professional directions to pursue in the future. She wants to go to law school to study medical law. When Denise claims that Eric is more ambitious than she is, she obscures the inequity that in their family he has the freedom to pursue his ambitions and she does not. Ironically, it is Eric who reveals that Denise has been more single-minded in pursuit of her professional goals than he has. Whereas she went to graduate school and has consistently followed a profession so that she now has a "decent wage," he calls himself a "real dilettante." Nonetheless, the talk in their family is about her nurturance and his ambition.

When the other unequal couples are asked why the mother contributes more to childcare in their families than the father, like Denise and Eric, about three fourths of them cite some kind of individual need, characteristic, interest, or goal. (They may give other reasons as well.) The men who proffer this type of explanation are most likely to invoke the difference between their interests and their wives': they want to emphasize career; their wives want to focus on the home. However, some claim that the unequal division stems from their wives' choices, their wives' need for control, and their wives' superior abilities in parenting. This myth of woman's power within the home is invoked even more readily by mothers. A third of the unequal women explain their disproportionate share of childcare as their individual choice. Another 10 percent invoke their need for control, while still others (18 percent) tout their superior parenting.[7]

Notably absent from these explanations of the division of labor in the family is any mention of male power in resisting the work at home. In fact, there was not one instance of an unequal woman whose explanation for the inequality at home explicitly targeted her husband's resistance, or the male privilege from which it stems. A couple of men did give answers that alluded to their own power to get out of the work when they described personality differences between themselves and their wives, calling themselves "weasel" or "lazy."

I am calling these explanations the "myth of women's power at home" because there is ample evidence from these same women that their husbands do resist.[8] Over three quarters of the women who explained the inequality in parenting as their own choice also complained about the division of work at home at some other point in the interview. When asked what they would change, the unequal women usually wanted their husbands to do more work or do the work without being asked.

Why are women unwilling to blame their husbands for refusing to do more at home? First, perhaps the unequal women want their husbands to do more, but don't want them to do half. They want the prerogative to retain primacy at home. Second, if women do want equality at home, they might not believe they have the power to achieve it. For those women, it is less distressing to believe they are living their lives out of choice rather than victimization. Over half of the women who invoke individual needs, choice, or interests have nothing to say about the gendered nature of their lives. They ignore socialization in their 1950s families, biology, and contemporary social pressures as possible explanations for the division of labor at home. They act as though their greater role at home is unrelated to their being women. This denial of gender is self-protective, because it allows the individual woman to retain a sense of control over her life. She avoids representing herself as simply being buffeted about by external forces. Moreover, when couples use individual needs and goals to explain inequality at home, they are implying an equivalency between husband and wife. As we saw in Denise and Eric's case, in theory each is getting to do what he or she wants. Such couples imply that the distribution of labor is fair.

Negotiating Inequality

By agreeing ahead of time that children would be Denise's "project" and that Eric would help "if he wanted to," Denise and Eric were explicitly choosing inequality at home. Yet, like Janet and Daniel, who explicitly endorse equality, Eric and Denise must resolve the practical issues of working out family arrangements on an ongoing basis. How much does Eric "want" to do? What does Denise feel she needs him to do, regardless of their earlier agreement?

As we saw among the equal sharers, the answers to these questions change over time, and are influenced by changing circumstances. Now that Eric has quit his job to focus his energies entirely on his business, he has increased flexibility, but also increased pressures. He is more willing to put in odd hours with the children, but may be less willing to cut back the total number of hours he works.

Even when you agree on the principle of equality, it's hard to figure out how to put that principle into practice. But for the unequal couples, even the principle involved is obscure. Unlike equality, which has a clear anchor point (a 50-50 split), the degree of inequality at home can vary along a wide continuum. The inequality from couple to couple differs not only in quality (as was true for the equal sharers), but in quantity. A split of 90-10 in the workload at home is quite different from a split of 60-40. The unequal families continually grapple with the question of how much participation from the father is enough.

Like many of the women in the 75-25 and 60-40 families, Denise accepts the role of primary parent. These women do not fight over the principle of equality, but they struggle over how much inequality will prevail. Like the other women I interviewed in unequal households, Denise tries to get Eric to do more.

Denise works part time, like half of the mothers in the 75-25 families, and still struggles under the burdens of caring for children. No wonder that struggle is intensified when women work full time and act as supermoms. Peg and Ethan illustrate some of the strains that emerge in families in which mothers are doing it all.

Peg and Ethan: Supermom and Slacker

Just to listen to Peg's description of her day makes me feel tired. She works forty-five hours a week as a school psychologist, administering diagnostic tests to elementary and secondary school students in a large public school system. Peg gets up at four in the morning to write some of her reports. With all her family responsibilities, the only way to get everything done is to get an early start. At five-thirty she goes downstairs to make breakfast for her three children: nine-year-old Florence, six-year-old Kenny, and five-year-old Wendy. At six o'clock it's upstairs again to supervise the before-school preparations: "In the mornings I generally lay out the clothing for the two younger kids. Florence is pretty self-directed. I'm the one who's saying brush your teeth. I make the lunches and make sure everybody's got their packs and everything." She negotiates disputes over clothing, and presides over breakfast, not only getting it, but responding to all three children's requests throughout the meal. It is easy to imagine the whirlwind of Peg's mornings, racing from one child to another pouring more juice.

Where is Ethan while all of this is going on? He gets up early as well to work on unfinished projects for his job. But when it comes to the domestic responsibilities to which Peg is attending, he is not available. Peg explains:

> He's not a morning person. He has coffee and sits. That's one of the biggest gripes. When I've had a tough morning, I'll say, "Am I the only one who hears people say, 'more orange juice'"?

They all leave the house at seven-thirty. He goes off to his job, and she drives the kids to the sitter where they later take the bus to school. She sums up their morning division of labor, which, in fact, isn't a division at all: "The morning is me."

The afternoon and evening is her too. She picks the children up at about four-thirty and then carts each of them to lessons—Florence to soccer, Kenny to karate, and Wendy to ballet. Then it's home to prepare the dinner while she supervises homework. They eat around seven, when Ethan gets home. After dinner she says that it's time for bed, but Ethan says there is an interlude before bedtime. If the children still have homework to do, Ethan reports, "She does the brunt of the inter- action on homework."

How does it happen that she supervises homework even when he is home? Ethan is a bit sheepish when he rationalizes, giving several rea- sons why she is more involved. First he says: "I'm going to cop out and say it's the nature of the homework they're bringing home right now." What could he mean by that? They are bringing home elemen- tary school homework. He then says that he sometimes helps Florence, who has spelling words to learn, because "it's very easy to do." "Kenny, on the other hand, is bringing home simple papers. He kind of migrates to Peg to assist him. It's like a natural thing the way I perceive it." The implication is that Ethan can't help with Kenny's homework because it is too difficult. Sensing that the difficulty of helping with a first-grader's homework is a pretty flimsy excuse for leaving it to his overworked wife, he quickly switches to emphasizing how little work homework supervision entails: "From my perspective the amount of homework they actually have to do is like fifteen minutes to a half an hour worth of work . . . I don't see it as being a major thing right now."

Nevertheless, some parent has to help. What actually happens, ac- cording to Ethan, is that Peg "just naturally jumps in . . . where I kind of wait for her to take the initiative." He reluctantly acknowledges, "Maybe I'm not helping as much as I could because sometimes I just feel like that." In other words, he just doesn't feel like doing it. Their evenings together parallel their mornings. Ethan sits in the morning while Peg responds to her children's requests for juice, and without a word spoken between them, he sits in the evening while she "jumps in" and helps them with their homework.

Peg is adamant that Ethan put the three children to bed: "They go up with their father and he tucks them all in. I stay downstairs. I don't do bedtime." Peg's no-nonsense tone conveys that this is one responsibility she refuses to take. But by Ethan's own report, bedtime responsibility and ritual are minimal in their family. He just tucks in his son and stands by while his daughters get ready for bed. No struggles are re- ported, but neither are any of the elaborate story-telling, singing, or book-reading rituals I heard about in other families. At most, Ethan occasionally sits with one of his daughters for five or ten minutes.

The division of responsibility is clearly quite "lopsided" in this household. Interestingly, though, it hasn't always been that way. Peg recalls that when their children were little, Ethan got up with all of them at night. He also did his share of staying home with their first child, Florence, when she was sick, and his share of taking Florence to dentist and doctor appointments. Ethan agrees that he was more involved at home: "when the children were younger . . . I perceived myself as being more of an aid to Peg."

In the intervening years Ethan's job has changed dramatically, and both he and Peg invoke this change to explain his lack of involvement at home. After they became parents, Peg put Ethan through college and then encouraged him to take advantage of a high-powered job opportunity that came his way. She describes the effects of his current job in a biotechnology business: "He's now with a high-achieving company . . . men don't stay home with children. You work sixty hours, so now I do all the sick care . . . His new job, while he's happier at it, has changed the dynamics of the family." Ethan says his job has eliminated occasions for him to interact with his children:

> There were opportunities (before) for me to take the children in the morning and there were opportunities for me to pick them up in the evening where today it's not even a question . . . A few years ago I was participating more in intramural activities with the children. I was coaching softball and soccer, and now again because of a job change . . . I don't have the opportunity or the desire.

Although his job has reduced the amount of time available for parenting, it doesn't entirely account for his almost complete withdrawal from family responsibilities during the week. "I don't have the opportunity *or the desire.*" The time away from home seems to make him feel like an outsider at home: "I do perceive myself to be more of a bystander observing the activities even though I'm in the same room. I'm not actually contributing."

Part of what he describes in his curiously detached way is his inability to adapt to the changing needs of his children, to carve out a role for himself as the children mature:

> I see the children becoming more independent. Whereas the youngest one, Wendy, couldn't put her pants on two years ago without some interaction. Now . . . she can get dressed by herself,

so I see myself watching her do that . . . I see myself watch that activity happen. I see my child putting on the clothes . . . Today she is going to ask me to help her with this, next day she's doing it by herself.

In the past, he relied on his children's requests for his help or their blatant need to elicit his involvement, and now as they become more independent, they make fewer requests. Even more discouraging, he sees them rejecting some of his wife's help. As children do, they sometimes refuse to wear the clothes she has laid out for them. Although Peg perseveres and chooses something else for them, he seems daunted by the prospect that some attempt to help might be thwarted: "If I was successful in finding something for them to wear, and they told me they didn't want to wear it, that would kind of deflate my balloon rather quickly . . . That would turn me off." Without both the specific, structured jobs of transporting children or coaching his daughter's team and the explicit demands of his children, an increased role for Ethan at home seems to require his initiative, which he seems unable or unwilling to muster.

It's hard for me to do anything during the week. If I come home at six-thirty, seven, I'm tired, basically fatigued . . . so when six A.M. rolls around and the kids are getting up, the last thing I think I really want to volunteer for is extra duties. I shouldn't say extra duties, but certainly not going out of my way.

Ethan knows that if he stands by passively Peg will get the job done. His lack of participation coupled with Peg's willingness to "jump in" seems to have engendered a downward spiral that they can't seem to reverse, even if their family arrangements aren't working very well. Periodically, however, Ethan's inability or unwillingness to take over more of the responsibilities when he is home becomes too much for Peg, and she starts a battle which is repeatedly lost:

Things build to a head and then I have what you call a meltdown. "I can't do this anymore. This isn't fair. This isn't right. I'm not the only adult in the house!" Then for a few days he'll try to make lunch . . . It's generally when I'm feeling pressured from everywhere and the stress level just gets to me and then I let it all out. It changes for a short period of time but then it reverts right back to the same.

His short-lived attempts to make lunch for the family illustrate part of the pattern that keeps them stuck in such unequal family arrangements.

Why does it "revert back" to her doing it all? It is not because Ethan fails to see the justice of her claims. He acknowledges that his wife's load is too heavy: "It's something that can't continue like this. It's too much of a burden for her." He agrees that she will plead with him to help, he'll make lunches for a few days, and then responsibility will revert back to her. But they have very different accounts of how that occurs. Each of them attributes it to the other. Ethan describes from his perspective what happens after one of her "meltdowns":

> We'll talk about what can I do to help and one thing naturally would be to help with lunches, so I'll take the responsibility for a day or two. Then the third or fourth day comes and she gets up before me and the lunches are made. Well, there's that opportunity gone for me to help.

When I asked why he thought his wife took over again, Ethan responded: "I really feel when she falls back, she's trying to do me a favor, where I'm not the one who really needs the favor . . . she's the one who's desperately demanding help, but it's very easy to sit back if the lunches are made and not worry about it."

When Peg starts making the lunches again she is not feeling as altruistic as Ethan thinks. In fact, she is seething with resentment. She takes over again because it is preferable to feeling angry over his continual requests for her advice. She explains:

> I don't like telling people what to do. I expect after so many years of being part of the family, you should know what your children like in their lunches . . . You should know what to put in them . . . When he says, "Who gets this? Who gets that?" I get annoyed. I'd rather do it myself than get annoyed at (Ethan).

She jumps in because it is easier just to do it herself. She is involved anyway in dispensing advice on how to make the lunches. And ironically, when Ethan does do anything to help, it emphasizes how little he is normally involved. Not only has he not made lunches for years, but he hasn't paid enough attention even to know how they are made. This stark reminder of his absence from the mental work of parenting is worse to her than the work of making lunches itself.

The ongoing dynamic between them is that she takes over and he stands passively by. Neither articulates how they feel about what is happening, and thus they continually repeat the process in which she periodically explodes over the unfairness of it all, he tries to pitch in for a short time, and then they revert to supermom and slacker. One is tempted to believe, as I did for a moment, that this is only a communication problem. If only Ethan would tell Peg about his frustration when she takes over, and Peg would reveal that she is not trying to do him a favor, but is angry that he can't seem to make the lunches without asking a million questions, all would be solved. But that optimistic scenario ignores the reason Ethan and Peg don't communicate more clearly. Both of them have conflicting motives. Although part of Ethan is frustrated when Peg takes over, part of him is also relieved. "It's easy for me to sit back and not worry about it if the lunches are made." Ethan's motivation is easy to understand. Their miscommunication lets him out of the "extra duties" he doesn't want to do.

But given her desperation for some help, what motivation would Peg have for letting Ethan believe that she takes over to do him a favor? Peg reveals that part of her feels responsible for all of the work at home: "I'm that perfect little girl who's got to do it all." She's angry at Ethan and angry at herself, while Ethan feels guilty. Nonetheless, each benefits from the dynamic that goes on between them. Ethan gets out of the work, and Peg gets to be that "perfect little girl."

Embarrassed, Peg admits another benefit of doing it all: "Another thing I can't ignore is I'm in control. That sounds terrible. That's not how I mean it, but I mean I'm able to structure things . . . I feel like I want to be in control." But it's a limited kind of control. She does get to plan the meals, the children's activities, the daily schedule of the household, but her descriptions of her meltdowns sound like anything but control. The demands on Peg are overwhelming; the stress is sometimes unbearable: "Sometimes I feel that I have no space or no time to myself *ever* . . . There are days when I just feel like I'm going crazy. It's just like I cannot do another thing."

Although the disadvantages of unequal family life to Peg are obvious, the loss to Ethan is no less profound. In retreating from responsibilities at home, he has broken a tie with his children. More than many of the men in the 75-25 families, Ethan seems to understand what he is missing, perhaps because he had been more involved in their lives earlier on. He describes the loss he felt when his new job precluded his coaching his daughter's team:

The coaching opportunity went right out the window with that decision, so that was painful, that was very difficult to do . . . I miss that interactive role with her. It was a wonderful, incredible experience to be coaching her team, to have her say, "Dad, I'm glad you're my coach."

He blames his job for the loss, but at a deeper level Ethan realizes that he doesn't take advantage of the opportunities he does have. He regrets not living up to his image of a father who will give what he didn't get from his own father. Time is rushing by, and although Ethan has the desire to be there for his children, he can't quite get himself to act on it: "I realize I'm losing a lot of valuable time with them, whereas having a desire is one thing but not acting through with it is another thing . . . It's a lot of guilt."

Ethan pays a price for his minimal role in family work, in terms of his relationship with his children, his self-respect, and his relationship with his wife. He focused on his relationship with Peg when he explained the advantages and disadvantages of the division of labor between them: "I get to have it a little bit easier than she has it to be truthful and honest with you. The disadvantage is that I pay the price for it later because she's tired, she's overworked, she's stressed out." It is not difficult for Ethan to see that her fatigue and stress have consequences for him and his relationship with her. Although all parents in dual-earner couples may be tired as a result of meeting the double demands of job and home life, when the demands are not shared equitably between husband and wife, a toll is taken on the marriage. Peg lives with resentment and Ethan with guilt. Nonetheless, neither imagines that much is going to change in the near future, although the children's growing independence will eventually lighten the load on Peg.

Dividing Family Work

Peg and Ethan are not the only parents who play the roles of supermom and slacker. Half of the women in the lowest paternal participation group are working full time. Not surprisingly, this group of women is the least satisfied with the division of childcare responsibility.[9] Their husbands are not particularly happy about the division of labor either, despite their own resistance to doing more.[10] Like Ethan, men in this group pay a price because of their wives' unhappiness.

Explaining Inequality

Both Peg and Ethan blame Ethan's job for the lopsided roles in the family. Yet deep down each knows that the constraints of Ethan's job do not tell the whole story. Otherwise, Peg wouldn't be so angry and Ethan wouldn't feel so guilty. The story that Ethan's job is the culprit is a myth that covers up the profound inequity that exists in their family. Of course Ethan's job does take him away from the family long hours. Yet some of the couples in which women work full time and men work even longer hours do not fall into the supermom/slacker pattern. Some hard-working men manage to come home after a sixty-hour workweek and still help their wives. The truth is that before and after his job, Ethan often sits while his wife works. When pressed, Ethan launches into numerous excuses. Peg blames herself. Neither acknowledges that Ethan resists the work at home. He doesn't want to do it after a long workweek, and his passivity at home is the perfect strategy for avoiding it.

Even if we accept that Ethan's job does limit his involvement, we must ask: Why did Ethan take a job that would put him so far on the margin of his family that he refers to himself as "a bystander"? Why does Peg enthusiastically endorse his job choice when it leaves her sometimes feeling that she is "going crazy"?

They have little to say about these work-related choices, despite the havoc that they have wreaked on family life. Even now, with so many women working in the paid labor force, the traditional expectation that men should maximize career success seems assumed in their family. They do not question whether any parent should choose a job solely based on its benefits to career without considering its effects on family life. Nor do they examine the gender inequality of Ethan's actualizing his career ambitions while Peg does not.

Although the inequality at home needs some explanation for it to make sense to them, the inequality in terms of their paid-work roles does not. Unlike Denise, who attributes the differential valuing of Eric's career over hers to the difference in their ambitiousness, Peg makes no such claim. She and Ethan both seem to take it for granted that his work life will be treated as the important one in the family. Ironically, when their first child was born, Peg already had a master's degree, whereas Ethan had not even finished college. Neither seemed to question that she would put him through school and then support his career moves, while putting aside her own ambition to get a doctorate in neuropsychology. Although she still has a rewarding career as a school psychologist, and has not made the profound compromises in work that Denise has, it is clear that her job is treated as the secondary one at home.

This taken-for-granted quality of inequality with respect to paid work is common among the unequal families, even ones where the women had high-powered professions. When I asked why it was the mother who cut back to part-time paid work in many of these families, the question didn't seem to make sense to them. That the father could be the one to stay home had never been discussed, or even given a moment's thought. The choice considered was whether the mother could, or would, cut back, not which parent would do so.

Negotiating Inequality

Peg and Ethan's story beautifully illustrates that neither the behavior of a supermom, juggling an endless onslaught of tasks and responsibilities, nor the behavior of a slacker, standing by passively while the work gets done around him, reflects ingrained or immutable personality traits of wife and husband. Instead, supermom and slacker are roles created within a particular family. Ethan went from acting as a very involved helper to acting as a slacker who contributes little at home. Peg went from sharing the work at home to acting as a supermom.

Ethan isn't lazy; he is a hard-working guy with a high-pressure job. Peg isn't simply a workaholic or a glutton for punishment. Peg and Ethan are a living example of how the roles of supermom and slacker (as well as any roles at home) develop out of the innumerable small interactions between husband and wife. Each time Ethan ignores his children's requests for juice while Peg rushes to meet them they are creating a picture of unequal family life, a picture neither feels particularly happy about when they look closely.

Although Peg may plead with Ethan intermittently to help, on an everyday basis she lets him get away with "sitting." Their real-life interactions, in which Peg takes over making the lunches in response to Ethan's awkward attempts, remind me of the hypothetical scenario described by Daniel, the equally sharing dad we met in the last chapter. In that scenario, which Daniel used to explain how inequality is created in families, the mother gets out of a shower dripping wet to take over for a father fumbling over diapering the baby. As Daniel put it, "Mothers can make it very easy for dads to disappear." Perhaps that is what Peg has done by jumping in rather than standing back: made it easy for Ethan to disappear. But Daniel added, underlining the joint responsibility of parents, "It's easy for dads to disappear, *if they're so inclined.*" Mothers' behavior gives fathers the excuse they may be looking for.

But didn't Peg even admit that she likes to have control? Could Peg's need for control account for their supermom/slacker syndrome? It's easy to blame Peg, and thereby let Ethan off the hook. But consider the contrast between Peg and Ethan's household and Janet and Daniel's. Both Peg and Janet describe themselves as women who like to have control. Yet Peg has become a supermom and Janet equally shares childcare with her husband. One major difference between the two couples is in the different ways the husbands respond to their wives' need for control. Ethan acquiesces to it, and takes advantage of it to excuse himself from the work. Daniel fights with Janet to retain control when her need for control threatens his involvement.

If Ethan challenged Peg when she took over, she might not act like a supermom. If Peg insisted that Ethan participate more, he might not behave like a slacker. If Ethan hadn't taken a job with a "high-achieving" company, the roles at home might be different. The unequal division of labor in Peg and Ethan's family has developed out of a set of choices, opportunities, and serendipitous events in which what each of them does alters the context in which the other acts, and together they create inequality at home.

Denise and Eric, Peg and Ethan represent two major patterns among the unequal couples: in the first the mother cuts back significantly on paid work, works part time, and assumes the majority of responsibility for the work at home; in the second she continues with full-time employment and juggles it all. Each of these patterns can have significant costs for women. In the first, illustrated by Denise and Eric, women compromise paid work, often with serious long-term consequences for their careers or their earning potential. In the second, depicted by Peg and Ethan, women face the impossible demands of the second shift.

Although these two stories represent what is happening in many of the unequal families, they are not exhaustive. In the creation of inequality, the negative consequences of either of the paths taken by Denise and Peg are moderated by several factors: women's attachment to the paid labor force, the demands of home life, and the stance of fathers. Unlike Denise, who experienced the diminution of her paid work as a loss, some women find it a relief to be freed from full-time labor outside the home. Moreover, in both of these families, the demands of home life were relatively high. Compare the stresses on them to those of one mother who worked part time as a secretary while assuming the primary parenting role for a ten-year-old son. Compared to Denise and Peg's lives, hers seemed like a life of leisure. Another mother, a magazine editor, happy to be working part time and spending the rest of the time at home with her new baby, had considerably less to do than did Denise and Peg, despite her 75 percent share of the work at home. Finally, both Denise and Peg were disadvantaged compared to women whose husbands were either sharers, who pitched in fully when they were home, or helpers, who despite their secondary role, still managed to contribute 40 percent of the household labor.

Denise and Eric and Peg and Ethan as well as the three equally sharing couples in the last chapter illustrate the bumpy process by which family life is created, fraught with struggle and continual revision. The process is the same for all of the couples: parenting arrangements are worked out within the constraints of work, ideology, social context, and identity, and those same constraints are transformed by the nature of the family arrangements created. Yet equality in all its diverse forms is a solution to the problem of modern family life radically different from gender inequality. Although the equal and unequal husbands and wives are alike in many ways, they differ in one important sense: what each feels he or she deserves and owes in the family. In the next chapter we will examine this sense of entitlement and how it influences the nature of conflict over the division of family work.

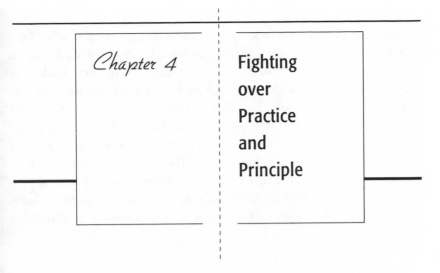

**Fighting
over
Practice
and
Principle**

The voices of equally sharing women sound different from those of unequally sharing women. They are more self-confident; they are surer of what they deserve. These women were often clear from the start that they expected their husbands to be equal partners in parenting and in sharing the chores of the household:

> I wasn't going to marry someone who wouldn't do it. I don't like domestic labor that much. The thought of having to do it was inconceivable.

> I never thought that I would be 100 percent everything and he would be watching—never, never, nor would I stand for that.

> I don't think my husband ever dreamed that if he married me I would do all the housework . . . or even that I'd appreciate him helping out with the dishes once in a while.

Equally sharing women feel entitled to equality.[1] But sometimes they had to fight to convince their husbands. By embracing equality unambivalently, they were able to be steadfast in their demands.

Unequally sharing women also argue over domestic labor, but because of their different senses of entitlement, equal and unequal couples differ in what they argue about, and in how they argue. Equally sharing women, who feel entitled to equality and expect it, fight over principles. They fight straightforward and direct battles with husbands.

In contrast, unequal women, who are ambivalent about what they are entitled to at home, ask for less and ask less directly. Like Peg, with her meltdowns, women in unequal households often tried to do as much as they possibly could at home, regardless of their husbands' contributions. They fought with their husbands when the demands became too much for them, but they fought over practice rather than principle. Or if there was a principle implicitly invoked, it was not equality but need. Wives thought their husbands should help them not because to do so was fair, but because they really needed their husbands' help. Although, like Ethan, many of the unequal men did respond, at least temporarily, when their wives pressed them to do more at home, they also resisted the work with a stunning array of indirect strategies.

Women's Fight for Equality

In a third of the equally sharing families, women reported battles with their husbands over establishing the principles that underlie equality at home: both parents are equally responsible for family work; the demands of their paid jobs must be given equal consideration; and the work at home must be valued. I have included several of their stories to illustrate how these women's senses of entitlement to equality were reflected in their conflicts with their husbands.

Consider Dorothy, a lively, animated woman who battled her shy, soft-spoken husband, Sam, over who was responsible for family work. She transformed her traditional marriage to one of the most equal arrangements I encountered. When I asked her how she had changed things at home, she attributed it to strikes, which she used to express her adamant refusal to be a traditional wife:

When we were first married, he was much more the chauvinist and expected me to clean, cook, and do every little thing and box his collars . . . I actually went on strike a couple of times. That's how it changed . . . There are times when, I remember, he used to come (home) for lunch and he would leave a mess. I'd come home at dinner and there's this mess from lunch . . . I just said, "This is ridiculous. I'm not doing this." So I stopped cleaning up after him. I said, "That's your mess; you clean it up" . . . I just kind of went on strike. And every now and then I'd go on strike. I didn't care how many times I'd walk past the mess, I refused to touch it . . . He couldn't stand it after a while. It didn't bother me. Stay there until doomsday . . . And then when the kids came I just said, "You have to help me."[2]

And he did. She praised Sam unstintingly for his efforts to change. Today, with their two girls, aged four and six: "It's about a 50-50 split with him doing everything that I do. I mean cooking, cleaning, washing, dressing children, feeding children. We both do all of that." Her voice is filled with pride when she explains that equal sharing means he does "everything" she does.

In Roberta and George's family conflict developed over the relative importance of their paid jobs. The turning point came when they made a decision to have a second child. Roberta reported that she needed to be convinced to have that child because her work as a theoretical physicist had been derailed by parenthood. Since it was ostensibly such flexible work, she felt that it had not been given equal consideration with her husband's work as a pediatric dentist, and the result was an unequal division of labor at home: "One of the things that happens when you do something as research is that it always seems that it's time that can be imposed on . . . You're not doing anything, you're just sitting at your desk." The decision to have another child brought this issue to the fore and enabled Roberta to claim the right to equality even though the nature of her work and her husband's differed:

> That is when we entered into our hard negotiations . . . We just had some really straight talks . . . I think what I began to insist on was that (my work) be given the same kind of consideration that a late patient would have for him. I think I sort of learned to talk back— to sort of stand up for myself . . . I had to sort of build a barricade around that time in a way that I hadn't done and that he had to learn to respect more than he (had).

In some families, like Roberta's, women developed a sense of entitlement to equality after their children were born.[3] Feelings of entitlement grow or shrink through the actual experience of family life. Roberta, whose work by any standards carried as much prestige outside the family as her husband's, was unable to assert its importance effectively in the early years of parenting. Her frustration with the compromises in her professional life eventually pushed her to demand more respect for that part of her life. By learning to stand up for herself, Roberta set the stage for equal sharing in her family: "I think a lot of this . . . had to do with my learning how to articulate my needs instead of just put them in the closet and wish somebody would pay attention to them without my having to say anything about it."

Women also set the stage for equal sharing by insisting that family work be valued as strongly as paid work. Mothers who eventually became equal sharers had often worked part time or taken time off from work entirely and done the majority of childcare when their children were young. Yet they had fought for the principle that domestic labor carries the same importance as paid work. In practice that meant that when their husbands came home from their jobs they had not earned the right to relax any more than their wives, who had been caring for the children. Like their wives, they were expected to be on duty when they returned home. For example, Rita asserted in no uncertain terms that her fatigue counted as much as her husband's: "We both have tough days. Maybe his is one way and mine is the other way, but that doesn't mean at five one of us can come home and take a nap. That pretty much established the fact that from the time we get up until the time we go to bed we both better pitch in." Establishing the principle that unpaid work counts as much as paid work makes for a smooth transition to equally shared parenting when women return to full-time paid jobs.

Agreeing on the principle of equality, however, doesn't mean that couples readily agree on how that principle will be put into practice. Even when couples agree to share, they argue about who should do what. Grinning, one equally sharing father described their daily routine:

We wake up in the morning and yell at each other about who is going to take what responsibility for what on any given day . . . I think ultimately it winds up we make a pretty much 50-50 split . . . Of course we are always arguing about which way it is tilted . . . We always each think it's the other one who's been doing not quite their share, but I think it pretty much strikes a balance that way.

The sense of entitlement to equality encourages equally sharing mothers to communicate their expectations clearly and directly. Like Dorothy with her strikes, Roberta, who learned to stand up for herself, and Rita, who directly challenged her husband's assumption that his day had been harder than hers, equally sharing mothers have not been shy about expressing their claim to equality. Their success reinforces their belief that communication is the key. As one mother said, "If you are clear about what you want, you get it."

The equally sharing mothers are also not afraid to use power, and the language of power. Dorothy's "strikes" and Roberta's "hard negotiations" reflect men's resistance to doing domestic labor. Simply communicating one's expectations in a clear and direct way doesn't always work; it may take the exercise of power to change the division of labor at home.[4] For some women, shared family work was a precondition or even an ongoing condition of their marital commitment:

> I wouldn't have married him if he wasn't like that.

> It was a deal we made when we had kids . . . "If you (her husband) don't do half, you'll be a single parent."

Like Roberta, a few mothers used their husbands' desire for children as a bargaining chip to win their agreement to equally share childcare. Consider this mother's story:

> I didn't want to have kids because I didn't think I knew how to do it . . . and thought I'd be totally overwhelmed and wreck my life . . . I finally said, "Okay, I'll do it if we split the work." He said, "No!" . . . Now he's into it, but he didn't like me saying that's what I wanted . . . I had to fight him a long time before we had a kid, though, about this 50-50. He did not want to agree on it.

Her husband wanted to have children enough to agree to her terms. This case provides an interesting counterpoint to Denise and Eric's: Eric refused to have children until Denise agreed that they would be her "project" and he would be released from responsibility for their care, while this mother refused to have children until her husband agreed to take half the responsibility.

Although feelings of entitlement may inform women's willingness to use power, their strategies may also reflect their sense of what will work.[5] Compared to the unequal women, equally sharing mothers may simply possess more power in their relationships because they are relatively less attached to their husbands than their husbands are to them, or because compared to other men, their husbands care more about having children and their relationships with children or care less about career success.[6] In short, equally sharing mothers may use power more because they have more power.[7]

Interestingly, by and large, the power equally sharing women report using is not economic power. Their power is derived from their husbands' love for them and their husbands' desire to have children. These women make it clear that they wouldn't get married, stay married, or have children if their husbands failed to live up to their equal ideals. Although equally sharing mothers don't use the word "divorce," the implication is clear.[8] Arlie Hochschild argues in *The Second Shift* that the implicit threat of divorce leads many women to give up the fight for equality. My findings suggest that the reverse is also true. Men succumb to the threat of divorce by agreeing to carry the load at home. Although Hochschild's argument that men are advantaged in the marital marketplace is well taken, when the human heart and love are at issue, marketplace considerations do not always rule.[9] The equal sharers in my study have bet successfully that their husbands' love for them is strong enough to withstand their exercise of power. In their fight for equality, however, the equally sharing mothers are the exceptions.

Women's Fight for Help and Appreciation

Peg and Denise represent the millions of women who, despite doing a disproportionate share of domestic labor, don't seem to feel outraged or exploited by inequality per se.[10] They don't expect much from their husbands. In fact, although their husbands are not cleaning the bathroom or cooking the dinners, a few wives praised them for not complaining that their wives weren't doing it:

> Never in a million years has he said anything to me like, "Why isn't this bathroom cleaned?" . . . He certainly has never in any way, shape, or form tried to lay a trip on me about "That's your job."

> He's notorious for his never ever ever ever, in our ten years of marriage . . . he never ever expects that there needs to be a meal on the table. It's incredible, because I may sometimes feel a little guilty about spending all this money eating out all the time.

Yet all is not well in these households. Peg, the supermom who tried to do it all, periodically exploded with rage. Although she does not expect equality, she is angry. She is not alone in her discontent. Consider another mother, Carol, a resource coordinator for museums, who changed jobs so she could be home at three o'clock to enable her children to participate in after-school activities. Previously her nights had been free, but now she is encumbered by work at night. She's dissatisfied because her husband is unwilling to compromise his work time at all. "I think he spends too many hours there . . . I think he spends too many hours away from us . . . I knew that (about his job commitments) when I got married, but I still think he could make some changes in his schedule that would benefit his kids."

Carol works fifty-two hours a week at her job and also does virtually all the housework. When her husband is home he plays with the kids while she does the work. He admits to doing no housework and seems to feel entitled not to. When I asked how he responded to her desire for him to do more he said, "I just chuckle."

Although tired and stressed, working a double day, Carol doesn't expect him to do much:

> I just want him to pick up after himself. I don't particularly expect that he is going to vacuum . . . My husband doesn't even know how dishes go in the dishwasher . . . All I would really like him to do is pick up behind himself. I really don't ask him more than that, and to be considerate of things like not walk across the floor I've just washed with his boots on . . . those little things too, not that I want him to wash the floor, but if he just wouldn't get it dirty quite so quickly, that's all I ask.

Take the case of still another full-time employed mother who complains about the burdens on her. The mornings are the hardest, when she has to get her five- and six-year-old daughters ready for the day. She wishes her husband would pitch in more: "I'd like to see him get more involved with putting them on the bus, making sure they've got everything for school . . . I wish he was around more in the morning." What does he do in the morning? "Oh, he'll get up and take a shower and go to work." Her husband also reports that the morning routine is a bone of contention, but seems undaunted in his entitlement to leave when he does. In the midst of her protests, he says, "I open the door and I go to work."

When they are both home, her biggest gripe is his failure to do laundry: "I get so sick of doing laundry. I do laundry constantly . . . he won't . . . lay a finger on laundry." Why doesn't he help with the laundry? He says: "Never done it. Even when I was on my own, I always brought it to a laundromat and had them clean it, fold it, hang it, press it. I've never done it on my own. Probably never will." He doesn't help because he feels entitled not to, just as he feels entitled to relax when he comes home from work, and on Sundays:

> She probably won't sit still on a Sunday . . . Sundays I usually relax . . . She's not happy unless she's doing something. That's the difference between her and I. She's not happy unless she's making a cake, making supper, doing laundry. She very rarely can sit down and watch television, take a break . . . She's not happy unless she's doing something. I'm different. I can relax.

What this husband describes as a personality difference between him and his wife really reflects their different senses of entitlement. As long as there is work to be done, she doesn't feel entitled to relax. She does the work, complains, but isn't overly angry about it. Although she thinks things should be different, she seems resigned, perhaps because his behavior seems so normal: "I think it's different for guys (becoming a parent) . . . I see it in a lot of the guys. The guys still go about their personal things."

Although resigned to inequality, she and other unequal women do fight with their husbands intermittently. Their most common refrains are pleas for more help. "If only he'd help in the morning, if only he'd do some laundry, if only he'd make dinner occasionally!"

Women today want more help, but they also want appreciation for the work they do at home and for what they've given up. Mothers who don't protest the second place their scaled-back careers take in the family still want their husbands to appreciate their sacrifice. For example, consider the plight of a mother with a Ph.D. who cut back to a twenty-hour part-time job and gave up opportunities for a higher-status, more responsible managerial position, while her husband continued to progress in his career. They fight sometimes because she wants his gratitude.[11] She doesn't demand equality, but does want recognition for the costs inequality has imposed on her:

> Every once in a while, I have this need to make sure that he recognizes what I've given up, and how hard that is on me . . . I would say to him, "Can you imagine if you worked twenty hours a week

... or if you ... hadn't taken a manager's position?" I can't take a manager's position part time. I mean, they just don't have them.

Other women struggle for appreciation of the value of the work at home: "What I wanted from him was appreciation. I don't know, a back rub ... Some sense that what I had done that day was not considerably less than what he had done." This woman, who had severely, yet happily, compromised her career to be home with her children wanted her husband to acknowledge her efforts: "'You are at work with all these bigwigs and I'm home with children playing blocks. I've had a hard day too.' And he'll appreciate it. But he needs to be reminded every time."

Unlike Rita, who insisted that her husband pitch in when he got home because of the underlying principle that the work at home has equal value with the work outside the home, this unequal mother, who wants her work to be valued, does not insist on its being *equally* valued. She readily reports that she has less leisure time because after her children go to bed she is left doing household chores while her husband is doing the *New York Times* crossword puzzle. If the work at home were given the value of work outside, why would he earn the right to relax while she continues to work? It is not clear how much value she wants him to ascribe to her work, nor is it clear how much of it she thinks he should do.

But some unequal women, even if not fighting for equal parenting, or equal entitlement to the pursuit of career, do fight on principle to get their husbands to share the work at home when they are available, rather than just to help. For example, one mother works fewer hours in paid labor than her husband, wants a primary role with her children, but fights to get her husband to take responsibility for family work when he returns home from his full-time paid job:

I've gone the whole route from making a list of his things to my things, and just sitting down and talking about it, and trying to get away from (the idea that) the housework and those types of things are my responsibility. Because I don't think they are.

The struggle between them is over which role he will have in the family: sharer or helper. She struggles to get him to adopt the role of sharer, which would acknowledge that the work at home is not simply her responsibility. He, however, feels entitled to the role of helper, which would leave her with the ultimate responsibility:

He always tells me, "I'll do anything you want me to do, just tell
me what." But I don't want to have to tell him what. I want him to
see that the floor is dirty and it needs to be swept or to take the
initiative because if I'm always telling him what to do then I feel
like I'm harping on him all the time.

But although she complains vociferously about her husband's unwillingness to take the initiative for household work, she also admits that
her own ambivalence about her responsibility for family work makes it
difficult to change the division of labor:

Part of it's probably my own fault because I don't know if I feel I
should be doing it or if there's still a part of me that feels it's my
responsibility still—the housework, the raising of the kids, all that
stuff. Because you hear that through your whole childhood and
your parents believe that. Your mother believes that. So there's
probably a part of me that thinks I should be the big superperson
that can do everything. But the reality is you can't do it all.

The unequal women are in a bind. They need help, but are unsure of
how much help they can justify to themselves, let alone their husbands.
For their part, husbands in the unequal families often resist family
work.[12] Even when they help, they may refuse to take the initiative,
performing the work while still leaving their wives with the responsibility for making sure it gets done. Yet many of these men are unsure
about their obligations. Like Peg's husband, Ethan, some feel guilty
when they see their wives working harder than they do.[13] Although
they may secretly believe they shouldn't have to do the work at home,
they don't simply feel entitled to claim male rights or roles to get out of
it. Today when conflict over domestic labor erupts it is colored by this
uncertainty.

Most of the unequal women simply resign themselves to doing more
than half of the work at home. But sometimes juggling it all simply
gets to be too much and the supermoms go over the edge. Their bursts
of irrationality are an implicit claim on their husband's participation.
Rather than a rational claim of a principle by which family work should
be organized, these "meltdowns" speak to women's need for their husband's help. Consider the family dynamics when this mother worked
full time:

He would just run around and stay out of my way as much as he could. He would say, "Tell me what to do and I'll do it" . . . He knew I would just blow at him for anything . . . I was not myself physically or mentally. It was too much.

Men can respond to this kind of irrational transformation in their wives without accepting responsibility for a share of the work. They can merely help in an emergency situation, without promising help in the future. Becoming irrational also means that women do not have to eschew responsibility for family work. They can say to themselves that they are trying to live up to their responsibilities, but are simply unable to do so. No change occurs in husbands' and wives' differing senses of entitlement. Therefore, as we saw with Peg and Ethan, the stage is set for periodic recurrences of the "meltdown."

One father described the repeated scenario in his household this way:

Periodically, my wife rages about, "Can't you help me clean up the house more?" I'll say all right, fine. Fold a few more loads. If the cars have needed a lot of work lately, I can ride on that for a bit because then I can have something quantifiable I point to that I have been doing.

He pleads that his breadwinning should excuse him: "What's left out of the scale, of course, is the fact that I go out for forty hours a week and do something that brings in the paycheck." When his wife rages about his lack of help, however, he doesn't say that. Instead he tries to accommodate a bit. Perhaps he knows that his wife would not accept his blatant claims, given that she works too, or perhaps he accommodates because it doesn't cost much to do a few things more until the storm blows over. These conflicts come up again and again because underlying senses of entitlement and responsibility for family work don't change.

When women hold themselves accountable for the work in the house, they have a hard time demanding more from their husbands, even when they believe they should. Peg articulated the nature of this inner conflict: "I get angry at myself because it is hard to do it all and I should ask for (help) . . . It's difficult to be asking somebody to assume what you've always assumed was your role."

Her ambivalence is echoed by other women. Even some women who saw themselves as feminists had conflicting motivations and expectations. One highly insightful woman told me about her struggle with this ambivalence. Although ostensibly looking for a man who would co-parent, June reveals that underneath she really feels that men's careers are more important than women's: "I think (I had an) entrenched notion that a real man isn't that interested in his kids . . . You really can't expect it . . . I'm so conflicted because I've low expectations but I'm angry about them." She acknowledges the cost of her ambivalence:

> Even though I'm pissed off at the ways in which I think Al is not doing enough, there's a way that I encourage it and I won't let him in. I have a certain view of what they (the children) need educationally and I don't want to leave it up to him.

It is difficult to win a battle that rages on two fronts. Women fight with their husbands to get them to do more work, but they also fight within themselves. Despite their periodic explosions, for these women fighting for real change is usually a losing battle. The best they can hope for is temporary respite. Nevertheless, change does occur in some unequal households. Unequal women who don't claim equality in any sphere do feel entitled to considerations beyond what their mothers received. Women today are not willing to be consigned to the serving role they witnessed growing up. Marianne, who got her husband to help, put it this way: "(My father) is the ultimate chauvinist. [Sarcastically] I would see the day that my husband would come home and sit in a chair and I would run around like a servant like my mother does . . . I'm not a maid; I'm not doing that."

At times, the unequal women do make demands, state their bottom line, reason with their husbands. In fact, occasionally an explosion propels a woman to take a stronger stand and limit the degree of inequality between her husband and her. In one of the most dramatic stories I heard, one husband learned that there was a limit to his wife's willingness to take on a traditional role at home. She recounts an incident that occurred when she was home with her infant son:

The Moo Shu Pork Story

Seth was about six weeks old and I had been cooking meals for them every night when Jacob would come home. I grew up that that's what should be done. Before we had Seth, for me to cook was great. I loved it. I really enjoyed it. But then, I had this baby who used to start screaming at four or five in the afternoon and Jacob wasn't coming home until seven to have dinner so I would have had three hours of screaming while trying to cook . . . We only had one car so I was driving Jacob to the train station and picking him up in February, and with the baby who was screaming. I just broke down in hysterics. "I can't do it. I can't cook. Could we please just get some take-out. I can't. I just am falling apart. There's nothing left" . . . "Oh sure, we can have take-out Chinese." (We) go out and get Chinese food to go. We sit down and he says, "You shouldn't put the food in serving bowls and make tea?" I'll never forgive him for that. He got up and made the tea. I threw the containers of Moo Shu Pork on the floor and grabbed my screaming child and left. I was just beyond myself. I didn't know what else to do. So now, I'll say, "I'm going to order take-out, and you can make yourself tea if you want. But when the food comes, I'm sitting down and eating it with the kids, and it's going to be hot."

Although not demanding equality, the unequal women, worn out, do reach a point beyond which they will not go—Peg's staunch refusal to do bedtimes, Marianne's refusal to wait on her husband, and this mother's refusal to make tea to go with take-out Chinese food. When they reach that limit, uncertainty disappears from their voices and they articulate their demands without an explosion. When women feel entitled to help, they don't need to go over the edge.

Strategies Men Use to Resist

Women's ambivalence alone certainly doesn't account for the unequal division of labor at home. The unequal men are hardly fighting to do an equal share of the work. In part, they feel entitled to their wives' domestic services, entitled to pursue unfettered careers, and entitled to relax after their day at the job. Yet they don't feel as entitled as their fathers did. They recognize that their wives are out doing paid labor as well. The men in my study virtually never justified their lack of involvement in household work by invoking some inherent right or privilege they held as men. Although even recent statistics show that women do much more of the household labor, the raw spoken claim of male privilege seems to have become taboo.[14] Men do resist, but their strategies are largely indirect. They include: passive resistance, strategic incompetence, strategic use of praise, the adherence to inferior standards, and denial.[15]

Passive Resistance

"Just say nothing!" seems to be the motto of some men who resist their wives' efforts to involve them in household work. The most obvious form of passive resistance is simply to ignore the request. When I asked one father how he responded to his wife's entreaties, he answered, "In one ear, and out the other."

Obliviousness can be another form of passive resistance. Ethan sits with his coffee oblivious to his children's requests for juice. Another mother reports a similar scene at her house:

> He plants himself on the couch. As soon as he's home from work sometimes . . . If there's something going on with kids, the kids could be screaming and yelling. He's totally oblivious to it. I'm listening to it (while preparing dinner) and I have to come out here and say something to them.

Sometimes men give in and perform a particular household duty, but their grouchiness while doing so becomes another form of passive resistance:

> He'll help do dishes once in a while . . . He might put up a stink, but he'll end up doing it.

> I think I . . . try to sleaze out of it (responsibility when at home) as much as I can . . . I try to dicker or make an excuse or something as my first response, but I usually end up, perhaps somewhat nastily, taking care of them (household chores).

Passive resistance is effective because it requires so much energy to overcome. Women, already tired from their double day, may give up the struggle if the cost of getting help looks higher than the benefits of that help. Having to ask a husband to pour the juice when a child asks may feel like more effort than it's worth. As one mother put it: "I have to direct him and it's easier for me to just do it." The sulking, unpleasant compliance of a husband who clearly resents doing a chore will probably cloud whatever satisfaction his wife feels in getting help.

Small wonder that the next time she may very well shrink from trying to obtain his help.

Incompetence
Ruining the laundry, leaving grease on the dishes, ignoring children when one is supposed to be watching them, and forgetting to pick them up from activities are all examples of the strategy of incompetence. Incompetence has its rewards. It allows men to justify the gender-based distribution of domestic labor.

> Getting the kids dressed—these buttons are so tiny I can't do these tiny buttons . . . Poor kids, they're always getting dressed backwards.

> Dinnertime. Mom is the cook. When the kids hear that Daddy's going to be making dinner, they'd rather eat out. I'm not talented. I'm just not very good in the kitchen.

> I just don't possess the tools to deal with girls' clothing, whereas she can.

Women may think twice about trying to get their husbands to take more responsibility at home when the way they carry out those responsibilities creates more problems than it solves: "From time to time he's taken on laundry, but that always ends up really a disaster, something being stained or shrunk, so I don't want him to do laundry."

Ruined laundry or mismatched children's outfits may be annoying, but incompetent care for children can be downright frightening. One mother recounted an incident in which her husband forgot her specific instructions to pick up his eight-year-old son before the older one so that the younger child wouldn't be waiting alone. The eight-year-old did end up waiting on a corner for his father, not alone only because another mother discovered his predicament and waited with him. Not surprisingly, she concludes, "Sometimes I don't trust (my husband) . . . He just doesn't pay attention."

Likewise, another mother explained why she worries when her husband watches their two-year-old:

> The other day he was outside with her and he was sitting there reading the newspaper. I never do that, never sit there and read a

newspaper, not because I have to see everything that she does. It was more of a safety thing . . . I would like to feel more confident that when he's alone with her he is watching out for her safety-wise. I sometimes think he's not as conscious of safety.

One might argue that men's "incompetence" in household chores is not a strategy, but simply reflects their lack of skill because of the way they were raised. Boys aren't taught how to take care of children and how to do laundry. According to this argument, even if their incompetence functions to relieve them of domestic responsibility, it doesn't mean that the incompetence is by design. There are two flaws in this argument.

First, although women may be socialized to feel the responsibility for childcare, many have not learned any of the necessary skills before they actually become parents. The difference between them and their husbands is that they know they have no choice. They have to learn how to button those tiny buttons, how to feed solid food, and how to soothe a crying infant. Although these women may have begun parenthood as incompetently as their husbands, the expectations that they and others hold for them as mothers mean that they simply learn what is necessary to learn.

Second, the skills in question can readily be learned. If one took the descriptions of men's incompetence at face value, one would wonder how these men held down jobs. Can it really be the case that a machinist or a man who holds a Ph.D. is incapable of running a washing machine? Women and men often say that women are the managers at home because the women are more organized, but how then do these "disorganized" men manage at work? If a man "forgot" important responsibilities at work the way the father just described "forgot" to pick up his eight-year-old son, he might soon be out of a job.

At heart the issue is not competence, but motivation. If someone wants to learn how to cook, do laundry, take care of children, and manage the household chores she or he can certainly do so. The equally sharing (and alternating-shift) fathers make eminently clear that competence in household skills is not the exclusive domain of women. Some women are not fooled by their husbands' cries of incompetence. Listen to this mother's take on what happens when she asks for some help:

He plays, you know, "How do you do this kind of thing?" and asks me fifteen questions so it would almost be easier for me to do it myself than to sit there and answer all his questions. That makes me angry because I feel like he's just playing stupid because he doesn't want to do it.

The strategy of incompetence often works. Like passive resistance, it is a way of making the cost of the struggle over the work at home too high. This mother sums it up succinctly: "If they act incompetent, then we have to act competent . . . I have this fear that if I didn't do it, then it wouldn't get done or it would be done incompetently." It is a fear that has basis in fact.

Praise

The flip side of men's self-portrayals of incompetence is their praise of their wives' skill in domestic labor. Although praise may be a sincere expression of appreciation, a benefit to its recipient, praise at home may also have the insidious effect of keeping the work within women's domain. The underlying message from men to their wives may sometimes be: "You're so good at it, you should do it." Sometimes the message is hardly subtle: "It would be a struggle for me to do the laundry. I don't think I do it as well as Roz. I think she is better with sort of the *peasant* stuff of life." And the father who said the kids wanted to eat out when they heard Dad was the cook told me: "I only eat to survive, but Dale is just wonderful. She makes these fabulous dinners." In a few couples men used the praise they heaped on their wives to justify why childcare was divided traditionally in their households:

I definitely wasn't as good as Roz. Roz's just good. She's good if they get a splinter. She's just good at all that stuff.

She's wonderful (as a mother) . . . Some women, like I say, are geared to be businesswomen; Florence is geared to be a mother. She loves it. She's good at it. I feel real lucky to have her as a partner because it takes a lot of the burden off me.

Praise can be insidious precisely because women do derive satisfaction from a job well done at home and from receiving recognition for it. Ironically, praise may undermine women's struggle for more help because they don't want to lose the self-esteem they derive from husbands' admiring accolades.

Different Standards

Another strategy men use to resist work at home is to maintain different and lower standards. Their spoken or unspoken claim is that they don't care as much as their wives if the house is clean, if a nutritious dinner is served, or if children have after-school activities.

There are three ways that couples might respond to this difference. First, men could raise their standards to meet their wives'. This rarely happens among the unequal couples. Second, women could lower their standards, which occasionally does occur among this group. Most commonly, however, the difference in standards becomes a driving force behind an unequal division. The person who cares more takes the responsibility and does the work.[16]

Women usually care more about keeping the house neat and clean because they, and not their husbands, are judged to be lacking if the house is a mess: "He wouldn't care if it wasn't dusted once every six months. I care because it's a reflection on me. Now that's another problem. Why should it be a reflection on me? He lives here too. But if anybody comes in here and the house is dirty, they're going to think that I'm a slob." Nonetheless, women are lowering their standards for household care, as sales of paper plates have increased and sales of floor wax have declined.[17]

The problem of what children need is a more troubling one. When the welfare of children is involved, women often feel they can't compromise their standards. Denise gave up a camping trip because she thought one parent should be home with her kids. Other mothers changed their jobs so they could meet the school bus when their husbands wouldn't do it or take their children to the after-school activities that they cared about more than their husbands did.

Denial

Just as a magician tricks us by directing our gaze elsewhere while he makes his move, some fathers deny there is a problem by focusing attention elsewhere while their wives do the work at home. Denial takes a variety of forms. Men exaggerate their own contributions by comparing themselves to previous generations, attribute greater contributions of their wives to their wives' personalities or preferences, and obscure who's doing what by invoking rules and patterns that sound fair and equal.

Men often recall their own fathers' roles at home in order to underline their superior contributions. Ironically, some men who do far less than their wives even see themselves as progressive role models. One father in a dual-earner family said he did 35 percent of the childcare; his wife said 25 percent. Nevertheless, he sees himself as a model of equality. His exaggerated view of his contributions seems to stem from his implicit comparison of himself and his father. When I asked why mothers usually did more at home, he said, "Because of the roles of our parents." (His analysis, of course, ignores that his wife leads a very different life from that of his mother, who was never employed outside the home.) He went on to describe his own contributions in glowing terms:

> We've joked and talked about many of the things that I try and do as far as helping and participating . . . I'm hoping that as our girls are selecting mates later in life, they will remember how much I helped out and how caring and listening I was . . . One of the advantages for kids that I'm involved with parenting (is) that they will expect their spouses will be involved. I'm a strong advocate of equal rights of women.

No doubt he is a loving and caring father, but he is far from contributing an equal share at home. He does help out, but his enthusiasm for the benefits of their modern division of labor must be considered in light of the inequality between him and his wife and her response to their division: "Sometimes I get overwhelmed and tired, real tired." By focusing on what he is doing that his father didn't, this man seems to miss what his wife is doing that he is not.

Men sometimes obscure an unequal division of labor by talking about and perhaps thinking about themselves and their wives as interchangeable. When I asked men to describe a typical day, indicating who did what, they sometimes used the word "we." "We get the kids ready for school." "We unload the dishwasher." Invariably, on further investigation, "we" meant that their wives were doing it.

Men also suggested a false interchangeability between themselves and their wives by invoking a rule for dividing household labor that ostensibly applied equally to each, but actually worked in their favor. For example, parents commonly reported that whoever was available did the task at hand. Although that might sound like an equitable procedure, it is not if the father arranges to be unavailable. Consider this family. The father describes the division of responsibility at night: "As far as helping with the homework it's fairly equal . . . We both tend to try to help out—whoever's free that night . . . It's not you're going to do the help in math or I'm going to help in math. It's who's free." That sounds equitable, but listen to his wife's description of what happens in the evening:

> That's been a bone of contention lately. Sawyer goes out a lot . . . He still runs a lot at night so that leaves me to deal with the homework . . . She (one of their children) needs a lot of help with math, so that any homework issues I've been dealing with, and getting the youngest ready for bed.

He goes out, so guess who is available?

Finally, fathers sometimes engage in denial when they acknowledge an inequity in the distribution of labor but attribute it to personality characteristics or personal preferences of their wives. Men exaggerated their wives' enjoyment of family work. For example, this 75-25 father told me: "Cooking relaxes her. She likes to do it and she likes to keep busy for the most part." But when I talked to his wife, she *complained* that he didn't make dinner when he got home from work early.

By imagining their wives' desire and need to do the domestic labor, these men avoid acknowledging the inequity within the couple. This denial allows them to resist not only the work, but also the guilt they might feel if they viewed the situation accurately.

Clearly, men in the unequal families resist the work at home. But the unequal men are not villains. In fact, most are helpers, not slackers. They do relinquish some male privileges, even while they resist giving up others.[18] However, they also ignore the need for their help, feign incompetence, manipulate their wives with praise, discourage them with very low household and parental standards, and avoid work by denying that there is any conflict at all. All of these strategies work to relieve men of household work without their having to admit directly that they simply don't feel responsible for it. Despite the time their wives spend earning a paycheck, the unequal men often feel entitled to avoid picking up the slack at home. The myth implicitly promulgated by these men is that their wives do the work at home not simply because they are women, but because they notice it, they're better at it, and they enjoy it more.

Although these work-resisting strategies are used mostly by the unequal husbands, the equally sharing husbands are not perfect either. Some resist giving up at least a few traditional male privileges. Housework, in particular, seemed an area of contention. For example, in one of the most explicitly feminist equally sharing couples I interviewed, the father's "incompetence" in doing laundry sounded remarkably familiar. Even in the most equal of households, there may be vestiges of the old ways. Still, even if there are some pockets of resistance, for the most part the equally sharing fathers honor their wives' claims to equality.

Strong Women and Reasonable Men

Strong women and reasonable men resolve the conflict over domestic work by inventing equality. Equally sharing mothers are an assertive crew. They communicate in a clear and direct manner, and use whatever clout they have to elicit their husbands' cooperation. Their husbands acknowledge the strength of these women in establishing equality at home:

> Sally is very strong. There's no question about that. I think it's partly that Sally . . . makes it that we both share. She feels very strongly about that.

> I think the most important reason is that Bernice absolutely, completely insists on it.

However, part of the reason these women appear strong is their success, and although women's strength may be necessary in the fight for equality, it is not sufficient. The strength and assertiveness of the equally sharing mothers is matched by the sense of fairness evident in the behavior of the equally sharing fathers. Equally sharing men have relinquished male privileges to which at least some had initially felt entitled.

In fact, the equally sharing women may argue for principles of equality because they sense they have a shot at success with their husbands. The unequally sharing mothers, realizing the futility of trying for equality in their families, settle for trying to get their husbands to do a bit more. The equally sharing mothers may not have to resort to meltdowns because their husbands have already responded. The rage of the unequal women may express more than the frustration of trying to do the impossible. It may be the rage of impotence at their failure to get more help.[19]

Compare the experience of the equally sharing mothers who won the battles for equality to that of Madeline, a legal services attorney with two children, who began parenthood with strong views about equal sharing. She and her husband agreed that when their first child was born each of them would take parental leave, and subsequently each of them would cut back on paid work to care for their new baby to avoid using too much daycare. Her husband, Aaron, was thrilled with his equally sharing role in the early years of parenting: "I was very excited about it. I had a paternity leave and . . . did sole care . . . and then worked a three- or four-day week for another year . . . There was a lot of time when I was just with my son and I considered that a privilege." Equal sharing was initially achieved in this family with little conflict. But perhaps signs of the dénouement were evident in the meaning Aaron ascribed to his sharing. The language he uses as he enthusiastically describes his role as a new parent is telling. It is the language of personal choice: "It was just great. It completely felt like my own choice and not something that I should do or that I had to do."

It is difficult to imagine a mother speaking these words. No matter how thrilled she is at spending time with a new infant, there is no denying that caring for a new baby is something she "should do." Aaron expresses the thrill of parenting at the same time that he asserts his entitlement not to do it. He immerses himself in parenthood the first time around because he wants to, not because he feels ultimately that it is his responsibility to do so. Thus, after their second child was born, when his career was getting off the ground and he had less passion and energy for parenting, he felt entitled to refuse to do it. He refused to take parental leave or cut back to part-time work. His wife told me:

> If you had come a year after William was born, then you would have found us struggling more about whose responsibility was what. I was feeling very much like Aaron was reneging on the commitment that we made about being with William . . . I had made my commitment and he wasn't keeping his part of the bargain.

Madeline was every bit as assertive as the equally sharing mothers. Yet, although she fought for her belief in equal responsibility for childcare clearly and directly, today she compromises her career while her husband takes a helper role at home. Aaron's analysis of what happens in "society" aptly describes what happened in his own family: "I think probably men feel they have the option to invest or not invest, whereas I think women feel they're the bottom line and they can't count on anyone else to do that."

Madeline may not appear as strong as other equally sharing mothers simply because she failed. Her husband did not honor her claims of equality. Aaron differed from the equally sharing men because those men accepted the justice of their wives' claims, even if they hadn't internalized as strong a feeling of responsibility for family life as their wives had. One extraordinarily honest equally sharing father acknowledged that although he "irrationally" wished his wife would create a more traditional family life, "rationally" he recognized that it wouldn't be fair: "I'm hardly a raging feminist, but I do have enough sense to see that that's a completely unfair distribution of labor."

Thus a sense of fairness motivates some of the equally sharing men to accept their wives' well-argued claims. Moreover, that sense of fairness drives some of the men to share even without a struggle. Let's not forget Paul, the father of five, who jumped in to help without prompting from his wife. His sense of fairness and his love for his wife dictated that it wouldn't be right to shirk while she worked.

The sense of entitlement that men and women bring to marriage affects the content and conduct of their conflicts, but it also changes and develops over time. Feelings of entitlement lead women to fight for principles, make clear and rational demands, and back them up with power-assertive strategies. But the feelings of entitlement expressed by the equally sharing mothers can also be a product, rather than a precursor, of their success. When their husbands accept principles of equality, respond to their demands, or indicate that their relationships are more important than male privilege, they promote a feeling of entitlement in their wives.

For example, consider Paul's wife, Mary, the equally sharing mother of five who didn't demand equality or even fight for it. When I asked her whether she or Paul had more leisure time, she reflected for a few seconds (indicating there wasn't much difference between them) and then replied, "I don't know, maybe he has a little bit more," adding in a light-hearted tone, "I'll have to do something about that." Once achieved, equality feels like a right.

Conversely, when the unequal husbands resist, they undermine their wives' sense of entitlement to their help. Listen to this mother's story:

> There's some things that aren't worth fighting over. I always know when (my husband) has been babysitting for a couple of hours because the living room looks like a demolition derby has come through. And the bathroom looks the same way . . . the dirty diapers are in there and all the dirty clothes are all over the bathroom floor . . . So I just have learned that it's just not worth wasting all kinds of extra energy. I just kind of do it, not necessarily that I like it. *He helps much more than a lot of fathers help.*

The futility of some struggles leads women to give up and to readjust their expectations. Instead of comparing their husbands' contributions to their own, they shift to comparing their husbands' contributions to those of other men. It is precisely that focus on within-gender comparison that maintains different senses of entitlement between men and women.[20] If a husband does more than his peers, his wife may then conclude she is getting a good deal. But although she may be getting a good deal relative to other women, it's not so good when you compare it to what her husband is getting. The shift in comparisons, however, allows women to live with resistant husbands and not feel exploited.[21]

Men's senses of entitlement are also, in part, products of the struggle with their wives. When you look at the equally sharing men now, they all seem eminently reasonable. For some, that reasonable stance was born out of serious strife with their wives. Interestingly, sometimes these men don't mention the conflicts that led up to their equally sharing role. For example, the husband who had expected his wife to "cook, clean, . . . and box his collars" made no mention of the strikes his wife used to get him to change. His transformation occurred so thoroughly that now his explanation for equal sharing refers only to his own sense of responsibility to do right by his children.

Discovering themselves acting like egalitarians, equally sharing fathers often pat themselves on the back for their enlightened stance. Meanwhile, their wives tout their own assertiveness and strength. Although they look like they have always been strong women and reasonable men, it is important not to forget that female strength and male reason are qualities that are sustained, lost, or developed in the creation of family life.

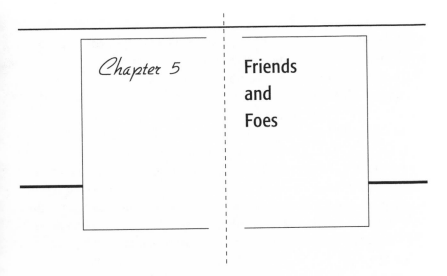

Chapter 5

Friends and Foes

Friends, coworkers, parents, in-laws, and neighbors are sometimes the enemies of equality. They undermine equality by assuming that inequality is inevitable, and by criticizing mothers who refuse to limit their lives to motherhood or fathers who favor time with their children over time at their jobs.[1] Unlikely as it sounds, onlookers also unwittingly undermine equality when they praise the nontraditional ways of equally sharing fathers. Praise, even when well-meaning, creates a double standard for mothers and fathers in which women owe their husbands gratitude for simply doing what they themselves do routinely.

Equal sharers resist and transform the dominant social messages of our times. By exposing the social expectations for inequality, by refusing to accept double standards for mothers and fathers, and by finding friends who also equally share parenting, these nontraditional parents create their own equality-friendly social world.

Unquestioned Assumptions and Self-fulfilling Prophecies

Parents, especially mothers, are well aware that when a child is born the spotlight is on Mom. Over and over again I heard women complain or simply observe that as far as parenthood goes, not much has changed. In one way or another, everyone seems to be telling new mothers that they should be more responsible than their husbands: "A mother who is working is still expected to be the same type of mother as a mother who's home. I think a father typically isn't expected to be anything other than what they traditionally were."

The belief that women are better at parenting than men can quickly become a self-fulfilling prophecy.[2] No one laughs at a new mother's fumbling attempts to diaper or dress her newborn, but people do joke about a new father's awkwardness. Usually, a crying baby is handed back to her mother to be soothed, not to her father. Questions about the new baby's temperament and habits, perhaps initially no more well known to the mother than to the father, are addressed to the mother. The expectation that the mother knows what she is doing and the father does not may quickly turn to a reality, simply by virtue of the practice and encouragement women receive. Forty-eight hours' practice of soothing a fussy baby may quickly teach the caregiver what works.

Powerful social expectations are conveyed even before the baby is born. One father, Larry, who took time off from work so he and his wife could equally share the care of their new baby, describes the differences in the questions he and his wife were asked about life after the baby:

> When Joyce was pregnant, people would say to her, "So when are you quitting work?" and saying to me, "So, you're going to be working more," something like that. Joyce would say, "No, I'm not quitting work." And I would say, "Actually, I'm working less." I really remember being struck by it, this automatic expectation that with pregnancy came the male role, that he had to be more of a provider, and the female role, that she was now going to stay home. That meant I had to think and clearly decide to go against the grain of that.

Inequality is so "normal" that it can blind people to the equality that does exist. This social blindness can subtly sabotage equal sharing.[3]

Fathers are often treated like invisible parents. Imagine this scenario. The mother of a child's friend calls to arrange a play date. Dad answers the phone. The mother who has called asks to speak to the child's mother. So far, so ordinary—but something important has happened. In this very normal everyday occurrence, that father, who is not expected to know anything about play dates, has been told that he is superfluous. Even the most equal fathers may feel embarrassed about correcting these mistaken assumptions, so sometimes they just hand over the phone.

Fathers committed to equal sharing chafe when their involvement is blatantly ignored:

> It's the one time where a white male can experience some sense of discrimination—when your invisibility is made apparent to you by the waitress. When (our daughter) Vivian was six months (old) and we were in a restaurant, she was sitting with me, and Rhona had gone to the bathroom or something. This woman kept on walking by and looking and smiling at the baby. Then as soon as Rhona came back and sat down (the waitress said), "How old is the baby? What's the baby's name? blah blah blah!"

Sometimes the equally sharing fathers fight back. Listen to this mother's story of a bystander who pushed her husband too far:

> We went on an airplane ride and Ollie was screaming his head off . . . Edward was holding Ollie (who) was screaming and screaming, and this bastard said, "What's wrong with this child's mother? Why doesn't the mother take care of this baby?" Edward turns to the man and says, "Because I'm his father and I am perfectly capable of taking care of him."

Discouraged, though, some men may give up rather than fighting back.

The invisibility of fathers' commitments to parenting is often matched by the invisibility of mothers' commitments to their jobs or careers. Janet, the political scientist we met in Chapter 2, went to great lengths to keep her career going when she was a new mother. She told me that she had written an op-ed piece on her laptop with four-day-old Noah sitting in an infant seat next to her.

When Janet told me this story, I felt simultaneously sad, angry, and awestruck. Sad because Janet never had the chance to give herself over to a few magical days of simply holding newborn Noah and gazing into his eyes, angry at a society that doesn't allow parents that luxury, and awestruck that she actually could do some professional work four days after giving birth. Given her superhuman efforts, Janet's frustration with colleagues in the department where she and her husband both taught is easy to understand:

> It drove me crazy that no matter what I would do . . . they would just assume, "Well, she's a mother now, she's not going to be as effective." So, it made me mad that people weren't recognizing that

hey, actually, I was working against all odds . . . I had to do it on no sleep . . . I felt I was maintaining my productivity and also doing it despite tremendous odds and difficulties . . . It also got me mad because there was no recognition of Daniel's contribution . . . They never recognized that "Gee, he's staying up all night too so maybe he's tired." People just expected him to do everything the way he'd done it before.

Mothers sometimes felt that almost anything could be used against them at their jobs. They were scrutinized in a way that their husbands and male colleagues were not. One mother regretted that when she went to a weekend work meeting she had been encouraged to attend, she brought her infant daughter and nursed her discreetly. From then on she believed that in her coworkers' eyes she was a "mother" who was not serious about her job as a public health program developer in the large HMO where she worked. Another mother, a hospital administrator, told me that she never mentioned her children at work, and did not even put up their pictures, because doing so would be seen as unprofessional: "As much as I think of myself as a mother before I think of myself as an administrator, I've learned that in terms of survival and success you almost have to pretend that they (the children) are not there."

Men also suffer from family-unfriendly workplaces. Fathers may be given even less leeway than mothers at work, because they are expected to put their jobs before parenting. Ethan once tried to use a sick day to stay home and care for a child who was ill, but was strongly reprimanded for doing so. Peg told me that at his job real men don't take care of sick children. Likewise, Jake, an economist who worked at a nonprofit research institute, was completely disgusted by his colleagues' attitudes about children. He shook his head when he told me about a man who worked down the hall. When Jake announced that he was going to a Little League game, the colleague bragged that he never attended any of his son's Little League games and recommended that Jake do the same: "It is such a waste of time."

But although fathers may suffer from the inflexibility of the workplace or the disapproval of coworkers, they are less readily dismissed as serious workers. The leeway given women may come at the cost of their professional reputations. Colleagues may nod sympathetically when a mother has to leave work early to take her child to the doctor, but no matter how many extra hours she puts in to make up for her early departure, those same colleagues may also be thinking that work is no longer a priority for her.

Women's paid work is also ignored when they leave the office. Even when it is obvious that a woman is employed, expectations are subtly communicated that she is or should be available. Mothers often do go the extra mile because they are expected to. As one father pointed out, when potluck dinners are planned, no one seems to notice that it may not be feasible for working mothers to cook: "Seventy-five percent, at least, have some work commitments that makes preparing something often beyond the norm, but it is expected because they are the mothers and it's not expected because you're the father." Mothers concur:

There's an assumption that women's schedules are freer.

It's always easy to infringe upon mother. Mothers are supposed to be infringed upon.

Coworkers and bosses expect fathers, but not mothers, to take on that big project, even when it involves weekends at the office. Friends ask mothers, but not fathers, what they are doing about after-school care. Even if a father declines a tempting opportunity at work, the offer announces that his professional identity is intact. Even if a mother knows her husband is signing the kids up for the after-school sports program, being asked about after-school plans proclaims that she is ultimately responsible. And even if she isn't making the arrangements, what mother could avoid thinking about how those after-school plans will work?

Criticism

Women's move into the workplace is widely accepted today.[4] The problem is that the acceptance of women as paid workers has not been accompanied by an equal acceptance of a decrease of women's involvement at home or an increase in men's involvement.[5] The social message that it is OK for women to work as long as nothing changes at home defies logic, and puts women and the men who support them in no-win positions.

When I asked the parents I interviewed what kind of criticism they got from other people, I discovered a double standard.[6] Fathers were

more likely to be criticized than mothers if they passed up a night out
with their friends to spend time with their children, or if they left work
to tend to a sick child. Mothers were more likely to be criticized than
fathers if they were employed full time or if their children were in
daycare. In short, when men and women stepped out of their traditional roles in the family, they risked criticism.[7]

Roughly half of the men who reported criticism said that someone
had made fun of them, or critically questioned them, because they were
doing too much childcare or housework. Almost all of these gibes came
from other men. Jack, who has been an equally sharing father since his
children were small, still gets ribbed by his brothers-in-law for changing
diapers. Men confided that male friends, relatives, and coworkers were
exasperated or contemptuous when they turned down time with the
guys because they needed to be at home. For example, a father working
the second shift in a dye factory described his exchanges with coworkers who called to see if he wanted to go out before the three o'clock
shift:

> I'll say, "Man I've got a ton of things to do, I really can't—'cause
> like I told you it's like my time between ten and two it's not fun
> time, it's not social—it's like we got stuff do to here." I try to tell
> that to people who want me to go out and they'll say, "Well what
> are you doing?" "Well, I might be vacuuming or grocery shop-
> ping"—*"Oh, for crying out loud!"* . . . It's like a lot of people got
> wives that will do that.

Other men told similar stories of putting their masculinity on the line.
Aaron said:

> My stepfather always harangues me that I should be out on the
> tennis court . . . He doesn't really say less time with family, he says,
> "Take the afternoon off." But I got the feeling he . . . feels . . .
> when I say, "I can't because we gotta divvy up the childcare," . . . I
> sorta feel like he thinks I'm a wimp.

Critical male peers either said or implied that the willingness to give up
leisure in favor of work at home meant that wives had too much power.
The critics seemed to be worried that these new fathers were undermin-
ing male privilege.

Colleagues also often questioned men who left their jobs early to
take care of their kids. Why couldn't their wives do it? Men who didn't

put in the long hours of their coworkers or who refused to attend late or early meetings suffered the disapproval of the workaholic men who surrounded them. One father, who anguished over the conflicting demands of work and family, spent sixty to sixty-five hours a week in his office. Yet, he still incurred questioning looks when he announced at six o'clock that he was leaving an interminable meeting to be with his family.

Men were especially criticized when they made work choices that sacrificed money for time with children. Even men with wives who work full time are expected to be the breadwinners. Donald, a freelance film editor, left a secure job so that he and his wife could equally share and spend a lot of time with their kids. He was bitter about the flak he got for not making more money:

> All of what I'm saying (about the rewards of parenting) has to be put in the context of the significant economic penalty that I pay as a man . . . Your alternative community might be going around saying, "Nice job, Don. Look at Don, he's a really involved father and that's great!" But out there in the world I'm being ridiculed. "You fool, you're struggling along here with your freelance independent projects and you're not making any money."

Wives, when criticized, were taken to task for compromising at home rather than at work. Mothers-in-law figured prominently in complaints directed at their sons' wives:

> My mother-in-law thinks I don't do enough. "Cliff does so much; it's amazing that he makes dinner!"

> She (my mother-in-law) has the typical idea that the mother is supposed to do certain things and then the father just sits there . . . (She thinks) Frank shouldn't be expected to do that . . . like he's the breadearner and you're the housewife type mentality.

> She (my mother-in-law) thinks it's terrible that her poor son is so burdened.

The women I interviewed easily dismissed the charge that they aren't doing enough for their husbands; they weren't worried about fulfilling wifely duties. However, criticisms about mothering hurt. Women who worked outside the home often did worry about the effects on their children; so criticism stirred up their deepest fears. Anxious questions and comments from their parents when they returned to their jobs made the transition back to work much more difficult:

> The weekend before my first day back, I remember him (my father) saying something like, "Poor Teddy (her son)." So I wanted to bash him. "Poor Teddy's going to have to be with a babysitter because his Mommy's getting a job." And I remember saying, "Dad, that's not fair, this isn't exactly my choice here." At the time I did not want to go back to work. I was very upset.

Yet despite the criticism that comes from some quarters, today all of us inhabit multiple social worlds. We may live on a street where all the mothers stay home with their kids, but go to a job where women drop their children off at daycare. Men's mothers may think their sons are getting a bad deal, but women's mothers may envy and encourage their daughters' freedom and achievements.

The notion that men are wimps if they cave in to demands from their wives coexists with a new view of fatherhood. One equally sharing chemistry professor noted that when he refused to go to a Saturday department meeting, although some of his colleagues looked askance, one came to him afterward saying, "I wish I had the courage to do that." Even among his harshest critics, he sensed ambivalence: "Some of these people who cut me for not being a prolific researcher—vicious men—they know they missed it (their children's lives) and work even harder. At fifty they miss it." Another equally sharing father, who talked about living in a world that failed to make room for parenting, remarked that his commitment to parenting was greeted by men in power with mixed responses:

> They're just not geared to taking kids into account. On the other hand, I also get a lot of wistful looks from men, say fifty or fifty-five . . . "Gee it's nice you're spending so much time with your kids." The unstated implication being that they feel their kids' childhoods are gone and they have nothing to show for it.

I expected that equal sharers would come in for the most severe and frequent criticism. After all, their family lives deviate most radically from what is conventionally expected. However, instead I discovered that equal sharers often travel in circles friendly to their nontraditional ways, which shelters them from criticism. Don, who complained about the criticism he suffered when he gave up a secure job, also alluded to an "alternative community" that applauded his involvement with his children. Equal sharers were no more likely to be the targets of criticism than fathers and mothers who divided childcare 60-40 or 75-25, but whose peers were less tolerant of any changes in traditional family roles.

The alternating-shift fathers, however, got the worst of both worlds. These fire fighters, police officers, electricians, mechanics, and factory workers spend more time taking care of their children than other men, but they also live in social worlds that hardly even pay lip service to changing gender roles. Many of them reported criticism for their involvement at home:

> I get teased at work once in a while . . . my wife will call up about where the kids are . . . and they pick on me and they'll snicker in the background.

> They (his family) comment about it. "Well, how come you change the baby's diapers? Why don't you let your wife do it?"

> The husbands think I'm pussy-whipped . . . There are friends of mine that think I'm a wuss.

For men like them, adopting larger roles at home often means coping with other men's disdain.

Nevertheless, even in the relatively conservative communities of the alternating-shift fathers, a growing segment does accept changing gender roles. A full 65 percent of these men say they have never received any criticism for their unusual involvement at home. Likewise, although most of the criticisms leveled at equal sharers support traditional norms, it is quite possible for them to escape criticisms entirely. It may be more difficult, however, for equally sharing parents to escape praise.

Praise

Ironically, praise can undermine equality. The problem is that fathers are much more likely to be praised than mothers. Men, particularly equally sharing men, are more likely than their wives to be praised for feeding and diapering an infant, or for taking time off from their jobs to go to a child's school play. One equally sharing father joked, "I change one diaper, I'm a hero, man of the nineties." This dramatic double standard of praise neglects women's contributions to an equally sharing family, and creates an imbalance in the "economy of gratitude."[8] How can mothers and fathers truly be equal at home if despite equally sharing the work of the family, wives owe their husbands more gratitude than their husbands owe them?

That is exactly what people seem to be telling them implicitly by praising their husbands. Over half of the equally sharing fathers are praised by someone outside the family, usually a woman, for their investment in parenting. The corresponding figure for their wives, mothers who are contributing just as much as the fathers, is 4 percent! When men share childcare, women notice it and reward them with praise. Fathers, like this one, acknowledge that it doesn't take much to get praise: "Men do stuff that women have conventionally done and never get praise for it, but men do . . . It's very easy to impress. It's just so easy to impress women who are used to traditional marriages." In the few cases in which equally sharing fathers took time off from work for childcare, their decision was viewed as a rare and special event: "Jonathan stayed home with our second child. He took a paternity leave. It was the first, the only paternity leave that I know of, that's ever been requested. The human resources department, which was largely women, stood up and applauded."

People, again predominantly women, go out of their way to tell equally sharing mothers positive things about their husbands. When Mary complained about Paul to a friend, she didn't get much sympathy:

> I was upset for a day or so with Paul. I was saying something to one of my friends. She stood in front of me and she had her hand on her hip. She said, "How can you be upset with him? He cooks every night. He does the dishes. He keeps the kids."

Husbands, however, are hardly inundated with positive remarks about their wives. Whereas 36 percent of the equally sharing women receive compliments about their husbands, only 2 percent of their husbands receive compliments about them. One might question whether praise of husbands from women, which ostensibly supports equality, is really so benign. Possibly this so-called praise is an insidious form of criticism of the woman to whom it is directed. Also, women who praise other women's husbands may be protecting themselves. When their own husbands do less, they may comfort themselves by emphasizing the exceptional nature of more involved husbands, rather than the skill of their wives in getting them to share.

Mothers complain about the inequity in perceptions of them and their equally sharing husbands. The mothers who care about equality, like Janet, are resentful:

> They see Daniel doing a lot with the baby and they see me working full time. I always get a negative reaction and for him anything that he does—he could just pick up the kid, "Wow, a family man, isn't that wonderful!" So he's always applauded and I'm always, "Well, maybe she's not a good mother."

At some point most of the equally sharing mothers have been told by someone that they are very lucky to have the husbands they do. "Lucky" implies two things. First, it suggests that these women had no influence in getting their husbands to share; they just fell into it. Second, and even more important, "lucky" implies that as women, they are getting a good deal, a better deal than their husbands are. Because their husbands do more than other men, they should be correspondingly appreciative.

The equally sharing mothers are virtually unanimous in rejecting the idea that they were lucky or any luckier than their husbands. Most of them resent this message because it ignores their role in creating an equally sharing household, choosing the right husband, and committing themselves to equality:

> It's not luck. It's planned and it's teamwork and it's talked about and I wouldn't have it any other way.

> Everything is always how lucky I've been rather than isn't it wonderful that you've been competent enough to . . . marry the right person.

> I don't feel lucky . . . I guess it's better for me than having one of those other husbands.

> My mother doesn't give me credit for having created a 50-50 partnership . . . She just thinks that it was a matter of extraordinary

luck that I found a husband who was willing to share in the parenting.

I constantly hear how lucky I am . . . (My mother says,) "He does so much more for you than my husband ever did." I felt like saying, "Well, you just didn't educate your husband."

Even when women seem to be conceding that they are lucky in one breath, they counter it in the next. They admit that they are lucky, but then remind whoever's listening that their spouses are lucky too: "I don't feel I'm really lucky to have him because I feel like he's lucky to have me too. We both do this together. We're both getting benefit from this. I don't feel like he's doing me a favor."

The most troubling aspect of the message "You're so lucky" is that it conveys that women are not really entitled to equality. As one mother put it: "I think it's ridiculous . . . My view from the beginning was it was my expectation that we do this this way. I think it basically downplays the woman to tell her that she's so lucky. Again, she should basically be doing everything, isn't she lucky if he does anything?" Another woman echoed similar sentiments when she explained why she felt "crummy" when people told her she was lucky: "Because the presumption is that I should be doing it all and isn't he generous to help me out with what is normally my job."

Twenty percent of the women reported praise for "doing it all," juggling the dual demands of home and employment, whereas men almost never did. Although this mother-only praise makes some sense in unequal families where only mothers *are* doing it all, it also conveys that women *should* be doing it all. By implicitly endorsing inequality, that kind of praise might discourage the unequal women from trying to get their husbands to share. Consciously or unconsciously, the praisers are holding up the superwoman as the ideal. And when people praise only mothers in the equally sharing families for juggling, they are ignoring that fathers are juggling too.

Double standards of praise and criticism are rampant. But there is one very peculiar exception to this rule. Women are not praised for making money. Thirty percent of the equally sharing mothers are outearning their husbands, and another 10 percent are bringing in salaries that match their husbands' incomes. Yet not one woman reported praise for her financial contributions. Nor did any of the women mention how much more money they contribute than their mothers had. If men get praised for changing diapers, why don't women get praised for earning money?

Apparently, it is inappropriate, impolite, or downright emasculating to mention the embarrassing fact that a wife outearns her husband. Instead of getting credit the way her husband does for pitching in at home, the outearning wife might have to compensate to prove she isn't trying to show him up.[9] Public praise for women's earnings might be construed as public humiliation of their husbands, even when women don't outearn their husbands. In the "economy of gratitude" money usually doesn't do much for women. Women are as likely to have to apologize for their incomes as to be appreciated for them.

Internalizing the Double Standard

In many of the unequal families, double standards were accepted without question. When one 75-25 father answered my query, "Do you think anything different goes into being a good mother versus a good father?" he spoke for them: "I think it's much easier for me to be what I consider a good father than for her to be what I consider a good mother. I don't need the patience. I don't need the endurance. I don't need the tolerance. I don't need to give up my whole everything to devote to a developing child."

This double standard also lives on in the psyches of parents even in the most equal families I interviewed, much to their chagrin. Equally sharing mothers are often tougher on themselves than on their husbands, and more appreciative of their husbands' contributions than their own, even when they don't think that makes sense. Donna is the perfect example. When I asked her if she held herself and her husband to a different standard, she replied emphatically: "Oh yeah, sure, absolutely, absolutely. That's all there is to it." She was hardly atypical among the equally sharing mothers:

> He gets so much credit for how much time he spends. I'm spending more and still feeling like he spends a lot.

> I guess my perspective is that somehow I should be leading their emotional and intellectual lives along in a way that I don't expect from him.

I don't feel like I should expect more of myself than I do of him, but yet I do.

Because of this internalized double standard, women who share parenting are more likely to feel guilty than their husbands are. Over 60 percent of the equally sharing mothers mentioned feeling guilty about their parenting, whereas fewer than 20 percent of their husbands did.

Involved fathers are satisfied with themselves and the time they spend with their children; mothers often question whether their time with children is enough. Donna, who worried about whether she was being selfish in taking time to exercise when she got home from work, compared herself unfavorably to her husband, Kevin: "For me to be a good parent and for me to be the best I can be and be happy I need to think of myself . . . so I really feel myself comes first. He feels the children come first. That's a big difference; that's a big issue." Donna ignores that it was *she* who took a number of years off from work to take care of her children when they were younger. Recall that although they both thought a parent should be there, Kevin admitted that he wouldn't have been the one to stay home. Because Donna holds herself to a stricter standard than her husband, she barely gives herself credit.

Mothers, at least upper-middle-class mothers, also felt guilty about working or guilty about how much they were working. An equally sharing mother, a professional whose income was higher than her husband's, noted: "There's this illusion of choice for a woman . . . Certainly when I was growing up there were many more mothers who didn't work. So there's always that (message) that it's OK not to work for women. Society says that's OK." Do women really have the choice to stay home or is it an illusion? Certainly, their families' material well-being would be drastically curtailed by cutting back to one income. Moreover, women who grew up with opportunities to achieve and excel in careers may pay a heavy price for staying home, in some cases as heavy as their husbands would pay for making the same "choice."

This ostensible choice to work outside, however, creates a dilemma for women that almost never exists for men, even when they equally share. As one insightful father told me: "Men, I don't think, have this profound issue of should I work or stay home. I mean, men never internally debate that at all in the transition to parenthood."

Fathers take it for granted that after becoming parents they will continue to work. Unlike mothers, who believe that they are choosing to work rather than to be with their children, fathers who are involved believe that they are choosing their children over work or leisure. Women who have invested in their work lives are left feeling that they have chosen to be there less for their children, chosen in some sense against their children. Conversely, men who have invested in fatherhood feel that they have chosen in favor of their children. Because of these different vantage points, mothers end up feeling guilty and fathers do not.

Finally, looking back at what their own parents did can make mothers feel more guilty than their husbands.[10] Today's parents sometimes describe a childhood in which only mothers were there for them emotionally. Their fathers were often so busy with work that they were virtually absent. As one woman told me: "A good mother is what my mother did. A good father is what my father didn't do." Certainly, in that context, it is easy for today's fathers to shine. Larry explains:

> My father never did this. He never nurtured this way or spent his time or took on these roles. You know, our fathers never changed diapers . . . "Hey, I'm changing a diaper, I'm a good dad."

An equally sharing mother finds it harder to pat herself on the back:

> My father and most of the men growing up—to some extent I'm comparing my husband with them and he comes out with gold stars . . . but for myself as a mother . . . it's much more convoluted, because there were some things that were really wonderful about those mothers.

The change required of men to become equally sharing fathers requires them to sacrifice money, power, or prestige, sacrifices that feel virtuous. The change required of women is more morally ambiguous. Women who strive for equally sharing households have to make their own needs for achievement, success, and autonomy more central than their mothers did. Men who compromise their careers and devote more to family may have to put up with criticism from the outside and the loss of status, and they may question their choice because of their own personal losses; but among the men I interviewed at least, they virtually never question it in a moral sense. Women, by contrast, must grapple with the moral issue of whether they are doing right by their children.[11] One equally sharing father who grew up in the sixties compared the costs of nontraditionalism for him and his wife: "I'm bucking something that's fine for our generation to buck—it's materialism, but she's bucking maternalism. That's not so good to buck. So I think the disadvantage is much more there for her."

Creating a New Social World

Equal sharers use two important strategies to buttress equality in their homes. First, they delegitimize double standards and social pressures for inequality by ignoring, subverting, or directly countering them. Second, they construct alternative social worlds, which encourage or at least legitimize their nontraditional lifestyles.

Delegitimizing goes on both outside and inside the family. Parents who expect to be derided by friends or colleagues often keep quiet about their activities. Aaron didn't tell his bowling buddies, "a pretty straight crowd," why he was declining their offers to go out for a beer. Mary confided that sometimes she didn't tell people about what Paul did at home because of questions it might raise about her. Jake, the economist whose work culture devalued children, had enough autonomy at work to slip out early without raising eyebrows, as long as he didn't mention that he was doing it for the kids. These parents all recognize the pressure to conform, but they ignore it. They avoid calling attention to their nontraditional ways, hoping to stave off criticism. Although hiding their behavior this way does nothing to change social norms, it allows parents under pressure to carry on without censure.

Subversion and countering require more confrontation. The mothers who pointed out that their husbands were as lucky as they, the fathers who publicly refused to accede to excessive demands at work because they wanted to be with their kids, and the equal sharers who called people on their mistaken assumptions that every family is unequal—all had the guts to directly challenge social norms, even when it was awkward to do so. They had the guts, but they may have also had more freedom than some parents who hid their behavior. The chemist who refused to attend Saturday meetings acknowledged his privileged position as a tenured professor: "I'm in a position where I don't have to worry about money or other things other people have to worry about . . . I don't know if you can do it in business. I'm not going to lose my job." Equally sharing fathers who were in business *did* stand up to the pressure exerted on them to ignore family responsibilities. Barry, the purchasing manager of a chain of health food stores, told me he didn't hesitate to set his male coworkers straight when they complained that he should get his wife to pick up his kids instead of leaving work early to do so himself: "One of my counterparts at work has made a comment a couple of times and I actually lost my temper over it."

When equal sharers confront their detractors, they risk increasing the pressure on themselves to conform, but they also bolster their own commitment to equality.[12] There is nothing like standing up for an unpopular ideal to shore up your position. The force with which some men stood up to their critics belied a struggle with their own ambivalence. In their passionate defense of equality, men just might be convincing themselves that the sacrifice of ambitions is worth it.

A funny thing happens when you stand up to the crowd. You often find out you have allies. It only takes one person to destroy unanimity, and when that one has taken the hardest step, others may soon follow.[13] The majority is almost never monolithic. Out of the equality closet, the chemist became a role model for men who wanted to resist the pressure to make work everything:

Men come and ask me, "How do you do it?" I tell them, "Just say 'no'!" You *can* do it here.

The hardest work of dismantling double standards, however, may be done not at the office, but at home. Praised outside for their unusual role, equally sharing men, even those heroes who have fought the good fight at work, may expect to be especially appreciated inside the family. One equally sharing mother said, "I think sometimes there's the male view of if they're doing anything at all it's, 'Aren't I wonderful? It's not expected so anything I do is great.'"

Wives have a lot to gain by convincing their husbands that the comparisons between them and other men are not legitimate, that the only comparison that should count is between themselves and their wives. One mother, who complained that her equally sharing husband didn't pay enough attention to the management of parenting tasks, explicitly identified the new standard. Men should contribute the way women do: "He definitely gets higher marks on that than any man I know, but it's still not enough. It's very good, but it's not a woman. I'm sorry." Other women, like Donna, shifted standards more subtly by simply emphasizing the similarity between themselves and their husbands. Donna said: "I feel that I'm working full time and Kevin is working full time. The jobs should pretty much be split in half."

The double standard outside the home undermines equal sharing inside because it encourages men to expect more appreciation than they give. But conversation between equal husbands and wives inside a marriage can delegitimize double standards promoted outside.[14] One can easily picture Janet railing to Daniel about the unfairness of their colleagues who expect her productivity to be diminished, but expect him to carry on normally. Similarly, several of the men reported conversations in which their irritated wives complained about how easy it was for their husbands to elicit praise for their parenting. Husbands heard their wives' implicit warnings: "That praise is not legitimate so don't expect me to be grateful."

But sometimes simple conversation wasn't enough. In the home of one fiercely feminist mother, Bernice, a battle over appreciation raged bitterly in the first year of her daughter's life. She demanded real equality within the household, equality that would mean that her husband, Kyle, not only would share the work of parenting, but would do so on the same terms as she did:

> Why should I appreciate him any more than he appreciates me?
> ... Often it would come down to that, that I should be grateful that he does half and I would say, "Look, why should I be grateful, are you grateful that I do half?"

Kyle was resentful and complained that he was doing more than his share. Furious, Bernice would add up the hours and show him that he wasn't doing any more than she was. She was very unhappy: "What was going on for me was that I was paying too high a price for equality. It wasn't that I wasn't getting the equal sharing, but that the price was just too high." Looking back, Kyle admits: "I would do half, but in return the price I required was that I be praised and appreciated and told how wonderful it was. Bernice steadfastly resisted doing that." Their marriage was at stake. Both intensely committed to their young daughter, they questioned their closeness and commitment to each other. At times things got so bad that Bernice dared Kyle to leave.

But Kyle didn't leave; he changed. Although still wistfully wishing he could get more appreciation, Kyle embraced the hardest part of transformed roles at home: that he wasn't entitled to more appreciation than Bernice. Kyle's commitment to his beliefs, to Bernice, and to their daughter helped him change. They still argue over the details of how to share equally, but not bitterly. The battle over appreciation is over.

Kyle wasn't the only equally sharing man who seemed reluctant to compare himself to his wife instead of other men. It's difficult to relinquish a standard that is so flattering. This father good-naturedly recounted how his wife challenged his self-serving comparisons:

> If we'd had a fight I'd say, "Well, look at me, I'm doing this and I'm doing that and nobody, none of the other fathers do that, why are you so mad at me?" She would say, "We're different . . . we always had the expectation that you would do this."

In his heart of hearts, he did recognize the contradiction between his ostensible commitment to equality and his invocation of an all-male comparison: "It's kind of (like) those ploys that one uses when one argues that in retrospect is totally unfair. Her response was the correct response."

Other fathers seemed unaware of the contradiction. Despite his professed egalitarianism, one 50-50 dad proudly reported that his participation had extended back to the pregnancy: "I'll put it this way . . . I don't know anybody else who went to every single . . . obstetrics appointment." Another father boasted: "Very few men on the face of this earth ever diapered as many bottoms as I have." It's easy to understand their pride and to applaud them. These fathers *are* extraordinary if you compare them to other men, but once the standard shifts to a comparison with their wives, their pride and the applause seem misplaced.

Like Kyle, other equally sharing fathers seemed to be wrestling with the injustice of a double standard. For example, Kevin was apprehensive about his children's welfare when Donna returned to full-time employment, but at the same time knew it wouldn't be fair to discourage her: "I was really worried . . . that there would not be as much kid time . . . (But) it wouldn't be fair for me to say to Donna, 'You can't do that.' It's as much my responsibility to spend time with the kids as hers." Kevin almost sounds as if he is reminding himself about the new standard of comparison in which he is just as responsible for children as she is.

Another equally sharing father caught himself unconsciously assuming a double standard. When I asked him how his wife's job affected their family life he responded: "Making the mornings chaotic. Well, I mean sometimes it'll make the mornings chaotic when we both work. It's not her working, it's both working." The implication is that men's employment is expected, but women's is not. Realizing that he had inadvertently reverted to a double standard, he corrected himself.

While some men ignored the double standard and some wrestled with it, still others, who had clearly come to reject it, were ready and armed to counter criticism directed at them from outside the family. When I asked one equally sharing father, a police officer, if he ever received criticism for his nontraditional role, he responded adamantly:

> If I was taking care of the kids and somebody said something (critical) . . . I could give a shit what they say. That's the way I feel. A lot of guys have that macho image or something like that. I don't have that. I hope I don't have that.

The voices exhorting women and men to adhere to traditional roles at home may be loud but, as we have seen, they are not unanimous. A virtual cacophony of conflicting voices can be heard today: "Women should have careers." "Daycare is bad for children." "Fathers should be more involved." "Mothers are more nurturing than fathers." Equal sharers often choose to live in a particular social world that amplifies nontraditional voices.[15] Despite the rarity of equally shared parenthood, three quarters of the equally sharing fathers know other men who are also sharing childcare equally. In contrast, only 18 percent of the 75-25 fathers know even one equally sharing family.

The importance of an alternative community was highlighted by one mother who moved from Hartville to Amity. In Hartville, women like her, with high-powered careers and supportive, involved husbands, were not unusual. The wealthy surburb of Amity, however, was a different kind of place. Women stayed home with young children and their husbands took responsibility for breadwinning. In the absence of a nontraditional group of peers, that mother found herself reevaluating her choices: "Coming to Amity has probably had some influence . . . too. Much more conventional community than Hartville. There are many many women who don't work . . . Seeing examples around makes you question more the commitment to career."

Equal sharers do not simply find themselves in egalitarian social circles that now shape their everyday family life. Instead, they actively work to create this alternative world. For example, when considering to whom to compare themselves, they intentionally choose their more progressive peers. When I asked one equally sharing mother if her husband did more, less, or the same amount of work at home compared to other men, she answered: "I have a colleague who does as much as my husband. They have two (kids) so he does more. I compare my husband to that father. I don't know why I should compare him to anybody else."

Equal sharers seek out social circles that support their nontraditional lifestyles and avoid those that don't. Kyle made this point when I asked how his involvement in parenting compared to that of other men in his social circle: "This may surprise you. I think the same. Our circle of friends is very carefully drawn." Another father reported: "I'm pretty selective in who I hang out with." And when Aaron hung out with his old-fashioned bowling buddies, he didn't think of them as his closest friends.

A difference in values about roles at home can strain or even destroy friendships. As Janet put it: "We've found that there are people who are critical of the kind of roles we play. We probably wouldn't be friends with them very long." Kevin reported that after refusing a few invitations to go out drinking with "the guys," they stopped calling: "They knew my role was different and I think they were critical of that."

Finding a group of peers who support nontraditional efforts at home is as crucial as avoiding those who undermine them. Two of the equally sharing fathers went as far as starting or joining men's groups that were specifically focused on changing men's roles. One of them decided to start a men's group to help himself deal with the contradictory messages he received for compromising his work life and devoting himself to fatherhood. He hoped the group would defuse criticism and provide approval for equally shared parenting. The group would be a refuge where men could legitimately pat each other on the back.

The other father who participated in a men's group was looking for role models. His longstanding group had disbanded, but he was joining another men's group: "I'm joining a group that has been going for twelve years . . . There are some great dads in there. I really value their wisdom, (and) their experience."

In perhaps the most dramatic example of a family's creating an alternative and nontraditional social world for itself, an equally sharing father recounted how he and his wife had moved to the town where they now live to join a parent collective: "They (friends) started telling us about Harmony (the collective), which at that point was defined as not only non but antiracist, antisexist, as opposed to non . . . It was the reason that we moved here, those few people in that organization." This community provided him with role models for equally shared parenting: "From the very beginning I had some good role models around here for that (being an involved father), fathers in the Harmony group who did that kind of thing, who kind of showed me that it could be done that way."

Peers are powerful models. They encourage equal sharing by simply conveying that it can be done. Most of the equal sharers had not gone as far as joining men's groups or collectives, but they did know other equal sharers. How did they find each other? I think they simply kept their eyes open. Equal sharers are out there if you just look carefully. That father who takes his daughter to daycare every day just might be one. At the pool, that mother who sits in a lounge chair while her husband diapers the toddler might be an equally sharing mother. Striking up a conversation is one way to find out. There is nothing mysterious about it. Friendships blossom among equal sharers, just as they do among all people who share values and lifestyles.[16] In an unselfconscious way, the similarities we notice draw us to other people, make us feel comfortable, and encourage us to pursue friendships.

The Insidious Invisibility of Social Pressure

Admittedly, the unequal families don't have to look nearly as hard to find examples of people who are living just as they are. Whereas the equal sharers understand the power of similar peers, the unequal couples often fail to recognize that their inequality looks normal only because the people around them are also unequal. The power of social norms becomes invisible when you conform.

Several years ago I lived with my husband and then six-year-old son in Bologna. Watching Italian families, I was continually struck by how much of my family's daily life is dictated by American conventions. Our child has a specific bedtime, designed to ensure that he gets enough sleep, a common practice in the United States. Italians, however, were universally horrified at our son's eight-thirty bedtime. We must not like children, they thought. Otherwise how could we cruelly exclude him from the nightly social life of the family?[17]

When I had to take my son to school late one day because of a doctor's appointment, we tried to enter unobtrusively without disrupting the class, forgetting that comings and goings in Italy must always be recognized.[18] The teacher stopped the class and told the children to greet my son. Up from their desks they jumped, showering him with "ciaos" and kisses. I wasn't surprised that things were done differently in another country; what surprised me was how much of my behavior was guided by conventions and social pressures that were invisible to me. By watching the Italian alternative, I discovered that without ever noticing American expectations, I had conformed to them.

To unequal families not privy to alternatives, the social pressures that legitimize inequality are similarly invisible. Maternal roles with children seem a result not of conformity, but of nature. Note the language these fathers used:

> I think kids might just naturally seem to gravitate towards the mother more than they do to the father.

> I think it's just more of a natural instinct because I always feel that they're (children are) closer with Mom up until a certain age.

The invisibility of social pressure is invidious. At one extreme, it allows the illusion that we are freely choosing inequality. At the other extreme, it keeps us believing in biological constructs like maternal instinct, or believing that biological differences constrain mothers and fathers to be unequal parents. As we will see in the next chapter, parents' beliefs in biological differences may be a bigger barrier to equal sharing than the differences themselves. It's not nature that keeps us stuck in unequal roles.

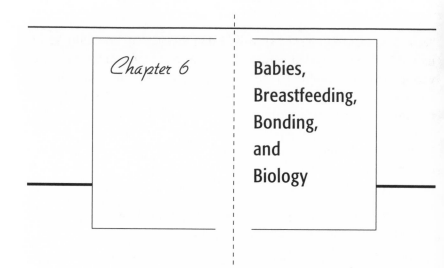

Babies, Breastfeeding, Bonding, and Biology

Equal sharers have a lot to teach us about the limits of biology. True, only women can gestate a baby, give birth, and lactate. Women also experience hormonal changes that accompany pregnancy, birth, and breastfeeding that men, of course, do not.[1] Those biological facts, however, do not explain why women parent more than men.[2] Breastfeeding is an extremely powerful experience for many women, one that men simply can't duplicate. Yet despite the fervent beliefs of many of the unequal couples that breasts, wombs, and hormones give women a unique ability to care for infants, to "bond" with their babies, or to nurture children, the fathers in the equal families show that men can capably share the care of the smallest infants, and can develop deep and nurturing relationships with their children.

Breastfeeding and Equality

How much do breasts matter? Breasts, of course, give biological mothers the capacity to breastfeed their babies. Today, pediatricians and health experts are quick to encourage women to use that capacity to give their children the much-touted benefits of breast milk as well as the warm secure feeling that comes from skin-to-skin contact with their mothers.[3] Middle-class women are increasingly heeding the call to nurse their children. Whereas in 1955 only 29 percent of middle-class women breastfed, by 1996 the figure had jumped to 59 percent.[4]

Women are pressured from all sides when deciding whether to nurse and if so, for how long.[5] Trying to do best for their babies, women weigh the nutritional benefits of breast milk against the inconvenience of lugging breast pumps to the job.[6] The decisions are unending, and everyone seems to have an opinion about what women should do, whether it is breastfeed in public, use supplemental formula, or wean before the baby is a year old. Pediatricians can be the worst offenders, making women feel guilty if they don't breastfeed and ashamed if they do it for "too long."[7]

Although I am not going to venture an opinion on any of these personal decisions, there is one question about breastfeeding that I can answer definitively. Does breastfeeding pose a serious barrier to equally shared parenting? The answer, I discovered, is a resounding "NO!"

Anatomy is not destiny. Equality or inequality coexisted with breastfeeding or without it. Equal sharers followed three different approaches to breastfeeding: deference—they acknowledged the mother's special role but treated it as temporary; substitution—they bottle-fed; and compensation—they created a special role for the father that symbolically involved him in breastfeeding.

Deference

Deference was the strategy of choice for a bit more than a half of the equal sharers.[8] These couples believed that there was no way for men to do half of the baby care while the mother was breastfeeding. The time, energy, and physical commitment entailed in nursing are certainly undeniable.[9] A few of the mothers who were most committed to equal sharing revised their views about equality in the early days of infancy: "I think that the physiology of being a mom is a much more intense commitment than I had ever imagined before . . . I still believe that everything should be 50–50. I just think that it becomes easier to do that after six months or a year . . . I think that when I was nursing and pregnant . . . no matter how much work he did that physical burden pushed me up another 10 percent."

Although all of the equal sharers who deferred believed the mother was the leading parent, they varied in how they conceived of the father's role while the mother was nursing. Mothers often enjoyed being in the number-one position. A few, like Sharon, didn't expect much from their husbands while they were nursing:

I think like any new nursing mother I spent more time with Nicole in my arms and that probably extended for the first nine months while I was nursing her. I think Peter was really excited about her birth and very involved, but, as you know, there just isn't that much for him to do when the child is eating and sleeping most of the time. So that was a period that was more intense for me. After that I think we started to share more equally. We've done that consistently since Nicole was old enough to be away from me for any period of time, to be out of my arms.

Although Sharon asserts that "there isn't much to do when the child is eating and sleeping most of the time," surely by the age of three months babies do a great deal more than that.[10] Even in the first weeks, when babies may seem to be only sleeping, eating, and crying, they produce a lot of laundry. In contrast to Sharon, other equally sharing mothers who wanted and enjoyed a central role with their new infants, as she did, expected their husbands to adopt a supportive role. Sally, an equally sharing mother who loved the intensity of being a new mom, describes the supporting role her husband took, but also how this secondary position for fathers ultimately results in more "on" time for the new mothers:

> He would take laundry into town, cook all our meals. For about two weeks I just stayed with Nina in this back room. It was just kind of dimly lit and I felt like I was in a cocoon. It was pretty wonderful. There was this intensity about the relationship that I wanted I think to have with this baby which started to translate into my being more on at nights.[11]

Nursing gives women an instant relationship with infants. Nursing babies demand attention and action from their mothers. Breastfeeding often gives mothers an easy way to gratify their newborn babies.[12] There is no way for a nursing mother to stand on the sidelines. Not so for fathers. Fathers also acknowledged the "intensity" of the nursing relationship:

> The beginning of the motherhood and the breastfeeding were sometimes pretty intense. It was intense for me too, but there was no way I could do it.

> She breastfed them. There was a kind of closeness, a bond that the mother seems to have that's a little more direct than the father.

For men who want to be equal sharers, the number-two spot can be difficult or even painful:

If you want to be involved, it's as a secondary citizen, and I think it is very difficult for men to accept that. I think if you want to be an involved father it's tough because you don't have a breast. You have nothing to give. The kid makes the initial hook-up with the mother. You're definitely a second-class citizen.

Kyle, the equally sharing father who battled over appreciation, astutely noted, however, that breastfeeding per se does not prevent men from taking care of infants. Mothers sometimes push their husbands out. He resigned himself to being a backstage parent while Bernice was nursing, but saw that as Bernice's choice. She wanted him to do "the logistical things that supported her being with an infant," while retaining the prerogative to actually care for their daughter, Kate. Kyle implies that the exclusive closeness between nursing mothers and infants is not a biological imperative, but the preference of mothers like Bernice. Kyle described what happened when Kate cried: "Bernice would be rushing to Kate and I would be rushing too. She'd kind of just nudge me out of the way. They were as babies and nursing mothers are—they were very close, *which is to say Bernice was very close.*"

A few fathers who eventually shared the care of their children expressed difficulties in connecting with their new infants:

I probably didn't really relate to him all that much the first six months until he actually started crawling and stuff. It was like this blob here. What do you do with it?

I mean those little ones are just so close to the womb and the all-enveloping embrace of the mother, you know, they just . . . There's nothing a father can do for them and there's nothing they can do for a father. It wasn't I guess until he began to be able to do something that could arouse my curiosity and then I could interact with him . . . Then I became interested in it and . . . well I was interested, there's no question about that, but I kept waiting. When's he gonna do something here? I guess six months.

Often men who couldn't connect were married to women who didn't expect them to or who wanted an exclusive relationship with their newborns. Proprietary mothers often discouraged fathers, or disconnected fathers encouraged mothers to forge an exclusive link with their babies. But fathers who couldn't connect were atypical among the equal sharers. While acknowledging the special role of breastfeeding, most were undaunted in developing relationships with their nursing infants:

> She breastfed, so she . . . had a little bit more closeness in that manner, but other than that I think it was a 50-50 thing, changing the diapers and so forth . . . On the weekends . . . I would take them (both children when they were infants) . . . and have them for the weekend pretty much . . . I used to have a little backpack and used to go walk them around the woods . . . make them go to sleep . . . I enjoyed that.

Changing diapers is not glamorous, but it gave men a chance to contribute, to interact with their new babies, and to feel competent as fathers. New fathers could also bathe their infants, hold them, cuddle them, and get up at night with them.[13] The more fathers did for their newborns, the more connected they felt. In several of the equally sharing families, fathers would get up, change the baby, bring the baby to the mother to be nursed, and then put the baby back to bed. In one, the father was in charge of vomit! Fathers found ways to be very involved even if they conceived of the breastfeeding period as an unequal time.

The primacy of nursing, the gratification women obtain from their experience of this central and unique role, and the fathers' experience of being secondary do not distinguish these equal sharers from couples who divide childcare more unequally. These deferring equal sharers, however, differed from their unequal counterparts because they treated the nursing-induced inequality as temporary. When mothers stopped nursing, fathers who had slept through the night took their turn in waking:

> I think when the nursing went, it means a lot of things . . . because he would nurse going to sleep . . . At some stage in there when he was one to two, I probably became equal in terms of diapering, baths and bedtime, and feeding and play, and getting up in the middle of the night.

Those fathers who had been waking all along upped their involvement to include feeding:

> If he cried I would go in and get him as much as she would. I would feed him and change the diapers. I mean when he was first born, of course, she was more involved because she was breastfeeding, so

she would spend more time with him than I was. But after he started drinking a bottle, of course I would feed him as often as she did.

And as for Peter, the father who said of small infants, "there's nothing a father can do for them and there's nothing they can do for a father," he was equally sharing the care of his daughter, Nicole, by the time she was nine months old.

Substitution

Some parents bottle-feed babies from the start. Slightly more than a third of the equally sharing families chose that option. The potential for bottle-feeding to immediately equalize parents' involvement strongly influenced the decision to bottle-feed in a few equally sharing families. Janet explained her thinking: "I didn't have an overwhelming desire to breastfeed, though I recognize the advantages . . . I'd have to say that it was also part of the consideration that my husband could get up in the middle of the night." Bottle-feeding was part of the rationale she used to argue for equality:

> I didn't breastfeed, so from the beginning there just seemed like no reason why he couldn't wake up as often as I did and feed the baby as often as I did. He could make a bottle as well as I could . . . It wasn't rational for us to do anything separate.

In three families the second child was bottle-fed, whereas the first one was breastfed. In each of those families, parents saw bottle-feeding as an aid to equal sharing. In one of them, for example, the mother stopped nursing because of a "terrible breast infection" during the first week of the baby's life. "The positive aspect of it," she told me, "was that he (her husband) could jump in more." Her husband became a very strong advocate of bottle-feeding:

> Romantically, it might be nice for the baby to breastfeed, but it really imposes a limitation on our equally sharing some component of caring for the child. So, retrospectively I realize that . . . my advice to new parents would be . . . stop as soon as you can, particularly if it seems to start being an issue . . . That would be my advice to my friends . . . She's cranky, tired, and upset and doesn't feel it's fair and you feel helpless and you're stuck. You want to change it, change it.

George, an equally sharing adoptive father, also implied that breast-feeding can be a big disadvantage for fathers:

> In a way I was a very fortunate father to be an adoptive father. I liked holding the babies and feeding them. I liked having as much share in their early caretaking . . . If I had been a father where Roberta biologically had the baby and she had the baby all to herself, I would have been an intensely jealous and disappointed father.

Despite these testimonials from fathers, bottle-feeding is far from a panacea for inequality. In George's family, for example, equality was established only after their second child was born. Although highly involved in infant care the first time around, he did not reduce his work hours as much as his wife did until the second baby arrived. In fact, couples who became equal only after an extended period of inequality were just as likely to have bottle-fed as breastfed. Certainly, we know that the prevalence of bottle-feeding in the 1950s did not encourage equal sharing.

Compensation

Breastfeeding posed no barrier at all according to approximately 15 percent of the equally sharing couples. Unlike the deferrers and substi-tuters, who believed that nursing precluded equal roles, albeit tempo-rarily, the compensators insisted that they had been equal from the get-go. When I asked one of these fathers if he had ever felt that breast-feeding interfered with equal sharing, he was adamant: "No, never, never even thought about it, never occurred to me. No, the kids used to suck on my chest and stuff like that . . . no." He wasn't the only father who pretended to nurse. Another father told me: "I was one of those kooks who would put her on my nipple . . . kind of joke around." But was it a joke or was it a symbolic attempt to participate?

Parents who denied that nursing was an obstacle to equality worked to make it a shared enterprise, as one father reported:

> At two weeks *we* introduced (a) bottle of the breast milk, ex-pressed breast milk. Starting (at) two weeks, every evening feed-ing. Then I guess *we* increased it, I would feed Vivian, thereby increasing my contact with her in that kind of a special way and

freeing up Rhona to not be on this tether . . . We were pretty much inseparable then.

A mother described an elaborate ritual for "sharing" nighttime feedings: "He would get Nicholas up and change his diaper. I would get up and go to the bathroom, flip the TV on, and prop the pillows up. He would bring Nicholas to me. He would lay there awake and just rub him and stuff while *we* were feeding." Beth also reported that Steve was eager to participate in all aspects of parenting:

He was very intent on being sure that he could feed Stephanie even though I was nursing. He right away wanted to introduce formula with the breastfeeding because he thought the baby would be more attached to me than to him and he didn't want that. He clearly, from the very beginning, wanted to be an equal parent with me . . . I even expressed breast milk sometimes and let him feed her. So, he definitely did everything.

Fathers who compensated gave bottles of expressed breast milk, stayed physically close to mothers and nursing infants, jocularly simulated nursing themselves, and used the word "we" to describe nursing. These strategies increased their involvement in breastfeeding and reflected their belief that even nursing, the most female of activities, could be shared.

Whether they deferred, substituted, or compensated, equal sharers were undaunted by the mother's biological capacity to breastfeed. When both parents thought fathers could and should be involved in infant care, they made it happen. Mothers made room and fathers jumped in.

Breastfeeding and Inequality

I discovered that even among the 75-25 couples, the most unequal group I interviewed, breastfeeding did not prevent paternal participation. Approximately half of these fathers participated substantially in infant care, despite their wives' breastfeeding.[14] They sounded remarkably like the equal sharers when they recounted their contributions to nighttime feedings. One father described this scene during the first week home with a newborn:

Marianne had a Caesarean . . . so . . . both of them were in the hospital for five days or so. And I took that week off . . . the week after they came home . . . so that I could help as much as I could. And . . . glad I did because . . . the baby's schedule was totally flip-flop. He slept all day and was awake all night. Marianne and I both had to take . . . four- or five-hour shifts. One would get some sleep while the other stayed up with the baby . . . We don't have cable so we don't get around-the-clock television . . . So I was smart; I did tape some preseason Monday night football. And I was able to keep my sanity.

Other fathers told similar tales. In one 75-25 family the mother expressed breast milk so the father could do the nighttime feeding by himself. Another father told me he did a disproportionate share of the nighttime wakings because if his wife got up, the baby would want to nurse rather than go back to sleep. Clearly, even in the families that were to become highly unequal, breastfeeding was not the culprit.

Yet, in the other half of the unequal families (and a few of the 50-50 families), breastfeeding was blamed for the father's early distance from infant care. Explaining in a tone of voice that suggested they were belaboring the obvious, both men and women told me that the mother exclusively awoke with their infant at night *because* she was nursing. But as we can see from the experiences of the equal sharers and the other 75-25 couples, it is not obvious at all. Instead, in some families breastfeeding becomes the excuse or justification for fathers' absence from the nitty-gritty work of responding to infants' needs.[15] Men's resistance, often expressed as an inability to hear a crying infant at night, can lead couples to latch on to breastfeeding as the answer to why Mom is up yet again in the middle of the night.

Men sometimes used breastfeeding to resist infant care, and their wives sometimes colluded in their resistance. But in other families, women themselves used breastfeeding to ensure and emphasize that they retained the most important role. Women sometimes resisted sharing at this early juncture, or downplayed their husbands' contributions, because they felt possessive about their own special role with their babies. In one case, a father played an exceptionally supportive part during infancy: getting up when the baby cried at night, changing her, bringing her to Mom in bed, and putting the baby back to bed when she was finished nursing. That father was incredulous that other men didn't do diapers; he was not afraid to bathe an infant; and he willingly took over for his wife during her maternity leave when she fled the house as soon as he came home from work. Yet when I asked her what his role had been when they first became parents, the first thing she said was that he couldn't help with the feeding because she was nursing.

In another family, nursing seemed to be the linchpin in a new mother's negotiations to retain the primary role. Worried that her husband would preempt her relationship with her newborn because he had been the primary parent in a first marriage, she emphasized that things would be different in this marriage because she was breastfeeding, whereas his first wife had bottle-fed.

> I was concerned that I was going to end up in this position of this is my baby and I'm asking permission to take care of it . . . Initially, we had had this discussion . . . even around breastfeeding . . . His first position was well, we'll do both; we'll do bottle-feeding and breastfeeding. I said I didn't want to do that . . . So a lot of the discussion initially was around that issue of breastfeeding and nursing. If I was doing that, what was his role?

He still found many ways to interact with his then five-month-old, who had started to use bottles, was playing patty-cake, and of course, needed diapering. Yet, when I asked about the division of childcare, all the talk was about breastfeeding. While I was at their home for the interview, there was a tense moment when they jockeyed for who would first attend to little Phoebe, the father who wanted to diaper her or the mother who said repeatedly that she was the only one who could nurse. Nursing won.

Equal or not equal, what parents believed about breastfeeding shaped the roles they adopted during their children's infancy, and the roles they adopted, in turn, reinforced their beliefs. For example, Pedro, the father who passionately endorsed bottle-feeding as the key to equal sharing, invoked his experiences with his second child. He explained that once he and his wife were bottle-feeding they could alternate the two o'clock and four-thirty nighttime feedings. In contrast, he didn't waken with his first child, who was breastfed, because "it would be a question of me going, getting the baby, and then coming and waking up Eva and saying the baby's ready to feed, which accomplishes nothing. Then we're both awake."

Extolling the advantages of bottle-feeding, he was unaware that he was also less involved with his first child than other fathers of breastfed infants. Parents' own experience can be a compelling, but misleading, teacher. Experience can mislead with lessons that are nothing more than self-fulfilling prophecies.

Bonding and Biology

Just as many of the unequal parents learned false lessons from the way they handled breastfeeding, they mistakenly took children's preferences for mothers in their own families as evidence of a unique biological "bond" between mothers and children. According to many of the unequal men and some of the unequal women, an ineffable difference separates mothers and fathers. Convinced of its significance, they were hard pressed to explain it. Nevertheless, they believed that no connection to a father could rival the special "bond" that babies and children automatically have with their mothers.[16] As one father said: "Mommy is this very essential, deep kind of relationship . . . Daddy is sort of cozy, teddy bear, fun, good to have . . . a real different kind of quality . . . I don't feel like I (have) an essential relationship with the kids."

These fathers saw in their own families that when their children were hurt, Dad wouldn't do. Their kids wanted Mom. When they looked around, all the children they knew seemed to gravitate to their mothers. The evidence of their own eyes convinced them that the depth of a mother's bond with a child could never be equaled by a father's. As we shall see, however, evidence based on the experiences of the unequal families is deeply flawed.

Unequal parents used biologically based words like "natural" and "bioprogramming" to describe the differences between a child's relationship with her mother and with her father. And even when they didn't explicitly invoke biological concepts to explain the difference between mothers and fathers, they may as well have, because some of the unequal parents thought the difference was universal and immutable. Of course his relationship with his children was different from his wife's, this unequal father told me:

> There's no one that can tell me in a normal situation that they didn't run to Mom first before Dad. I mean it was always that way. I mean . . . every family that I've ever been around. That was the way it was . . . Whether it's a little girl or a little boy . . . where's

Mom? Or if they fall down and they get hurt, they look for Mom first.

He was wrong. Families exist today that are different from every family he's ever been around. These families show that the universality of an unrivaled bond with mothers is greatly exaggerated. In equally sharing families today, even the youngest children looked to their dads for comfort as readily as they looked to their moms. Equal parents also reported that the preferences of very young children shifted between the mother and the father. Recall Janet's observation that Noah goes through Mommy and Daddy phases. And Peter, one of the equally sharing fathers who had trouble connecting initially, mused: "I can't figure out how Nicole chooses who she goes to if she's hurt . . . It just seems to go back and forth." In another family, a two-year-old boy seemed to merge his parents into a "Mommy/Daddy concept," protesting if either left the room when he was upset, and demanding that both be present to put him to bed.

Parents' Behavior and Children's Attachments

What parents did mattered. In general, children seemed to be more attached to the parent who was relatively more available.[17] Children of equal sharers often shifted allegiance to the parent who had spent time with them most recently, occasionally to the chagrin of the other parent.[18] For example, Bernice recounted that when she returned from an extended trip to take care of an ailing parent she discovered that her three-year-old daughter had developed a preference for her father:

> She may have been real mad at me for going away . . . They had just gotten tight somehow in my absence . . . I was furious . . . I was jet-lagged and I was tired . . . I missed her so much, I wanted to put her to bed, and she said, "I want Daddy to put me to bed." I didn't express (it) . . . but I felt very slighted. This only went on for about two days; I felt horribly slighted. In my jet-lag I was so fatigued, I thought I was going to have a temper tantrum.

When both parents are physically present they may still not be equally available. Matt, the two-year-old with the Mommy/Daddy concept, though wanting both parents to put him to bed, preferred Mom to do the last part. Notably, Mom was willing to lie down with him until he fell asleep, whereas Dad was not. On vacation, when Dad carried him and supplied nonstop attention, Dad became the parent of choice. George, a father who just loved sitting, holding, and cuddling his children when they were babies, was their preferred parent when both were small. A few other equal sharers observed that their perceptive children sought out the more relaxed parent.

Children sometimes preferred fathers for very specific functions they had embraced in their otherwise unequal families. One workaholic father seemed very removed from most of the everyday care of his daughter, but had, from her infancy, been the parent to waken and tend to her at night. At the age of ten, she still invariably called for Dad when she woke up from a nightmare, or was sick at night, or got scared by a thunderstorm. The children of another relatively uninvolved father have clamored for him to put them to bed ever since he created a serial bedtime story for them.

The attachments of children reflect the arrangements of parents. In two thirds of the equally sharing families with young children (under six years of age), parents reported that their children were equally attached to both of them.[19] Although in a third of these families the children preferred their mothers to comfort them, put them to bed, or stay with them, they were attached to their fathers too. As long as fathers were available to comfort children in the equally sharing families, there was none of the desperate crying for mothers I heard about in some of the 75-25 families. Surprisingly, though, even in 45 percent of these highly unequal families with young children, parents reported equal attachments.[20] The disparity between the equally sharing families and the 75-25 families increases, however, when we consider families with older children. In all but two of the 75-25 families, children clearly feel closer to their mothers, whereas in the 50-50 families, the percentage who prefer Mom drops to under a third.

Biased Evidence: What Unequal Parents Ignore

The unequal parents who insisted that children are "naturally" more attached to their mothers ignored the ways in which they had produced lopsided attachments in their own families. For example, James, an uninvolved father, spent long hours at his job and paid little attention to his two-year-old son, whom he viewed as a "simple creature." He discounted his wife's greater attention and availability when explaining his son's attachment to her: "(There's a) certain naturalness about it . . . Teddy clings to his mother—*I don't think it's because she's here more.*"

A couple of the unequal fathers invoked their own experiences as sons to support their belief that children always felt closer to their mothers. Growing up, they had turned to their mothers for comfort, sympathy, advice, and support. These men ignored that mothers were there for them and fathers often were not. At best, their fathers had been interested and playful, but removed from the everyday care of children. At worst, the fathers they described were distant, alcoholic, or abusive, fathers whose behavior would hardly inspire a loving attachment.

One of the unequal fathers who equally cared for his first son, Henry, but dropped out with his second, William, paid with William's intermittent rejections. Yet despite the evidence of his own uneven involvement, he too invoked biology to explain William's stronger attachment to his mother:

> It makes me think of this whole bonding and mother bonding and how important that is, you know, to have one person. I sort of didn't believe in that with Henry. I think the result is he's (Henry's) pretty bonded to both of us. With William, once he showed a strong preference, we just got in the habit. I didn't have the energy to try to balance it out. So Madeline did most of the waking up at night. I don't know, maybe at those very early stages I think the nursing . . . some quality of that nurturing and sustaining and stuff remains to those associations.

He can't quite deny the glaring evidence in his own family. Although he starts by touting maternal bonding, he recognizes that rejecting the belief in an exclusive maternal bond allowed him to develop a strong relationship with Henry, his first child. Ironically, though, he falls back on nursing as an explanation, ignoring that his first child was also nursed.

In most of the unequal families the belief in maternal bonds, however, was never challenged by the parents' own experiences. The parents who believed most in biological bonds arranged their lives to ensure that mothers were more available, and by doing so promoted the bonds they believed in. Or once having arranged for mothers to be more available, unequal parents often used biology to justify their choices and pointed to their own experiences as proof that they had been right all along.

The Myth of Women's Superiority

Unequal parents sometimes believed that women possessed a superior capacity to nurture. "She's their Mommy," one father told me as if that statement completely explained the difference between his relationship with his children and his wife's. When pressed about what he meant by "their Mommy," he said:

> What kind of question is that? . . . There are obvious sex differences . . . She's the woman. What does that mean? It means really nothing more than, I don't know, that I'm quite comfortable with those roles. It turned out in this case that she's much more able to give comfort to these kids . . . Whether this is biologically determined or sociologically determined, I don't care because, you know, I don't feel like I have the power to change it, nor do I want to change it.

Although acknowledging the role of "socialization," his wife agreed:

> I think women are socialized very dramatically to be nurturers and that we are good at it and we expect it of ourselves and get enormous pleasure out of it . . . Men are socialized to be warriors and it's hard to be a good nurturer of a baby when you're a warrior and especially a warrior without titties. The patterns get set then to a large degree.

The men and their wives who equally shared infant care from the start didn't believe for a minute that there were biological differences between men's and women's capacity to give that care.[21] One father turned the notion of maternal instinct on its head when he told me, "I really believe in paternal instinct." Daniel ridiculed biological beliefs by noting that "there was no reason to think that the mother . . . (had) this instinctive ability to change a diaper." In most families today, parents have little previous experience with infants; both mothers and fathers have to learn how to take care of them. Women often seem better at it simply because almost immediately they get more practice. Daniel can't understand why women don't answer their husbands' protests of "I don't know how to do it" with "I didn't either when he was born, but I learned." His advice to new mothers reflects his belief that, given the opportunity, men can learn: "Hand him the kid and leave and tell him you're going to a movie. Then go someplace else so he absolutely can't find you and be gone for five or six hours. You'd be amazed at how much he could learn in five or six hours."

A few parents who became equal sharers after an initial period of inequality, like Edward, did maintain that women had an edge in nurturance: "Most women find certain things easier to do than most men with regard to kids . . . traditionally stereotypically female, empathy, being able to pick up subtle cues or not so subtle cues about how people feel, being able to deal with feelings." However, the equal sharers who believed that women found it easier to nurture differed in one important way from the unequal parents. Although they talked about women's biological superiority in parenting, they didn't doubt men's capacity to learn or their responsibility to try harder. For example, Edward thought women's greater aptitude for parenting did not "justify having distinct ideals about what a father and mother should be." Biological differences could be overcome.

The equal sharers unanimously agreed that the ingredients of good parenting were the same for mothers and fathers; the essence is nurturance. This father speaks for most of them: "Show your love, show your affection, show your concern, guide them, help them, help them grow. I think it's equal. I think it should be no different. That's my own feelings."

Men in the equally sharing families who initially felt awkward or inhibited with their children developed a greater capacity to nurture through their relationships with them.[22] Edward, who admired his wife's ability to respond to subtle emotional cues, discovered an untapped empathic part of himself by taking care of his second child from early infancy:

I'm Ollie's primary parent . . . When push comes to shove and he's crying and screaming he wants me . . . I could very easily have fallen into a traditional fatherhood role because dealing with feelings is not easy for me . . . So I think I've had the advantage of having to be what I want to be, but probably wouldn't be if I were simply given a free choice . . . Part of me likes to believe I'm a very special kind of father . . . so I feel kind of proud of myself.

Maternal bonds don't arise automatically. They are created in the work and attention required by the everyday care of children. Children have remarkably sensitive antennae for who will meet their needs. Mothers are chosen by children because of the care they give and the needs they meet, not simply because they are mothers. Fathers can respond to children's needs, and when they do they are chosen as well.[23] Theories about maternal instinct don't get in the way for children. Kevin told me that when his children were two and four years old he was reading them a bedtime story about a mother cat putting her kittens to bed in a basket in the closet. They were "adamant" that it was a father cat. It couldn't possibly be a mother cat because in their family Kevin tended to their nighttime and bedtime routines. Visibly touched, Kevin confided that their insistence that the cat was a daddy was "one of the nicest things my kids ever did to me."

When equally sharing parents told me about differences between their children's relationships with mothers and fathers, they focused on the idiosyncrasies of their own particular families. In one family, the mother was the disciplinarian and the father the softie; in another the children went for walks in the woods with their father and to amusement parks with their mother; and in yet another, one high-strung daughter gravitated to a mother who was short-tempered like her, while her quieter sister confided more in their introverted dad. Often the differences reflected gender stereotypes. On average, even in the equally sharing families, mothers did quieter activities at home with children, like arts and crafts, sewing, and cooking. Fathers encouraged children's adventurousness and challenged them in sports. None of the parents claimed, however, that these stereotypical activities were universal or biologically based. Nor did they think these activities imply a deeper bond with mothers.

The belief in biological explanations for differences between mothers and fathers was useful to parents in the unequal families. First, it justified the low participation of fathers. How could they be expected to participate as much as their wives if they are "naturally" less equipped to nurture? Second, it freed men from having to appreciate their wives' individual contributions or talents as childrearers. If women are only doing what comes naturally, they don't especially deserve any credit for it. Third, it assuaged the pain men felt when their children rejected them. If small children "always" want their mothers, then when a given man's child turns away from him, he doesn't have to ask why. He doesn't have to examine any personal inadequacies in himself that children might detect. It is not that he personally can't give, but that men simply don't have the same capacity for nurturance as women.

Although consoling themselves by conceding that men are incapable of nurturing small children, aren't these men also giving up a part of their humanity? Sometimes they seemed a bit sad to me. Explaining why specialized roles in the families made sense, they groped for some superior male ability that would match their wives' maternal one. With women out in the workforce, achieving in all domains, however, none of the men was comfortable arguing that men were innately superior computer scientists, carpenters, dentists, or salespeople. Embarrassed that they couldn't come up with something comparable to maternal instinct, several fathers resorted to joking that they "go out and hunt the big game."

We don't have to solve the mystery of maternal instinct or deny the effect of a lifetime of gender lessons to endorse paternal participation in the care of the smallest infants. The question should not be, "Are women better at parenting?"[24] Instead we should be asking, "Can men be the kind of parents we want for our children?"[25] Edward's relationship with Ollie, like those of the other equally sharing men with their children, shows that men can.

Men can, but they usually don't. Perhaps the most intriguing issue is what happened to those men who dropped out, the men who involved themselves in infant care early on but were decidedly secondary parents by the time I interviewed them. In most cases they turned their attention from home to work. Making a living or advancing in a career was the primary focus of unequal fathers. Many of the parents I interviewed who eschewed biological explanations looked to their work lives to explain why they were equal or unequal. But as I will show in the next chapter, jobs and families are inextricably intertwined. Family lives shape work lives every bit as much as work lives shape family.

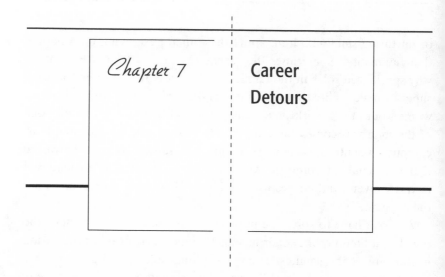

Chapter 7

Career
Detours

Our jobs often seem to control our family lives. Money and time constrain when families can sit down to dinner together, whether a parent greets a child getting off the school bus, and which parent gets the children ready for school in the morning. Some sociologists and social psychologists, in fact, have argued that job-related factors are the key to gender inequality at home. Because women work fewer hours in the paid labor force, earn less money, and have more flexible jobs than men, they end up with the bulk of childcare.[1] Notwithstanding the power of jobs to shape our everyday lives, the different kinds of jobs men and women hold don't tell the whole story. When I examined the employment histories of the men and women I interviewed, I was surprised to discover that parents had often exerted more control than they realized. Parents' decisions about which jobs to take, how many hours to work, and how to interpret the demands of their jobs often created constraints to which they were then bound. In short, parents' decisions about employment, which were profoundly affected by their genders, influenced the equality or inequality between them both at home and on the job.

Time, Money, and Equality

Why do women do more parenting? When I asked the unequal couples, many invoked time. Mothers said:

I think the biggest factor is time. I have a lot more time. I work probably half as many hours as he does.

I think because my husband is gone most of the time working . . . I think it's just because I'm here more.

Men's answers echoed women's:

Why she does? . . . just because . . . I don't physically have the time and I'm not physically here I guess.

A lot of it is because she's around more, she's available more, she's there more.

I guess it's because I spend more time at work . . . I never really thought about it.

Time available certainly shapes who takes care of children. Jobs are key to how much time parents have available. If one parent works nine to five and the other doesn't leave the job until six, chances are the nine-to-five parent will cook dinner for the children. Numerous studies have documented that fathers' and mothers' shares of childcare partially reflect the relative time men and women spend in paid work.[2] In my study, likewise, in the 75-25 families fathers worked for pay fourteen hours more per week than their wives, compared to only one additional hour per week in the 50-50 families.

Money was also mentioned by unequal husbands and wives when they reflected on the inequality in their childcare responsibilities. As Clifford, a carpenter, told me: "It's easy, it's economics. It's got me facing a certain direction so . . . somebody's gotta cover the home front." Their relatively higher incomes put pressure on men to turn their attention to earning money rather than taking care of children. Larry began parenthood as an equal sharer but later sadly relinquished his desire to spend as much time with his child as his wife did because of the pressure on him to earn money. "It's still a struggle to come to terms with that," he confided to me. His income as an optometrist is substantially higher than the salary his wife, Joyce, makes as a nutritionist at the state psychiatric hospital. Moreover, because he is in private practice in a community with a high demand for his services, the more hours he works, the more money he makes. Larry articulated the dilemma in trying to share equally:

I make more money . . . The private practice has the potential to make more money or to have some sort of elasticity in what I can add to the family income. Just in terms of sort of economic efficiency it makes sense . . . It doesn't make sense economically to say we're gonna each work 50-50. There's a huge differential between what you work per hour. It makes sense to tilt to the work, in some ways the way Joyce and I did. I don't think we did it in this planned way but it's sort of like, all right, I work forty hours, she works thirty hours, that kind of thing . . . So I think it's economically driven . . . That's my theory . . . I mean it's speculative, but if Joyce were a doctor I could imagine my staying home a lot more. And doing more than half of the childcare.

Larry puts more hours in at his job because it seems to make sense economically for their family. Fathers' and mothers' shares of childcare partially reflect their relative incomes.[3] When I compared the income differences between husbands and wives in the three groups of couples I interviewed, I found that on average, equally sharing husbands and wives had the most similar incomes.[4]

Gender counts, however, when families are counting up money.[5] As we will see, families don't simply maximize the amount of money they could earn without reference to the gender of the parent who is doing the earning. For example, Dorothy, an extremely assertive woman who later became an equal sharer, lost the argument that her husband should quit his job to stay home with their new baby, despite earning twice her husband's salary. A mild-mannered, gentle man, Sam put his foot down. Why did he refuse to do it, even though it made so much sense financially? The logic of money is not gender-blind. As Dorothy said: "It's a gut feeling of men don't stay home with their children . . . Mothers stay home and fathers work. And so it was more of a social thing that worked on us than . . . a logical . . . because if we were being logical, he would have stayed home." Money may give both men and women power, but women's dollars don't buy as much domestic power as men's.

Men did earn relatively more than women per year in the 75-25 and 60-40 families than in the 50-50 families, which suggests that the division of labor was economically based. But when I delved deeper into the relation between money and the division of labor, I was stunned to discover that the difference between husbands and wives in the hourly rate of pay in the three groups does not vary. In other words, the income difference between husbands and wives in the three groups of parents (50-50, 60-40, 75-25) is entirely explained by the choices about time devoted to paid work. Men earned more because they worked longer hours, period.[6] Among the parents I interviewed, at least, money cannot begin to explain couples' decisions about jobs.

When we take a snapshot of families at one moment in time, their division of labor, whether unequal or equal, can often look like the inevitable result of money earned or time demanded by the two parents' jobs. We might think to ourselves: maybe a few couples can work out equal parenting arrangements, but only because the demands and financial rewards of jobs are so similar. A glance at the unequal couples shows that equality at work is not the norm for mothers and fathers. In most families fathers outearn and outwork mothers at their jobs.[7]

The problem with the snapshot is that it ignores how parents construct unequal or equal work lives. We need a video, and we need to rewind and replay it until we can find the key decisions that set parents on a course that facilitated equality or made it nearly impossible to achieve.

To illustrate this process, let's compare two couples: Tammy and Thomas, an unequal couple, and Joan and Mark, equal sharers. Tammy and Thomas work at jobs that are as unequal as their roles at home. Mark and Joan's equality at home is matched by their equality at work.

Tammy and Thomas: Climbing up and down the Corporate Ladder

Tammy and Thomas met in college. She was an excellent student who had majored in business with an eye toward climbing the corporate ladder. Thomas was more relaxed about his college education and had set his goals somewhat lower. As a student all he wanted to do was graduate from college and get a job as a baseball coach. Yet today, less than six years later, Thomas is a successful sales representative for a water-bottling company, and earns more than twice as much as Tammy. Tammy works full time in a brokerage firm as a senior client management associate, but she has cut back on her career aspirations and on her extra hours at work. Thomas's job entails a great deal of travel away from home, and Tammy ends up shouldering much more of the parenting responsibility.

Interestingly, in the initial stages of parenting Tammy and Thomas had more equal roles. After being at home for a few months, Tammy got a job with the company for which she still works:

> Thomas's career didn't take off like mine did so I was able to put in a lot of time and effort in this company. I could still start a move on my career. Thomas had a strict eight-thirty to five job and was home. I would be putting in the overtime . . . I would work a lot and Thomas would feed and change Shannon and they would do a lot. He was actually excellent.

The balance between them changed dramatically two years ago. Thomas came to her and argued that the only way he could advance in his job was to travel. If he traveled, she would have to take more responsibility for their preschool-aged child. She would also have to cut back at work. Tammy agreed:

> I started taking on more of a role of "let's focus on his career" because the company started to slow down. I've changed because I've put things in perspective. To me, the family . . . is more important than my career right now, but there are times when you say, "God, I could have really been something else!"

Thomas is pressuring her to cut back even further. She related a recent conversation between them and her reflections about it:

> He said to me Friday night, "You know, you have a stressful job, I have a stressful job. It's just important that your job is not as stressful as mine." And he had a point. He does the traveling. He's made a decision, we've made a decision that this is going to be his career. He's going to focus on it so that I can ease up on the hours and . . . be home a little more.

She is considering working only part time when they have a second child.

Thomas and Tammy's relative shares of the parenting have become more unequal over time. This increasing inequality seems to be directly related to his increasing and her decreasing investment in career. Why, though, did they make the decision to move in this traditional direction? When asked, each attributes it to money. Tammy says: "It was money . . . How could I get ahead? . . . His salary plus the company car plus the bonuses they get every year based on the amount of business they bring in. There's a potential for a lot more. They're a small company that does very well." Thomas concurs: "My potential for earning power in a sales position would have been more than hers in mostly an administrative position . . . I think that Tammy really saw that in corporate America the male had a better shot in getting to such and such an earning power or position than a female did." Nevertheless, at the time they made this important decision the two of them were earning approximately the same salary. They both ignored that she might have had a lucrative future in management, possibly with a higher earning potential than his in sales. Although we can't know for sure, they probably wouldn't have ended up with such disparate salaries had each been able to invest equally in career. Yet Thomas's argument, that he possessed the greater earning potential, went unchallenged.

They both hinted that gender influenced their decision. Thomas described Tammy repeatedly as a woman whose identity had been transformed by becoming a mother: "When we were both in school, she was more career-oriented and going out and finding a high tech job in New York—the whole bit. I think now by having Shannon she's come around full circle and she really enjoys the other aspect of having and raising a family." He uses this change to explain her willingness to cede the career focus to him: "She'd say, 'The hell with this corporate climbing ladders and all that stuff,' . . . Shannon was just more important to her than chasing a career." Tammy also notes the change in herself but expresses more ambivalence. When I asked if her attitude toward work had changed after Shannon was born, she said:

> I don't know if it was a drastic change because . . . I'm very competitive . . . and I don't want the working mother thing to be a drawback or a crutch . . . But it's changed a little because I don't think it is as important as it was to reach the top and become Vice President or President of a corporation . . . To me the most important job is being a parent.

However, Tammy did not push to change the balance in their work and family roles; Thomas did. Although neither has ever said so, his desire to have the central breadwinning role may have been critical in how they now divide childcare. Thomas talked about how his career plans were affected by becoming a father: "Your responsibility goes up a notch of course. You then think of a plan, steps or maybe a guideline on how you can get to a position where you can enhance your earning power." That's exactly what he did. His feeling of responsibility for the breadwinning is matched by her feeling of responsibility for childcare. When I asked why she does more of the childcare, her voice carried a note of resignation: "I think you just feel like you've got to do it. You're the mom and that's the way it's always been."

Joan and Mark: Creating Equal Careers

Mark is a police officer, a line sergeant in the police department of a mid-sized northeastern city. His wife, Joan, is a manager in a public utilities company, responsible for the training and development of twenty-five to thirty customer service representatives. Although neither of them went to college, their joint income of over $80,000 a year allows them a very comfortable lifestyle. Mark works forty-two hours a week; Joan works a fifty-hour week and earns about $8,000 more than he. They equally share the care of their fifteen-year-old son and eight-year-old daughter. Joan invokes their work hours to describe how they share childcare:

> It's all based around our crazy hours. With Mark, he works two days and two nights and when he works the nights, he works all night . . . I also put in a lot of hours. I don't just work an eight-hour day. Sometimes I can go ten, twelve hours, depending on meetings that I might have at my job. So how we share is basically whoever gets home first usually does the cooking or starts the cooking . . . We try to share our household duties as much as possible . . . It's whoever's available, (we) basically take turns.

Mark doesn't shirk taking any responsibility with children, from getting their lunches to discussing their days at school with them. He's a veteran because Mark and Joan have been equally sharing childcare since their son was a few months old.

Joan is a real go-getter in her career. She took a job with the utilities company right out of high school and has worked her way up from there. While many women, like Tammy, cut back on their careers in order to assume primary care of their children, Joan persuaded her husband to assume equal responsibility in order to allow her to continue to advance at her job.

> When I had Alexander, I was in a position at work where I was in line for a promotion. Alex was born at the end of May and I had to

be back to work by July in order to maintain that position . . . to get this job . . . It was a good opportunity and it was something I had been working for so I went back to work in July . . . That's when my husband became Mr. Mom.

They worked different hours and each took care of the children while the other was at work, supplementing when necessary with babysitters. Mark fondly describes his life as Mr. Mom: "I was home with the kids, the baby, from zero to preschool and even in preschool I was taking care of them . . . taking them out . . . We used to live near Verona Park so we always went to Verona Park. I enjoyed that, I really enjoyed that."

Mark is not a father who began his marriage with ideals of equality in mind. Joan describes the evolution of their sharing as predating the birth of their children. When they first got married she was doing most of the work at home:

I can remember I got upset one day and I said, "This is not the way this house is going to be run" . . . This was many moons ago. This was before the kids, before children. "I need help; I can't do everything on my own." I remember sitting down and having a discussion on it. "Well, what do you want me to do?" "Well, if the bed isn't made, I want it made" . . . "We've got to help each other out, it can't be on one person."

He agreed, and though there were fits and starts, the stage was set for equally sharing the care of their children. Over the years Mark has taken over an increasing amount of responsibility not only for time spent with children, but for the associated chores. For example, Joan used to have dinner ready to be cooked when she was working at night. Gradually, he took over that chore, despite not having known how to cook at all when they first got married: "I got him a subscription to *Food and Wine* . . . I don't know how it really happened, to be honest with you. It just seemed like little by little I was coming out of the kitchen more and more . . . I think the *Food and Wine* magazine really helped."

Why do Mark and Joan differ from so many American couples? Yes, their work lives are more equal, but it is not an accident that they became equal. Joan's choice to go back to work full time meant that she continued to advance in her job. Although Mark's willingness to take over much of the childcare did not compromise his position at work, it did take away leisure and some of the freedom that he might have had. By relinquishing some traditional male prerogatives, though, Mark has reaped the advantages of sharing with his wife:

> The biggest advantage is we both get to share the kids. I mean not like my father, he had hardly any time really and whatever time he did have he tried as best he could. The other thing I would say is the lifestyle, her job and mine. It makes things very comfortable . . . I know guys who have to go out and hold two jobs, three jobs trying to support their family.

In this family, equal sharing has meant career success for Mark's wife and important time with children for him. Mark genuinely cherishes the relationship he has with his children. He appreciates the material advantages his wife's job affords, and the quality of life he has attained because of not having the total responsibility for breadwinning. Mark and Joan have created not only an equally sharing family, but a very happy one. When I asked if he was satisfied with the trade-offs he has made, Mark answered: "Oh, I think it's great. I love the way I live." Joan's answer echoes his: "I don't know what the disadvantage is to be honest with you, I really don't. I just like the way our life is."

Couples make choices about their jobs that propel them toward equal or unequal arrangements at home. Tammy and Thomas's story might be quite different today if their conversation two years ago had gone in another direction. Tammy might have resisted compromising her career more adamantly. She might have argued that although her company was falling on hard times, with experience under her belt she could look for another job. Thomas might have decided that the increase in his pay wasn't worth the sacrifice of so much time with his daughter or the loss of Tammy's future earnings. Imagine what could have happened if Thomas had turned down the job that entailed travel.[8] They might have become the equal sharers instead of Mark and Joan.

In a similar thought experiment for Mark and Joan, we can see that a critical moment for them came when Joan was home on maternity leave. Despite the offer of a better job, it is easy to imagine Joan as a new mother deciding to turn it down. Or Mark might have refused to take the extraordinary role of an alternating-shift father. They could have survived on his income as a police officer and her wages as a customer service representative. Or, like some of his friends, Mark might have taken a second job to help make ends meet. Joan could have become the wife who earns half of her husband's income; Mark, the father who rarely sees his children.

When couples are faced with the kind of decision that Tammy and Thomas and Joan and Mark confronted, money is far from the only factor they consider. Gender bias enters. Women's choices about jobs are constrained by the expectation that parenting comes first; men's are not. Gender influences three important types of job-related decisions that parents make: how much time to allocate to paid employment, whether to take or give up opportunities for career advancement, and how to take advantage of the potential flexibility in their jobs. When women become parents, they are expected to cut back on their work hours (or take time off from paid employment), sacrifice career advancement if it interferes with parenting responsibilities, and take advantage of whatever flexibility exists on the job, even if doing so hurts their careers. Although expectations for men may be changing, men are still expected to work at least full time, and to take advantage of opportunities for advancement.[9] No one expects them to press for job flexibility so they can meet parenting responsibilities.

We can readily see how these gender biases operate by comparing the decisions made in equal and unequal families. Unequal couples moved toward inequality when they gave in to gender pressures; equal sharers moved toward equality by resisting them. The stories that follow illustrate couples' contrasting approaches.

First, let's compare the cases of Judy and Ben and Edward and Jane. These two couples will illustrate how the trajectory toward equality changes when women take up instead of turning down career opportunities. They will also show that husbands' interpretations of their own job demands are linked to their support of their wives' careers, support that is critical in shaping the career choices of women.[10]

Ben and Edward are both college professors and both are married to professional women. Judy is a dermatologist; Jane is a dentist. Despite these similarities, Judy and Ben's story is a tale of becoming unequal, Edward and Jane's a story of pursuing equality. They differ because Judy gave up opportunities whereas Jane pursued them. Edward supported Jane's aspirations; Ben undermined Judy's. Edward took advantage of the flexibility of his job and cut back his work hours. Ben saw the same job as inflexible.

Judy and Ben: Money and Status Do Not Buy Equality

Judy is an outgoing, vivacious, articulate woman who sat me down at her kitchen table, made an exceptionally good cup of coffee, and proceeded to chat as though we were old friends. I had come to interview her on a day when she wasn't going to work. Judy works part time; her husband works full time. As might be expected, Judy does more childcare than he. She says she takes about 75 percent of the parental load of caring for two children, a six-year-old and a three-year-old. He basically concurs, attributing 70 percent to her. These facts are not unusual. What is unusual is her profession, dermatology. Both she and her husband, Ben, a college professor who teaches economics, have very high-status professions, although he does not earn nearly as much as she. Even working part time, Judy earns almost twice as much money as her husband. Their joint income puts them in the top 5 percent of American households.[11]

Ben seems like a loving father. He certainly attends to his children when he is at home: bathing them, diapering them when they were younger, playing with them, and worrying about them. Indeed, both parents report that at least at some stages the kids were more attached to him. Nonetheless, Judy spends three afternoons a week with them to his one, and at night, when Ben often goes back to work, it is Judy who gets everything prepared for the next day, including his lunch. Judy seems to be responsible for the overall management of the household, but does not seem especially overburdened, both because she is able to afford household help and because she works thirty hours a week while Ben works forty-five. But if we knew only their professions, we would have no reason to expect that one worked more than the other. College professors don't spend more time at their jobs than physicians. How then did this work structure get established in their family, a structure that supports the mother's greater involvement in childcare?

Perhaps the critical moment came when Ben got his first academic job. At the time they were both in very high-status training programs. Judy had gone to one of the best medical schools in the country, and was then in a very demanding fast-track internship. She had been accepted to go on to a very competitive residency in surgery, the kind of training that leads to a high-powered academic job, the top of the profession for doctors. Ben was working as a postdoctoral fellow in economics at a top-rated university.

When Ben told Judy that he was applying for a job as assistant professor at a university far from the hospital where her residency was, her reaction was: "Fine, you go there. I'm not interested. You go alone." He applied for the job anyway, and got it. It was his best job offer, although he could have spent another year as a postdoc. Over the course of time Judy changed her mind.

> I was working 80 to 100 hours a week and in some ways it was . . . the most socially acceptable way of bugging out on something that's more of an intense commitment than what I really wanted to do . . . At a certain point I said, yeah, yeah, it's an out for me. I can leave this program and . . . I'm not screaming uncle. I'm going with my husband, that's perfectly socially acceptable.

She gave up the idea of becoming a surgeon and started in a new training program in dermatology, a much less prestigious one: "Their program wasn't tough enough for me. I did some research projects on the side . . . I was looking for more stimulation because it felt easy compared to the very intense program I had been in." Incredibly, she was taking on some of these additional commitments while pregnant and suffering from severe morning sickness. Some things started to pall: "I was doing some of those things because I felt I should be doing them . . . It is not like I was absolutely, necessarily enjoying that."

When her first child was born and her residency complete, she stayed home for four months, describing it as "a really very happy time." The job she took when she went back to work was a far cry from the high-powered academic medicine she had envisioned. She took a job in private practice and negotiated part-time hours. She got off the fast-track career path, and found a job that would allow her to spend more time at home:

> I felt like I was kind of selling my career ambitions short and that I was doing something that at the time felt like a sacrifice . . . going from wanting a high-powered academic job as a surgeon to being a private dermatologist. It felt like I was shorting some of my dreams, although, in fact, I can't imagine that I would actually want to stay on the other track. I just can't imagine how that would have worked into my life.

Judy seems happy for the moment. In many ways, her choice makes a lot of sense. What sane parent would want to work the grueling schedule that she described in her training program? Her career is lucrative enough to allow her to escape some of the crazy juggling many parents do, without incurring any economic hardship. However, something about her story is unsettling. Ben's unwillingness to compromise much in his career meant that she had to totally alter her course. Wasn't there some middle ground where they could have split the difference, each compromising a bit? Can a woman who was as achievement-oriented as Judy truly be happy with the vicarious rewards of seeing her husband succeed at his career instead of achieving herself? And if she really is happy now, will she be as satisfied with her dramatically scaled-down career when her children are older and need less care?

Ben's career has been affected much less by having children. Ben's compromises have been much smaller. When asked if his attitude toward work had changed since he became a parent, he replied: "I think I'm a little bit less invested . . . not a whole lot less, but the amount of time I put into it has declined from fifty hours to forty-five hours a week . . . I don't know that that's a big change though." He reflects on the idea of both parents working part time in an equally sharing arrangement, but clearly rejects it as feasible for himself, based on the way he interprets his career:

> I think there are a lot of careers, of which doing research is one and you probably know this as well as I do, that doing them part-time doesn't quite make it . . . The whole field goes at a certain speed and requires a certain investment. If you do it for twenty hours a week, you're kidding yourself that you're really doing it.

Although he didn't specifically mention Judy, it is clear that he was talking about his own family in one of his concluding comments: "I think it's certainly the case that women make more sacrifices about that (career) than men, although I certainly feel that I have made compromises too that were just not part of the scheme of the 1950s."

Edward and Jane: It Takes a Husband to Support a Wife's Career

Edward is a tenured classics professor. His wife, Jane, has an entry-level position as a dentist at a health maintenance organization. Since they were married, Edward has earned most of the family's income. Last year Edward's salary was more than eight times Jane's.

Edward and Jane's children are the same age as Ben and Judy's: one, six years old, the other, three years old. But unlike Ben and Judy, Edward and Jane equally share childcare. In some spheres Edward even does a bit more. Here's how he describes their division:

> I'd have to say 50-50 because there's some things that I do more. I think I do more of the routine stuff . . . Simply because she needs more sleep, I'm much more likely to be on early and on late and I'm mostly the middle of the night person. I'm the one they call when they get up, so I do a lot more of that I think. She does a lot more of the nonroutine stuff, a lot more of the planning.

He later elaborates that "on early" means that he is the parent responsible for getting both children up, dressed, and fed in the morning.

Jane agrees that Edward puts equal time into parenting, and also shares the nitty-gritty work of caring for young children. Although in this modern professional couple equality at home parallels their equal-status careers, that equality was not a foregone conclusion in their family.

Early in their marriage Jane started dental school in Washington, D.C., and Edward started his academic position in New England. They commuted back and forth on weekends to be together. After a short time, however, Jane was unhappy commuting and decided to leave dental school to join Edward. She wanted to start a family right away, but he felt strongly that she should continue her training. It was very important to him that the mother of his future children invest in her work life, and not just in parenting.

She took his advice and went back to dental school, but then took a leave when they had their first child. While on leave, she did more of the parenting. When the leave came to an end, again Edward urged Jane to go back to school. She had doubts:

> I wasn't sure I wanted to go back. I found parenting Emma to be really fun. I had a very easy life, all I did was exercise three mornings a week and then I would take care of Emma. I enjoyed it . . . When I went back to school that September with Emma, Edward was very instrumental in that. I was very opposed to going back because I really was devastated by my first-year grades.

Jane completed her dental school education on a reduced schedule, all the while continuing to do more of the childcare:

I think I did a lot more of the parenting as a result of his career needs at that point in time. Oftentimes he would come home and I would have dinner ready. He would interact with Emma until she went to bed and then he would take off and I would finish up whatever needed to be done.

According to Jane, childcare really became equal only after their second child was born and Edward had gotten tenure. Jane started to put more time into dental school. Edward's increased share of the parenting necessitated compromises in his work:

I feel very negative about my work right now. I haven't really been able to get much of my own work (this is how academics refer to their research—their own work) done since Ollie was born . . . I mean I finished my second book just before he was born and did some editing on it . . . I haven't really been able to get into a new research project since he was born.

Edward reports that he spends about thirty to thirty-five hours a week working:

I don't do early morning or late in the afternoon meetings for the most part . . . I don't work most evenings . . . My family life, I think, greatly constrains how much I work and when I can work. I think in that sense it has probably limited my ability to really get into a research project.

He acknowledges that Jane has compromised too:

We both in different ways limited our careers . . . I've managed to get tenure and . . . to get a fair amount of work done and Jane's made sacrifices right along. On the other hand I know I have never . . . very rarely been able to work the kind of sixty- or seventy-hour workweek that some of my colleagues seem to have . . . because I'm busy with the kids one way or another. Life's been busier and more difficult than we ever imagined it would be . . . at least than I ever imagined.

Although Ben and Edward are both tenured college professors, they interpret the constraints of their jobs quite differently. Ben spends forty-five hours a week working, Edward, thirty to thirty-five hours. Their relative shares of parenting reflect this disparity. Ben invests less time in parenting than his professional wife; Edward devotes equal time to parenting. Clearly, each has *chosen* how much time to invest in his profession. Time spent on their jobs is not an inevitable result of their professions.[12]

College professors are not the only workers who have flexibility in the interpretation of their job demands. (I used the example of college professors only because I know it so well.) In many jobs there is room for a lot of interpretation and negotiation. One equally sharing contractor described how he had cut back his work hours in order to be home when his child got home from school. His job can easily consume ninety hours a week, because there is always something more that could be done to drum up new business, but he limits himself to thirty hours a week. Another equally sharing father who sells commercial real estate limits his hours to thirty a week, despite his working on commission. Even clerical workers, who contend with fixed work hours and inflexible bureaucratic rules, find ways to creatively take advantage of the "flexibility" of their jobs to juggle family responsibilities while at work. They negotiate with their immediate supervisors to bend the rules, use the telephone to keep track of children, refuse to stay late, and surreptitiously do household planning while performing their job duties.[13]

Parents also negotiate with employers in numerous ways to change the constraints of their jobs in order to spend more time with their children. An accounts receivable clerk convinced her employer to let her work at night so she and her husband could alternate childcare. Tammy, in a corporate job that had entailed a great deal of overtime, made it clear that she would work no more than an eight-thirty-to-five day at the office. In many cases parents were able to negotiate with their employers to work less than full time. However, mothers, rather than fathers, usually do the negotiating. Often men see the same kinds of jobs as more constraining. One mail carrier described the hours of his own job as fixed, but thought his wife's job as a seamstress was more flexible and she could cut back her hours. But he later mentioned that some of the mothers in the post office who were mail carriers had arranged to cut back their hours to spend more time at home. A male lawyer and a male obstetrician told me similar stories. The lawyer explained that his wife could cut back to a part-time commitment in her career as a college writing instructor, but as an associate lawyer aspiring to partnership he certainly couldn't cut back. He later revealed, however, that two associates in his firm had done just that. The obstetrician reported that in his private practice his colleagues thought it was acceptable for a female physician to negotiate a part-time schedule but not for him to do so.[14]

Who could have a more perfect set-up for equally shared parenting than couples who share the same profession? A number of the couples I interviewed possessed this advantage: two dentists, two college professors, two lawyers, two physical therapists. And some of these same-profession couples work in private practices, which could readily be structured to allow for both parents to work outside and inside the home equally. Yet sharing a profession by no means ensures equality. Some of the husbands and wives with identical professions make gendered choices about how to balance paid work and family work. Women do a disproportionate share of childcare, while their husbands do a disproportionate share of paid labor.

Those same-profession couples who have achieved equal sharing have not had an easy time of it just because their jobs are now so friendly to equal sharing. A current snapshot would not capture the often difficult decisions that have kept them equal at work. Although their circumstances may be the most favorable imaginable, sometimes men's sacrifices of job-related opportunities were critical in maintaining those circumstances.

Let's compare two same-profession couples to see how their choices led to very different family arrangements: an unequal couple, Rosalind and Joe, both lawyers in small general private practices, and an equal couple, Jonathan and Ruth, two high school teachers. The most striking contrast in these two families has been in how parents have allocated their time between careers and home. When Rosalind and Joe became parents, Rosalind took time off and cut back her work hours; Joe maintained or increased his work hours. Jonathan and Ruth *both* took time off from work to raise their young children. The two stories also contrast the effects of men's and women's career sacrifices. Rosalind relinquished some of her career dreams; Jonathan relinquished some of his. Rosalind's gendered choices contributed to inequality in her home; Jonathan's gender-resisting choices contributed to equality in his.

Rosalind and Joe: Mirrored Images and Inequality

Joe and Rosalind are the parents of two school-aged children, a ten-year-old son, Luke, and a six-year-old daughter, Bridget. Joe works sixty hours a week at his law practice; Rosalind works about twenty hours a week at hers. Despite their shared profession, they have highly asymmetrical work lives and family lives. Their disproportionate shares of childcare are the mirror image of their division of paid work. Joe describes it:

> It's incredibly traditional, it's really incredible . . . I mean we put each other through graduate school and we each picked relatively equivalent careers . . . We have been incredibly traditional and we would not have predicted that . . . Rosalind does 90 percent of the household running, I work a lot out in the world . . . I log a lot more hours outside of the home than she logs. She's outside the home, but she logs a lot more inside the home.

Rosalind agrees:

> I do mostly all the childcare . . . Joe does a little bit, but it's not much, so it's always been the same . . . Since Luke was born, that pretty much he has his work life and . . . then I worked as much as I felt was going to work given what the kids' lives were like at each stage . . . It never involved Joe's life really.

Rosalind does not seem unhappy with this state of affairs. Although she had been working in private practice full time before her children were born, from pregnancy she expected things to be different: "It was just set up like I would change my life completely, which was completely fine with me. It didn't feel like a compromise in any way. It was something I was looking forward to. I would become this person who took care of kids and worked in whatever fashion emerged."

Although Rosalind ended up with a career of equal status to that of her husband, it is not a career that she finds equally satisfying. As a child, Rosalind had wanted to be a geologist, but got the message that her scientific bent was not appropriate for women. She switched to geography, which she loved. But instead of pursuing graduate work herself, she followed her husband to the Southwest for law school. At one point they decided to try to come back east; again she applied for graduate programs and was accepted, but because he was not accepted as a transfer student, they remained in Texas, where he finished his training. Rosalind imagines that her work life would have been different had he been accepted:

If he had, I bet I would have gone to one of those (programs) . . .
I'm sure I would have gone to one of them. I don't know if I would
have made it or lasted, but I bet I would have gone because I felt
comfortable . . . I think I would have felt like I can handle this, like
this was the right arena for my level of smartness.

Instead, surrounded by law students, she too became an attorney. But,
Rosalind confided, it was not an entirely satisfying choice. It "didn't
quite fit" with her inquisitive "nature."

Motherhood afforded her an escape from some of the struggles that
she had experienced over her work life:

When I had a family, I stopped worrying about my work life so
much in terms of my identity. The identity of being a mother feels
like in combination (with work) that I'm taken care of . . . I mean I
think if I didn't work at all I'd feel really uptight about that. It's
like, that's good, I'm doing enough, I don't have to do more . . . I've
been happy to have a reason to not be out there in the world.[15]

Although sometimes she wants her husband to be more involved at
home and to work outside less, she is also relieved not to have major
responsibility for breadwinning: "It seems very scary to think about
working more . . . letting go of the connection to home and kids. But
then also, I have no experience of what it's like to get a lot of help so I
don't know how freed up I'd feel."

Joe expresses more ambivalence about the traditional way they've
structured their lives. He sometimes feels burdened by the responsibility of maintaining the family income: "I've been so driven to make a
living for us . . . part of me thinks if I were with a partner who was as
driven in that way . . . I would gladly give that up and do a lot more at
home." Joe is torn between his desire to be the breadwinner and his
desire to flee the responsibility.[16] He admits that his fantasy of marriage
to a high-earning woman reflects only part of the truth. In fact, when
Rosalind lobbied for him to take the children on Friday afternoons
when they get off early from school so they wouldn't need a babysitter,
he balked: "Rosalind has always wanted me to stay home then and she's
been bugging me all these years. I think she's sort of resigned that I
wouldn't . . . It is a strain to find someone every year and the strain's
fallen more on Rosalind because she's run the ad (for a babysitter) and
interviewed the people."

Joe and Rosalind are well aware that they created the job structures under which they now operate. Each has imagined it otherwise, but neither really wants to change the balance between them. When asked why, as in most American households, the mother is the primary parent, Joe answers in terms that make clear the gender pressures that drive them:

> I think I feel more responsibility to be the bread-earner and she feels more responsibility to be at home. We're just products of the way we were . . . sort of the fifties sociologically, rather than just what's emerged as women's roles have changed over the last twenty years.

Jonathan and Ruth: Downshifting to Equality

Jonathan and Ruth also have a son and a daughter, but their children are older than Joe and Rosalind's. When I interviewed them, their son, Ryan, had just begun college. Their daughter, Hannah, was fourteen. Jonathan and Ruth teach at the same public high school. He teaches music; she teaches art. They work approximately the same number of hours per week, and earn roughly the same amount of money. They both take summers off. Unlike Joe and Rosalind, they divide the work at home equally. Ruth links their home lives to their work lives: "We knew that if we were going to have children, it had to be a 50-50 arrangement because we worked the same kind of job, exactly the same hours." Their shared profession does fit well with their shared parenting. Ruth explains:

> We were all here at home at the same time, so one could start dinner and the other could go run. Or one could play with Ryan and the other could run. So it fell into sort of a natural division, maybe because we both had exactly the same schedule and worked in the same town and traveled back and forth together. It just made the equality work better.

Jonathan credits his job, not any special effort of his, for giving him time with his family: "My job allows me, and it always has allowed me to spend a lot of time with my family . . . I think being a teacher has given me a lot more time. It hasn't given me a lot of money, but it has given me time to be with my family."

Nevertheless, they began parenthood more traditionally. Even though they had the same jobs, Ruth was the one who stayed home for the first three years of her son's life, and for a year and a half with her second child. At that point, however, they made a radical change. Jonathan took a paternity leave to stay home for a year with his daughter:

> It was very difficult for Ruth to be home. It was very very hard. I think it was for that reason that I took a year off to be with Hannah . . . I would come home and Ruth would be very, very unhappy. She was a very outgoing gregarious social person and she felt really stuck being at home.

This choice, although rewarding in many ways for Jonathan, did have its down side:

> It turned out to have a lot of good things about it. In terms of my life with Hannah, it was very good, but I remember at the time, it was very hard because it seemed bizarre to a lot of people . . . There were times . . . when it was very difficult. Everybody was going to work and what was I doing at eight in the morning? It was very strange and much about my identity was lost.

But perhaps the bigger compromise for Jonathan had come earlier in the decisions that led to their sharing similar work lives. When their first child was born, Jonathan, a talented violist who had attended Juilliard, was trying to establish a career performing with chamber music groups. But because Jonathan and Ruth both thought it was necessary for Ruth to be home with the new baby, Jonathan accepted a job as a high school music teacher to support them. He tried for a year to continue part time with his performance career, but after a year dropped out. Ruth's unhappiness at being the sole full-time parent influenced his decision. Jonathan explains:

> I really felt ground down by my teaching all day and finding time to do difficult work . . . and Ruth was very unhappy. She was home and she was going crazy . . . I mean not literally going crazy, but it was a great stress for her. It was very hard so I just said screw it after a year and a half.

Jonathan's job as a music teacher is a compromise for him, perhaps more of a compromise than he had originally anticipated:

I never really felt, to tell you the truth, that I was going to be doing this for the rest of my life . . . There was never a time early on when I felt like I'm a teacher . . . It's just like I'm a person who happens to be teaching right at this moment . . . I think part of me always felt a little embarrassed because my expectation was always to perform and play, to be teaching at a university, to be doing some interesting work.

He has some nagging doubts about his choice:

I guess I feel that I'm good at it and I think the job is important, but it's always been a problem for me . . . not making very much money . . . Part of me can't avoid feeling failure as an American man not making much money. I think no matter how much I rationalize it and how much I say it doesn't matter, I think it always has mattered. So I would not do it again.

Nevertheless, both express deep satisfaction over the kind of family they have created. Despite his regrets about his work life, Jonathan has few regrets about the kind of father he has been:

I always got a lot of pleasure in being with my children, especially when they were young. I think that the happiest times of my life were when they were really little and they were so precious . . . It was a great deal of deep physical pleasure out of a child's existence . . . It would be hard to imagine doing it any other way. It's not like you have to think about, "Well, shall I find time to tell my daughter a story every night when she's in bed?" I mean there's nothing you'd rather do anyway.

Ruth feels no ambivalence. She recognizes that in conventional terms her husband might have had a more prestigious career:

Many of the people who know Jonathan will say to me, "Jonathan is so underemployed. He really should be performing or at least teaching at college level." What I say inside myself is that I wouldn't want him to have a career that was so overwhelmingly important that he didn't have time to create the texture of the dad in the family that we want to have.

She experienced the cost of a father's high-powered career in her own childhood:

My father was this very very brilliant mathematician who had no time at all for his family. No time. He would come home and go directly to bed. "Feed the kids, get them out of my way. When they're asleep let me know and I'll wake up and work all night" . . . I would never have agreed to have children married to a man who was that single-minded about a career.

These two couples, Rosalind and Joe and Jonathan and Ruth, both share professions, but in opposite ways their feelings about family life have shaped decisions about their work lives. Identical professions notwithstanding, Rosalind and Joe's decisions led them to inequality, Jonathan and Ruth's to equality.

Cutting Back and Cutting Down on Careers

Jonathan and Ruth believed that parental care was better than daycare for young children, a belief that is widely shared in the United States. When economically feasible, it is common for one parent in a family to stop working for at least a year after the birth of a child.[17] Regardless of the relative incomes of the two parents, if one of them stops working, it is almost always the mother. And often when the mother resumes employment, she works part time.[18]

Taking time off from work or reducing to a part-time schedule often means resigning from a satisfying job and later finding one that is less satisfying. Recall the painful experience of Denise, the nurse-midwife we met in Chapter 3, who couldn't arrange to work part time at the job she loved, so instead stepped down to a less challenging and less fulfilling job. Interruptions in work history can also mean lowered earning potential.[19] If subsequent jobs are less satisfying or have fewer options for advancement, women have less incentive to invest in work outside the home. Meanwhile, men who are free to take advantage of the best jobs are investing more and reaping the benefits of those investments at work. Taking time off can have career-long consequences.

Rosalind's story illustrates, moreover, that women's compromises in careers often begin even before children are born. Thwarted at times by sex discrimination in school or in the marketplace, women may be pushed more quickly than men to give up their career dreams and aspirations. Relationships with men further complicate women's pursuit of satisfying or remunerative work. When the two career paths of spouses clash, men usually win. Even highly educated professional women defer to their husbands' careers more often than husbands defer to theirs.[20] Women defer partly because they anticipate shouldering most of the responsibility for childcare. They may worry that it isn't fair to ask men to follow them to a job that motherhood will compromise later anyway. Ironically, the unequal job circumstances then become the justification for women's making career compromises. Men rarely anticipate interrupting their work lives and thus maximize the advantages of their jobs. When the time comes to balance family and work, they've already created more obstacles to cutting back than women have. Women routinely think about how motherhood can be combined with a particular career. Daniel was the only man I interviewed who had taken his future fatherhood into account when he contemplated his career.

Male investment and female disinvestment in jobs then fuels the inequality in parenting. The asymmetries between the parents in pursuing their aspirations, deferring to spouses, and taking time off or reducing time in paid work may perpetuate an unequal balance at home and at work.[21] When these asymmetries result in men's deriving greater financial and psychological rewards at work than their wives, inequality at home just seems to make sense.[22]

But when men like Jonathan start making the same kinds of choices as women, putting family ahead of career, the logic of inequality is no longer compelling. He shows us that just as women have always done, men can limit their time working and even sacrifice some of their dreams for achievement. It isn't easy. Even Jonathan lives with regrets about his career, but he also knows that his career sacrifices have allowed him the happiest parts of his life, caring for his children.

Child-centered versus Career-centered Families

Equal sharers do not reject child-centered families in favor of career-centered families. Jonathan and Ruth certainly show us that. But one might wrongly conclude from stories like Mark and Joan's that careers are all-important to the equal sharers, because in some of these families women were more likely to resist gender pressures and pursue careers, despite motherhood. But a family is created by *both* a mother and a father. We need to stop assuming that only women create the texture of family life. Husbands and wives do it together.

In fact, when I carefully examined time spent with children, I discovered that equally sharing couples spent virtually the same number of parental hours with children as 60-40 or 75-25 couples.[23] The differences between the groups are in how that time was distributed. Equally sharing mothers spent less time alone with their children than unequal mothers, but the equally sharing fathers compensated for that by spending more time alone with children than unequal fathers.[24] Moreover, equally sharing parents spent more time together with their children than their unequal counterparts.[25]

Families varied in how much time they devoted to children relative to jobs, but once we widen our lens to include fathers and mothers, we can see that career-centered families are as common among unequal couples as equal ones, and that child-centered families are as prevalent among equal sharers as unequal families. Child-friendly equality is created when men like Jonathan, Edward, and Mark devote significant amounts of time to parenting. Sometimes they take it out of what would have been leisure time; sometimes they sacrifice work. Child-friendly equality survives also because although the equally sharing mothers spend less time with their children than more traditional women, they have not switched from traditional motherhood to traditional fatherhood. They are present in their children's lives. Even as these equally sharing women pursue jobs or careers, their commitment to mothering, as well as their husbands' work at home, ensures that children are not left behind.

Job Structure Is Not All-Determining

The link between equality at work and at home isn't a hard and fast rule. Equality at home certainly made it easier for men and women to establish equality on the job. Conversely, jobs that ensured equal time and money for men and women made it easier to establish equality at home. The women I interviewed who earned as much or more than their husbands were most likely to be equal sharers, but I also interviewed equal couples in which women earned only a quarter to a half of their husbands' salaries. Mary and Donna, the equally sharing women I introduced in Chapter 2, for example, both earned about half of their husbands' (Paul's and Kevin's) incomes.

Even more striking, equality on the job by no means ensures equality at home. "Time available" doesn't work exactly the same way for men and women. Women who are working outside the home more than other women do a smaller percentage of the childcare in their families. But when both husbands' and wives' "time available" is taken into account, women still do a great deal more childcare than their husbands. In two extreme examples among the couples I interviewed, mothers worked much more on the job and still worked more at home than their husbands did. One mother clocked seventy-five hours as a clinical social worker in a residential treatment program, compared to the forty-one hours her husband put in as a speech and language pathologist. Another mother worked full time as an occupational therapist, while her husband worked part time as a draftsperson for an architectural firm. Despite these women's disproportionate shares of time worked outside the home, they also did the majority of the work inside the home. When I asked their husbands why they didn't do a bigger share of the work at home, the speech pathologist said that he didn't enjoy and wasn't interested in doing the cooking or laundry. The draftsperson said that he "faded away" when his wife was at home because she was able to do things more "naturally" with their children than he. It is hard to imagine these situations reversed. Money doesn't guarantee equality either. In approximately a quarter of the unequal couples, women earned the same or more than their husbands.

As we have seen, decisions couples make about jobs set them on trajectories toward or away from equality. Nonetheless, couples also change course. The deck may be stacked against women when they and their husbands make gendered choices about paid work, but even a stacked deck sometimes yields a good hand. When women give up opportunities, they are certainly putting themselves at a disadvantage in the job market, but not always fatally. Recall that Donna, the ESL teacher, dropped out of the paid workforce to care for her young children. But when an opportunity for the perfect job came along later, she grabbed it. Although her previously equal earnings are now half of her husband's, her job is just as rewarding. And Kevin, the husband who couldn't bring himself to drop out, now equally shares. Gendered choices at one moment in time do not preclude gender-resisting choices at another. It's never too late to edit that video.

Chapter 8

Why Couples Don't Practice What They Preach

Shelley and Dick seem to be perfect candidates for equal sharing. Shelley's jeans and sweatshirt fit her casual style. With his long hair and beard, Dick looks like he could have been a student in the sixties, although he was only a toddler then. Both are avowed feminists. Shelley works as an internship coordinator for a women's studies program; Dick has a job as a daycare teacher in a Head Start program. Dick works hard with his young charges to break down gender stereotypes and to show by example that men can be nurturers. When Shelley and Dick filled out my standardized survey assessing their views about gender, they scored as egalitarian as anyone can. "No, mothers shouldn't be responsible for children's birthday parties"; "No, when a child awakens at night, it shouldn't be the mother's responsibility to take care of the child's needs"; "Yes, cleaning up the dishes should be the joint responsibility of husbands and wives"; "Yes, men and women should be given equal opportunities for professional training"; and so on. Yet by their own accounts Shelley is doing 75 to 80 percent of the childcare. What's going on here?

Preaching and practicing often don't go together.[1] As we can see in Shelley and Dick's case and in many of our own lives, believing in gender equality is not enough to ensure equally shared parenting. That doesn't mean that Shelley and Dick or other parents are hypocrites. We shouldn't be surprised about the tenuous connection between principle and practice, because translating egalitarian beliefs into the mundane everyday exercise of equality requires effort. It requires us to make difficult choices that promote the circumstances in which equality can thrive. We saw in the last chapter how gender-resisting choices about work created job situations that promoted equality. But equality also requires conditions that are friendly to new relations between men and women at home, and friendly to a new kind of parenthood. Sometimes we have to try out new ways of living in families that don't feel entirely comfortable so that egalitarian feelings can develop to support our egalitarian ideals. Many of the unequal couples fail to live up to their own ideals of gender equality because those ideals meet practical difficulties, don't feel right, or clash with gendered beliefs, goals, and prerogatives that deep down are more important to them.

The transition to parenting is often accompanied by overwhelming feelings about what parents should be doing as men and women. All parents grapple with the cultural ideals of masculinity and femininity that they've internalized and continue to confront every day. Men feel their self-worth is tied to paid work, whereas women may feel they have the prerogative to abandon their jobs without suffering the same loss in self-image. The flip side of the prerogative to quit paid work, however, is the deep sense of responsibility women bring to parenting. A woman's self-worth is usually more tied to motherhood than her husband's is to fatherhood.[2] Men often act as though they have the prerogative to bow out of parenting, either by making incompatible commitments to their jobs or by actively or passively resisting the work at home. It's hard to build equality on this scaffold of gender differences.[3]

Egalitarian Ideology Meets Parenthood

Gender equality often just doesn't feel right. Even when couples intend to equally share, their feelings get in the way.[4] Shelley, for example, couldn't bring herself to go back to her job after her maternity leave while Dick stayed home, as they had initially planned. When the time came, she felt strongly that she wanted to be home instead of him. She admitted to feeling "a little bit of uneasiness about trying to do it 50-50 at that point."

Parents themselves recognize the contradictions, like this father who wished that his wife, a veterinarian, would quit and find a part-time job:

I agree with all these things about equality and not having stereo-typical sexual roles and all that, but when it comes right down to it, I wish she (his wife) wanted to spend more time with them (the children) . . . Intellectually, I believe all the right things. I don't always feel them correctly.

The egalitarian beliefs he sported before children were no match for the reality of parenthood: "It's easier to talk about too before you have kids. I remember at one point thinking I was going to split everything even-steven. That's the right thing. That's the fair thing—right down the middle. No way, you know, I don't want to do that."

The unequal parents who believed in equality were sometimes shocked when they compared their own lives to an egalitarian vision. Some of these parents had grown up in the sixties and seventies and were amazed and embarrassed that the political and cultural move-ments of those times had had so little practical impact on their lives. Joe, the lawyer we met in the last chapter, noted the contradictions: "We were caught up in the sixties and principle-wise I'd say, oh, we'd share everything right down the middle. We don't, so I say it with some embarrassment and with some sense of incredulity." In the feminist so-cial circles Joe and his wife frequented, they kept their childcare ar-rangements to themselves. Like the equally sharing men who slunk out of work early and didn't tell anyone they were going to a child's soccer game, Joe kept quiet about the traditional division of labor at home.

Although these unequal parents may have believed in gender equal-ity for everyone else or for themselves in the abstract, they didn't feel comfortable with it in their own lives. This father spoke for many of them: "It's like abortion. I'm totally for abortion as long as it's other people." One mother was so ambivalent about the contradictions she faced within herself that she wept during the interview and blurted out: "I'm telling you what my feelings are. I'm not telling you what I believe 'cause I don't know what I believe . . . I mean . . . what I believe for me may not be what I believe for society."

Egalitarian gender ideology is often thwarted when it confronts men's and women's feelings about jobs, parenting, and children's needs. The powerful feelings each of these issues evoke can override reasoned beliefs that men and women should have the same rights and obliga-tions at home. Women are torn between ambition and their love for their children; men are torn between fairness and their need to achieve. Both are faced with quandaries born of their deeply internalized senses of identity and self-worth.

Men, Money, Jobs, and Careers

"Somebody's got to get the food that's gonna go in Deborah's mouth that's gonna come out those breasts," one father explained. Somebody does need to earn that bread. Often when men become fathers they suddenly feel their manhood is at stake in providing for their families. For example, Thomas's job ambitions developed only after he became a father. Kevin couldn't bring himself to stay home with children because it meant relinquishing paid work. For many men earning money was the measure of themselves as human beings. The loss of an income-producing job would have been too big a blow to their masculinity for them to bear.

Jobs were often seen as a given, nonnegotiable part of men's identities. We saw in the last chapter that men usually maximize their job opportunities. Although some of the unequal men and women might have been all for equality when answering theoretical questions about it, that didn't seem to influence them when men contemplated jobs. They might not have set out to make their situations unequal, but neither did they consider how their choices would affect the possibilities for equality in their families.

Achievement, rather than breadwinning, seems central to the identities of many upper-middle-class men. They pursue careers without compromise because they feel driven to achieve professional success. As Ben put it, "Men in our society are brought up to feel that their worth is much more tied to work than women are."

But even if Ben is right and on average, men's self-worth is more tied to their work than women's, let's not forget that many women today also derive self-worth from their career-related achievements.[5] The problem is that there may not be room in a marriage for achievement on that scale for two, especially when children enter the picture. There certainly wasn't in Ben and Judy's marriage. Undaunted in pursuing his own career as an economist, Ben nonetheless recognized that the coexistence of equality and the unfettered pursuit of individual careers was impossible:

In comparison to my parents' generation, things are very confused and I don't have a good theory . . . I believe that women and men should be able to pursue careers to the extent that they feel satisfied by it. On the other hand, there seems to be a real problem with making the family run. I think that women and men are in situations that are stressful for both parties and undefined. The least stressful approach is certainly the stay-at-home mom or stay-at-home dad.

Women, Work, and Motherhood

Judy struggled with Ben over whose career would take precedence, but some women who believed in equality didn't put up a fuss over whose paid work would come first. Like Rosalind, the lawyer who cut back in her private practice while her husband revved up his, a few women welcomed the opportunity to cut back or quit their jobs. In those families the women's desire to deemphasize paid work and emphasize family work complemented their husbands' opposite desires. Their beliefs that the roles don't *have* to be gendered are irrelevant to the choices they've made. Despite its costs, inequality works for them.

Rosalind wholeheartedly embraced conventional motherhood and found it "incredibly fulfilling and satisfying to be a mother." Like her, a few of the other unequal women were overwhelmed by the powerful feelings motherhood elicited, whatever their beliefs about equality. For example, one previously career-driven woman precipitously quit her job when she was due to return because she just couldn't bring herself to part from her child. That mother told me that she discovered a "very strong gut feeling of wanting to be part of children's lives in a major way." Another mother, who wished she could quit work entirely, cut back to part time to care for her infant daughter. She explained, "I want to be with her every minute."

The mothers who wanted to be home with children expected their husbands to pick up the tab. Egalitarian principles notwithstanding, women often felt they had the prerogative to cut back on paid work, as long as their families could manage financially. Husbands almost never challenged these maternal prerogatives, even in the rare cases in which they might secretly have preferred to be the parent at home or not to have carried the entire financial burden alone. Shelley and Dick's experience is a case in point. Shelley reneged on their plan despite their previously shared egalitarian beliefs. If there was going to be one primary caretaker, she wanted to be the one. Her husband "acquiesced."

Children's Needs

Yet for every unequal mother who told me that she found infant care immensely satisfying, I found many more who were desperately unhappy during the years they spent at home without paid work. (Even the mother who quit her job got tired of being home after a few months.) Why then do they do it? In most families, women simply feel responsible for responding to their children's needs, or what they perceive as their children's needs. They want a certain level of care for their children and feel more responsible than their husbands for providing it. They do it because they would simply feel too guilty if they didn't. Their motherhood is at stake.

But what children need is neither obvious nor agreed upon.[6] Do infants need a parent at home? Donna and Kevin thought they did. So Donna, the parent who felt more responsible, quit her job and stayed home. When couples felt that full-time parental care was essential, almost invariably the mother provided the care, no matter how much they protested that in theory either parent would do.[7] For some mothers, like Donna, it was a sacrifice they bore because their husbands wouldn't. Other women couldn't tolerate the idea of losing the number-one position with their children. If their husbands cared more about their careers or earning money, so be it. The choice to stay home was uncontested.

Mothers usually sacrificed more of their work-related goals in families even when parents didn't think children needed full-time parental care. Women often gave elaborate answers to what they would be doing differently in careers if they weren't mothers, while their husbands were usually pursuing the career they wanted to. Mothers worried more than fathers did about too much daycare, so women altered their lives to reduce the amount of substitute care. They made sure their children got what they thought children needed, even when they resented that they were the only parent worrying about it. As one mother told me:

> I would love to feel that I could go to work, do what I have to do, and not wonder if the phone's gonna ring and not feel guilty

working past four. I could keep my kids in daycare till five-thirty. There's just a part of me that thinks it's too much time . . . I resent sometimes every day having to pick them up at four, be with them until six . . . For some reason, I will sacrifice more than he will. Short of divorce, what are you going to do? He's just not gonna change.

Another mother, an industrial psychologist who worked as a human resources consultant, went to extraordinary lengths to create a child-care situation that satisfied her conscience. She quit a full-time job with a large printing company, started freelance consulting part time, and set up a small daycare center in her house, which she personally managed. Some parent, she believed, had to put in a significant amount of time at home. Why was she that parent? She wondered: "Is it really just me who feels such a responsibility?" Yes, it is just she. Over the years she had persuaded her husband to take over much more of the parenting when he was home and available. By their third child he was getting children dressed in the morning and responding to their calls at night. But it was she who responded to the "need" for a parent to be home by dramatically altering her work life. His job remained untouchable.

Mothers often acted as the default parent past the preschool years as well. One frustrated mother had reduced her hours at work so she could chauffeur her ten-year-old son to after-school activities. She wanted him to be able to take clarinet lessons, to participate in sports, and to have play dates. In the absence of a husband who would share that kind of responsibility, she did it all. Egalitarian principles didn't matter as much to her as the quality of her son's life: "I want him (my husband) to be as involved as I want to be . . . If he took on more I might be able to do less and my son could still have the quality of life that I want him to have."

Sometimes even when both parents tried to live up to principles of gender equality, mothers and fathers didn't experience parenting the same way. That meant mothers did more. One couple, Meredith and Arthur, shared a vision of equal parenting in which neither mothers nor fathers would be the primary parent. They deeply believed in the principle of gender equality. But, Meredith explained, "Our vision is one thing, how it plays out in the day-to-day is a whole other ball game." Abashed to admit that she did more, Meredith couldn't help herself. Principles don't control thoughts and worries. No matter how evenly they divided the time with their child, the mental work of parenting was all hers.

> In terms of mentally worrying: making sure we have pediatric aspirin, talking to his teachers . . . I would say it's 75-25 . . . I will actually come to work and think we're out of Tylenol, I'd better go and get some . . . It wouldn't worry Arthur during his work day that there are no clean pajamas. It will actually worry me. I will make a note that if I don't do wash he has no clean pajamas. That would never worry Arthur . . . Never! So I carry more mental (stress).

Meredith also set aside one day a week as a day off from daycare, a special time to spend with her son. Committed to her work as a labor organizer as well, she found herself canceling the special day sometimes and hiring a babysitter because of job commitments. Her husband, Arthur, who worried less, felt that full-time care at the excellent center they used was just fine.

Daycare and Motherhood

Daycare is the crucible on which ideals of equality are often destroyed. The image of sending a small child off to group care clashes with treasured images we carry about mothers and children, images that, however far from reality, drive us to cling to traditional family arrangements. We know, however, that if we look back in time our ideal of one mother's attending single-mindedly to her young child has rarely been fulfilled. How much time did colonial mothers or pioneer women actually spend caring for their children, what with churning the butter, sewing the clothes, and tilling the fields with their husbands? Across the earth in Burundi today, children growing up in a subsistence village spend their days wandering about and playing with their friends, free of adult interference.[8] In this "traditional" life, children don't see their mothers for most of the day.

Historians have documented that the family we so fondly think of as traditional is decidedly not part of any longstanding tradition. The nuclear family comprised of a financially providing father and a stay-at-home mother whose major life task is child-raising was a historical anomaly of mid-twentieth-century America. Even at the time it was far from universal. Huge segments of the population could never hope to meet the ideal popularized in the *Donna Reed, Ozzie and Harriet,* and *Father Knows Best* families that some of us grew up watching on TV.[9]

I wonder too about the American mothers today who try to live up to this 1950s television ideal. How many feel like the mother I interviewed who had taken time off with her second child, but failed to do all the arts and crafts projects and cookie baking that she had always imagined she would do with her older child if paid work didn't interfere? Tortured by her impossible ideals, she cried when she admitted the distance between her everyday life at home with two children and that image. Are toddlers really better off at home watching TV with a mother nearby than in a well-run center, child-proofed and arranged every day with new things to explore, cared for by creative and nurturing caregivers whose chosen work is childcare?[10] Were and are the children of colonial, pioneer, subsistence-farming, and employed mothers really less happy, less well adjusted, and less secure than those whose mothers try to act out a 1950s ideal of motherhood?

Recent results from the National Institute of Child Health and Human Development (NICHD) Study of Early Child Care, the most comprehensive and rigorous research ever conducted on the effects of daycare, are quite reassuring. The kind of mothering children received when their mothers were available, and the quality of nonmaternal care, were much more important for children's welfare than the number of hours they spent in daycare. Children in full-time daycare from infancy were no less likely to be securely attached to their mothers by fifteen months old than were children at home with mothers. Moreover, two-year-old children whose mothers took care of them full time were less linguistically advanced than children who were in childcare, as long as that care was above average in quality.[11]

As questionable as parents' fears and distrust of daycare may be, mothers often sacrifice equality to save their children from it. For most families today, however, the issue is not whether or not to have daycare, but how much and what kind of daycare to have. By the time a child is one year old, a majority of mothers are back in paid work. But half of them are working part time, so they can limit the number of hours, haunted by the feeling that although a "good mother" may put her child in daycare, she doesn't do it full time.[12]

The mothers of school-aged children live with an equally powerful image of a "good mother": the mother standing at the door greeting her child coming home from school, the smell of fresh-baked cookies wafting through the kitchen. She welcomes the child home with a snack of milk and cookies while they talk over the day at school. One mother went so far as to create a highly unconventional career for herself as a buyer of Asian art so that she could create that image, at least some of the time. Ironically, she left town for weeks on end to travel to Asia, and probably spent less time overall with her children than many full-time working mothers. Yet, when in town, she met her returning children at the door.

I am not immune to these images myself. I had to laugh when, after I went to great lengths to readjust my work schedule to allow for after-school pick-ups, my child was less than enthusiastic about Mom's undivided attention. He much preferred play dates with friends, which were previously part of his after-school schedule. We have to keep in mind that children may not always care if we are there after school. After all, they didn't watch 1950s TV. Nonetheless, listening to the regrets of women who couldn't muster this after-school picture at home because paid work interfered, I often mused that if only employers would allow mothers a one-hour break at three o'clock so they could go home and enact this milk-and-cookies scenario, the guilt-relief might result in happier and more productive employees.

As much as some couples believed in equality, the fear of daycare, the desire to be home after school, and the worry about having enough time with children weighed more heavily on women than on men, and convinced many to take a significant amount of time off from paid work and to go back only part time. The gender bias behind these choices was based not on old-fashioned beliefs that mothers should be the parent doing these things, but on each woman's overwhelming feeling that she personally should do it for her child. Sometimes joyfully, sometimes reluctantly, and sometimes resentfully, women heeded the call of their own consciences, consciences very much shaped by their being women, and shaped by a culture that announces in no uncertain terms that maternal care is best.

Living with the Contradictions

People feel embarrassed and uncomfortable when they confront fractures between their convictions and their conduct. When reality conflicts with people's beliefs in gender equality their identities are threatened. Couples coped with this threat by changing their beliefs, emphasizing individual choice rather than general principles, fantasizing about reversing roles, and stressing other nontraditional aspects of their identities.[13]

Beliefs sometimes change when they confront the reality of parenting. One couple who attempted to share because of their beliefs gave up because the father didn't have the patience, the skill, or the desire to deal with the frustrations of infant care. He now dismisses his earlier beliefs in gender equality as an effort to be "politically correct":

> What we used to do was try to divide equally 'cause that was (politically) correct . . . Ten years ago if the solution seemed to be Dinah would spend more time with these kids . . . and I would be less involved, but do more support things, that wouldn't have worked out well, because it didn't seem like the right thing to do . . . That was the prevailing moralistic philosophy of the times . . . We were swayed by it.

We know that people are as likely or even more likely to change beliefs to fit behavior as to behave according to beliefs.[14] When mothers do 75 percent of the childcare, there is a big impetus for them and their husbands to endorse traditional family roles.[15] Although Shelley hadn't gone that far, her newfound beliefs in the importance of one primary caregiver did fit her choices.

Unequal women, like Shelley, often invoked their own choices when explaining why they carried more of the load at home: "Why I do more of the parenting? I think that's a choice on my part." By shifting the comparison from what they and their husbands were actually doing to their ostensible freedom to choose, women implied that gender equality exists in their families after all.

Although in one sense they are choosing, as we saw in the last chapter, the choice is not free of gender bias. The invocation of choice ignores how our genders affect what choices feel right and rewarding: what we feel responsibility for and what opportunities we are offered in life. In a world free of those differences, we can imagine truly equal families in which one parent emphasizes family work while the other puts his or her energy into paid work. But until the differences that foster gender inequality are erased, neither women nor men are entirely free to choose. It is telling that these "choices" are often barely discussed. What feels like a choice may be nothing more than the well-internalized deep sense of responsibility that women bring to parenting and men bring to breadwinning. As one father, embarrassed by the stereotypical roles in his family, explained, "You kinda go on automatic pilot in life. Sometimes you end up on these flight paths that your parents laid out for you."

Fantasizing about switching roles was another way of putting up with unequal arrangements while holding on to a feminist vision. The myth that fathers wish they could change places is comforting because it reinforces women's ideas that they are getting the better deal in the family. For example, Benita, who proudly called herself a feminist, imagined a future in which she reversed roles with her husband: "I would be in a business suit driving a car to Fieldville making fifty or sixty thousand dollars a year, and he would stay home and cook on his stove." Likewise, Joe imagined that with a more "career-driven," high-earning woman than Rosalind, he might have been the one to stay home.

These fantasies about role reversal often came with disclaimers, however, or clues revealing that they would never be actualized. Joe admitted his fantasy might be a myth. Benita too admitted her ambivalence about role reversal, considering what it would really be like to have the burden of breadwinning:

It's no small task to come up with that amount of money . . . no small psychic task, to deal with that burden every month . . . I enjoy having my problems to be dealing with (like a child's sore neck), if I had to choose between dealing with that and coming up with $2,000 tomorrow to pay a bill . . . That's a heavy burden.

Apparently, role reversal was a frequent topic of conversation between her and her husband, Clifford. She seriously thought Clifford would trade places in a minute. He humored her in their banter about reversed roles, but thought it was just a joke:

We have this standing joke that she's just going to become a lawyer . . . Then I'm gonna semi-retire and become a house father, except I wonder if the kids will still be home when that happens . . . I can't imagine having my own business and then having Benita be the breadwinner . . . But that's her joke, she's gonna be the breadwinner.

Two other mothers I interviewed, happily working part time, saw themselves as relatively advantaged compared to their husbands. Like Benita, both women claimed that their husbands would love to change places with them. One, like Benita, felt sorry for her husband because, although she worked, he had the real responsibility for earning money. The other talked about what her husband had missed: "I felt like he was missing out on stuff once my son was past a certain age. It wasn't because I was resentful, it was because I thought that he was missing something because I spent time with our child and he didn't." Despite these mothers' claims, their husbands weren't the least bit interested in changing roles. One compared his two-year-old to a puppy, resented even minor suggestions that he spend more time with him on the weekend, and talked with markedly more animation and interest about his new job than about his new son. The other stated he could never sacrifice his personal goals the way his wife had: "I could never turn everything off for four or five years so that the kid would come first and drop everything that you're thinking of doing because the kid had a need . . . I don't think I would want to do that. Maybe I could if I had to. It would have been hard."

Parents who believed in gender equality most strongly were most troubled by their own traditionalism. Sometimes they seemed to be trying to convince me and themselves that, inequality notwithstanding, they were nontraditional people after all.[16] For example, Meredith, the labor organizer, took pains during the interview to report on her left-leaning and feminist activism. Likewise, the mother who had changed her job so she could manage her own daycare center described her set-up as "an incredibly creative nontraditional way of balancing."

Poignantly, although living gender inequality themselves, many wanted equality for their children. Sometimes parents seemed to be grasping at straws when they focused on the nontraditional lessons children were learning by having a working mother or a father who "helped." As surely as my Mount Holyoke students, who tell tales of their own harried mothers working a first shift for pay and a second at home without pay, the children of today's unequal parents are also witnessing the price of inequality. The daughters of these overworked women are especially paying attention. Won't they too, like my students, question whether such an unbalanced life is worth it?

Although some of the unequal parents kidded themselves about the examples they were setting, others noted the gender lessons they were inadvertently providing and regretted them. Some tried to compensate by encouraging antistereotypical activities in their daughters, making it a point to play ball with them and teach them how to hammer a nail.

Occasionally, though, their children demonstrated all too clearly what good teachers their unequal parents were. Nathan, the four-year-old son of an unequal mother, gave his mother pause when she overheard him at play:

> Nathan had two girls over and they were playing house. They were laying on the living room floor 'cause it was nighttime . . . Nathan was laying in the middle. Nathan said, "The baby's crying," to one of the girls, "I think you'd better go get it." I thought, "This isn't happening." I guess maybe that's what he thinks because when he gets up at night, he comes to me. I said, "Dads can get the baby too" . . . I remember thinking I'm doing this all wrong. I want to bring Nathan up more neutral about things.

Some of the unequal couples, however, especially the 60-40 couples who were trying hard to share, did provide substantial nontraditional lessons, even if they weren't exactly equal. Timmy, Meredith and Arthur's four-year-old son, sees his father and mother engaged in many nonstereotypical tasks. Meredith reported:

> Timmy gets to see his daddy cooking . . . and gets lots of private time with him. He also gets me in the late afternoons . . . We each do special things with him and he sees us together at home sharing work. You know, "You collect the garbage, I'll take it out." His daddy picks him up; his daddy knows his school. I pick him up; I know his school. I think Timmy's getting to see two people engaged in the world. I go to work; Daddy goes to work. I go on business trips; Daddy goes on business trips . . . I think he thinks, you know, people can grow up and be lots of different things.

Timmy also got to see his parents struggling together to create an equally sharing household. Meredith sighed, though, when she explained why, despite their best efforts, she still did more at home:

> Even when we try and break out, we tend to teach what we were taught, live what we saw lived. It's very hard to break out of a cycle that is reinforced by a culture that is very deeply and profoundly sexist. You can swim against the tide just so hard . . . It takes conscious work all the time to not fall into what were very well-ingrained patterns, so I feel like we're living our upbringing and we have rebelled against a lot of it.

Equal Sharers: Practicing What They Preach and Sometimes More

Changing the patterns we've grown up with and seen all around us can feel awkward or uncomfortable. For men, it requires the sacrifice of some privileges. Some of the equally sharing men forced themselves to live with the discomfort simply because they believed it was the right thing to do.[17] They practiced what they preached because they couldn't have lived with themselves if they didn't. Like Daniel, they couldn't argue with their wives' insistence on their shared principles. But they sometimes struggled:

> It's one thing intellectually to know that you have married a woman who is a professional and has a career and is not at all intending to adopt the role your mother had. You have been well-schooled and now you know that it is your duty to do an equal share of these things, but it's quite another thing actually finding yourself in that situation and to find out there is really too much to do.

Peter does do his "duty." Despite his emphatic belief in women's intellectual equality and right to a career, however, he admitted to some of his "irrational" yearnings for a more traditional family:

> Wouldn't it be great if somehow Sharon had a career and baked cookies and was there to meet Nicole when she came home from school . . . that kind of warm and nourishing aspect of motherhood . . . I wish there were more of that in our home, but there's just no way it can be that way if we're all going to have jobs that are demanding.

When I asked whether the two of them could cut back on work to create that fantasy together, he answered honestly: "Bah! . . . What I'm fantasizing about is Sharon creating that family and I'm going off to write a Pulitzer Prize–winning book or traveling as a foreign correspondent to Bosnia by myself."

Creating equality didn't mean that parents were always comfortable with nontraditional roles. Edward had to push himself to become the kind of parent he wanted to be. Janet persevered despite her worries that Noah would be more attached to his daycare providers than to her. Daniel took care of Noah even when he was scared. And Jonathan, the musician turned high school teacher, never felt entirely comfortable with the career sacrifices he made. All of these equal sharers, however, believed that parenting should be shared and were willing to put up with some uncomfortable compromises and choices to practice what they preached.[18]

For many of them, as Meredith said, "It takes conscious work all the time to not fall into what were very well-ingrained patterns." But efforts get easier and feel less unnatural over time. The equally sharing mothers who watched their young children having fun at daycare relaxed and focused on the benefits of group care. The fathers who felt awkward got more comfortable. As for Meredith and Arthur, I ran into them recently. I didn't ask, but as I watched Arthur monitoring Timmy and talked to him about his son, I wondered what they would say about the division of labor now. If it isn't equal, it is certainly very close.

Gender ideology may become less important as circumstances change. Mothers who felt strongly about staying at home with young children, and cut back on work to do so, felt less of that pressure as their children got older. Equal sharing at that point often grew out of pragmatism rather than principle, and with little rhetoric about gender equality. Mothers who willingly did a disproportionate share of the childcare at first balked when that share got to be too much for them. Returning to a full-time job or having a second child tipped the scales. Doing 60 to 75 percent of the childcare with a part-time job and one child is a lot different from doing it with a full-time job and two kids. Equality solved the problem of too much work. Facing an unwieldy family workload, with a lot of struggle or a little, some men pitched in, and before they knew it, they were doing as much as their wives.

Although some of the equal sharers struggled against gender lessons, others had never learned those lessons very well. One father explained: "We're flaky, we're not normal, so I would attribute it (equal sharing) to our own quirkiness rather than to any enlightened state . . . I think we're just odd ducks." For the men who recoiled from the macho models they saw growing up and the women who dreaded becoming like their mothers, the ideology of gender equality offered a way out. Their stated ideals gave voice to feelings they already had.

For equal sharers, just like the unequal couples, egalitarian principles don't tell the whole story. Some of the equal couples testified that the sixties had transformed them, but those "transforming" ideals may simply have facilitated the equally sharing lives they wished for anyway. Ideology often looks more powerful in the lives of equal sharers than in the unequal families simply because that ideology is consistent with the lives they are living.

Even for Beth and Steve, with their passionate politics, the strong belief in equality coexists with other reasons to share. Steve said, "I think that it (equal sharing) has its roots in the sixties . . . I rebelled against most of my family's values, the ones that didn't seem right . . . the sexism fit in with the racism . . . What brought us (Beth and me) together as people is our rejection of traditional values." Beth pointed out, however, that her whole generation had gone through the same political movements. What set them apart, according to her, was Steve's personality. Unambitious in conventional terms, Steve has always had a lot of "feminine qualities." He was very close to his Italian grandmother, who lived with his family when he was growing up and taught him all her recipes, including the one telling how to make pasta by hand. He didn't like sports and "didn't get into the whole macho thing." Steve's nurturing qualities were complemented by Beth's engagement in and enthusiasm for her work. Equal sharing fit their politics and their gender ideology, but it also fit who they were and who they wanted to be at home and at work. Steve could throw himself into parenting as much as he wanted to. He didn't have to achieve much outside the home for Beth to love and admire him, and she could achieve like crazy. The egalitarian ideas of our times liberated them from old roles that would have constricted and constrained them.

To share or not to share? Ideology doesn't give an easy answer. We saw in this chapter that believing in nontraditional families doesn't mean that couples will equally share. In the next we'll see that believing in traditional families doesn't mean that they won't.

Chapter 9	**The Mother and Mr. Mom**

If you stopped to watch at the construction site of a new office building going up in Worcester, Massachusetts, you might catch a glimpse of Stan pouring cement for the foundation. Stan is a lean, muscular, good-looking guy whose job as a laborer in the construction industry means hard work for low wages. Some facts about Stan would probably not surprise you. A high school graduate, Stan is an avid Red Sox fan, thinks his mother is the world's best cook, and is known among his friends as a great story-teller. As you might expect, especially once you know that he is the father of two children, Stan worries about how to make ends meet.

However, if you believe, as I did once, that the gender revolution of today is limited to affluent, highly educated families, you might be surprised to find out what Stan does when he gets off his shift.[1] Every day at three o'clock, Stan rushes home just in time for his wife, Maureen, to go to her job as a retail clerk at a convenience store nearby. From quarter of four until ten o'clock, when Maureen gets off, Stan is home taking care of his two daughters, four-year-old Annie and the baby, Sarah, now seven months old. Stan plays with them for a while, gets them their dinners, gives them baths if Maureen hasn't already done so, and puts them to bed by eight-thirty. Usually he washes the dinner dishes, but sometimes he leaves them for Maureen because he wants to relax after the kids are in bed. In his wildest imagination, Stan never pictured himself as the father he is today, doing all the tasks that used to be Mom's: diapering babies, giving baths, even taking his four-year-old daughter to ballet lessons.

There's a revolution brewing in the homes of blue-collar families. Alternating work shifts has become a solution for a growing number of dual-earner couples.[2] In families like Stan and Maureen's, mothers and fathers are taking turns taking care of their children while their spouses work at paid jobs. Blue-collar fathers are taking on responsibilities that their own fathers would never have dreamed of and that they themselves had never imagined. None of these men set out to be trailblazers. "Mr. Mom," the label many of these men have bestowed on themselves, conveys their feeling that there is something topsy-turvy about it all.

Mr. Mom was the title character in a movie about a man who loses his job and stays home to take care of his children while his wife goes to work. Strikingly different from the alternating shifters on a superficial level, Mr. Mom of the movie was a high-paid executive who had lost his job. Those details were unimportant to the alternating-shift fathers, however, in the face of their identification with a man who was humorously assuming a role for which he was ill prepared. "Mr. Mom" connotes that the movie father, just like the alternating-shift dads, was acting a bit odd by doing what mothers are supposed to do. Despite the time men like Stan spend taking care of their children, they protest that they are not really the mothers. They are the "Mr. Moms." Their wives are "the mothers."

Who Are the Alternating-Shift Couples?

Approximately twenty-three million workers in the United States work an evening, night, or rotating shift: a fifth of all employed workers.[3] Among dual-earner couples with children under fifteen years of age, the numbers are even more startling. In 51 percent of these families, at least one parent is working a nonday shift. These off-shifts encourage paternal caretaking.[4] Fathers are the primary caregivers of 11.4 percent of all preschool children whose mothers are employed, and of 28 percent of preschoolers whose mothers work a nonday shift.[5]

Who are these fathers who are involved so intensively in the care of their children? Occupations that rely heavily on shift work are predominantly working-class occupations: mining and manufacturing, health care, fire fighting, police and correctional work, and other forms of service work.[6] The alternating-shift fathers I interviewed worked in diverse jobs; they included a bellman, a delivery man, an aircraft mechanic, an oil burner technician, a powder processor, a stock handler, a police officer, a fire fighter, a custodian, a chef, two electricians, and a foreman. Their wives were nurses, pink-collar workers, retail clerks, service workers, or blue-collar workers themselves.[7]

How Do Couples Alternate Shifts?

Consider Diane and Patrick. Patrick works days as an electrician, earning about $15.00 an hour. He leaves for work around seven-thirty in the morning after having breakfast with Diane and their two boys, a five-year-old and a three-year-old, who send him off every day with waves and kisses. Diane does "the duties during the morning and afternoon." She gets the older child off to and back from kindergarten, feeds both children breakfast and lunch, plays with them, and does some housework, although she admits housework is not her first priority: "the kids are more important than the cleaning." On most afternoons she packs them up and is off visiting friends or doing errands. Patrick gets off work at four-thirty. Unlike most of the alternating-shift families, they eat dinner together before she leaves at 5:30 for her job as a sandwich maker at a delicatessen, where she works until ten o'clock four nights a week, and from eight until twelve on most Saturday and Sunday mornings. When she leaves for work on weekdays, Patrick is "on." He cleans up after dinner, gives the kids their baths, takes them outside to play when the weather is nice, and puts them to bed. Before she gets home, he tries to do some housework and usually does a load of laundry.

Patrick strikes me as a sweet, earnest man. I was touched by his efforts to understand his young children's feelings and to express his own, something that was not encouraged in the male world he grew up in. Although he thinks Diane is more attuned to the emotional side of life, he keeps trying: "She's more open with her feelings and I'm more closed and more harder than she is. I've always been that way. It's really hard for me to tell about feelings . . . I do it, but it's hard. The children know her better." Patrick's efforts and the time he spends with his sons at night have paid off: "We got to know each other a little bit. I got to be more attuned to their feelings and their emotions and stuff, so it was good."

Diane and Patrick are not equal sharers. Diane works fewer hours for pay than Patrick (about twenty-four hours to his fifty) and spends more time with their children. In fact, when we look at the blue-collar alternating-shift families as a group, only two of them could be classified as equal sharers. As in Patrick and Diane's family, in two thirds of them mothers work many fewer hours for pay than their husbands, and the husbands work correspondingly fewer hours at home. But the variations in paid work don't entirely explain the variations at home. Fathers differ in how they define their responsibilities when at home with their children. Diane brags about how much more Patrick contributes than other men who alternate shifts with their wives:

> I don't think I've ever met a man that's taken such an interest in his kids plus done housework at the same time. It's . . . "Okay, if you wanna work at night I'll watch the kids, but don't expect me to do the dishes, don't expect me to put a load of wash in . . . I'll be the father but I won't be anything else."

She's partly right. There are a few alternating-shift fathers who do childcare and nothing else. Their wives prepare the dinner, and they just warm it up in the microwave. After dinner, they leave the dishes in the sink. One father admitted that he called his wife at work five or six times a night, implicitly refusing to take responsibility: "I'll have to know where something is or what should I do. Even when she's not here, she is still kind of running the show." He acknowledges that she does 75 percent of the work despite their both working full time. "I don't know how she does it. I really don't."

Although partly right, Diane is largely wrong. Many of the alternating-shift fathers did as much housework as Patrick and some did a lot more. In one family of six children, a father who took care of his children three days a week while his wife worked didn't stop for a minute. After putting the youngest down for a nap in the morning, he reported,

> I usually go down to the cellar and put in a load of laundry . . . I just kind of spend the day . . . doing whatever's got to be done . . . I don't think I was put here to do nothing. I have to stay busy; that's why I do most of the stuff around the house. I'll vacuum the floors; I mop the floors; I do the laundry.

Other men learned how to cook instead of just heating up what their wives had prepared.

When we view the alternating-shift families in the light of traditional gender standards, they are every bit as extraordinary as the middle-class equal sharers. Because the parents do virtually all of the childcare themselves, even if fathers do a smaller *percentage* than their wives, these dads may be doing a greater total *amount* of parenting than even the equally sharing fathers. This is certainly true if we consider the time fathers spend with children by themselves. On average, the alternating-shift fathers spent twenty-eight and a half hours a week in solo care of their children, as compared to the fourteen and a half hours spent by middle-class equally sharing fathers.

Alternating-shift fathers resemble the equally sharing fathers on some tasks, but not others. For example, since the majority of these fathers work the early shift, they have relatively little to do with supervising children's morning routines, whereas among the equal sharers the morning jobs are some of the most equally divided.[8] Bedtime routine, however, is a different story. Fathers who alternate work shifts put their children to bed just as frequently as their wives do, just as frequently as the equally sharing fathers, and more frequently than the fathers in the 75-25 families.[9] In short, alternating-shift fathers do what needs to be done for children when their wives are not home, and that turns out to be quite a bit.[10]

The demands of childcare were especially intense in the homes of alternating shifters because their children were younger than the children of the equally sharing families.[11] The care required is a far cry from the stereotypical paternal jobs of roughhousing, playing sports, or teaching kids how to ride their bikes. I saw how deftly men managed the demands of preschool-aged children firsthand because I often interviewed the alternating-shift fathers at their homes while they fielded their young children's questions, warmed their babies' bottles, and rocked crying infants, sometimes all at once, with great aplomb.

Let's also not forget that these families can't afford paid help for housework. Men may have fought more with their wives over housework, but that was partly because they couldn't buy out of the problem the way a number of the middle-class equal sharers had.[12] Cleaning and laundry figured much more prominently in the typical day of alternating-shift fathers than in the typical day of middle-class fathers who were equally sharing.

Why Do Couples Alternate Shifts?

Money. There's no doubt about it; it is cheaper to avoid using paid childcare.[13] In over 80 percent of the alternating-shift couples, at least one spouse mentioned money when asked why they share the care of their children the way they do. The alternating shifters have the lowest incomes among the groups I interviewed. Yet they differ in how constrained they feel. Some thought they simply couldn't afford daycare; others maintained that they could have afforded it, but believed alternating work shifts was economically wise.

For some it wasn't a choice. As these parents explained:

> Can't afford daycare. Obviously, with three kids it would just be horrendous to pay for it.

> We can't afford childcare. I mean childcare would be over $140, $120 a week and that's just too much because we don't make that much. With the rest of our bills, to be able to have a mortgage and vehicles and getting to and from work, and then plus trying to pay childcare, we could never do it.

> I mean it was just money, economics. We can't afford to pay for a babysitter five days a week unless you got a pretty good job or something. I don't know how some of these people do it.

Others reasoned that it was impractical to spend so much of their income on daycare. It seems especially costly because it is often calculated as a deduction from mothers' incomes.[14] As this mother indicates: "I couldn't see myself working for all of this money on a weekly basis that would come in and half of it going right out to somebody else to raise my children. I didn't think it was right." A few reported that they chose alternating shifts to provide a more comfortable life for their families:

> Different shifts . . . because we really wanted to build our own house and have our own house and there was no way we could do it working the same shift and not more income.

> We could have more and we could take them more places, take a vacation. They could even go to college.

Money matters, but money is not the only reason, or even the most important reason, that parents invoke for alternating shifts. Many of the couples believed that children should only be cared for by family.[15] Adamant about not wanting his children in daycare, this father conveys what many of the parents feel:

> I've been proud of that actually . . . Each parent is in contact with them at any given point . . . I know people . . . just drop them off

and leave them for an endless time. That to me is, you're not being a parent, you're paying somebody to do your job and how healthy is that? "Oh, there's good daycare," and all this crap. It's not as good as the real thing.

When middle-class parents object to daycare, they often do so for subtle psychological reasons, because they believe it doesn't promote the child's optimal development or because they think it will damage the bond between parent and child. The blue-collar alternating-shift parents give different reasons for avoiding daycare. First, they fear that terrible dangers await children who are cared for by strangers. These fears were pervasive among mothers:

> You hear too many things on the TV about what could happen and I just, I don't want to take the chance.

> I get nervous having to trust somebody . . . There's too many crazy people out there and you can never tell.

> I'm leery of having someone that I don't know real well in my house . . . I can't see what they're doing with my daughter . . . I'm not comfortable enough with it to put myself in that position.

And fathers said:

> I don't let people outside my family watch my kids . . . You don't know those other people. It doesn't matter that they got a sign out that says that we're certified . . . There's a lot of things out there that happen to kids . . . I don't want nothing to happen to my kids.

> . . . the fear of some of these perverts out there and stuff. We'd just as soon take care of our children ourselves.

> You hear the horror stories about childcare . . . people hitting kids on the head with spoons to leaving them in a dark room, to tossing them in a crib and whacking them. It's so hard to know what another person's going to do with your child . . . I'd just as soon take care of her than let some stranger take her.

> It may sound silly but you hear the horror stories all the time. Deep down inside we've always felt that we don't want anyone else to take care of our children. They're going to be exposed to enough trash soon enough anyway.

You see stuff all the time—childcare people abusing children and everything.

The second reason alternating-shift parents give for avoiding daycare is their resolve to inculcate their children with their own values. As one father said: "I didn't want Marie to learn things from other people. I want her to learn from us. We are not the most intelligent people in the world, but we know right from wrong." Like many of the alternating-shift mothers, Diane trusted that her husband's caregiving would reflect their shared values:

> When I go to work at night I have a clear conscience and a clear feeling that he will do everything exactly like I would if I was home . . . We have always said that . . . a parent has to be here at all times . . . We both have the same understanding of how we want to raise our kids . . . with all the same goals and morals.

Repeatedly, I heard from these blue-collar parents that they didn't want strangers raising their children. Yet surely the middle-class couples who send their children to childcare don't conceive of it as ceding control of childrearing to someone else. Daycare may provide care for part of the day, but ultimately these middle-class parents believe that they will have more influence over their children than any substitute caregiver. Both of the criticisms leveled at daycare by blue-collar families reflect their concerns about losing control over their children's care. In contrast, middle-class parents don't seem to worry about having that kind of control. They take it for granted.

Two reasons might account for this difference. First, because blue-collar families have less money, the childcare that they can pay for might be worse. Their fears may have some basis in fact.[16] Second, even if the blue-collar families could avail themselves of the "best" institutional daycare, they might still suffer from a relative lack of control. The so-called best institutions might reflect middle-class values, and be less responsive to their concerns than to the concerns of middle-class couples.

Values are at the heart of how many of these parents talked about alternating work shifts. They conceived of parenthood as a responsibility and an opportunity to convey their own values. Although in "normal" times the mother is the direct conduit of this influence, if the mother works outside the home responsibility shifts to the father. When driven or justified by cherished values that are shared by both parents, the alternating of work shifts is not simply a practical accommodation to financial constraints; it is a way of life that has meaning and substance.

But when husbands and wives felt they had no choice because they couldn't afford daycare, the loss of time together was a bitter pill to swallow. The physical separation symbolized a spiritual separation as well. One mother, who attributed her family's arrangements entirely to financial necessity, said: "I'd rather have him work days. I'd rather have him home at night with us as a family, not a divided family . . . I like it when he's home at night. We're participating in the family. I like it that way. That's the way it should be."

Choosing to alternate shifts obviously creates hardships. Husbands and wives missed having time together with each other and as a family. That loss is a cost for all of the families. A few families bore the cost painfully as a symbol of the parents' inability to create the kind of family they wanted. But other parents, those who intentionally chose to alternate shifts, bore the costs philosophically, as a symbol of their willingness to sacrifice for their children and create, if not the perfect family, at least one in which they are doing right by their children. While acknowledging the price of their choice, they stress the rewards of a shared sense of purpose and moral rightness. Listen to this father of two young sons, aged two and three:

> If I'm going to have kids . . . I'm going to be the one who instills their morals and ethics and I wasn't going to leave that to someone else . . . From the start we considered parenting very, very important . . . Whatever the sacrifice it takes as far as maybe the time me and Brenda spend together, we consider it worth it. I consider it worth it.

Theresa, a mother who had been alternating work shifts with her husband for thirteen years, expressed similar sentiments:

> Before we even had the kids we had agreed we basically didn't trust anyone else. We knew how we wanted our kids raised. We knew what was important to us, what we wanted to give them. It has been a struggle because there have been times when neither one of us has been happy with the hours or the lack of sleep or the lack of contact with each other. There have been years where we've laughingly said to other people the kids have the best of

Mom and Dad when they don't have much of each other . . . Looking backwards, it's worked out and I think that's why they're as
good as they are because we have given 100 percent of what they
needed.

Even some parents who adopted the alternating-shift pattern only because it seemed sensible, and worried initially about the loss of time
together, came to appreciate the advantages:

I am thrilled at the way this worked out . . . We never planned . . .
we need jobs like this because we have kids. It just worked out that
way. Then after we had the kids we saw that this is a good thing.
This is not a bad thing. It's hectic and it's crazy, but I think it's good
for us as a family.

In their belief that parental care is best, alternating shifters are similar to the professional families in which women sacrifice time at work
to stay home with their young children. In the blue-collar families,
however, it is a change in the father's life that makes parental care of
children possible. When middle-class families opposed daycare, the solution was usually for the mother to stay home, whereas when working-
class families felt the same way, fathers' roles changed drastically. Paradoxically, staunchly adhering to some facets of traditional family life led
these blue-collar fathers to assume very nontraditional roles. In doing
so, they had to change.

Change and Resistance to Change

No father has changed more than David. David and Theresa have been
alternating work shifts longer than any of the other couples. Theresa is
an inhalation therapist who works thirty-two hours a week and earns
$32,000 a year. David is an installer for the phone company who works
forty hours a week and earns $31,000 a year. Currently, David works
days from seven to about four, and Theresa works the second shift four
nights, from three-thirty to eleven-thirty. The parents of three children,
Veronica, thirteen, Betsy, ten, and Nicholas, six, Theresa and David
have been sharing the care of their children by working different shifts
since their firstborn, Veronica, was five and a half weeks old.

David and Theresa's relationship is exceptionally egalitarian. She
claims it is 50-50; he says it is 60-40 in her favor. But both agree that

each pitches in with whatever needs to be done. On a typical day, David is the first to awaken: "My day starts at five-thirty in the morning. I get up and take a shower, put wood in the stove if it's wintertime, and then I eat breakfast . . . I make sure that her (Veronica's) light is on. I go upstairs and get dressed and in the course of my leaving I wake Theresa up to start her day." She takes care of the morning tasks: getting the other children up, making all their breakfasts, and getting them all off to school. She does errands, volunteer work, or housework until Nicholas returns from kindergarten at eleven-thirty. She gets his lunch and spends a couple of hours with him until she needs to leave for work at about a quarter to three.

David gets home about four o'clock. (Their oldest daughter, Veronica, gets paid to babysit until he gets there.) His evenings are full. He drives the children to their activities, makes their dinners, and cleans up. Four nights of the week, he's the parent who asks about their days at school, helps them with their homework, and plays with them. He handles all the bedtimes: "I make sure the showers are taken care of, then we have some type of a snack and then around eight-thirty I get Nicholas ready. I do half-hour increments. Nicholas between eight and eight-thirty, Betsy between eight-thirty and nine, and Veronica . . . between nine and nine-thirty." At bedtime he spends time with all of them, but especially with the youngest: reading, talking, calming his fears. After that, he makes the lunches for the next day, and then relaxes for a few minutes before he drops into bed. Theresa wakes him when she gets home so they can talk.

Today, David looks like the model of the new man, but he confided how much he had changed and still continues to change. He's learned the practical skills of taking care of children, has become more emotionally attuned to them, and has developed a different understanding of men's and women's roles in the family: "This is nothing that I was born with or I was brought up to see . . . It's something I had to learn, I had to get used to."

David laughs when he reminisces about how scared he was to take care of an infant:

I remember when we had just had Veronica. Theresa said, "Well, I'll give her a bath tonight if you give her one tomorrow night." I'm saying, "Geez, I've got to give her one tomorrow night." Now it's second nature . . . It's something I had to learn, I had to get used to

... Once I started to catch steam on this thing there was no stopping me. I told Theresa tonight I was going to make some cookies.

He learned more than just the mechanics of cooking dinner and bathing babies, however; he learned how to really listen to his children. Just the week before I interviewed him, his daughter Veronica had come home upset about a problem with a friend at school. Although at first he dismissed it, telling her not to worry, he soon realized he had made a mistake, and invited his daughter to sit down and talk to him about what was bothering her. "It's a growing thing . . . I'm developing, believe it or not, a soft side, but it doesn't come natural. Fathers don't have that natural ability. It's something you have to develop."

David expresses little reluctance to take on "women's work." Like many of the alternating-shift men who are unable to earn an income sufficient to support the family, he feels beholden to his wife for helping him with that responsibility. Perhaps David feels more grateful than most, because he gave up an opportunity to make more money.

A few years back David was promoted to a management position. Theresa confesses that it was a terrible period for their marriage and their family. His anger and distress about events on the job infected their home life. They decided together that it would be better for all of them if David stepped down and went back to his old job as an installer, despite the cut in pay and the need for Theresa to work more "to fill in the dollar end of it." David is very conscious of the trade-off: "I took . . . a 33 percent cut in pay and left . . . If I was earning now what I was earning then, perhaps Theresa wouldn't have to work as hard as she is now."

Although David has not changed his idea that mothers are ultimately responsible for childcare and fathers for breadwinning, his strong sense of fairness requires him to contribute as much as he does at home:

I look at Theresa . . . She is working on equal terms as myself. Theresa started out like this . . . her primary job is the family and running the household, the father is the outside job. When the mother steps out of that primary role and goes into another role, I feel it is the obligation of the father to step out of his primary role as the breadwinner and . . . go into the mother's part. When Theresa's at work, I am at home doing the motherly functions to the best of my ability . . . I only consider that fair.

Virtually all the alternating-shift couples exhibited a tension between change and resistance to that change. There is no doubt that, like David, many of the alternating-shift fathers have changed their views about the appropriateness of their doing "women's work." By doing the work of the family, men learn that it is worthy of respect. Listen to this father's account:

> I've learned from this where a lot of men would never understand the respect for women. If I had never gone through this I would be in the same chauvinistic "It's a woman's job" but when you actually do what you have to do, you gain a lot more respect for what it takes.

Another father, as his wife observed, changed after he spent some time at home: "I think it was the first time he really realized it just wasn't so easy being home . . . It wasn't the old husband come home, 'Well, what did you do all day?' Now you know what I did all day."

Women led the way amidst varying degrees of struggle with their husbands. The mounting unpaid bills helped Eileen succeed in convincing her husband to alternate shifts and pick up some of the housework, but only after her second child was born:

> When we first married, Larry felt like I was there to be his wife: to do the dishes, to clean the house, to take care of the kids. Things have changed since then. We're more equals. It's more like I'm his wife, not his slave.

Diane had an easier time with Patrick: "I always thought that he should share in the responsibilities and he never disagreed, so I kind of just showed him the way."

Interestingly, in the alternating-shift families the wives' jobs carry leverage that they often do not in more affluent middle-class families. Because pay scales for blue-collar jobs are narrower than for white-collar jobs, when the wives of blue-collar men get paid jobs, the ratio of their income to their husbands' is often better than the wife-to-husband pay ratio among wealthier families. Moreover, upper-middle-class men do not have to acknowledge that they couldn't make it without their wives' incomes; blue-collar men do.[17]

Ironically, in these alternating-shift families the claim on men to share the work of the household derives from the belief in traditional gender roles. Because most working-class families cannot financially afford to have the mother at home, it is impossible for men to live up to a traditional standard of the breadwinner, however much they might believe in it. Failing to provide their wives with the possibility of a traditional life means that their wives can legitimately expect them to contribute to "women's work." As one mother bluntly put it:

> I don't consider myself to be a women's rights activist type person, but . . . if he wants me to stay home and cook and clean and do laundry and have meals on the table . . . that's fine, but he's going to live up to the male standard of you are the breadwinner . . . Until that point, if I'm going to be going my way with the financial end of this family, he's going to pull his weight with helping out with everything else that I can't be doing because I'm out forty hours a week.

In the "economy of gratitude" that operates in these alternating-shift families, women's paid work counts. The work men do at home is often viewed as a payback for the gift they are receiving of their wives' employment.

Men who alternate work shifts receive another, even more important gift. They get to know their children and their children get to know them. Time spent with children translates into a closeness that surprises and delights them. Fathers were thrilled to be admitted to a relationship they previously thought was reserved for mothers. One father, who thoroughly enjoyed bath time with his kids, said: "There's other stuff that I help out and I get to see. Like when it's bath time. They love bubbles and they're always calling me in there. They take my old razor and make like they're shaving their bubble beards off." These men are visible figures in their children's lives, in contrast to the shadowy images cast by many of their own fathers. These caregiving fathers often came from working-class families in which many of the fathers worked two or three jobs and were barely seen at home. The alternating-shift fathers work hard too, but they are not strangers to their children. As this father said: "They've been able to bond so much more with me . . . One of the greatest things—they really got to appreciate their Dad . . . It has made me keep going back for more."

The remarkable changes in these families are real, but they are sometimes accompanied by resistance to change as well. A number of the alternating-shift fathers take primary responsibility for their children when their wives are at work, but abdicate if both parents are present. For example, one mother reported that she cooked and fed the children when both she and her husband were home because he was busy doing other things. When I asked what he was usually busy doing, she replied, "watching television." Another mother said: "On the weekends, if I'm going out to the store, I always feel guilty if I don't take them (the children) with me . . . because, oh gosh, leaving them alone with him . . . It's not them, it's him. He doesn't like it if I'm to leave them with him if I'm not going to work."

This resistance to changing roles when the mother and father are together is significant because it portends more traditional arrangements in the future. Many of the alternating-shift mothers who work the evening shift while their children are little plan to get day jobs when their children go to school. In these couples, I asked the mothers what they thought would happen to the division of labor if both husband and wife were working the same shift and thus home together in the evening. Although about half of the women expected their relatively egalitarian arrangements to persist, the rest saw their husbands' backsliding as indicative of their future:

> Probably, I'd be doing most of it, because on my days off I get them to bed. I make sure they brush their teeth and they take their fluoride, and they get into their pajamas. He, if he could, he'd leave me their baths too. He doesn't like to give baths.

Some still hoped. As one mother said, "I'm hoping (that the division of labor won't change). I kind of wonder about that though . . . When I'm not here he has no choice but to take care of them." But her husband's answer left little doubt about what was going to happen: "I definitely see less, I mean I see less for myself because I just see she is so giving. She wants to be a mother." Another father had a bit more insight into his own motives: "If she was home at night I guess there might be a point of laziness that I might acquire. When things change and you get the opportunity to take it easy, that could become a habit."

Although gender ideas in these families have changed enough to allow men to take over domestic duties when their wives are at work without any loss of manhood, often these ideas have not changed enough to really shift the ultimate responsibility. Mothers are still "in charge" of the work at home; fathers help because their wives are unavailable.

Clinging to Gender Identities

Despite the liberalization of gender ideology among all social classes over the past fifteen years, there is more support for traditional gender ideology within the working class than among more highly educated groups in the United States.[18] Many of the blue-collar couples I interviewed carry with them images of an ideal of traditional family life, featuring the men going to work while their wives stay at home to tend young children. None of them live that ideal. Yet by clinging to some core aspects of that picture, they can convince themselves that they are maintaining traditional gender identities despite their nontraditional arrangements. These couples try hardest to keep intact three aspects of gender identity: the father is the breadwinner; the mother does not derive a primary sense of identity from work—she works outside the home only to ensure the economic survival of the family; and the mother is the primary parent.

The Father as Breadwinner

Ironically, even though alternating-shift men have lower salaries and earn a lower proportion of the family income than their middle-class counterparts, both they and their wives readily invoke the father's role as breadwinner. An overwhelming majority emphasized that though both parents are employed the men are the breadwinners in their families.[19]

There is no doubt that the alternating-shift men feel a profound responsibility to make money to provide for their families. Patrick's simple statement emphasized that there was no choice in the matter: "I have to work and I have to be the breadwinner." Several men noted that becoming a father intensified their need to be breadwinners. Fatherhood made them feel more responsible, and for many, responsibility meant providing financially. One father, discussing how his attitude changed after he had children, said that he wanted "to do better at my job so I'd make more money." Another said: "It's made me more responsible only because now I have to provide for three more children and everything that goes with it: the home, the bills." One father was on the verge of taking a job he knew he would hate because it provided "stability and benefits." He worried that, despite the close relationship he was developing with his infant son, if he did not succeed in conventional breadwinning terms, ultimately his son would be ashamed of him:

> I mean as far as our relationship goes I think it's wonderful, but there's that money, success kind of thing. "Oh, what does your father do?" "He stays home and makes peanut butter and jelly sandwiches."

The most poignant statement about the father's role as a breadwinner came from a man who had been laid off. Despite taking care of his children when his wife went to work in the evening, he didn't see himself as contributing to the family: "I feel I'm not contributing anymore, I'll say because of finances. I'm supposed to be the one to support my family." Another father, who had been laid off previously, echoed the devastating effects of the loss of the breadwinner role: "I had no self-esteem. I felt terrible about myself."

In almost all the alternating-shift families, the parents stressed men's breadwinning roles by treating the father's job as the more important job in the family.[20] Superficially, it seems to make some sense to treat the man's job as more important because in almost all the families men earned more money than their wives. But closer examination suggests that a number of couples in these families structured their work lives to enable the father to retain the role of principal breadwinner. In eight families the women's rate of pay was either higher than or equal to their husbands'. But in only two of the families did the women earn higher overall salaries. The more typical scenario was this: when women earned a higher rate of pay, their husbands worked a substantially greater number of hours. For example, in one family in which a nurse earned about $17.50 an hour to her foreman husband's $13.50, he worked fifty hours a week to her twenty-four, resulting in his earning approximately $12,000 a year more than she. In an even more dramatic example, the mother's hourly wage rate was double that of her husband's ($14.00 an hour versus $7.00), but he worked more than twice as many hours as she, thus ending up with a higher income. It appears that couples organize family and work life to make sure that despite two incomes, and despite the woman's greater earning capacity in some families, men in the alternating-shift families are still recognized as the principal breadwinners.[21]

Like many of the alternating-shift wives, Diane doesn't dispute that

Patrick is the breadwinner in their family: "We have always established that he was the head of the household. I think it was because our dads were. He just knows consciously that he's the one with the education, and he's the one that makes the most money. His job is more important than mine." In terms of overall pay, and even rate of pay, her husband *is* the principal breadwinner in their family, but as she herself points out, that was by design. After they had children he went back to school: "We kind of made sure that he got the education before I did so that he would make the most money and I could just take care of the kids during the day and work at night to supplement. That was, I think, the big thing, that he is the head of the household."

The Mother as Worker

The image of the mother at home complements the ideal of the father as breadwinner. But the ideal of a mother without paid employment is problematic for these families. First, there is no way to get around the fact that these mothers are in the paid labor force. Second, in most of the families the mothers' incomes are critical to maintaining the family's economic well-being, so they do not really have a choice in the matter. Third, and perhaps most disturbing to their images of ideal family life, most of the mothers enjoy being in the paid labor force, and wouldn't choose to be home full time if that choice were available. In fact, only a handful maintained that they would prefer to be housewives. Yet the prevailing myth in these families is that the mothers work only for financial reasons.

Men in the alternating-shift families wish that their wives could be home, and believe that they would be if finances allowed. Nonetheless, almost all of their wives want to work outside the home, at least part time. When I asked a number of the full-time working women about their preferences, initially some said they would prefer to stay home. But when I questioned them further, most admitted that they did not want to quit their jobs entirely, but would prefer to work part time:

I'd rather stay working. I like to get out of the house.

People work not just for the income, but because we each are people and there are certain parts of us that need to be used. You can't just be a parent if there are other things that you're good at and need to do.

These mothers derive a variety of rewards from their paid work: a sense of independence in bringing in money, a chance to get out of the house and be with other adults, a feeling of accomplishment and recognition for a job well done, time away from children. Listen to this account receivables clerk:

I look forward to (going to work) every night, I really do . . . taking off in the car by myself . . . I really enjoy it . . . I love it, I love my job . . . I love doing the paperwork and working with numbers . . . anyone asks me a question, nine out of ten times I have an answer for them and it's wonderful. I feel very successful.

The obvious satisfaction many of the alternating-shift mothers derive from their jobs contradicts the mythology that they are working only for financial reasons.[22]

Mythology often masks potential conflicts over an issue between husbands and wives. Husbands sometimes downplayed their wives' desire to work by invoking the financial need for them to be employed. One man said, "I would prefer that she didn't have to work. She only has to work because it helps supplement the family income . . . She would have loved to be home. I would have rather had her here, but living in this state you need five incomes, so two isn't hardly enough." But his wife told a different story: "I wanted to go to work. I wanted to get out of the house."

In almost half of the alternating-shift families wives and husbands gave very different accounts of why the women were working. The men said simply that the reason was finances, but the women gave much more elaborate answers, indicating that money wasn't the only reason. Ivy, a phlebotomist, acknowledged the need for additional income, but also revealed other motives for working: "the need to get out . . . it is good to eat supper by yourself without somebody saying 'I need juice.' I enjoy the two days that I do go . . . I couldn't quite totally (stay home) even if I could afford to."

Patrick and Diane were one of the few couples who had fought openly about the wife's working.[23] She explains: "He, at first, didn't want me to go to work ever. I said, 'I cannot be a person, a whole person (without working).'" He gave in, but balked again when they had two children. She held her ground: "As much as he pressured me and made me feel guilty, I was not going to give in." Nevertheless, she describes the decision for her to go back to work as a mutual one, because finances had the final say. They needed her income. He still has the fantasy of her not working. When asked what he would change, he answered: "I wish she didn't have to work . . . I'd love her not to have to work, but she works for different reasons, for money. She needs a sense of purpose, a sense of helping out . . . It gets her out of the house."

Perhaps Patrick and Diane could have scraped by with one income. In most of the alternating-shift families, however, the economic necessity for two incomes allows the men to ignore other reasons that their wives work, reasons that would contradict their traditional ideas about family life. This mythology is reinforced because women themselves often exaggerate the financial motivations for working and their desire to be at home. One mother, a nursing assistant, complained bitterly about having to work for financial reasons: "I can't be here (at home) and I greatly resent that, just the fact that I can't be here all the time." But when asked directly if she would choose not to work at all, she responded, "No, I would have to work part time." In fact, she was among those most enthusiastic about her job: "It would take a lot for me to leave . . . It's wonderful when it's hectic and busy. It's very challenging . . . It makes you realize you can have a very great impact on people." It is no wonder that men are sometimes confused.

Because of the financial pressures working-class families operate under, women are not required to make a choice between traditional family life and being employed. Freedom from actually having to make that choice means women are free to imagine themselves choosing to be home. Consequently, in some families both the women and their husbands can maintain the myth that even though the women work outside the home, paid work is not a central part of their identities.

The power dynamics underlying the suppression of this conflict are intriguing. The importance of their income to the families' survival gives these women the power to work despite their husbands' preferences. Yet the lack of conflict over this issue and the mythology surrounding it suggest the latent power of the husbands. Power can be expressed not only in whose preferences are honored, but in the way conflict is managed or avoided.[24]

In truth, however, most of these alternating-shift mothers do not aspire to equal gender roles in the family. Despite being employed, women don't identify with work and breadwinning as much as their husbands do. They don't want to be in the paid labor force as much as their husbands, but they do want to be there more than their husbands want them to.

Take the case of Sue, who has a clerical job in a department store, working for $7.75 an hour part time in the evenings, and her carpenter husband, who is currently working odd jobs. In a good year when he is working forty hours a week, he can earn $25,000 to $30,000, but times are bad and he rarely works that many hours. The underlying conflict in this family is typical of the alternating-shift couples. He wishes she could be home: "If I can get a better job, she'll be 100 percent Mom then. If she wants to quit work, I'll let her. Right now, it's just for finances. That's why she works, we work two jobs." She sings a very different tune: "I just finally decided I had to go back to work. I had to get out of the house. It wasn't for financial reasons, I just had to get out. I couldn't stand being in the house anymore." Work provides quite a contrast for Sue:

> I love my job. I love my job, I really do. I'm probably one of the only people in the world who loves their job as much as I do . . . It's the people I work with . . . They all have young children. We all have the same types of problems. It's more like a counseling session every night for six hours.

Although her husband began by emphasizing the financial motivations behind his wife's working, her enthusiasm for her job has not entirely escaped him. He later admitted that being home might not be her first choice: "That's what I would like. But she would just like to have a job so she doesn't have to be talking to little kids all day long, so she could talk with adults besides me . . . That's why she likes working." When asked what would happen if he did get a higher-paying job, he predicted that his preferences would prevail: "I'd say she might quit. That's my feelings."

Chances are it will never be put to a test. Because these families can't afford to do without women's incomes, it is possible for men and even women themselves to cling to the belief that the only importance of work outside the home is to bring in income. The underlying conflicts about the real meaning of paid work, between husbands and wives and within women themselves, can remain buried. For women to earn money without embracing the work role is less threatening to traditional gender identities in the family. The financial constraints allow this myth to reign.

The Mother as the Mother

Mothers in the alternating-shift families are still regarded as the number-one parent, regardless of how much time fathers spend with their children. Dads may take over many of the functions that mothers have traditionally performed. They may feed their children, give them baths, read them bedtime stories, kiss their boo-boos, but the mother is still "the mother." Women retain this special role in two ways.

First, the mothers try to tailor their work lives so that they can be with children at times they define as key times, or they redefine the key times as those when they are available. Theresa, who has spent most of the thirteen years she has been a parent on the evening shift, says of her role: "I'm very much what I consider a traditional mom in that I've had my days home. I can do the mommy stuff with the kids and volunteer in the school, or have a friend over, or be with them for whatever they want to do during the day."[25] Another mother, who works a day shift and leaves the care of younger children to her husband while she spends more time with the older ones in the evening, sees the crux of motherhood as her role with the older children: "I'm starting to feel like a true mother with the fourteen-year-old, with growing up and getting into high school and the peer pressure . . . I'm beginning to really feel like a real mother, have to direct her to which the right path is."

Time is mentioned most often by mothers who work an evening shift while they have preschool-aged children, but expect to change their shift when their children go to school. Being there when children arrive home from a day at school is part of their image of being a good mother. One mother explained why she changed from an evening schedule to a weekend schedule: "I liked the idea of being there every day when he (her son) came home from school." She works the same number of hours and misses time with him on the weekend. But it seemed more important to her to be there at that critical time of the day. Other mothers reported similar plans:

> I always said that when my kids went to school I'd rather be home during the day in case they were sick or in case they wanted to go on a field trip, and they needed a chaperon.

> I'd go days, working maybe the mother hours, the school hours.

They are not called "mothers' hours" for nothing. Women want to be home at those times, and not simply because they think a parent should be there. At those key moments their husbands will not suffice, because it is their identities as mothers that are at stake. One woman put it bluntly:

> Once she (her daughter) goes into school, I'll be (on) days because I don't want her coming home from school and telling just Bill what happened, or telling the babysitter what happened during the day. I want to be the one that she's telling these things to.

There is no doubt that by claiming this time of the day as central and insisting on her right to be there, this mother is claiming the right and the desire to be the number-one parent.

The second way that mothers retain their primary position is through the claim that they are still the center of emotional life in the family, and that they should be. By and large, the alternating-shift mothers strongly believe that all mothers (including themselves) are more nurturing, closer to their children, and more attuned to their emotional needs than fathers:

> As a mother, I worry more about their emotional needs.

> The mother feels more strong. It's like if I had to choose I'd do something for my kids first . . . I don't think he sees it that way.

> Moms are more tender than fathers are. My husband is compassionate, but I think I'm more compassionate than he is, and they look to me for that.

These are prescriptions as well as descriptions. Mothers should possess these qualities and hold these responsibilities in greater measure than their husbands:

> As much as we try to do everything 50–50, if Freddy gets hurt and he cries, I think I'm the one that should take care of him.

> Somewhere in my head I think that she (her daughter) should depend on me more.

Mothers seemed disturbed if the balance shifted too much toward their husbands. When asked about the parents' division of responsibility for their child's emotional life, one mother was reluctant to admit that it was equal: "I would hope it would be me more . . . I don't know why I would hope that, but I would hope it would be me . . . but I would say 50 (percent)." Another mother was disappointed that her knowledge of how to do things with her baby wasn't automatically superior to her husband's:

> He taught her how to eat. I couldn't do that for some reason, which bothered me because I'm supposed to know all these things and I didn't. People told me, "Well, you're a mother, you'll know." I didn't.

Men seemed just as invested as their wives in retaining the notion that the mother is the primary parent. Despite spending much more time than his wife with their infant daughter because of their work schedules, one father was flabbergasted that his infant daughter would crawl to him to be comforted instead of to his wife. "It just throws me off," he said with obvious embarrassment. Other researchers have noted that even men who anchor their identities in involved fatherhood usually remain "mother's helpers" who avoid responsibility for the less desirable tasks of parenting.[26] The interesting difference in my findings is that the alternating-shift fathers often take on the responsibility for doing the tasks but still define their contribution as "helping."

Even when men were very nurturant themselves, they clung to the image of the mother as the nurturing parent. One father who does at least half of the childcare and housework, including very stereotypically maternal tasks such as getting up at night to rock infants back to sleep, still wants his wife to have a more nurturant role than he: "Women can provide the more softer end . . . I mean they don't call them the fairer sex for nothing . . . Let her show that sympathy end of it." He is willing to do his fair share of the household work, but wants her to be "the mother," the one who nurtures. The reality is that when fathers are home caring for young children they become nurturers themselves, however much that contradicts their gender beliefs. As this father puts it:

> You picture the mother when the kids skin their knees, that she comes running up and hugs them and kisses the boo-boo. Well, that's something I do, and I suppose . . . the reason it's like that is because she's not here. I think if we had more overlap times she would probably do more of the traditional mother things and I would do less of them . . . I know that when they need something it's attended to.

In the absence of his wife, this father cared for his children just the way she would.[27] Yet, many of the fathers insist that their wives provide something that they cannot:

A mother's never going to do the same thing as a father. Even if they do the same things . . . the feeling is different.

There's something about that sense of nurturing that the children can sense from the mother . . . I can't probably provide for them in that way.

Even after thirteen years of nurturing his children, David deferred to Theresa:

Theresa can just zing; she's right there with them. I have to believe that's a mother's touch, something a father can work on and perhaps get, but probably never come into the capacity that a mother has. A mother's got that special—they always know what to say at the right place at the right time to kids, whereas a father is a little bit more jagged on the edges.

When the alternating-shift fathers care for their children, they believe that they are substituting for their wives. These men stress that their participation in no way detracts from the importance of their wives' gender identities in the family: "She's still the mom because, as close as we all are, if one of them falls down, if she's there, they're going to go to her first . . . She's the mother."

Traditional Ideologies, Nontraditional Lives

Alternating-shift couples believe in an ideal of family life that features breadwinning fathers and stay-at-home mothers. They are far from living that ideal. For at least part of every week mothers in these families are out in the paid workforce, while fathers are caring for their children at home. In contrast to middle-class couples, who often don't practice as much egalitarianism as they preach, these working-class couples practice more than they preach. They manage the marked difference between their behavior and their ideology by maintaining core aspects of parental gender identity.[28] Despite their nontraditional arrangements, they still regard the father as the breadwinner and the mother as the central parent.

Old notions of gender identity die hard.[29] When the mother goes to work outside the home, she does so not as a breadwinner, regardless of how much money she makes, but to help when her husband can't provide sufficiently. She goes as his proxy. Likewise, when the father cares for his children, he does it because his wife is unavailable. Regardless of his ability to nurture, he is merely there as her substitute.[30] It is permissible for each to expand his or her role to allow for nontraditional behavior, as long as that behavior is seen as constrained by circumstance, and thus not relevant to the core of gender identity.[31] Making money doesn't make a person a breadwinner any more than doing maternal things makes a person a mother.

In one domain at least, though, gender identity is changing within this group. Although these mothers are not about to usurp their husbands' roles as primary breadwinners, they are more committed to their work roles than traditional gender ideology would allow. As we have seen, interviews with these women reveal that work provides them with a variety of satisfactions beyond the financial ones, and that most would choose paid work, regardless of financial considerations.[32] The economic realities that they do face, however, mean that clashing views over this issue between husbands and wives need not be addressed.

Despite the ways in which these working-class men and their wives assert traditional gender identities, it is important to note the egalitarianism of these couples' lives. Although they may not be arguing for a genderless world in which the roles of men and women are the same, they are standing up for a world in which men and women work together to create a reasonable family life. Ironically, and perhaps without the feminist rhetoric touted by many middle-class men, the alternating-shift fathers eloquently argue for equality:

> I mean you have a kid, it's for the both of you. You both have to pitch in and do it. I mean it's not just, "Well, I'm the man. I'm going to work and do what the hell I want and you take care of the kid." It doesn't work that way because she's got to work too. If we're going to make it, she's got to work too.

In the end, it is simply a question of fairness, as this father put it:

> I think my wife works as hard as I do when she's at work so . . . I don't think she should have to come home and do all the work when she gets home . . . What the heck, she goes out and earns a living too. I don't see how anybody could think it would be fair otherwise.

Chapter 10	Constructing Identities as Parents and Professionals

The birth of a first child brings with it the birth of new parents. Perhaps no event in adulthood so profoundly transforms identity as becoming a parent. So much changes: from the shifts in parents' relationships with spouses, friends, and their own parents, to the way they spend their leisure time, to changes in their most cherished beliefs. All these changes transform the way parents think about themselves, but none affects their identities more than how they balance work and childcare.[1] Negotiations in couples over the division of labor are often intense because the decisions affect not only who will do what, but who each will be as a parent and as a worker.[2] Equally sharing parents create nontraditional identities as both parents and professionals.[3]

Equally sharing mothers invest more of themselves in work than do other mothers; equally sharing fathers invest more of themselves in parenting than other fathers.[4] These women reject or compromise traditional notions of motherhood, while their husbands do the same with respect to career. Traditional motherhood is incompatible with professional achievement, and traditional male careers are incompatible with primary parenting. Nontraditional identities in either domain promote equal sharing, and equal sharing, in turn, promotes the development of nontraditional parenthood and nontraditional careers. Finally, all of this occurs in the context of the couple's relationship because the husband's and wife's identities as parents and professionals are inextricably linked. Nontraditional parenting is a tango for two; you can't be an equal sharer if your spouse isn't doing half.

Expanding Identities

Equal sharing allows both men and women to expand their identities to include characteristics that have been reserved for the other gender.[5] Women are freer to develop as workers and men are freer to develop as parents.[6]

Mothers as Workers

A majority of mothers today have paid jobs, but for some the jobs are merely a way to make money or a chance to get out of the house. For other women, however, the achievements of career or the recognition for providing for their families are central to their senses of self. As a group, the equally sharing mothers commit themselves more to work, and define themselves more by career, than do more traditional mothers. On average, equally sharing mothers have education comparable to that of the 75-25 and 60-40 women, yet earn more money and feel more excited and engaged by their work.[7] In both senses, they are more successful.

Joan, for example, talked about her career with pride:

> I work for the regional utilities company and I'm a manager for customer service representatives . . . I'm responsible for their training, their development, keeping them abreast of changes . . . and making sure they are giving the best possible service . . . This is my twenty-fourth year with the company. I went to work with them right out of high school. I started out as a customer service rep; I went up to supervisor a few years later . . . I am very good at my job and I know I am.

Rosemary, also a high school but not a college graduate, has been extremely successful in her career as a marketing director for a cosmetics company, getting one promotion after another:

> I just got promoted so of course I feel great about it. I feel that I am successful at it and I find it very stimulating . . . I've had a lot of flexibility and growth. Whenever I've wanted to grow they've found room for me somewhere and have placed me. So I have been very fortunate . . . I am career-driven. I have always wanted to have a career.

Some, like Sharon, thought about their life's work long before they considered having children:

> I love what I do . . . I am very much engaged by it . . . I don't think I ever thought about balancing career and raising children. I always felt I would work. I decided I wanted to be a math teacher when I was about fourth grade. I wanted to be a teacher and that was my model—teacher, teacher.

Equally sharing women were most likely to worry about keeping their professional identities intact after they became mothers. A hospital administrator who took some time off to be home with her new daughter said:

> It was really important to me to make sure that people recognized I wasn't abandoning my new career to stay home . . . I don't look at work as a job. It's my career and it's extremely important to my feeling fulfilled and satisfied as a person . . . My work is very important . . . (I'm) not just working to make money.

In many cases, that commitment to work enabled women to make the gender-resisting choices discussed earlier, either to limit how much they were willing to cut back or to insist that their husbands cut back as much as they did and share the load at home. When they became parents, work often came second to a child's needs, but for many it wasn't going to come second to their husbands' jobs.

Women's career commitment alone was not enough to maintain a strong work-related identity after children were born. Career women do not automatically become equal sharers. Many of the unequal women also began marriage with strong work-related identities. Husbands' support was critical.

Equally sharing women needed and, if necessary, insisted upon their work getting equal billing in the family. One mother, a dentist who shared a dental practice with her husband, could barely contain her disgust when she described the inequality in another two-dentist marriage:

> I have even known dental couples—I heard this and I was absolutely repulsed; it just drove me up a wall—this dental couple, he's a dentist and she's a dentist and she did all the fillings and he did all the crowns and root canals. Ugh! That was horrible!

Husbands had their own reasons for championing their wives' careers. They too recognized the importance of their wives' work in establishing equality. Barry, who left his own job early every day, said:

> Rosemary's a great mother and a great wife and she's also incredibly good at what she does as far as her career is concerned . . . I work very hard to accommodate her . . . so that she has the time to devote to her job . . . I don't mean this to be demeaning . . . but if Rosemary was strictly a nine-to-four secretary somewhere who could leave her work at work that would be one (a different) thing.

Husbands encourage their wives' work identities for a variety of reasons: because it is fair to do so, because it is important to their wives, and for some, because of the money. The salaries some women earned enabled their families to enjoy affluent lifestyles. Equally sharing men were not threatened by their high-earning wives. Bruce followed his wife, Laura, when she got a job as a certified public accountant paying over $60,000 a year. He looked for and found a new job as a financial aid director at a small college. He bragged about her salary: "I took a pay cut to come down here and she makes more money than I do. It doesn't hurt my ego. It's pretty cool."

Many of the equally sharing men enjoyed being married to women who were fully their equals. Peter, the journalist who bemoaned the loss of the "nourishing" traditional mother in his family, explained why he was willing to give up the advantages that men had enjoyed in the past, which he himself had called "a pretty good situation": "I think men and women are intellectually equal and should have equal opportunities . . . It has not been one of my aspirations to marry a woman to whom I was intellectually superior, over whom I would have a certain amount of control and could therefore shift duties on to." It's the right thing to do. But it also gives Peter the kind of marriage that he wants with a woman he not only loves, but deeply respects.

Even though work commitments are more central to the lives of equally sharing mothers than to other women, their work does not go uncompromised. When I asked how parenting had affected their work, a number of them reported reducing the time and intensity of work. Some reformed workaholics among them admitted working sixty to seventy hours a week before children. Bernice, for example, is still a committed clinical psychologist, but said, "I spend much less time working. I was a workaholic. I worked every weekend and now I just squeeze out a few hours. I do what I have to do with my work and put the rest aside for a while." Sometimes torn by the dual commitments of work and parenthood, Sharon, the math teacher, speaks for many equally sharing women when she comments on the positive balance parenthood has brought to her life:

> I divide my day very carefully. I think having a child is a source of sanity for me. At the same time it makes it very hard to get everything done. I do appreciate the way that having Nicole puts my life in perspective. I don't think my job is the only thing that I care about or have to be good at. (It) reminds me how important it is to have a family. I don't wish that I was all teacher or all parent. I'm glad to be both.

Fathers as Parents

Fatherhood is central to the identities of the equally sharing men. Fathers' self-definitions as parents complemented their wives' as workers.[8] Some envisioned themselves as fathers long in advance. Daniel, for example, reported that his experiences as a "big brother" working with inner-city youth convinced him that he wanted to be a parent. Others fantasized about the superfathers they would become, and often they initiated the decision to have children in their families. Benjamin, the father who moved to a different town to participate in a parenting cooperative, couldn't wait:

> I was the one pushing harder to have children from the very beginning. I wanted to be a father ... I knew that for me it was not going to be—go to work, make money, come home, and do something else while Faye took care of the kids. That was very clear from the outset ... I had this fantasy image of myself as this great father, but I had no idea what that really meant.

Some equally sharing fathers embraced the more "feminine" parts of parenting as part of a longstanding refusal to adopt a traditional male identity. Beth reported that Steve had always been unconventional: "You're talking about a person who got in trouble in high school because he wanted to take home economics instead of shop." These unconventional men were dissatisfied if parenting broke down along gender lines. Kyle complained when his daughter turned to her mother for cuddles and him for excitement: "I see this as a gender stereotype which I don't like. I'd like to do more cuddling with her."

Interestingly, a few of the equally sharing men approached parenting with a sense of competence about the feminine parts of the role, not so much because they had rejected male socialization, but because their mothers had either died or been disabled when they were children, thrusting them into a "feminine" parenting role for themselves or for younger brothers and sisters. The skills they developed translated to greater competence when they later became parents. Barry's mother died when he was twelve and he became a "parent" for his siblings. He described the "easy" transition to parenthood with his own children:

> It struck me as incredibly easy when I first became a parent. I come from a large family and my mother died when I was twelve . . . At the time, I had a six-month-old brother, a two-year-old sister, a four-year-old sister, and a six-year-old brother. So it was up to my-self and my older brother to raise the kids. I never thought much about being a parent because I feel like I had already been one . . . since I was so used to raising babies from a young age and doing my own cleaning and my own laundry. (I still to this day do most of Rosemary's ironing.) Those kinds of things were neither beneath me nor seemed like a chore to me.

Of course, childhood trauma is neither necessary nor desirable for men to become equal sharers. But Barry's example does show that competence encourages fathers to be involved with children and to embrace parenthood. Like most people, fathers are more likely to identify with and invest in the successful parts of their lives.[9]

It might have been easier for men like Daniel and Barry to develop into equally sharing fathers because their unconventional gender identity or competence in caretaking predated parenting, but most of the men, without histories of rejecting conventional masculinity or caring for children, developed in ways they had never anticipated when they shared equally. Peter, the journalist who sometimes fantasized about having a more traditional family, acknowledged what equal parenthood brought to his own development as a person: "I think being very much involved in raising a child opens up a whole realm of the human experience that you've been cut off from, particularly as a man, I think, in conventional male roles. So I think I've changed and it's been extremely good for me."

Whether fathers came to parenting reluctantly or eager to embrace a new identity, their direct experience with their infants, and their wives' encouragement (or insistence) influenced how much they came to identify as fathers. Donald, whose wife, Rhona, had threatened that he'd better do half or he was going to be a single parent, made infant care his first priority. By immersing himself in parenting, he developed into a nurturer: "That caregiver side of me just got to blossom . . . that part of me that can just really give, be really nurturing and supportive. I feel really great about it." Rhona happily acknowledged his "maternal" fatherhood when she described him this way: "Very, very like a mother, except for not being able to nurse . . . no squeamishness around diapers and puke and stuff. He's totally cool with all that."

Ironically, the more enthusiastically women embraced motherhood, and the more competent they seemed, the harder it was for men to play an equal role.[10] Women's insecurity about their ability to take care of an infant sometimes gave men more room to share (although Janet's insecurity made it harder for her to make room for Daniel to share). Whether the wives were insecure or not, however, their encouragement was extremely important for men to become nurturers. Mary, for example, wasn't the least bit insecure, but from the day she and Paul became parents, she welcomed all of Paul's offers to "help."

Role models sometimes made nontraditional fatherhood easier. Although the equally sharing men were more likely than the unequal fathers to know other equal sharers, a quarter of them did not know any. The few who sought out and joined men's groups were looking for examples that they could follow, models of a new kind of identity. The lives of their own fathers provided little guidance for most of the men, except as anti-models.[11] Many of the equally sharing men are far from the fathers they grew up with, and proud of it.

Nevertheless, although none of the equally sharing men had fathers who took as large and nontraditional a role as they did, a few lucky ones did derive some helpful lessons from their fathers' lives. Kevin, for example, invoked his father as a role model: "My father was described once as a person who's gentle, but not meek . . . I think that one statement about my father more than anything has guided me towards the type of person I would want to be. Part of that means being gentle with my family and caring about them and involved in the process. It's not a sissy thing to do."

Men create new selves through nurturing their children and taking responsibility for their development. As they reflect on these experiences, they see that they've changed and embrace those changes. They often begin to look away from work and toward family for their sense of self-worth, as this father did: "It was kind of like my work was my baby, but once I had babies I saw it quite differently . . . saying that this is really more important—more important for me and more gratifying for me to be available and involved." Jake, another equally sharing father, never expected parenthood to be so compelling:

> I really had no interest in becoming a parent and stalled it for as long as possible, but I really enjoy it. I find it really fulfilling. It's displaced a lot of my interest in my job. Since I've been here, my job has become less interesting to me and less important to me. Being a dad has become more interesting to me, much more important.

Even without fathers like Kevin's, the equally sharing men often became men like him: gentle, but not meek.

Relinquishing Identities

The women who achieved at work and the men who nurtured at home enriched their lives by expanding their identities. But equal sharing also meant relinquishing potential parts of the self. Fathers gave up the unchecked pursuit of career success, and mothers gave up their conventional prerogative to be the number-one parent. Some of the equal sharers were relieved to shed these roles. Equal sharing freed men who weren't ambitious and women who rejected traditional motherhood. But some equal sharers found the loss of "male" careers or traditional motherhood harder to bear.

Fathers as Workers

The equally sharing men are less ambitious, on average, than the unequal men. Some fathers never cared about career success; some changed their priorities dramatically after their children were born. Several discovered that they simply no longer cared as much about their careers. But others found putting career second more painful. Fatherhood is important to them, but it doesn't entirely mitigate the career losses.

Steve is a prime example of a father who has never been ambitious, and whose identity is not primarily derived from paid work. He says about his job teaching Spanish at a community college: "I like it . . . I don't love it . . . it's okay. I love the hours, and I love the fact that I'm working with kids, and I love my vacations." Steve gets a lot of opportunities to consult and make extra money because he speaks Spanish, but he turns them all down. He loves to read and to get involved in local political causes. He guards the time with his children. When Stephanie was born, career was no competition for fatherhood: "When I first became a father I was just overwhelmed. I would have easily if I could have, quit work and become a housewife. It would have been fine with me."

In fact, about a year later that's exactly what he did. During Stephanie's first year, Beth had worked part time while Steve worked full time. When they decided to move back east from the West Coast, both thought it made sense for Beth to look for a job and for Steve to take the year off. Steve didn't do it as a favor to Beth; staying home with Stephanie was a benefit to which he felt equally entitled. Staying home wasn't the perfect idyll that he anticipated, however. Like many mothers, he suffered from the social isolation, but the loss of paid work posed no threat to his identity.

Other equally sharing men were happy to shed the identity of primary provider and appreciated the relief from pressure that their wives' incomes afforded them. Fathers mentioned several advantages: the freedom to pursue risky job alternatives themselves; more leisure time; less conflict with their wives over money. Mark, the police officer married to Joan, said: "(Her income) . . . eliminates one of the big reasons I guess that people argue all the time—dough." Although many men willingly accept the pressure of earning in return for the power and identity of being *the* earner, these men either didn't want the pressure or didn't care about the power. One father joked about the big disadvantage, "Nobody calls me 'Your Majesty.'"

For equally sharing men who were more ambitious about their careers, parenthood tempered those ambitions, as it had for their wives. As men cut back they also cared less, and caring less made it easier to cut back. Daniel explained the changes in his feelings about his career since Noah was born: "Success as an academic and getting things like tenure used to be foremost . . . Since he's been born, my feeling is much more that he's more important. I'm not as tied up in the goals of a specific career . . . any job is fine." Frank, another equally sharing father, was a successful sales representative, earning about $50,000 a year working for a growing commercial real estate company. After his first child was born, he limited his work to thirty hours a week, even though he worked on commission. He was ambivalent about his job; he didn't feel particularly challenged or stimulated by it: "The thing I like about it is the fact that I'm home every night. My workday's flexible around my family. So, I know if I change jobs for more money that I'll be away more . . . which I don't think I'll like too much." During my interview Frank suddenly realized just how important his identity as a father had become to him. Almost imperceptively, fatherhood had taken precedence over his career: "I often wondered why I haven't changed jobs before . . . I could have picked better jobs, higher-paying jobs. I think the main reason I haven't is because of the things we've been talking about. I really do."

Equally sharing men who care about their careers also make compromises in their work lives: cutting back their hours, taking time off from work, choosing particular jobs, or even changing careers to accommodate parenting. They compromise far more than their 60-40 or 75-25 counterparts, and those compromises have consequences for identity, and for how successful they feel. Some are lucky or creative enough to alter their work lives without sacrificing success. The pediatric dentist joined a group practice that promised him a lucrative income and a nine-to-five job. Another father was thrilled with the new career he developed as a stock broker working out of his home so he could spend time with his new daughter. He was extraordinarily successful, and had earned over $100,000 the year before I interviewed him.

Still other men created satisfying careers by redefining what success meant. One father decided to quit graduate school to get certified for teaching despite the low pay and status, so that he could be home for his children. He enjoyed teaching and felt he was doing something extremely worthwhile. He had "no qualms at all about not having finished graduate school." Likewise, the chemistry professor who refused to attend late meetings or early ones didn't care about becoming famous in his field, but derived satisfaction from teaching and from mentoring students: "I'm generally very satisfied with what I do, but I tend to have a different set of criteria for success than a lot of people I know . . . I don't feel that I have to get to the top of any heap."

But putting parenting first means real sacrifice for some men. Jonathan gave up a promising career as a musician. Likewise Barry, who talked with great animation and enthusiasm about his career in the health food industry, cut back dramatically when he became a parent by leaving early every day: "It (becoming a parent) changed my priorities. They (his children) are the most important thing in my life . . . I have an understanding with the people I work for . . . I'm going to leave my office between three and three-thirty to pick up my kids. I think that's the main way that they changed my life; they really changed my priorities." But Barry's career is very important to him. Sometimes he feels frustrated that he can't give work his all. When I asked about his job, he said: "I like it a lot. As far as engaging me I couldn't ask for anything that would give me more. As far as success, I'm successful at it, but I could do a heck of a lot better . . . I think I feel frustrated because I'm not as successful as I could be."

Putting the brakes on career is harder on ambitious equally sharing men than it is on women who are just as career-driven, because the men are giving up the privilege of an unfettered career, which they might have had in the past or with a different wife. The equally sharing women, despite career compromises, still have more freedom to achieve than their mothers did in years past or their unequal friends do today. Because our fantasies are often born of our gendered worlds, what's difficult about equal sharing differs for men and women. Giving up career dreams can be as painful for men as renouncing a special maternal bond is for women.

Women as Parents

Italian children refer to their own mothers not as "my mother," but as "La Mama," *the* mother, as if each individual mother is the incarnation of a quasi-religious ideal. Similarly, in the United States if you ask people what they associate with the phrase "the mother," you are likely to elicit a series of laudatory adjectives: loving, nurturant, patient, available, caring, and self-sacrificing.

Two other deeply internalized cultural ideas also inform our idealization of motherhood. First, mothers are irreplaceable, unique, and the best caretakers of their children. A mother is and should be the uncontested number-one person in her children's lives. Any other caretaker, including the children's father, is second-best. Second, motherhood forms the core of a woman's identity once she has a child. Children need maternal care if they are to thrive and grow up to be healthy and happy adults. Mothers need children to need them if they are to become this idealized mother.[12]

It is not news that this image of motherhood is problematic for any woman, but it is especially troublesome for equally sharing mothers.[13] If mothers are really best for children, and motherhood is the core of identity, then what kind of woman would share parenting with her husband?

In the face of this ideal, some equally sharing mothers initially rejected parenthood itself; some tried to live up to the ideal and failed; some enacted a part of the ideal when their children were small and then changed; and some knew from the start that they would have to create a different kind of motherhood and become a different kind of mother.

When some women looked ahead to the life laid out for them, they didn't like what they saw. The idealized image of motherhood either had little appeal, seemed completely beyond their reach, or was incompatible with their aspirations for achievement. If this was motherhood, then they wouldn't become mothers at all. Sharon, the math teacher whose passion for teaching developed when she was a little girl, said: "I remember astonishing my mother by announcing that I was never going to have any children . . . I always wondered how I would find time for a child and would I be sufficiently affectionate with a child. Where would that extra energy and affection come from?"

Equally sharing women were more likely than other women to be reluctant mothers. Some put motherhood off for years. Worried about whether they could relate to children, unsure they had the patience, afraid and never feeling ready, some had trouble imagining themselves living up to those daunting images. One mother said outright what several of them implied, "I never saw myself as a mother." Ironically, sometimes this initial rejection of motherhood helped them achieve equality. Husbands who wanted children had to convince their wives that they wouldn't have to do it all, and their wives held them to their word.

But the power of images of motherhood initially led some of the women who later became equal sharers to try making themselves into traditional mothers at first. Some found it very hard to realize that ideal, and painful when they couldn't. Jonathan described how Ruth had suffered because she believed that as a good mother she should be home with young children: "She felt trapped and very unhappy and guilty at the same time because . . . according to her values, it was more important to raise her child the right way and live a good life than to be going back to work . . . She thought she'd go crazy if she had to stay home anymore." As we saw in Chapter 7, her unhappiness propelled him into equal parenthood. Jonathan said: "There was a conscious attempt on my part to share what seemed to be from Ruth's point of view too much of a burden on her."

Women who are unhappy at home taking care of young children do not simply suffer from boredom or from an aversion to endless diapering and dishwashing. They suffer from a loss of identity. First, because women discover they can't be endlessly patient, responsive, and self-sacrificing, they doubt that they are good mothers. Second, in creating themselves as traditional mothers, they often relinquish achievements and job-related status. Ruth was a high school art teacher, with a job that challenged her, engaged her, and brought out her artistic and pedagogical talents, a job where she was recognized for those talents. At home with a one-year-old, she had no place to express those talents and no one except Jonathan to applaud her.

Even when people consciously intend to do things differently, the forces pulling them toward inequality can be overwhelming. Rhona, a poet, found herself taking on more and more of the childcare after the birth of her second child despite her explicit agreement with her husband, Donald, to co-parent. She explained:

Something really funny happened for me because I'm really a feminist . . . All my internalized oppression came out with the second kid. "I shouldn't be a poet; it's a waste of my time." Somehow part of me just sort of laid down and died for a while. I just felt really flattened, worthless, unattractive . . . Six months after I stopped nursing her . . . it was like the beginning of me getting up and saying, "What is going on?" Something's wrong with this picture. This isn't the deal. This isn't what I contracted for. I look exactly like my mother . . . That precipitated this deep reevaluation of our relationship and our roles.

What she was doing in the family was only the outer manifestation of the problem. The struggle for Rhona, as for Ruth, was over identity. Something inside her finally sounded an alarm:

When I found myself being a traditional mother more, it was like, "Wake up. This is not who you are. Get real. You're not a traditional person. You're not a traditional mother. You're not traditional in any way shape or form, so this is phony for you."[14]

The crises in both of these families led them to change how they did parenting. Jonathan and Donald took on more of the childcare, but no less significantly, Ruth and Rhona changed who they thought they should be as parents.

Ruth realized it was OK for her to step aside while Jonathan took paternity leave to care for their daughter. Rhona, after feeling she was being "buried alive" by motherhood, came to a new conception of it. She decided that her children wouldn't suffer if their father gave them breakfast instead of her some mornings. "The sex of the person feeding them isn't relevant." She found a way to mother her children less and without the total self-abnegation that she had unconsciously felt was required of her. Her conversion to this new way, fully sharing with her husband Donald, still allows her to feel like a good mother. Her own transformation into an equally sharing mother models the ideals she holds for her daughters, so she's happy about the kind of mother she has become:

> I'm very proud of my parenting . . . I have been so conscious of giving to my daughters (the idea) that "You are beautiful, you are strong, and you are brilliant. You don't have to choose" . . . They are really free to be who they are.

The power of the motherhood ideal has affected and continues to affect the lives of all the equally sharing mothers. Often they invoke it as a standard used to judge themselves, even when they don't agree with it. One mother explained why she had stayed home for four years after her second child was born:

> I'm not that nontraditional. I wanted to be a mom. It was my job to stay home with the baby . . . I wanted to see what it was like to be a mother. Could I do it? I was scared to death. It was never something easy. I was very anxious about it . . . just to prove to myself I could do it . . . to be a more full human being or woman.

"To prove to myself that I could do it." Sadly, these words reminded me of the self-criticisms of a few equally sharing mothers who shared the primary role when their children were young. As one put it: "This feeling of being a little untested as the total mother . . . Maybe I have the feeling I'd like to prove my competence . . . reach down within (myself) and find out (I) did a good job . . . Maybe motherhood is a bit like that." And another:

I keep wondering if there's some sort of selfless, self-effacing, all-giving, nurturing core somewhere inside me that is waiting to blossom, but I don't really think it's there . . . It should be satisfying for you to love your children . . . in this selfless, giving everything, everything, everything . . . I don't think there's really ever been a point that I felt like I could just let go of the rest of the world and devote myself in entirety to my children.

Women sometimes manage these images of the ideal mother by incorporating a part of them into their own ways of being mothers. Several women told me they did "good mom" things occasionally, like letting a daughter have five friends over for a sleepover or making cookies with their children. There is nothing remarkable about these activities. What was remarkable was their emotional power and the deliberate use of them to help women feel like good mothers.

And despite sharing parenting overall, some mothers clung to a special role with children that they didn't want to share: putting them to bed, taking care of them when they were sick, managing their affairs, or acting as their confidant. Listen to this busy professional woman:

I think that clearly I'm the manager for the children . . . My husband couldn't wrest that from me if he wanted it. You have got to take a stand at some point . . . I don't want to be a traditional father. I'm a mother. It's different.

And this mother:

I spend more time on an emotional level talking to my kids about their friends and what they're going through in adolescence . . . They don't talk about those things with their dad . . . I think I'll probably have a pretty large role and I'm delighted. That's what I think the essence of being a mother is. Being able to reassure and see them change and grow and just be there for them at times like that.

Interestingly, her claim that she was *the* confidant was disputed by her husband.

Impossible motherhood ideals made it difficult for some equally sharing mothers to escape the guilt that working mothers in all groups felt for not becoming what Donna called "Susie Homemaker."[15] Repeatedly, I heard mothers criticize themselves if they didn't bake cookies, do arts and crafts projects, get on the floor and give themselves over to creative play, or feel patient and loving every single moment. The equal mothers might have been the most likely to intellectually reject those images, but that doesn't mean they weren't affected by them. Donna's vehement response to this Susie Homemaker image reveals its power: "I hate it! I hate it! I don't like it. Well, for some people it's great. I think it depends on who you are. Some people really like that. I just don't like it . . . There's the pressure, but I try to tell myself that it doesn't matter."

All mothers wrestle with these unreachable ideals, but equally sharing mothers have one very significant additional issue to confront. Nothing is a more powerful reminder to a woman that she is not living up to the cultural ideal of motherhood than the realization that she is not number one to her child. In a few families in which fathers fully shared the nurturing of young children, those children turned to their fathers as their primary source of comfort, at times preferring them to their mothers. For some mothers, this was a relief, but for others the loss of the central position in a child's emotional life could be devastating. One anguished mother explained: "That doesn't feel good emotionally. It doesn't feel good in terms of society. How can this baby prefer his father to his mother? . . . Isn't that at the core of motherhood, your child preferring you, the special bond between mother and child?"

The equally sharing mothers have something to lose by relinquishing the kind of motherhood that puts women at the center of the family. (Usually, the loss only meant sharing the center rather than ceding it to their husbands.) But they also have something very important to gain. The new kind of motherhood that equal sharers created allowed for a human, rather than a superhuman, standard.

With somewhat less angst than Rhona, several women struggled with guilt before adopting a more attainable definition of good motherhood. Roberta, the physicist, said: "I did have a sort of idealized notion of what a mother ought to be and then I found myself dissatisfied and unable to function inside that idealized context. So, I sort of had to find my own way through it." Ironically, sharing the responsibility allowed these women to feel that they were better mothers. Because equally sharing mothers have not sacrificed their work identities, and can often bow out when they feel irritable, they don't resent their children. The love they felt and the joyful relationships they developed with their children justified their nontraditional arrangements and convinced them that they were good mothers after all.

In fact, mothers who initially felt guilty because of their work commitments saw over time that, paradoxically, they could wholeheartedly embrace motherhood once it was defined as an important part of, but not their entire, identities. Helen, a hospital administrator, said:

> It's really a couple of hours in the afternoon, say from four to six, that I wish I were here. And yet, having seen how unsatisfied, dissatisfied my mother was ultimately with what she did her whole life, I just think that we're all kind of better off this way, because I'm happy most of the time. I think that when I spend time with them, I'm happy with them.

Sharon, the math teacher who has shared equally with her husband, Peter, since their daughter Nicole was nine months old, has also changed over time:

> There were times that I felt the guilt that women who work feel, but I feel a lot less guilty now and much more able to put my heart and energy into the time I spend with her . . . I feel like I can be a more wholehearted mother in the times that I'm a mother now, so I feel that I'm a good mother.

The mothers with the strongest preparenthood fears fared well when they created a motherhood that didn't imply absolute responsibility. Irene, the mother who refused to have children until her husband agreed to a 50-50 split of childcare, was extremely gratified by her success at mothering her son. Keeping part of her identity anchored in her work as a writer acted as a source of sanity for her. She said:

> I have never ever ever in my whole life wanted to stay home with children . . . I never had very much in the way of maternal instincts, although I feel like they're coming out now that I have a child . . . For someone who really didn't think she could do it, I think I'm doing a great job . . . I couldn't do the family life without the work . . . I'm a much better parent when I'm away for a day or two. I have much more energy. I'm much less irritable.

Relinquishing a traditional maternal identity wasn't always easy. But when mothers saw that their own freedom to work and achieve meant that they actually felt happier with their children, it was easier to adopt a new standard of motherhood.[16] This mother speaks for many:

> I feel great. I really really love my kids so much. I figure if I love them this much something's got to be going right. I mean they barely ever bug me. They're very much a part of my life. *I haven't had to not have a life to just be with them.*

The Link between Husbands' and Wives' Identities

Achieving women don't just happen to marry nurturing men. Husbands and wives interdependently create equally sharing identities. Mothers' freedom to pursue their careers may depend on their husbands' interest and willingness to share the demands of parenthood. Fathers' freedom to develop a nurturing relationship with their children may depend on their wives' willingness to cede some of the mother's traditional prerogatives, which in turn may depend on those mothers' involvement in outside work. It is obvious that one can't be an equally sharing father or mother without a partner who is willing to cede half or to do the other half of the parenting. It is less obvious, but equally true, that the work identity each parent creates also depends on what his or her partner does at home. Men have less freedom to compromise work to concentrate on parenting if they don't have wives who share the burdens of breadwinning. Women are less free to develop their careers and to invest in work if their husbands are unwilling to take up the slack at home. The birth of two parents commences a journey of identity development for each of them, a journey in which their individual identities are ineluctably connected.

The three stories that follow show some of the diverse routes that equal sharers may take on this journey. Grace and Brian easily established and maintained equal sharing through the nontraditional, complementary, and satisfying identities they created within their marriage. Rita and Charles had a bumpier road to follow. They were not nearly as nontraditional as Grace and Brian when they embarked on parenthood together. Susan and Jake established equally shared parenting early on, but now find that the pressure of two high-powered careers and the care of three children are pushing them toward inequality. Susan and Jake show us that nothing in the family is settled once and for all. The division of labor with its consequences for parents' identities is continually recreated.

Grace and Brian: "He Is a Daddy!"

Brian and Grace, two architects, share a deep love of music and a peaceful, welcoming home that made me feel at ease immediately. They also equally share the care of their two children, a four-year-old daughter, Lily, and an eight-year-old son, Christopher. Lily is in daycare and Christopher, a third-grader, goes to after-school care three days a week. Lily and Christopher's lives are filled with interesting and lively activities. Their father takes them ice-skating and their mother takes them to piano lessons. Brian and Grace have arranged their schedules so that each has some time off during the week to spend with their children. Parenting is a rewarding part of both of their lives. Grace said: "It's fulfilled me enormously . . . because it gives meaning to life . . . I had all sorts of good things in my life up until then, but 'Why?' was always the question. Now . . . this is why, because of them . . . They're everything." Brian, who looked forward to becoming a father for a long time, said, "It fulfilled a hope."

According to Grace, being a father is central to Brian's identity:

> I can't imagine Brian *not* being a parent and I can imagine me not being a parent. That is his primary job. He likes being an architect and he has all sorts of other interests . . . He loves computers; he likes to ride his bike; he likes friends. He is a very fulfilled human being. But as a Daddy, that's it. I mean that's his number-one over-whelming fulfillment of life . . . I mean deep deep down it's not a sideline to him. He is a daddy!

In his understated way, Brian tells me: "I take on a lot of roles of the traditional mother. I don't know, I just think it's what it should be for the two parents."

Brian and Grace share an architecture practice. Of the two, Grace seems more intensely involved with work. She says:

> It's my life. It's my ego and it's my life . . . I'm working on someone's plans and if they don't look beautiful I get depressed, and if they look beautiful I feel wonderful . . . I get insomnia if something in the office didn't work right . . . My ego is attached to what I do.

If she were not a parent she would be spending more time at work: "I would love to get to work early and really plan my day and plan my activities, and I would love to stay at work a little later . . . I'm drawn to spend more time at work." Brian's feelings about work are more measured: "I like it a lot. I like working with people as clients a lot, but I can leave it at the end of the day. I feel I'm pretty good at it; I feel satisfied with what I do."

One thing is crystal clear, just as Brian and Grace are equals at home, they are equals at work. Grace is adamant: "I wasn't going to play second fiddle to anybody in the office." The importance of her profession predated parenthood. According to Grace, Brian knew what he was getting into:

> When we got married, I was already an architect and my ego structure was already established . . . There was no way I was ever going to be a housewife . . . It always has been important to have my career be fulfilling and Brian knew that when he married me. I think for his ego he wanted a career woman to be proud of.

Even when an "ego structure" is already established, however, it can change. Grace's didn't. For a brief time Grace stayed home after each of her children was born, while Brian continued to work. Neither was happy. He didn't want to be an overworked, pressured provider, and she didn't want to be a traditional mother. Brian recounts: "I was definitely a more traditional working father, out in the morning and then busy all day, double-time type of thing . . . We had two offices and I was the only architect . . . I remember it was a very anxiety, work-wise anxiety, problem time." He was relieved when Grace went back to work. She was too: "I couldn't be a mommy at home. I just couldn't . . . I'm incapable of it and so I'm very happy, very fortunate it works out. I love being a mommy during the times that I'm a mommy, but if it was all day without work I would go crazy."

Both Brian and Grace embraced identities that are unusual for their genders. Grace is free to achieve at work; he to nurture at home. Brian's ego isn't threatened by a wife who is in the same career and highly invested in it. Grace can shed those parts of traditional mothering that are unsuited to her because she knows Brian is more than willing to take them over. Grace doesn't need to be the number-one parent in the family. She is not the least bit threatened by shared parenting: "If you're not having your ego gratified by a career and your ego is being gratified totally by your children and your home, then you might not want to share it . . . My ego is not bound up with them coming to me." Grace admits to competitive feelings sometimes at work, but not when it comes to her children's welfare; she told me:

> I did literally steal his clients. I didn't do it on purpose to steal them from him. I just wanted them for me. But that would never happen at home because I want the best for Lily and Christopher. Like right now I'm delighted he's taking the kids ice-skating. I get to have fun with you, but I don't have to feel guilty at all about them, because they're with him having a positive time.

Grace exaggerates a bit when she says: "I always tell people that Brian is the mommy and I'm the daddy in a lot of ways in the old-fashioned sense." After all, Grace spends as much time, does as many chores, and is at least as emotionally involved with her children as Brian, and much more than a traditional father would be. Moreover, although Brian is an unusually warm and "maternal" father in many ways, Grace receives most of Christopher's confidences, and Lily runs to her for comfort. No gender reversal has occurred in this family.

Strikingly, role reversal came up in a number of other equal families. Donna divulged, "I always tell him, he'd make a better mom than myself." But the equal sharers who refer to "role reversal" are overstating the case. Mothers in the equally sharing families are nothing like the fathers of yesteryear. There is not one among them who comes home from work, puts up her feet, and reads the newspaper while her husband scurries around cooking the dinner, managing meanwhile to keep the children out of her hair. That image is so funny because it is so far from the truth. These equally sharing mothers are fully engaged and responsible parents. Similarly, none of their husbands are currently househusbands. On average, they work as many hours a week as their wives.

Equality sometimes feels like role reversal because parents are so different from their same-gender peers. Although equal couples have not reversed roles, they have developed identities that incorporate the stereotypical characteristics associated with both genders: nurturance and assertiveness, sensitivity and drive, a commitment both to caring for children and to achieving in paid work. Parent and professional—combining these in one enriched self renders gender irrelevant.

Grace and Brian seem ideally suited to equal sharing because of the identities they brought to parenting. Yet couples in which women aren't highly invested in career and are attracted to traditional motherhood at first can also become equal sharers. And couples in which men are highly committed to their careers, or don't start out longing to be fathers, can also create equally sharing families. People change.

Rita and Charles: "You Can't Raise Children by Spectating"

Rita and Charles defy all stereotypes about equal sharers. Although Rita claims that Charles is no longer "as straight as an arrow," as he was before they had children, that is exactly the phrase that comes to mind when one meets Charles. He seems responsible, serious, conventional, and conservative. In certain ways their life together has been extremely traditional. His career takes priority in the family, and has since the day they were married. Rita supports his career aspirations unambivalently:

> Charles is mobile. Charles has career goals that he laid down on the table before we got married . . . I'm not real career-oriented and that was one thing I was very excited about. He has definite career goals . . . Since we've been married, we've moved four times across country . . . But I love it. I mean I really do. I love it.

Charles has worked his way up into a position as a director of program development for the State Division of Air Quality of the Environmental Protection Agency, a position that carries a salary of over $50,000 a year. Rita, a full-time secretary for the board of education, earns less than half of his salary. Rita is happy to have a job now that her children are "self-sufficient" (potty-trained), but the job itself is not satisfying: "I'm a very frustrated worker because my job entails a lot of tedious routine things and it's not fulfilling in the least. I'm not happy at all with really any aspect of it except the pay. The paycheck, I'm happy with that."

Rita and Charles have two children, seven-year-old Mae and four-year-old Andrew. Rita stayed home for six years after Mae was born. There was no question that she was going to be the one to do that: "I wanted to (stay home) . . . I'm in total support of his career moves because that's important to him. I'm very proud of him and I know he's going to get to where he wants to get, but I wanted to stay home with the kids." So far, this looks like a pretty traditional middle-class American household: Dad has the career; Mom stays home with small children. Today, however, the scene does not look typical at all. Dad is every bit as involved in taking care of his children as Mom. Now they both work full time, but Mom is not doing the "second shift" alone. Rita says:

> He bathes them most of the time. He fixes their lunches most of the time. He gets them their breakfast in the morning and dresses them in the morning . . . I always do the laundry . . . It's just who's there at the time. If the dishes are dirty and he comes into the kitchen, he cleans up the kitchen . . . We do what we like to do and the things that no one likes to do, we trade off.

Rita and Charles obviously weren't equally involved in parenting when Charles was the only earner, but the seeds of equal sharing were sown during that period. Rita expected Charles to pitch in when he came home. Traditional to a point, Rita didn't believe mothers should have to do it all:

> I expected help. I expected him to deal with the child because I needed a break . . . I think there was frustration on his part because, "Hey, I work all day and I come home and you want me to take over." "Well, I've had a hard day too."

Charles recalled an incident that was a turning point for him. Rita had gone away for a few days to visit her sick mother, and Charles had been home with their one-year-old:

> I forgot to wash out the diaper pail. She got home and found the diaper pail. She says, "My goodness gracious now, you've been a dad a whole year. It's taken a whole year and you didn't even . . ." and so after that I learned how to wash diapers.

When Rita decided to go back to work, Charles admits that his initial reaction was negative:

> I will confess for my own selfish reasons I kind of liked it when she was home . . . I got more of her emotional attention, I guess. I'd been raised in a house where the mother didn't work, so that when it came time that she would work, why then we had to find day school . . . and I worried a lot about that.

Despite his doubts, he supported her decision, and in doing so, supported the new identity she was trying to create for herself. Despite his own worries about daycare, he didn't play on the guilt she already felt about leaving a young child in daycare: "It was important to her . . . She's not the kind of person that is a stay-at-home-all-day person. That's not her, that's just not her . . . I knew that she needed to go back just for her own mental health."

Now that they both have full-time jobs, their contributions at home are equal. Unlike some of the other equally sharing fathers, Charles doesn't strike one as a very "maternal" father. In part, his description confirms that impression: "I guess when they want to be nurtured, they usually go to their mother. When there is a serious matter of discipline, not a routine matter . . . that's usually mine to deal with." But Rita's expectations and Charles's predilections have led him to become a more nontraditional father than is obvious at first. He accurately refers to himself as a "hands-on" father. He actively participates in all the basic caretaking work with his young children. Changing diapers, giving baths, and cutting up children's food are not beneath him. He is also "hands-on" in the time and thought he gives to raising his children. Charles took a week off from work to help ease Andrew's transition to daycare, and he currently leaves work for two hours every Thursday to take Mae for tutoring. In spite of characterizing Rita as the nurturer and himself as the disciplinarian, he doesn't think his young children are closer to her than to him:

> No, no, I don't think so. All our discipline is exercised in a loving fashion. Our kids know, and I think even the little one knows that when we have to discipline, it's because we love them and . . . we want them to have certain standards to live by.

The parent Charles has become matches the theory of parenting he has developed:

> You can't raise children by spectating. You have got to be with them. You have got to be there when the good things happen and praise them, and then you've got to be there to correct them when they need correction. You've got to be there.

Despite his job, Charles is there for them: "I have a demanding job . . . I'm career-oriented . . . but I'm not a workaholic. When there's priorities in the family, then sometimes the family takes (priority)."

In a sense, Charles has been able to have it all: a fulfilling career and a fundamental role in the family. He shares parenting equally without seriously jeopardizing his career. Rita has made it possible for him to do so by expecting and encouraging his participation at home, while at the same time accommodating his career needs. In turn, his willingness to be the only breadwinner gave her the opportunity to be home for six years and and be the mother she wanted to be.

But there is one piece of this happy picture that doesn't quite fit comfortably. Although Rita disclaims an interest in career, she is frustrated by a job that offers her little challenge and little sense of accomplishment. She hopes at some point to go back to school. Charles says he is encouraging her to do that, but Rita anticipates the potential problem if she becomes more invested in career and that conflicts with his career goals: "I've thought about it a little bit, because right now it's not an issue. I think when I intend to pursue something, it will be when I feel that Charles can maybe take a breather . . . I will spend some time to pursue something that I'd like to do." As parents and as professionals, their identities are linked.

Susan and Jake: "You Always Want to Be Reexamining Your Life"

Susan and Jake are both researchers with demanding, high-powered jobs that entail grant-getting and publishing. Susan is an epidemiologist who works at a medical school; Jake is an economist who works at a research institute. They both work fifty or more hours a week and equally care for their three children: Hector, aged ten, Anya, five, and the baby, Todd, eleven months old. Warm-hearted and idealistic people, they adopted Anya, a developmentally delayed child who had been physically abused, when she was two. Todd was a surprise, but no less welcomed into this loving family.

As one would imagine, Susan and Jake's lives are incredibly busy. In fact, they've decided that their lives are too busy, and they have embarked on a major change. In the long run, they intend for one of them to have a less intense job. Jake says: "Our lives were just too hectic. Two positions and three kids is pretty intense, where you're expected to get grants and publish papers . . . Something had to give . . . If you're both heavily committed at work, there's just not enough time." Susan tells the same story:

> Our life is too chaotic. We went out to dinner once a year on our anniversary . . . If everything's perfect, we can barely manage it, but if the slightest (problem occurs), if a child gets sick and a child has to stay home from school, if I have a paper due, if Jake has to

go to Washington, anything that perturbs the system is just unbearable. So we decided that one of us has to have a less powerful job.

The interesting twist is that although they have decided that one of them has to have a less intense job, they don't know who it will be. In the short run, Jake has resigned from his current position and is planning to spend next year as a househusband, doing some writing, while Susan, on leave from her job, works with collaborators at a medical school in the Midwest. After this year, either Susan will return to her current job while Jake takes a more primary role as a parent or, alternatively, Jake will try to get a more lucrative job in government or industry, while Susan looks for a less high-powered job that will allow her to devote more time to the family. Each seems open to both scenarios, despite the profound implications for their family life and for Susan's and Jake's individual identities. Susan says: "It could be him or me (who has the less intense job). I don't know who it's going to be . . . I like this job a lot . . . so if I'm the one who is going to have the intense career, I want to stay here." Jake says: "Maybe I'll decide that I like taking care of the kids full time and I'll do that and we'll just live off Susan's salary, or maybe I'll decide that I really love economics and can't live without it . . . and Susan will resign. I have no idea." Jake wasn't sure he wanted the kind of career that would bring in more money. When pressed, he said: "I really think it's more likely that Susan will be more involved in her work and I'll be less involved."

Arriving at this point appears to be the result of remarkable transformations for each of them. Despite Jake's initial lukewarm attitude toward parenting, he is now willing to contemplate becoming the primary parent. Despite Susan's exceptional career, she is willing to consider a major cutback in that career.

They did not begin parenting as an equally shared enterprise. Susan wanted children much more than Jake did and initially devoted herself more to taking care of Hector:

I was more likely to change his diapers . . . more likely to sing him to sleep at night. When Hector was little I really wanted to be home with him, so I took off this time . . . rearranged my whole schedule, but I didn't always like it . . . One day we went to Pizza Hut and I was sitting there. These two women came in behind me and literally discussed canned versus frozen peas for forty-five minutes. I thought, "I'm going nuts here. I can't do this."

When Hector started daycare, Jake became more of an equal partner in parenting. Both agree with Susan's statement: "When the work got to be too much for me to do, we just looked it over and divided it in half." Not only did Jake do more childcare, but he developed a new sense of the place of fatherhood in his life:

> I think maybe the most important thing I can do is help Anya straighten out her life or help Hector and Todd grow up. I came to this point where I said, "I've done some really good economics. I've published dynamite stuff . . . Maybe, that's the best I'll ever do . . . It's time to do something to shake up my life" . . . having this idea that I've got the family to redirect my energies to if I want to is interesting.

Susan's openness and flexibility about her role are no less remarkable. Susan has been a model of a woman creating a nontraditional identity, sometimes in opposition to her own mother. Her mother wanted her to learn to sew, cook, and type, and she refused to do any of them: "My mother sends me things like cookbooks called *Meatloaf Magic*. She sent me a whole booklet about what you could do with coffee filters recently. This is just not where my life is really."

Academic achievement was encouraged and expected in her family, although her parents were ambivalent about the unbridled aspirations of a daughter. Despite their objections, she went on to graduate school, received a Ph.D. in epidemiology, and succeeded brilliantly in the competitive world of grant-getting and research. But she can imagine herself changing:

> I enjoy what I'm doing, but it is not something I have to do. This is a big department that is run entirely on grant money. There's a lot of pressure and they count your publications every year and all this kind of nonsense . . . I think I would do fine in a different job.

Susan can envision two different future images of herself, the first as a mother spending more time at home: "It'd be kind of fun to be there more. I still have these images . . . I decided I was going to make Anya a sweater. This will probably be a wedding present at the rate it's going." The second image is of herself in the more high-powered career:

> It would be nicer than it is now, because I would have a little bit more leeway. I wouldn't have to leave work as many days. Jake

would do more of that kind of stuff and I could work more regular hours and be free more. I could read a novel at nine at night.

When Jake talks about their future, he conveys a sense of adventure and excitement. "You always want to be reexamining your life," he says. Reexamining their lives means renegotiating identities. Although in other families the link between parental identities may be less explicit and the renegotiation less obvious, in all of them in subtle ways the recreation of identity goes on continually.

For all of Susan and Jake's flexibility and willingness to change, however, they never really consider the alternative that most of the equal sharers have stumbled on: equality works best when couples transform their careers from male careers to family careers. Because Jake and Susan are stuck with the assumption that somebody has got to have the superhuman career, equality just doesn't seem to work. Unlike their traditional counterparts, they don't assume Jake has to be the career-driven spouse, but they don't question the wisdom of anyone sacrificing so much of family life for career. Until parents routinely ask that question, equality will be a tenuous achievement.

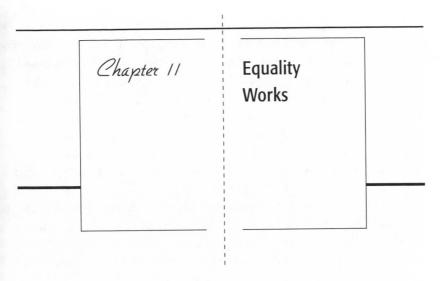

Chapter 11 | Equality Works

Many have mistakenly given up on gender equality. In a recent op-ed piece in the *New York Times,* Danielle Crittenden argued that pay parity between the sexes has gone as far as it can go. Single and childless professional women are getting paid the same as their male counterparts, but mothers will never be paid the same as their husbands because mothers put children first. Gender equality, Crittenden implied, can never be achieved because women are, and want to be, the primary caretakers of children.[1]

Despite the flood of mothers into the labor force over the past thirty years, women do indeed retain primary responsibility for childcare in most families today. Husbands are helping more than they used to, and even doing a lot more than their fathers did, but as dozens of studies over the past twenty-five years have shown, Mom is still number one at home. These modern moms, however, are not as sanguine about motherhood as Crittenden suggests. American women, who overwhelmingly want to work outside the home today, face excruciating choices when they become mothers: compromise the care of their children, curtail their careers, or become supermoms, struggling under the exhausting burdens of the double day. Couples talk about it, joke about it, and fight about it. Some couples even divorce over it. The inequality in the division of labor at home is the problem that won't go away for dual-earner couples today. The "stalled revolution" takes a terrible toll on men and women and on their marriages.[2] We pay the price of this inequality in lives of impossible demands, lost dreams, and lost intimacy.

But despite this pessimistic picture, in some families the revolution is alive and well. Some couples *are* equally sharing the care of their children and defying the naysayers. They show that inequality is not inevitable. But if the lessons we have learned from the equal sharers are to take root, we need to stop treating the problems of dual-earner couples as the plight of working women torn between their bonds with their children and intransigent employers. What husbands do at home matters. Yes, employers should adopt more family-friendly policies and women need to stop feeling so guilty. But changes in the workplace and in women's heads are not enough. We need to change the family. The changes may be difficult, but as we have seen, real husbands and wives are already transforming the family. Crittenden is wrong. We don't have to give up on gender equality. It *is* possible for both men and women to embrace the family and still pursue life beyond it.

Crittenden and I do agree about one thing. Parenting is the key to gender equality. No matter how equal couples have been before the birth of their first child, the pressures pushing them toward inequality increase dramatically after they become parents. The time, energy, and emotion required by one baby is unparalleled by anything else couples have experienced. Although theoretically creating equality at home without sharing parenting might seem possible, practically it rarely works. The magnitude and urgency of children's needs can't be compared to mundane household chores. Painting the house, cleaning the bathroom, and vacuuming the floor can wait, but a child has to be fed every single day. A sick child needs a parent's attention immediately whether or not that parent works outside the home. The worries and concerns of a fully involved parent take hold of one's mind and life as almost nothing else can.

Why Achieving Equality Is So Hard

There is no doubt that men resist doing half of the work at home. Yet male resistance is often fueled by women's ambivalence about equality. Fears may be preventing women from enthusiastically encouraging their husbands to share fully in the joys and burdens of parenthood, but these fears are unfounded.

Imagine for a moment that we could listen to the kinds of internal monologues that women construct when they think about equal parenting.[3]

I don't want to become just like a man, focused more on career than on family. I love my job, but my child is more important.

In the equally sharing couples I interviewed, mothers were intensely involved with their children. I had to change the first question of my interview from "Would you describe your children?" to "Would you *briefly* describe your children?" The difference between the equal sharers and other couples was not that mothers cared less, but that fathers cared more. Like all mothers, the equally sharing mothers compromised their careers for the good of their children, but so did their husbands. Recall that in several of these families, *both* fathers and mothers took leaves from their jobs or cut back to part-time paid work to care for their children. Yet paternal care may not always assuage women's worries.

No one can take care of my child the way I can. Especially during infancy, my baby needs me.

Mothers who believe that no substitute will suffice for their infants' well-being can take the primary role early in their children's lives, and still establish equality later on when they return to paid work. A majority of the equally sharing mothers were *the* parent in their family who took time off from the job to care for infants. When I began my study, I believed that if parents didn't share equally from birth, they were doomed to be forever unequal because it would be impossible to undo the patterns set up in the early days of parenting. I was wrong. Parenting continually changes during children's lives.

It was also true that in families committed to equality from the start, men made just as good "mothers" as their wives. These dads carved out significant roles for themselves even in the earliest days of parenting when their wives were nursing. Equally sharing fathers got up in the middle of the night to comfort their babies, diapered them, and lovingly handed them over to their wives to be fed. They encouraged their wives to use supplemental bottles so that they too could feed their sons and daughters. The intensity of attachment between these men and their infants was as strong as the bond we usually associate with mothers. One father joked that when his son started childcare at seven months, he and his wife each visited an hour every day. They paid for five hours of childcare and stayed with their baby two out of those five hours. That same father introduced solid food to his child. He fretted over how the baby was eating, and read articles about what was important for his nutrition: "I'm not Jewish, but I'm kind of a Jewish mother." When fathers equally shared infant care, they worried about all the little details. Fathers *can* meet the needs of infants. Nevertheless, even when the needs of children are met, equality may be threatening, because of the needs of mothers.

> I want to be a real mother. Isn't being number one to your child the essence of motherhood? I don't want to give that up.

Motherhood is central to the identities of most women with children. For many, as we have seen, being number one, at least when children are small, is part of the definition of being a good mother. For some, that belief precluded equal sharing when they first became parents. One self-perceptive mother admitted that she lacked confidence in her ability to nurture the way she thought a mother should. She told me she quit her high-powered job to be home with her two daughters for four years to prove to herself that she could do it. Married to a highly nurturant man, she made room for him to be an equal parent only after she felt secure about her own special relationship with her children.

But we also saw equally sharing women who transformed the meaning of motherhood. Some completely rejected the notion that mothers should perform a unique role in the family, and shared the central spot with their husbands in all ways. Other mothers, reluctant to relinquish all of the special meanings of motherhood, retained some particular part of parenting for themselves. Equal parenting doesn't mean that men and women had identical roles or relationships with their children. To some women, motherhood meant tucking their children in every night, or staying home when they were sick, or taking the lead when discussing problems with them. Most of their husbands honored these maternal prerogatives and found other ways to contribute. The mothers' view is:

> I like being in control. The truth, which I am embarrassed to admit even to myself, is that I like things done my way with my children. I can just imagine the kind of clothes he would put on my daughter!

Yes, equal sharing does mean that women have to give up a certain kind of control. Most men are not willing to do half the work of raising children without a say in how it is to be done. And who would blame them? Yet, even though the mothers ceded control overall, a few domains remained predominantly under their influence. Funnily enough, fashion headed the list. On average in the equally sharing families, mothers did over 80 percent of the clothes-buying.

It always seemed ironic to me when the supermoms I interviewed talked about wanting to keep control. Like jugglers with too many balls in the air, women who did the lioness's share of the work at home while handling the demands of paid work had tenuous control at best. Although these supermoms usually did get to plan the meals, the children's activities, and the daily schedule of the household, their descriptions of the stress created by relentless demands sounded like anything but control. One mother working a full-time job and managing three fourths of the work at home described the burnout she felt: "When I go to sleep at night, I'm not tired. I'm really exhausted. A lot of that is mental energy, it's keeping all the balls in the air." At times, she told me, it all "unravels." No woman, no matter how organized, efficient, loving, or self-sacrificing, can work full time and care for children with minimal help from her husband and really be in control. But these supermoms are worried about dividing things equally:

> I don't know if I want to share everything equally with my husband. It would be so hard to negotiate every little decision. I know a couple who did that and they ended up getting divorced.

Equal parents don't negotiate every little decision. Sharing a profound commitment to their children, equal parents trust each other to do what is best for them. Of course they negotiate about who's going to do what, but so do all dual-earner couples today. We live in an age that lacks consensus about the roles of mothers and fathers. In one sense, couples who agree on the principle of equality have less to negotiate than other couples. They simply have to figure out how to put the 50-50 principle into practice. Equal or not, couples vary dramatically in how much time they spend negotiating and discussing decisions, but these variations reflect their personal styles more than how they divide childcare.

There is nothing to fear from equality. Equally shared parenting doesn't mean giving up the commitment to children's needs, or adopting identical roles, or endless negotiating. It does mean sharing it all instead of doing it all. There is nothing to lose from equality and a world to gain.[4]

A World to Gain

I wrote this book because all around me I saw women compromising their dreams. Growing up at a time when the barriers to women's achievement were crumbling at an incredible rate, I was shocked to see what was happening in the family. When motherhood hit, egalitarian ideals went out the window. Women were either cutting back substantially on their careers (in the absence of husbands who did so as well) or working full time, trying to manage the unmanageable dual burdens of the supermom. It seemed to me that there must be a better way.

I admit that after having a child myself, I realized I had underestimated the intense pull of a fragile new person. The day my husband and I took our newborn son home from the hospital I sat on my bed with him in my arms. All of a sudden, I realized I was in love. It is an indescribable love, comparable to nothing else in life. I never would have believed it before becoming a parent, but when my child had surgery at the age of three, I would have changed places with him in a second. Now twelve, he knows exactly how to exasperate me, yet the love I feel for him today is as intense and passionate as when I held him in my arms on that beautiful fall day over a decade ago.

The fallacy we have accepted is that this uncompromising love for our children means that we have to give up on equality. The stories of the equal sharers I interviewed show that we don't. Love doesn't diminish when it is shared. Equality is good for children. It is simply easier for two devoted parents to meet children's needs than for one to do it.[5] Ironically, by doing less childcare, mothers can do more for their children and feel better about what they are doing. "It's just giving the kids more . . . They still have their mother as much as they would otherwise, but they also have their father." Two fully involved parents means neither is "burned-out, over-involved, fried or depressed." Mothers and fathers buffer each other. "Children benefit in that they have two adults. If one happens to be sick or in a bad mood on a particular day, they have someone else to rely on." The endlessly patient, totally nurturing mother is a fiction that exists neither in the families where mothers do it all nor in those where parenting is shared. The difference is that in the equally sharing families when Mom has had it, Dad is right there to comfort, help with homework, or answer the 7,000th "Why?" that day.[6]

Equally shared parenting benefits not just children, but women and men, and their marriages.[7] Women obtain the most obvious advantages. Secure in the knowledge that their children are getting the best of both parents, equally sharing mothers have room in their lives to invest in work outside the home without suffering the excessive burdens of an unshared double day. Some even make time to exercise or see a friend. They report that their marriages benefit because "there's a whole lot less conflict if you aren't always mad at your husband about how you're being a martyr."[8] Equal sharers don't fall into the syndrome that this mother observed: "Oh God, the number of marriages that seem to have difficulties because the husband is going full steam ahead (in his career) and the wife has kind of been left behind in the diaper pail."

Equal sharing can strengthen marriage because family work, when shared, becomes a bond rather than a barrier to intimacy.[9] The stuff of everyday life with children can seem pretty mundane to less involved fathers, but it is these seeming trivialities that connect parent and child, and parents to each other. Children's questions, their fumbling attempts to tie their shoes, their willingness to try a new food after months of resistance—all these ordinary details of life with children can be intensely interesting to a parent who is seriously involved in their care. Sometimes the hardest part of inequality was the loss of intimacy because the wonder of parenting wasn't shared. As one unequal mother confided: "There's a loneliness sometimes I feel . . . There are times when I feel alone in raising them." When parents share equally, interest and pleasure in the details become part of what they share as a couple. Sharon laughed that when she and Peter spend a rare night alone together, they go out to dinner and entertain each other with stories about their daughter, Nicole.

In truth, of course there is a price for men to pay when they fully shoulder the dual demands of home and paid work. Until now, juggling has been a woman's problem. When men pick up the slack at home, however, it becomes their problem as well. The equally sharing fathers were well aware of the cost to their careers entailed by their involvement in childcare. But just as so-called career women were amazed to discover the depth of their connection to their children, men who shared responsibility for daily childcare were surprised by the depth of their relationships with their children. One father, a factory worker who alternated work shifts with his wife, described the transformation that occurred after he started taking care of his infant son:

> Until I actually stayed home with him . . . (I knew) nothing. I mean in the deep-seated sense of knowing what he's like during the day, what he wants, what different looks are . . . I don't think our relationship developed to anything substantial until I started taking care of him . . . It was just a different closeness.

Perhaps these fathers cherish their relationships with their children all the more because they know how easy it would have been to miss out. Their own fathers missed what they are experiencing, and even now they know other men are missing it: "Now watching my children develop is just amazing. It's fantastic! It's really mind boggling! I can't imagine a parent who could miss that."

Poignantly, the fathers on the sidelines sometimes understood that they were missing something that could never be regained:

> I feel sad that I don't have the opportunity to do more with them, spend more time with them. I also know how quickly this time is passing by. Ten years from now my son won't be in the house more than likely and that's a scary feeling.

Equality means some sacrifices from men, but the men I interviewed told me, each in his own way, that the rewards reaped were well worth it. The bond they forged with their wives, the special relationships with their children, and the development they saw in themselves were priceless.[10] This equally sharing father of two teenage daughters expressed what many of them felt: "A lot of things I would change in my life. (Parenting) I wouldn't consider changing. It's the best thing I've done in my life."

How Couples Become Equal Sharers

Couples create equality by the accumulation of large and small decisions and acts that make up their everyday lives as parents. Couples become equal or unequal in working out the details: who makes children's breakfasts, washes out their diaper pails, kisses their boo-boos, takes off from work when they are sick, and teaches them to ride bikes. Like all dual-earner families today, the equal sharers grapple daily with how to manage the demands of work and family. It is not easy to create equality. Sometimes it seems that everything is stacked against it—from gender discrimination in the workplace and the seeming normalcy of the inequality in friends' relationships to the serious obstacles inside the marriage. Equal sharers must squarely confront all the complex feelings that arise when trying to change the "normal" course of family life: anger, resentment, frustration, and guilt.

The stories of Mary and Paul, Jonathan and Ruth, Donna and Kevin, Jake and Susan, and Rita and Charles show that equal sharers are not an elite group of gender radicals. They are ordinary couples grappling with how to manage two jobs and kids. Remember that over half did not start out sharing equally. Couples come to equality along diverse paths. A majority of the equal sharers in my study had comparable careers; some were self-consciously feminist; and many lived in social circles that touted gender equality. But although comparable careers, egalitarian ideology, and liberal friends facilitate equal sharing, they don't ensure it. And the couples we've met show that these things are not prerequisites to equality.

Almost all previous studies that examine gender inequality in the division of labor at home search for and examine its "causes." Inequality has been blamed on pay inequities between the sexes, men's longer hours in the workforce, old-fashioned ideas about men's and women's roles, maternal instinct, traditional social circles, and deep-seated male and female identities developed through childhood socialization. If only these obstacles could be overcome, then equality would prevail. So goes the implicit reasoning in much of current research.

This reasoning is fundamentally flawed, however, because it ignores the role that couples themselves play. The so-called causes of inequality are as likely to be consequences of decisions as they are to be forces driving inequality. For example, as we saw in Chapter 7, researchers and couples themselves often invoke inequality in paid work to explain inequality at home. Fathers work more hours and earn higher incomes, they argue, so it just makes sense that fathers would do less than mothers at home. But recall that both equal and unequal couples had often begun with very equal work schedules. Equal mothers were able to pursue jobs comparable to their husbands' by resisting the gendered decisions about careers often made by their unequal counterparts. Couples who created equality at home made choices and changed in other ways that supported equality. They found new friends, rejected the belief in maternal instinct, and developed nontraditional identities, resisting the pressures of conventional motherhood and conventional male careers.

From Male Careers to Family Careers

Careers are designed for men. Privileged men in traditional relationships with wives backstage have lives that best promote conventional careers, which, when closely examined, are really two-person careers.[11] In my first teaching job, over twenty years ago, I witnessed firsthand the advantages of the backstage support entailed in a two-person career. The wives of my male colleagues brought hot lunches to the office for them, entertained for them, kept the children out of their way, and sometimes even worked for them as unpaid research assistants. When our department meetings lasted until six o'clock, I knew those men would soon be home eating a nicely prepared dinner, while the other lone single female colleague and I would be rummaging around in the supermarket trying to find something quick to fix before we settled in to prepare the next day's lecture. It didn't seem quite fair.

Conventional careers demand the willingness to put in long working hours, to relocate for good job opportunities, to shield work from personal responsibilities, and to give work priority over family. Career building at its most intense occurs during childbearing years. Is it any wonder that these requirements mean that careers are gendered?[12] Men in traditional relationships are best situated to meet these requirements; mothers in traditional relationships are least able to meet them.

Dual-earner spouses without children, although disadvantaged as compared to men with wives at home, can still hope to compete, especially given that fewer and fewer men have the luxury of a wife backing them up at home. But when children appear, the picture changes entirely. As we have seen, in many unequal families, women drop out. When parents accept the conventional definition of career but reject the model of a "two-father" family, they have few options but to create an asymmetrical division of labor. Given the gender pressures, mothers give up on careers. No matter what their title and how educated they are, their paid jobs become jobs rather than careers.

In equally sharing families something very different happens on the way to equality. Parents de-gender careers by contesting the conventional career and turning to alternatives that fit primary parenting for two. What does it mean to de-gender career? It means limiting work hours, passing up opportunities, altering the career clock, and allowing family obligations to intrude on work, while still maintaining a commitment to work as a significant part of identity. When both husbands and wives made symmetrical adjustments, they avoided the spiral in which only the father ends up with a real career, but those adjustments meant that neither had a conventional male career. Equal sharers created family careers, one couple at a time with choices, compromises, and costs, some aided by the luxury of high-powered, well-paid work with plenty of room to cut back. Maybe, just maybe, by recreating themselves as professionals, the equal sharers can teach us a different model of family and professional life. Rather than pulling us back and forth, family and profession could work together like the two oars of a rowboat, each necessary to row us in the right direction.

From Motherhood and Fatherhood to Parenthood

De-gendering parenthood is just as important as transforming career.[13] Although, as we have seen, some of the equally sharing parents resist completely transforming motherhood and fatherhood to parenthood, others are doing exactly that. We can see de-gendered parenting in the relative amount of time equally sharing mothers and fathers spend with children, the nature of the tasks they take on, the behavior and beliefs they adopt about caring for infants, and their construction of primary parenting.

Equally sharing fathers spent virtually the same amount of time alone with their children as their wives did. But these fathers are not just "doing time" with their children or just playing with them; they are taking care of children.[14] The way equally sharing parents divide up specific tasks is telling. Even when faced with tasks we might think of as especially maternal—comforting, changing diapers, toilet-training, getting up at night with children, responding to their requests for attention, and taking care of them when they are sick—the equally sharing fathers are doing about half of the childcare.

Nevertheless, some of the tasks of parenting, like buying clothes and arranging play dates, were done mostly by mothers.[15] Moreover, in a majority of the equally sharing families, mothers managed more than fathers did. They were more likely than their husbands to keep track of the calendar: to make sure children had permission slips, got their hair cut, and had physical exams when they needed them for camp. One

equally sharing mother passed on a metaphor she had heard describing
this difference between men and women:

> A man's brain looks like one computer screen . . . whatever is on
> the screen is what they're looking at. A woman's brain is more like
> a security guard room. You walk in and there's like twelve screens
> and they're all going.

But we should not overstate the difference between fathers and
mothers in the equally sharing families. Although the mothers claimed
more than half the management, they were not faced with the "nagging" required of the unequal mothers.[16] And in equal families in which
mothers managed more, fathers often compensated in other ways.
Moreover, in about 20 percent of the equal families fathers did do half
of the management. Irene, for example, was pleasantly surprised that
her preparenthood fears about being responsible for everything were
unfounded:

> That was what really petrified me. I thought I was going to be in
> charge of all these details . . . I didn't think he'd be responsible
> about all of the details that women tend to keep in their heads
> about birthday parties and what to wear, what to buy . . . He keeps
> track of all these things . . . I don't feel as though I'm the only one
> thinking about whether she has sunscreen or she doesn't have sun-
> screen . . . He's really pretty good about that.

By changing what they do as parents, equal sharers help us change
our beliefs about parenting. For example, men's competence and involvement in early infant care debunks the notion that women have a
special superior instinctive ability for infant care. Although only mothers can breastfeed, even that obvious biological difference doesn't preclude the de-gendering of the rest of infant care. Men can nurture even
the smallest infants.

Equal sharers have gone a long way toward inventing a new kind of
genderless parenting. They not only do parenting differently, they create new meanings for it. As Grace put it: "People who have more traditional lifestyles (ask), 'Does he help you?' He never helps me, that
would be a ridiculous definition of it, because he takes the responsibility; he doesn't help me."

But perhaps the thorniest issue in inventing truly genderless parenting is how we can reconstruct the meaning of motherhood. I wonder

how most mothers would feel if their identity was simply expressed by the word "parent" instead of "mother." My guess is that many of us would resist because of the fear of losing our exclusive relationship with our children. The word "mother" proclaims that we are indisputably indispensable. One introspective mother answered candidly when I asked about the disadvantages of equality:

> The only disadvantage . . . someplace deep inside me, (I feel) it wouldn't be bad for me to be the key person that my kids always rely on . . . that would help me then answer a question like the kind of mother you are, to say, "Well, I know I'm always here for my kids" . . . So, it might be a disadvantage that I'm sort of not needed as much. Sometimes I wish I could be needed that much . . . I don't necessarily think that that would be a better life for me or my kids or for the family.

Despite admitting to these feelings of loss, that mother supported and encouraged her husband to share all aspects of parenting. In other families, however, mothers sometimes subtly tried to retain the central place in children's lives by taking over the more intimate moments with children, despite sharing the work and time and even emotional investment in parenting. In most families, in the face of these prerogatives, fathers deferred.

Other mothers, however, did not assert these prerogatives. They were relieved to shed the exclusive maternal tie with children. In fact, they disputed the prevailing idea that a primary role with children has to be exclusive. As this mother said:

> I think a child can have two number ones, I really do. The whole thing about primary caretaker—all the developmental theories always refer to the mother or some of the newer books will say, "the primary caretaker," but it's always one. I just don't think that. I think a child can have two primary caretakers . . . I am not afraid of losing my role.

When I asked Barry if he thought his children had two mothers or two fathers, he was surprised by his own answer: "Boy, that's a great question and as much as an affront to my masculinity as this is going to be, I think it's more like two mothers. Yeah, I really do." It was a trick question. Like the children of many of the equal sharers, his children had neither two mothers nor two fathers. They had two parents.

A Vision of the Future

Employers and government need to change their policies to help us create a child-friendly equality. I am hopeful that when men and women routinely share their children's care, our combined voices will be so loud that they will finally be heard. Imagine our country with generous family-friendly policies in every company that people were actually encouraged to use.[17] Imagine, too, a childcare system in which every family had access to high-quality daycare. And let's not forget that if pro-family policies are to be friendly to all families, they have to take economics into account; we can't close our eyes to the inequities of gender and class. Women have to make as much money as men. Unpaid leave for parenting doesn't work for families who need two incomes to survive.[18]

When I look ahead toward my son's future, I am hopeful that he will live in a world where his prodigious talents can be put to good use. Whatever his chosen work—mathematician or lawyer, jewelry store owner or game inventor—no doubt he will have the opportunity to achieve and find fulfillment in work. I want more for him. I want him to live in a world where his loving, nurturing self has as much room to flourish as his logical, productive, intellectual self, a world in which fathers routinely nurture their children as much as mothers.

If I had a daughter, I would want every door open to her too. Composing a symphony, curing cancer, writing a novel, organizing a union, or becoming President of the United States, should be as possible for her as it is for the son I do have. These possibilities should exist without her having to give up the opportunity women have now for intimate, involved, nurturing relationships with children.

I was so impressed with the mother who taught her daughter that she was brilliant, strong, and beautiful, that she didn't have to choose. Wouldn't it be a better world if our children didn't feel the pressure to choose between parenting and working, achieving and nurturing, loving and succeeding? We can make that world, not just for our children, but for ourselves; not in the future, but right now. The equal sharers' struggles and successes offer renewed hope that equality is not a utopian ideal. Equality works. I began my research by asking, "Why not equality?" I end it with the same question, "Why not?"

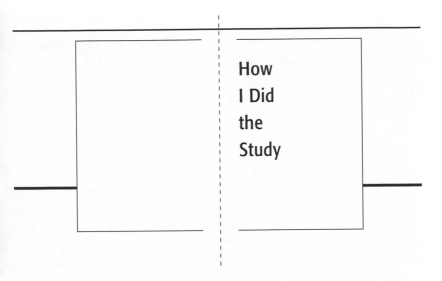

How
I Did
the
Study

I conducted the equally shared parenting study sponsored by the National Science Foundation in three phases: initial recruitment and telephone interviews of participants; selection of participants to be interviewed in depth and the face-to-face interviews; and refinement of the final sample and analysis of the audiotaped transcripts.

Recruitment and Telephone Interviews

Participants

Potential participants were recruited through letters soliciting volunteers for a study of dual-earner couples sent to daycare centers and schools in New England. My research assistants and I also used word of mouth to recruit, and a snowball sampling procedure in which couples who had volunteered were asked to recommend other couples who might be interested in participating. Finally, we recruited additional couples through random sampling, using a local telephone directory. In all, 429 couples were recruited to participate in the first phase of the study: the telephone interview. To be eligible, both husband and wife had to agree to participate (couples did not have to be legally married to participate, and one couple was not). Both had to speak English and work at least 20 hours a week for pay. They were also required to have at least one child under 18 living at home (including adopted children and/or step-children).[1]

The couples were overwhelmingly white (96 percent).[2] Thirty-six percent were Roman Catholic, 27 percent Protestant, 14 percent Jewish, and 23 percent claimed either no religion or another denomination. They had been married or living together from 1 to 36 years (M = 10.8). The mean number of children was 2. Children's ages ranged from 1 month old to 34 years old (this figure includes children no longer living at home), the youngest child averaging 5 and the oldest 8. The husbands' ages ranged from 25 to 60 (M = 38.5) and the wives' ages ranged from 23 to 58 (M = 36.2).

At this stage of the research we had no information about husbands' or wives' incomes, but their educational levels and occupational statuses give some indication of their socioeconomic status. Despite a wide range of participants, the sample overrepresents upper-middle-class, well-educated participants. Approximately half of both husbands and wives had received graduate degrees and another quarter had graduated from college. Only 13 percent of the men and 10 percent of the women had not earned more than a high school degree. Occupational prestige ratings for participants ranged from 1 (e.g., bellhop) to 9 (e.g., physician) on the Hollingshead scale.[3] The median occupational prestige rating for both husbands and wives was 7 (e.g., elementary school teacher, reporter, computer programmer).

Telephone Interviews

Several female research assistants and I conducted the interviews. We interviewed husbands and wives separately (beyond earshot of each other) by phone for 15 minutes each. First, we asked participants to estimate the overall percentage of childcare they and their spouses contribute, considering all the parenting the mother and father do over the course of a typical week. Then we asked them to estimate the number of their children's waking hours that each spouse spent alone with them, that the spouse's partner spent alone with them, that both spouses spent together with children, and that others spent caring for them. Next, we asked them to estimate their percentage contribution and their spouses' percentage contribution to each of 32 childcare tasks: feeding, comforting, bathing, dressing, changing diapers, toilet-training, supervising personal hygiene, supervising morning routine, picking up after, playing, reading, helping to learn, helping with problems, setting limits, disciplining, putting to bed, getting up at night, taking to the doctor or dentist, providing sick care, taking on outings, taking to birthday parties, taking to lessons, going to teacher conferences, buying clothes, supervising in social situations, supervising religious instruction, making arrangements with other parents to organize social life, planning activities, making arrangements for childcare, worrying, making decisions, and responding to requests or need for attention. Finally, we asked parents about their demographic characteristics, including age, occupation, number of hours worked per week, highest level of education achieved, religion, race, and number of years married.

Selection and Face-to-Face Interviews

Selection

The 150 couples I interviewed face to face were selected from the couples who were interviewed by phone. Thirty couples were interviewed from each of five groups: equal sharers; potential equal sharers; 60-40 couples; 75-25 couples; and alternating-shift couples.

The key question in the phone interview, which was used to select equal sharers, 60-40 couples, and 75-25 couples, was: "Considering everything that goes into parenting in a typical week, what percentage do you do and what percentage does your spouse do?" To be selected as an equally sharing couple, husbands and wives had to agree that each contributed 50 percent. This broad definition allowed for a diversity among the equal sharers. For example, in some families mothers spent more time interacting with children while fathers did more of the chores of parenting, or vice versa. Common sense dictates that these parents are no less equal than parents who precisely divide up each aspect of parenting.

Relying on self-reports does pose a thorny methodological dilemma. How do we know that these reports are accurate? Although we can't know for sure, here's what I did to maximize the probability of selecting equal sharers who are really equal. For a start, both parents had to agree that parenting was equally shared. However, we know that agreement about equality may not be enough. Couples develop shared mythologies about the division of labor at home, and may think that they are sharing the work at home even when they are not. In fact, we did find that when we asked couples about the overall division of labor, a surprisingly large number initially reported a 50-50 division. But their subsequent reports about the division of labor concerning concrete childcare tasks belied their claim of equality. The evidence of who is diapering the baby is visible and direct, and therefore less prone to distortion. Many participants who had initially reported an equal overall division revised their estimates after reporting and reflecting on the division of labor on the 32 childcare tasks, if those were clearly divided unequally. In addition, if they didn't spontaneously reconsider their overall childcare estimate when their estimates on the specific tasks contradicted it, we asked them about the discrepancy. In virtually all of those cases, parents then revised their original estimates. Their initial "50-50" answer often simply reflected their belief that the division between them was fair. We persuaded them, however, to make a distinction between equality and fairness.

I also selected couples for the interview whom I saw as potential equal sharers. In these couples at least one spouse reported that the husband was doing more than half of the childcare. Because men's contributions are sometimes exaggerated, I thought it would be wise to include this group, some of whom might turn out to be equal sharers.

I then chose two groups of unequal couples to interview whose agreed-upon estimates hovered around a division of either 75-25 or 60-40, the most commonly mentioned unequal divisions. I do not assume that these numbers are precise measures of the percentages of childcare undertaken by wives and husbands in these households, but I do think that 60-40 reflects relatively small inequalities between mothers and fathers, and 75-25 reflects relatively large ones.

Finally, the last group selected for the face-to-face interviews consisted of couples who were alternating work shifts. Husbands took care of children while their wives worked and vice versa. This group was included because it offered a window on blue-collar couples in which husbands did an unusually large amount of childcare. I included all couples who reported alternating shifts, regardless of their percentage of childcare estimates or whether they agreed on those estimates, as long as each spouse cared for the children by himself or herself at least 15 hours per week.

The 172 couples identified from the telephone interview who met the criteria for one of these five groups were asked if they would agree to be interviewed face to face. One hundred and fifty-eight (91 percent) agreed in principle. Interviews were actually scheduled and completed individually with members of 151 couples (87 percent). Because of scheduling problems, only one person in two of the couples was interviewed.

Face-to-Face Interviews

I interviewed all 300 participants myself. Each was interviewed at a place of her or his choice: the participant's or my home or place of work, most at their own homes. The interviews lasted from one to four hours, but most took approximately two hours. I always interviewed husband and wife separately. Some were interviewed in the same evening; others were interviewed at two different times. All interviews were audiotaped, although there were a few taping failures before I switched to a high-quality Marantz tape recorder.

Before the interview began, I asked participants to fill out three forms: two self-generated lists of characteristics describing themselves as parents and people; the Beere-King Sex Role Egalitarianism Scale; and the Spanier Dyadic Adjustment Scale.[4] The interview consisted of 34 structured and unstructured questions:

1. Briefly describe your children.
2. Do you think being a parent has changed you as a person? How?
3. Do you think being a parent has changed your spouse? How?
4. Can you describe how you and your spouse are dividing and sharing parenting responsibilities? (Take me through a typical day.)
5. Overall, what percentage of the parenting and childcare are you doing and what percentage is your spouse doing?
6. I am going to describe four different aspects of parenting: time, work, emotional parenting, and management. For each one, estimate the percentage that you and your spouse are each doing. Time refers to the percentage of parental time you spend with your children. Work entails the chores of being a parent (e.g., making lunches, diapering, picking up after them). Emotional parenting means being tuned in to children's emotional needs. Management is not necessarily doing the work, but keeping track and making sure that everything gets done.
7. On a scale of 1 to 10, how satisfied are you with the current division of responsibilities? If you could change anything about it, what would it be?
8. Can you tell me the history of the ways you have done things?
9. Do you expect the division of responsibilities to change in the future?
10. In what ways are you and your spouse similar as parents?

11. How are you different?

12. Do you think there are differences between your relationship with your children and your partner's relationship with your children? How would you describe those differences? Do you think that any of your children are closer to one of you than the other?

13. Most couples at one time or another experience some conflicts over parenting. On a scale of 1 to 10, how much conflict do you experience over parenting, if 1 indicates no conflict at all and 10 indicates a lot of conflict.

14. What would you be most likely to have a conflict about?

15. In a typical week, would you have more, less, or about the same amount of leisure time (e.g., reading, exercising, watching TV, going out with friends) as your spouse?

16. How many hours do you sleep on a typical night?

17. Where do you work and what do you do?

18. How many hours per week do you work?

19. What is your annual salary?

20. How do you feel about your job? How much do you like it? How involved are you? How successful do you feel?

21. How does your work life affect your family life and your family life affect your work life?

22. How does your spouse's job affect your family life?

23. What are your supplemental childcare arrangements? How satisfied are you with these arrangements?

24. Where or from whom have you learned the most about being a parent?

25. Can you describe the family you grew up in? What kind of roles did your parents take in the family?

26. How have your parents reacted to the two of you as parents? How did your spouse's parents respond?

27. Compared to other fathers with children around the same age as yours, do you / does your spouse take more, less, or about the same amount of responsibility for childcare?

28. Do you know any families in which the father is as involved in childcare as the mother?

29. Do you ever get criticism from any source about the way you are doing things? Praise? From whom are you likely to receive those messages?

30. How do you feel about the kind of mother/father you are and the kind of relationship you have with your children?
31. How do you feel about the kind of mother/father your spouse is and the kind of relationship she or he has with your children?
32. Does anything different go into what makes a good mother versus a good father?
33. There has been a lot of research recently about what is going on in the American family. There have been a lot of changes over the last 20 years. Most women now work outside the home, but are still responsible for most of the parenting and childcare. (The question was then varied depending on the group of the participant.)

> 75-25: In your family, the mother is the primary parent. What is the most important reason that childcare is divided that way?
>
> 60-40: You/your husband does more than the average father. How would you explain that? The flip side of the question is why does the mother still do more?
>
> Equal sharers, potential equal sharers, and alternating-shift couples: Why is your family different?
>
> Only alternating shifters: Why do you alternate work shifts?

34. Is there anything I have left out or that you want to add?

I always asked the questions in the same order, but each interview was different because I engaged each participant in conversation about his or her answers. I asked for elaboration about points that were unclear, questioned interviewees about the implications of what they told me, and explored internal contradictions in their stories. These probes helped me get a richer understanding of their answers.

Refinement of the Sample and Qualitative Analysis

Reclassification
I read all 300 transcribed interviews to get an initial sense of the themes, issues, and explanations that participants had expressed. (The interview for each couple contained about 50 pages of single-spaced text.) My next step was to reclassify participants into four stringently defined groups that could and would be used for all statistical analyses:

50-50, 60-40, 75-25, and alternating shift. We reclassified couples, taking into account additional information obtained in the face-to-face interviews, including changes in reports of the division of labor that had occurred since the telephone interview.[5] For example, if both husband and wife had reported a 50-50 split during the telephone interview, but a 60-40 division favoring the woman during the face-to-face interview, they were no longer classified as equal sharers (nor were they classified as 60-40 couples). Because their reports varied, they did not meet the criteria for either group and were dropped from subsequent statistical analyses, as were other couples whose reports varied. However, six couples who had been classified as potential equal sharers initially, because of the possibility that they exaggerated men's contributions, were reclassified as equal sharers because both said they divided childcare 50-50 in the face-to-face interview. If we consider the four reports of the division of labor (i.e., husbands' and wives' reports during each interview), the average estimate of husbands' contributions among the group finally classified as equal sharers never dropped below 47 percent and never exceeded 55 percent.[6]

Couples were dropped from the 60-40 and 75-25 groups if they no longer met the criteria for the study (e.g., a spouse was unemployed), or if their reports of the division of labor in the face-to-face interview diverged significantly from their initial reports.[7] Couples were eliminated from the alternating-shift group if they no longer met the original criteria for the study (e.g., the father was no longer caring for children on his own 15 hours per week). Six couples were also excluded from this group because although they met the original criteria, the husband did not have a blue-collar job. We eliminated these middle-class couples because I was specifically interested in studying alternating shifters to illuminate the gender dynamics of a nontraditional division of labor among working-class parents.

Demographic Profile
The reclassified sample included 88 couples: 26 equal sharers, 18 60-40 couples, 21 75-25 couples, and 23 alternating shifters. The 88 couples were predominantly white (97 percent of the women and 96 percent of the men). The couples had been married (or cohabiting in the case of the unmarried couple) an average of 11 years (with a range of 1 to 25). Couples had an average of two children, whose ages ranged from 1 month to 14 years. The mean ages of the oldest and youngest children

were 9 and 4, respectively. Thirty-five percent of the participants were Roman Catholic, 20 percent Protestant, and 20 percent Jewish; 5 percent practiced another religion, and 20 percent did not endorse any religion. The husbands' ages ranged from 25 to 52, with an average of 38.4. The wives' ages ranged from 25 to 49, with an average of 35.9.

The majority of couples were upper middle class with a skew toward high education and high occupational prestige. The participants' annual personal incomes varied between $5,000 and $100,000. The median income for husbands was $36,960, for wives $25,000. Half of the women and men possessed graduate degrees, and an additional 19 percent had graduated from college. Occupational prestige ratings ranged from 1 to 9; the median rating for both men and women was 7.

Demographic Comparisons across Groups
The four paternal participation groups did not differ statistically in ethnicity, religion, number of years married, number of children, or ages of the oldest and youngest child.[8] But there were significant differences for both women and men in occupational prestige, education, and age. There were also significant differences across paternal participation groups of husbands', wives', and family incomes. In general, these differences are attributable to differences between the working-class alternating-shift participants and their predominantly middle-class counterparts in the other three groups. For example, 83 percent of the alternating-shift husbands and 74 percent of the alternating-shift wives did not graduate from college, compared to 14 percent of the wives and 14 percent of the husbands in the other groups. The mean occupational prestige rating for the alternating-shift wives was 5, compared to 7.67 for the other women; that rating was 4 for the alternating-shift husbands, compared to 8 for the other men. On average, alternating-shift men and women were younger (33 and 31 years old, respectively) than men (40) and women (37) in the other groups.[9]

The median income of the alternating-shift men was lower ($28,226) than the median incomes of the men in the 75-25 ($46,750), 60-40 ($45,500), and equally sharing ($42,000) groups. Alternating-shift wives earned less ($16,640) than 75-25 ($26,500), 60-40 ($25,000), and equally sharing ($29,000) wives ($p < .05$). Finally, of course, the median family income of alternating-shift couples was lower ($43,654) than the median family incomes of couples in the 75-25 ($65,620), 60-40 ($73,200), and equally sharing ($75,000) groups.

In contrast, when the alternating shifters were excluded, and the remaining three paternal participation groups were compared to each other, there were no significant differences in wives' ages, husbands' ages, or occupational prestige levels for either husbands or wives. Nor were there statistically significant differences across the three groups in husbands' and wives' educations, or in their combined and separate incomes. But there was a marginal difference across groups in the difference between husbands' and wives' incomes. Although in all three groups (in fact, in all four groups) husbands made more money on average than their wives, equal sharers were the only group in which that difference was not statistically reliable. In the 75-25 and 60-40 couples, husbands earned about $19,000 more than their wives. In the alternating-shift couples husbands earned about $11,000 more per year. But in the 50-50 couples, on average, husbands outearned their wives by only $6,000.

Qualitative Analysis

I read and reread the transcribed transcripts many times to identify themes and patterns in them. My analytic-inductive approach borrowed from methods described by a number of qualitative researchers.[10] Although I had some initial working hypotheses and questions, informed by prevailing theories of the division of domestic labor, I soon discarded most of them in favor of conceptualizations that seemed better grounded in the data. For example, it seemed to make more sense to focus on the question of how people became equal sharers than on who became equal sharers.

For the most part, I personally developed the categories for analysis, and then I often (although not always) had student research assistants code and count instances of the behavior in question as a check on my perceptions, particularly when I was making comparisons across groups. I used Ethnograph, a computer-assisted qualitative analysis program, to sort the information so that it would be easier to analyze.[11]

Although some parts of the data were quantified (particularly those that involved comparisons between groups), much was not. Qualitative analysis, in my view, is as much art as science, and relies heavily on the insights and intuition of the researcher. For better or worse, I've used my own skills of observation and interpretation to make sense of what couples told me, and to uncover the complex dynamics of creating an equal or unequal family.

Ethical Issues

Two ethical issues are at odds in a study like this one. The paramount ethical concern is to protect the privacy and confidentiality of the participants.[12] I have done that by disguising identifying details in the stories and information presented. In addition to using pseudonyms in all cases, I changed jobs when it was appropriate to do so, and in some cases I changed the ages and/or genders of children. Occasionally, I transposed details from one story to another. Very rarely I changed a word in a direct quotation to protect the participant's identity, but for all intents and purposes, the quotations are unaltered.

The countervailing ethical issue is maintaining scientific truth. My goal was to disguise the details without misrepresenting the data. To do so, I made every effort to replace the identifying details with comparable ones. Obviously, when disguising a person's job, I replaced it with one of comparable status, and in addition I tried to find alternatives that were similar on dimensions of relevance to the analysis. Likewise, the genders or ages of children were not changed if they were relevant to the claim at hand. Throughout the process of disguising details I have consulted with many other people to verify the comparability of the details that were replaced.

Notes

1. Why Not Equality?

1. The names of all family members discussed in the book are pseudonyms, and other identifying details have been disguised. Arlie Hochschild (1989) popularized the term "second shift" to denote the hours of household labor required of many women after they complete a full shift of paid work. Numerous studies have found that employed women do significantly more household labor (housework and/or childcare) than their husbands. See, for example: Almeida, Maggs, & Galambos, 1993; Anderson, Golden, Umesh, & Weeks, 1992; Berardo, Shehan, & Leslie, 1987; Barnett & Baruch, 1987; Berk, 1985; Biernat & Wortman, 1991; Blair & Johnson, 1992; Deutsch, Lussier, & Servis, 1993; Geerken & Gove, 1983; Gunter & Gunter, 1990, 1991; Hersch & Stratton, 1994; Hiller & Philliber, 1986; Jones & Heermann, 1992; Kamo, 1988; Kim, Kim, & Hurh, 1979; Larson, Richards, & Perry-Jenkins, 1994; Meissner, Humphreys, Meis, & Scheu, 1975; Rexroat & Shehan, 1987; and Shelton, 1990, 1992.

2. Beth and Steve's negotiations over who should do what are unusual because they both feel responsible. Steve doesn't help Beth with "her" childcare responsibilities; he equally shares them. This distinction between role enactment and role responsibility is critical (Perry-Jenkins, 1988).

In separate studies, both Gerson (1993) and Coltrane (1989, 1996) found that "involved" fathers were often involved only as "helpers." According to Coltrane (1989), "Helper husbands often waited to be told what to do, when to do it, and how it should be done" (p. 480). The problem with helper husbands is that they may undertake the parts of their wives' roles that are the most appealing and leave the dirty work to the wives. Even when willing to do any type of work, helper husbands add to their wives' burdens the mental work of keeping track of what needs to be done, managing, and delegating. Small wonder that three fourths of the wives of helper husbands in Coltrane's study complained about the need to remind their husbands to get something done.

Like helper husbands who don't feel responsible for childcare, wives can work for pay without feeling responsible for providing. As Wilkie (1993) showed, by the 1980s people in the United States overwhelmingly approved of married women's working outside the home even when it was not financially necessary, but that approval did not extend to women's assuming *responsibility* for the provider role. Potuchek's (1992, 1997) analyses of the variations in meanings attached to women's paid work shows that there is no simple equation between earning income and assuming a provider role. Even when women earn more than their husbands do, they may not feel responsible for supporting the family.

3. Quotations are reported verbatim except that I occasionally deleted a word like "and" to increase clarity or changed a word to protect the participant's confidentiality. Sometimes I added parenthetical statements to clarify the speaker's meaning.

4. A random sample of fifty-five dual-earner families, contacted by phone by my students, reported that on average mothers did almost three fourths of the care of sick children.

5. In *Kidding Ourselves* (1995), Rhonda Mahony argues that negotiation is part and parcel of the day-to-day life of every family. Beth and Steve differ from most of the unequal couples described by Mahony, however, because Beth negotiates with Steve from a position of equal strength.

6. An electronic search of Psychological Abstracts and Sociological Abstracts from 1970 to 1995 identified 484 nonoverlapping references under the topics gender and domestic labor, gender and childcare, gender and roles at home, and gender and housework.

7. Young and Willmott (1973) represent the view that marriage would develop into an egalitarian institution. They described the predominant family type of the mid-twentieth century as the "symmetrical family," in which women work in paid labor, "helping" their husbands with breadwinning, while their husbands "help" with domestic chores. By the twenty-first century, however, Young and Willmott fully expected that the symmetrical family would give way to an egalitarian family in which men and women are equal with respect to their responsibilities for breadwinning and domestic labor.

For a contrasting view, see Blood and Wolfe (1960). Although they argued that the American family was becoming more egalitarian, their evidence was based on the increase in shared responsibility for decision-making between husbands and wives. With respect to domestic labor, however, they expected that husbands would "help" with traditionally female chores at home when their wives were working for pay, but they did not anticipate a breakdown of gender roles. To them, the separation of roles implied not inequality, but an appropriate response to the differing resources of men and women. They failed to address how this "equitable" arrangement could remain equitable when women worked as much as their husbands did in paid labor.

8. See, for example, Davis & Sanik, 1991; Douthitt, 1989; Geerken & Gove, 1983; and Larson, Richards, & Perry-Jenkins, 1994. Some researchers have disputed the claim that men don't increase their contributions at home when women

are employed (e.g., Bird, Bird, & Scruggs, 1984; Coverman, 1985; Davis, 1982; Hiller & Philliber, 1986; Maret & Finlay, 1984; Pleck, 1979). But the studies they invoke used relatively crude measures of men's participation, such as global time-use measures or checklists of whether specific tasks were shared at all or done exclusively by the wife.

One study that used more reliable measures, however, did show an effect for wives' employment on men's contributions to domestic labor. In that study, which examined forty predominantly working-class dual-earner couples, fathers whose wives were employed did more solo child care than fathers whose wives were full-time homemakers. Note that these were blue-collar families who might not have been able to afford paid childcare (Crouter, Perry-Jenkins, Huston, & McHale, 1987).

Generally though, with the exception of men who care for their children when their wives are out working for pay, the changes men make when their wives are employed, if any at all, are small ones. Coverman (1985) estimated, for example, that husbands spend a total of three more hours per week on housework and childcare when their wives are employed. Pleck's (1979) and Davis's (1982) estimates were slightly higher, but still very low, less than five hours per week. Finally, even authors who claim that men increase their work at home in response to their wives' employment admit that wives are still doing far more at home than their husbands. See Spitze (1986b), for example, whose data suggest that even when women work *full time* outside the home they are responsible for 68–70 percent of all household tasks.

9. See, for example, Beckman & Houser, 1979; Jones & Heermann, 1992; Piotrkowski & Repetti, 1984; and Ross, 1987. All use only proportional measures of husbands' and wives' contributions to household labor.

10. See, for example, Barnett & Baruch, 1987; Berardo et al., 1987; Meissner et al., 1975; and Shelton, 1990.

11. See, for example, Antill & Cotton, 1988; Barnett & Baruch, 1987; Bird, Bird, & Scruggs, 1984; Brayfield, 1992; Calasanti & Bailey, 1991; Charles & Hopflinger, 1992; Coltrane & Ishii-Kuntz, 1992; Farkas, 1976; Haas, 1993; Hersch & Stratton, 1994; Ishii-Kuntz & Coltrane, 1992a; Izraeli, 1994; Kamo, 1988; Maret & Finlay, 1984; Model, 1981; Perrucci, Potter, & Rhoads, 1978; Ross, 1987. For studies that failed to find evidence of the relative income effect, see Aytac, 1990; Coverman, 1985; Sanchez, 1993; and Shamir, 1986.

12. See, for example, Almeida, Maggs, & Galambos, 1993; Barnett & Baruch, 1987; Baruch & Barnett, 1981; Beckman & Houser, 1979; Biernat & Wortman, 1991; Brayfield, 1992; Charles & Hopflinger, 1992; Coltrane & Ishii-Kuntz, 1992; Coverman, 1985; Deutsch, Lussier, & Servis, 1993; Haas, 1993; Peterson & Gerson, 1992; Wright, Shire, Hwang, Dolan, & Baxter, 1992. For studies that failed to find that wives' work hours influenced husbands' participation in domestic labor, see Antill & Cotton, 1988; Berheide, 1984; Fox & Nickols, 1983; Haas, 1981, 1982b; Meissner, Humphreys, Meis, & Scheu, 1975; and Perrucci, Potter, & Rhoads, 1978.

13. See Antill & Cotton, 1988; Barnett & Baruch, 1987; Baruch & Barnett, 1981; Beckman & Houser, 1979; Bird, Bird, & Scruggs, 1984; Brayfield, 1992; Charles & Hopflinger, 1992; Coltrane & Ishii-Kuntz, 1992; Haas, 1993; Hiller & Philliber, 1986; Ishii-Kuntz & Coltrane, 1992a; Kamo, 1988; Levant, Slattery, &

Loiselle, 1987; Model, 1981; Perrucci, Potter, & Rhoads, 1978; Perry-Jenkins & Crouter, 1990; Radin & Harold-Goldsmith, 1989; Ross, 1987; Seccombe, 1986; Wright, Shire, Hwang, Dolan, & Baxter, 1992; and Yao, 1987. Several studies did not confirm the influence of liberal gender-role ideology on the division of domestic labor, including Baxter, 1988; Coverman, 1985; Huber & Spitze, 1981; Maret & Finlay, 1984; and McHale & Huston, 1984.

14. A highly unequal division of labor exists even in homes of women who have high-status careers (Biernat and Wortman, 1991). One study showed that mothers who were either college professors or businesswomen still ended up doing much more than half of the childcare, despite their liberal sex-role ideologies and high-status careers. Likewise, in a comprehensive study of a random sample of couples from both the United States and Sweden, Calasanti and Bailey (1991) statistically controlled the effects of relative income, sex-role ideology, and paid work hours, and showed the dramatic effects of gender above and beyond any of those variables. Women in both countries do more work at home even when they believe in gender equality and their incomes and work hours match their husbands'.

15. Hochschild, 1989. There is, however, no simple equation between women's happiness or marital satisfaction and their husbands' involvement in domestic labor. In fact, there are surprisingly few studies that document unqualified positive effects of men's contributions. For contradictory findings, see Baruch & Barnett, 1986; Biernat & Wortman, 1991; Nicola & Hawkes, 1985; Steil & Turetsky, 1987a, 1987b; and Suitor, 1991. If women's husbands do get involved in domestic labor, it may be at the cost of increased marital conflict or at the cost of compromising their wives' cherished identities as women.

Women who believe their situation is unfair, regardless of the actual division of labor, are the most unhappy (McDermid, Huston, & McHale, 1990; McHale & Crouter, 1992; Ross, Mirowsky, & Huber, 1983). However, even when women are doing a lot more than their husbands, they do not always perceive the situation as unfair.

The perception of inequity is tied to what women see as their legitimate role. Perry-Jenkins, Seery, and Crouter (1992) examined reactions to husbands' domestic help among women who could be characterized as co-providers (employed and believed they held equal responsibility with their husbands for financial support of the family), ambivalent providers (employed, but would rather be home), secondary co-providers (employed, but viewed husbands' jobs as primary), or housewives. The co-providers, whose husbands were doing twice as much household labor as the husbands of secondary providers, were less depressed and harried than other women, which suggests that men's contributions can have strong effects on women's happiness. Yet the ambivalent providers weren't nearly as happy, despite having husbands who did just as much at home. It is not simply the work done but the meaning attached to it that makes a difference. Presumably, the co-providers, who had a more egalitarian view of the family, could accept and benefit from their husbands' nontraditional role at home much as they constructed a new role for themselves outside the home, whereas the ambivalent providers, who clung to a more traditional identity despite working outside the home, needed their husbands' help, but could not enjoy it because it encroached on their domain.

Although ambivalent providers are in a no-win bind, they probably represent a shrinking group of women. A recent study of couples at Arizona State University showed less ambivalence on the part of wives. The more time their husbands spent on childcare and housework in those families, the more satisfied they were (Benin & Agostinelli, 1988).

16. There have been a few previous studies of equally sharing parents (DeFrain, 1979; Ehrensaft, 1987; Fish, New, & Van Cleave, 1992; Haas, 1982a; Risman & Johnson-Sumerford, 1998). Research on families with highly participant fathers, which has usually included some equal sharers, has been conducted in the United States (Carlson, 1981, 1984; Coltrane, 1996; Geiger, 1996; Radin, 1981, 1982; Radin & Goldsmith, 1985), Israel (Radin & Sagi, 1982; Sagi, 1982), and in Australia (Russell, 1982a, 1982b, 1989).

17. It is difficult to determine how many equal sharers there are. Hochschild (1989) estimated that approximately 20 percent of the couples she interviewed truly shared the "second shift." Russell (1982a) asserted that only 1–2 percent of families he studied in Australia could be classified as truly sharing caregiving. In a study of fifty-three high-status professional couples in the United States, Poloma and Garland (1971) reported that only one couple could be considered truly egalitarian. However, Rachlin (1987), who used a much less stringent measure of equality, classified 34 percent of the seventy dual-career couples as egalitarian. Inconsistencies in estimates of equal sharers occur even in random samples, because the definition of equal sharing varies, as do the criteria for including participants. For example, in some studies the couples included are not all parents (e.g., Ross, 1987). In others, housework but not childcare is considered in classifying a couple as egalitarian (e.g., Benin & Agostinelli, 1988). Despite the difficulty of pinpointing the precise percentage of couples who equally share childcare, most researchers would agree they are still a small minority.

18. The inequality between mothers' and fathers' responsibility for childcare has been demonstrated in surveys in Australia (Baxter, 1988; McAllister, 1990), the Netherlands (Tavecchio, van IJeendoorn, Goossens, & Vergeer, 1984), Sweden (Frankenhaeuser, Lundberg, & Mardberg, 1990; Wright, Shire, Hwang, Dolan, & Baxter, 1992), Switzerland (Charles & Hopflinger, 1992), and Taiwan (Yao, 1987). Cross-cultural observations confirm that in Brazil, Iceland, India, Ireland, Israel, Japan, Kenya, Senufo (Ivory Coast), and Taiwan children are more likely to be seen in public with women than with men (Day & Mackey, 1989). Time-diary studies also show that employed mothers spend more time with their children than employed fathers on both weekdays and weekends in every country researched, including Belgium, Bulgaria, Czechoslovakia, France, Germany, Hungary, Peru, Poland, the United States, Yugoslavia (Roby, 1975), and Russia (Robinson, Andreyenkov, & Patrushev, 1989).

Yet significant cross-cultural variations in the degree of parental inequality certainly exist. A few societies even approach egalitarian childcare arrangements. Observations in Iceland, for example, showed that only 10 percent more children were accompanied in public by women than by men, whereas the corresponding figure in Taiwan was 33 percent (Day & Mackey, 1989). Sweden has adopted public policies that are explicitly designed to encourage equally shared parenting (Haas, 1992). Some of the most equal parenting arrangements have been observed in non-Western, nonindustrialized countries. For example, in Scott Coltrane's

(1988) study of fatherhood in ninety nonindustrialized societies, he identified the Mbuti pygmies of the Ituri Forest in Africa as having a relatively equal division of childcare between parents. Among the Mbuti, children come to accept "the father as a kind of mother." Likewise, in *Intimate Fathers* (1991), Barry Hewlett's study of father-infant relationships among the Aka pygmies of the sub-Saharan rain forest, he reported that the Aka fathers were highly involved in the care of their babies and that the nature of that care is "maternal" by Western standards. Aka fathers didn't engage in rough-and-tumble play with their infants; they held, kissed, cleaned, and soothed them.

Nevertheless, childcare responsibilities of fathers are not truly equal to those of mothers in any of these "relatively" egalitarian societies. Hewlett's (1991) data on the Aka show that despite the fathers' intimate connections to infants, mothers hold infants more frequently than fathers and are in close proximity to them for more time during the day. Among the industrialized Western countries, even Sweden, probably the most egalitarian of them, falls short of its gender ideals (Haas, 1992).

19. In this book I elaborate the theory that emphasizes the ongoing and contested construction of gender. Some scholars may object to my use of the phrase "gender role" because it is often associated with the socialization theory, which emphasizes childhood socialization. (See Potuchek, 1997, for an excellent discussion of these two theoretical approaches.) I use "gender role," however, not to endorse a socialization approach but because most people understand it to mean an interconnected set of values and behaviors culturally endorsed for men and women at any given moment. Although I agree with gender theorists on the importance of adult experience in the creation of gender, I also show that the deep feelings people sometimes express about gender have their roots in childhood.

20. This reversion to traditionalism is described in two excellent books written over a decade apart by two different academic couples: *Transition to Parenthood: How Infants Change Families,* by LaRossa and LaRossa (1981), and *When Partners Become Parents,* by Cowan and Cowan (1992).

21. Although I use the term "traditional" throughout the book to denote gender roles in which mothers bear primary responsibility for childcare and fathers for breadwinning, I use it only as a practical shorthand. I am mindful that the term "traditional" is fraught with problems. See, for example, Stephanie Coontz's fascinating book, *The Way We Never Were* (1992), for a discussion of how infrequently the so-called traditional family has existed historically.

22. Longitudinal studies document that during the transition to parenthood women feel increasingly dissatisfied about their husbands' level of participation (Cowan & Cowan, 1992; LaRossa & LaRossa, 1981). For example, Moss, Bolland, Foxman, and Owen (1987) found that seven weeks postpartum only 16 percent of the new mothers they studied were dissatisfied with their husbands' involvement in childcare. After six months that number had jumped to 24 percent. Women whose husbands did relatively more childcare were less dissatisfied than other women (Belsky, Lang, & Huston, 1986; Moss et al., 1987). New mothers were particularly dissatisfied if they had expected more from their husbands (Belsky, 1985; Ruble, Fleming, Hackel, & Stangor, 1988).

23. See Hochschild (1989, pp. 277–279) for a description of how she arrived at the estimate of a one-month leisure gap between men and women. I reviewed all the studies I could find that compared the total number of hours that men and women worked (paid and unpaid work). Nine studies confirmed that women do substantially more labor overall than men: Barnett & Rivers, 1996 (among families with preschool-aged children); Coverman, 1983; Farkas, 1976 (among families in which women work more than twenty hours per week); Hill, 1985; Meissner et al., 1975; Rexroat & Shehan, 1987; Sanik, 1990; Shelton, 1992 (in the 1987 sample); and Yogev, 1981. However, thirteen studies reported either no differences in the total workload of men and women, trivial differences, or differences favoring men: Barnett & Rivers, 1996 (excluding parents of preschoolers); Berk, 1985; Farkas, 1976 (among families in which women work less than twenty hours per week); Ferree, 1991; Geerken & Gove, 1983; Larson et al., 1994; Leete-Guy & Schor, 1992; Nickols & Metzen, 1982; Nock & Kingston, 1989; Robinson, Andreyenkov, & Patrushev, 1989; Schor, 1991; Shelton & Firestone, 1988; and Zick & McCullough, 1991.

It is not surprising to find these inconsistent results given the diversity in the samples considered and the methods used in these studies. Only a few of these workload studies are really relevant here because, for my purposes, the key comparison is in the total workload of *mothers* and *fathers* who are both working *full time* in paid labor. In fact, only three of the studies I reviewed (Barnett & Rivers, 1996; Rexroat & Shehan, 1987; Yogev, 1981) compared the workloads of full-time working mothers and fathers. The gender gap uncovered in those studies is dramatic. Yogev found that the total workload (i.e., hours devoted to career, housework, and childcare) of faculty women with children was 108.2 hours per week, compared to the 78.5 hour workweek put in by their husbands. Likewise, Rexroat and Shehan (1987), who analyzed data from a national sample of white husbands and white full-time working wives, found a gender gap in total workload among mothers and fathers ranging from 16.5 hours per week for those whose oldest child was a teenager to a whopping 24 hours per week for those whose oldest child was three years old or younger. Mothers in those families had workloads of almost 90 hours per week. True, Barnett and Rivers's more recent research (1996) found no gap in the total work hours of the full-time employed mothers and fathers of school-aged children. However, their own data show that mothers of preschool-aged children still work 17 hours a week more than their husbands. The extra 884 hours per year translates to an extra month of work for this group of mothers.

Among the studies that failed to find that women did more work than men, none, except the Barnett and Rivers (1996) study, examined the comparison between full-time working mothers and fathers. Three other disconfirming studies did examine parents separately from nonparents, but none of those focused specifically on full-time workers. They all lumped together mothers who were full-time paid workers with mothers who were part-time workers (Larson et al., 1994; Leete-Guy & Schor, 1992; Zick & McCullough, 1991). In fact, in two of the studies, housewives' work hours were also included in the estimates of mothers' work hours (Larson et al., 1994; Zick & McCullough, 1991).

Perhaps the gender gap does not exist for all groups of men and women. In fact, women who are housewives may work fewer total hours than their husbands. But it is clear that among parents with young children who work at full-time jobs, women are working a lot harder than their husbands.

24. A different path means cutting back on paid work. This strategy is common even among women who have invested a great deal in their careers, such as academics, dentists, and lawyers (Statham, Vaughan, & Houseknecht, 1987). Mothers of young children are most likely to cut back (Yu, Wang, Kaltreider, & Chien, 1993).

25. In a study of the costs and benefits of women working full and part time, Barker (1993) discovered that women employed part time felt marginalized at work and at a greater occupational disadvantage than full-time working women. In male-dominated professions (such as engineering), women's work-related self-esteem dropped if they worked part time. For a vivid description of how a part-time worker can be marginalized, see Hochschild's story (1989, pp. 90–91) of what happened to Nina Tanagawa when she negotiated a part-time position in her firm.

Christensen (1988) articulates some other disadvantages of part-time work. See also Alice Rossi's (1965) analysis of how part-time work perpetuates women's subordinate status in the professions, and Deborah Jacobs's examples in "Back from the Mommy Track" (1994).

Despite the negative effects of cutting back, some researchers (e.g., Barker, 1993; Poloma & Garland, 1971; Statham et al., 1987) have reported that women who work part time are satisfied with the balance in their lives, and happier than women working full time. Although these findings seem to suggest that the availability of a "Mommy track" in which women accept a lower-level career so they can fulfill family obligations would be just fine (Schwartz, 1989), Smith (1983) argues that the so-called benefits of part-time work are only benefits because in a patriarchal society the alternative to working part time is working a double day.

Gronseth (1978) offers a more egalitarian vision of part-time work in which *both* men and women would cut back in their paid jobs when their children were young. No stigma would be attached to part-time work in this notion of career, and thus women would suffer no relative disadvantage vis-à-vis men.

26. Equally sharing husbands and wives spend almost an identical amount of time with their kids. On average, mothers and fathers each spent between 14 and 15 hours alone with their children, and about 33 hours jointly with spouses, for a total of 48 hours of kid time. (My estimates are based on averages of husbands' and wives' reports of each spouse's hours of childcare.) Statistical tests verified no differences between mothers and fathers in solo childcare hours, $t\,(40) = .43, p > .50$, and in total childcare hours, $t\,(40) = .43, p > .50$.

When asked to estimate how they divided the "work" of parenting, the "less glamorous aspects that someone has got to do," a quarter of the couples admitted that the wife did more of the work. But in the overwhelming majority, the work was evenly divided or close to it. A third of the couples agreed that it was split 50-50 between them. In slightly more than a third, either the wife or husband reported an equal division, but were contradicted by a spouse who claimed it was slightly tilted toward husband or wife. One equally sharing couple agreed that the father did the lion's share of the work of parenting. On twenty-four of thirty-two parenting tasks I asked about equally sharing fathers contribute at least 45 percent.

27. The primacy of fathers' roles in equally sharing families is illustrated dramatically by how these couples divide some caregiving tasks that have traditionally been tied to mothers. For example, equally sharing couples reported that on average, fathers did 48 percent of the putting children to bed, 46 percent of the comforting, 49 percent of the sick care, and 51 percent of the responding to children's pleas for attention. Among the couples whose children were still in diapers, fathers did slightly over half of the diapering. The five couples who were toilet-training their children at the time of the interview shared that responsibility equally. Amazingly, when children of equal sharers called out for their parents at night, 56 percent of the time it was the fathers who got up with them.

28. See Janice Steil's excellent book, *Marital Equality* (1997), for a thoughtful answer explaining why they can't.

29. Stress is associated with time spent doing stereotypically female tasks (Barnett & Rivers, 1996).

30. Coltrane's (1996) cross-cultural evidence shows that societies with distant father-child relationships tend to devalue women. In a truly equal society, Lorber (1994) argues, men and women would participate equally in every kind of work, with the ultimate effect of eliminating gender entirely.

31. I specifically chose groups of unequal couples to interview whose agreed-upon estimates hovered around a division of either 75–25 or 60–40 because these were the most commonly mentioned unequal divisions. I do not assume that these numbers are precise measures of the percentage of childcare undertaken in these households; rather I think that 60–40 reflects relatively small inequalities between mothers and fathers, and 75–25 reflects relatively large ones.

32. This lack of racial diversity among the couples I interviewed is a serious limitation of my research. A study of equal sharing among African American parents would be an especially important contribution to our understanding of gender equality. The sex-role egalitarianism among African Americans has been noted by many researchers. (See the articles cited in Wilson, Tolson, Hinton, & Kiernan, 1990, pp. 409–412.) Survey data collected in 1976 and 1988 confirm that black families are more egalitarian in their division of household labor than either white or Latino families (Beckett & Smith, 1981; Shelton & John, 1993). However, although married black men may do more at home than their white counterparts, on average, black women, like white women, still do the majority of childcare and housework in their families (Beckett & Smith, 1981; Hossain & Roopnarine, 1993; Shelton & John, 1993; Wilson et al., 1990). Nonetheless, because the exigencies of history often led black families in America to adhere less rigidly to "traditional" sex roles, the division of domestic labor involves different dynamics and carries different meanings for black than for white Americans (Jones, 1985).

33. Chapter 9 will be devoted entirely to a discussion of these nontraditional working-class couples and the special issues they face in grappling with the dilemmas of work and family life. In other parts of the book, I will note explicitly when they are included in my analysis.

34. This TV commercial advertised Enjoli perfume, "the eight-hour perfume for the twenty-four-hour woman." According to Jennie Jones at the American Advertising Museum in Portland, Oregon, the commercial, which was created in 1978, supposedly embodied the aspirations of contemporary women at the time. It was

incredibly successful and helped Enjoli to become the third best-selling perfume that year.

35. Articles in the *New York Times* that feature women who discovered the rewards of full-time motherhood after they abandoned careers include Chira, 1994; Klein, 1995; Klemesrud, 1983; Richardson, 1988; and Rimer, 1988. For a different and more humorous view of what happens when women on the fast track give up careers to stay home full time, see Mark Singer's article in the *New Yorker*, "Mom Overboard" (1996).

36. See Ferree (1976, 1984b) for evidence that working-class women are more satisfied with their lives when they are employed than when they stay home full time. Surveys reported in the *New York Times* also confirm that most employed women would prefer to continue working even in the absence of economic necessity (Klemesrud, 1981; Silverman, 1987). In a nationwide representative sample of married couples surveyed in 1987–88, the more hours wives spent in paid labor, the happier they said their marriages were (Greenstein, 1996).

37. Several national surveys have shown that housewives are more depressed than employed women (e.g., Glass & Fujimoto, 1994; Kessler & McRae, 1981, 1982). Likewise, Cowan and Cowan (1992) found that women who returned to their jobs by the time their children were eighteen months old were less depressed than those who remained at home. However, other studies have shown little difference in the rates of depression for housewives versus employed women (e.g., Lennon, 1994). In a rigorous examination of these inconsistencies, Rosenfield (1989) demonstrated that there was only one exception to the rule that housewives were more depressed and anxious than women with jobs outside the home. Housewives were less anxious and depressed than the most overloaded employed women, the full-time working women with children who got little help from spouses.

For studies showing the low self-esteem of full-time mothers, see Ferree, 1976, and Mackie, 1983. Betty Friedan's highly influential book *The Feminine Mystique* exposed the widespread malaise among housewives, calling it the "problem that has no name." Elizabeth Ness Nelson (1977) starkly described the alienation experienced by housewives. Also, see Faye Crosby's engaging book, *Juggling,* for women's descriptions (as well as hard evidence) of the benefits of balancing the roles of wife and mother with paid employment.

38. Consider this: In 1992 the poverty level for a family of four was $14,335 (U.S. Bureau of the Census, 1995). That year there were 14,970,000 two-parent families of two or more children with fathers in the paid workforce. Among those families, if the mothers were housewives, 14.3 percent had a total family income of less than $15,000 per year. That figure dropped to 3.71 percent if mothers were employed (U.S. Bureau of the Census, 1993).

2. Creating Equality at Home

1. According to the American Society for Psychoprophylaxis in Obstetrics, 150,000 Lamaze classes are held each year, attended by 2,000,000 expectant parents.

2. Ephron, 1983.

3. See LeMasters (1957) and Dyer (1963) for the argument that the transition to parenthood is a crisis for a majority of middle-class couples. Other researchers have argued that first-time parenthood is a major transition in the life of a family rather than a "crisis" (e.g., Hobbs, 1965; Hobbs & Cole, 1976; Russell, 1974). However, I think these researchers are quibbling over words rather than substance. LeMasters (1957) defined crisis as "any sharp or decisive change for which old patterns are inadequate." That sounds a lot like "major transition" to me. LaRossa and LaRossa (1981) make a similar observation.

4. See "How I Did the Study" for a detailed description of how equal sharers were classified. By the most stringent definition, 26 of the 150 couples that I interviewed were equal sharers. By a less strict definition, about 41 could be considered equal sharers. In all quantitative analyses I report, I used the more stringent definition.

5. I found changes in the division of labor between when I initially contacted the families for the telephone interview and when I interviewed them face to face, although the time that lapsed between the two interviews was never longer than two years and often much shorter than that. Of the 41 couples who agreed on the phone that childcare was equally shared, five later agreed that it was not split equally at the time of the face-to-face interview. Conversely, four couples who agreed they were equally sharing childcare during my interview had previously reported an unequal division. Overall, approximately 10 percent of the 300 men and women who were interviewed in person reported a change of 20 percent or more in the father's contribution to childcare.

6. Janet wanted to bottle-feed, in part, to eliminate any difference between her and her husband. But, as I will show in Chapter 6, breastfeeding need not be an obstacle to equal sharing.

7. Sixteen out of the twenty-six indisputable equal sharers started parenthood in unequal relationships.

8. The Internal Revenue Service estimates that two million American households hire domestic workers (Loose, 1993). However, this figure is only an estimate. It is difficult to get accurate statistics about the number of families that hire outside help because of widespread underreporting. Also it is not known how many of these families are dual earners.

9. The findings regarding the link between number of children and men's contributions to family work are mixed (Coltrane & Ishii-Kuntz, 1992; Hiller, 1984). Some studies have found that men's participation increases as the number of children increases (Coverman, 1985; Charles & Hopfiger, 1992). Others have found the reverse: that men's participation decreases with more children (Berardo, Shehan, & Leslie, 1987; Blair & Lichter, 1991), and still others have found no relation between the two (Baruch & Barnett, 1981; Baxter, 1988; Presser, 1988).

10. Ferree, 1976; Mackie, 1983.

11. Coltrane (1996) also noted that couples negotiate both the symbolic meanings and the practicalities of the division of labor.

12. See Risman and Johnson-Sumerford's (1998) alternative scheme for examining diversity in "postgender" couples.

13. On average, the equal sharers in my study relied on nonparental caregivers

approximately twenty-five hours per week. However, some families used no non-parental care at all, and two families used paid childcare forty-seven hours per week.

14. The children of equal sharers spend, on average, 62.5 hours per week being taken care of by at least one parent. In the typical equally sharing family, for a little over half of that time (i.e., 33.5 hours) both parents are available. In some families, however, 70 percent of parental time with children means time with both parents, whereas in families that rely on "tag-team parenting" as little as 15 percent of parental time is time families spend together.

15. Donna and Kevin mentioned the word "homework" four times as often as Mary and Paul did (twenty times versus five times) in their interviews. In fact, homework didn't come up once in Mary's interview.

3. Creating Inequality at Home

1. People usually go about their everyday lives with a taken-for-granted sense that their routines, customs, and practices are the only way to do things. Their social arrangements, which are, in fact, merely particular human inventions, appear natural and inevitable (Berger & Luckman, 1967; Marciano, 1986). But in times of rapid social change, alternative practices and ideologies can threaten that "taken-for-grantedness." People suddenly need justifications and explanations for their behavior. These explanations reinforce the wisdom and sense of the status quo and become crucial in maintaining it. See Berger and Kellner (1964) and Reiss (1981) for a discussion of how social reality is constructed within the family.

2. See Barbara Ehrenreich's humorous essay "Stop Ironing the Diapers" (1981) for commentary on the dangers of calling parenthood one's profession. She writes, "Being a mommy is a relationship, not a profession. Nothing could be worse for a child's self-esteem than to think that you think being with her is work. She may come to think that you are involved in some obscure manufacturing process in which she is only the raw material" (p. 149).

3. There is little research documenting how mothers at home with children actually spend their time. The one pertinent study I found compared employed and homemaker mothers on whether they had performed twelve childcare tasks within the last forty-eight hours, including reading to children, praising them for taking care of themselves, helping them learn a new skill, and stopping what they were doing to play with a child. There were no overall differences between the two groups, even though the homemaker mothers spent twice as much time with children. The only task homemaker mothers were more likely to have done was watching educational TV with their children (DeMeis & Perkins, 1996).

4. Approximately 60 percent of the fathers in both the 75-25 and 60-40 groups could be classified as helpers. The other unequal fathers in the 75-25 group were more likely to be slackers (33.3 percent) than sharers (4.8 percent), whereas fathers in the 60-40 group were more likely to be sharers (27.8 percent) than slackers (11.1 percent).

5. Lionesses are responsible for most of the hunting for the pride and all of the care of the cubs. Nevertheless, after a kill the male lions dominate. Male lions appear to do little more than protect the pride from other male lions (Bertram, 1978).

6. This seems remarkably similar to the mythology created by Nancy and Evan Holt in *The Second Shift* (Hochschild, 1989). Nancy gave up struggling over sharing the work at home and lived with the myth that she and Evan were "equal" because she was responsible for the upstairs, he for the downstairs. Denise, however, doesn't go quite that far. She implies an equivalency that suggests fairness, but never uses the word "equality."

7. This analysis was based on the fifty-one dual-earner couples who were dividing childcare unequally at the time of the interview (excluding the alternating-shift couples).

8. Blain (1994) argues similarly that "the discourse of individual choice" obscures power relations within the couple.

9. A comparison of wives' satisfaction with the division of responsibility for childcare across groups shows that women in the 75-25 group are more dissatisfied than women in the other three groups: $F (3, 84) = 8.46, p < .0001$. However, the difference among the three groups is primarily attributable to the supermoms, women working full time and receiving little paternal help. On average they rate themselves as 6.3 on a 10-point scale measuring satisfaction with the division of childcare, as compared to an average rating of 8.1 among the full-time working mothers in the 60-40 group, and 9.0 among the full-time working mothers in the equally sharing group.

10. Men married to women working full time were more satisfied with the division of labor themselves if they contributed more: $F (3, 50) = 3.2, p < .05$. Although Newman-Keuls tests found that only the 60-40 ($M = 7.5$) and 50-50 ($M = 8.8$) husbands were significantly different from one another, the 75-25 husbands actually had the lowest mean satisfaction ($M = 7.1$).

4. Fighting over Practice and Principle

1. See Major (1988, 1993) for a definition of entitlement.

2. Hood (1983) also mentions women's use of strikes to get their husbands to take more responsibility for domestic labor in her study of sixteen families that changed from single-earner to dual-earner families.

3. See LaRossa (1977), however, for a discussion of why women's power usually decreases relative to their husbands' power after the birth of a child.

4. Sometimes the unequal mothers avoided bringing up the division of labor because they didn't want to argue with their husbands. But arguing may set the stage for change. Arguing leads both women *and* men to see women's greater workload at home as unfair. Often the work is invisible to men until their wives lobby for change (John, Shelton, & Luschen, 1995).

5. Komter (1989) observed that power in marriage can be expressed as the ability to keep issues from coming up. The lack of conflict may reflect the weaker partner's resignation or fear about the consequences of conflict.

6. Willard Waller (1951) wrote that in an intimate relationship the person who loves less can dictate its terms, a phenomenon he dubbed the "principle of least interest." In an empirical demonstration of this principle, Safilios-Rothschild (1976) showed that among Greek and American couples, women who love their husbands less than they are loved in return have more say in important family deci-

sions. The principle of least interest also implies that this love-based power could be used to obtain a more equal division of family work.

7. In the absence of power, women may be reluctant to recognize the unfairness in the division of labor. Lack of viable alternatives leaves women feeling powerless. Lennon and Rosenfield (1994) documented that women who couldn't imagine finding a better marriage were less likely to think the division of labor was unfair than were women who thought they might be able to do better. Likewise, women who would fall into poverty if they had to rely on their own wages were less likely to view the division of labor as unfair than women whose wages could sustain them. Conversely, if men believed they had more options outside of their current marriage, they were less likely to think that the division of labor was unfair to their wives.

8. Of course, whether or not this is a bluff is unclear. Their husbands have not called their bluffs.

9. In second marriages husbands do a slightly greater share of domestic work than they do in first marriages (Demo & Acock, 1993; Ishii-Kuntz & Coltrane, 1992b), which suggests that men are at least as interested in avoiding divorce as their second wives. However, husbands in second marriages who were unfaithful to their first wives, or who are married to women whose first husbands cheated, do a smaller share of domestic work than other remarried husbands. What's going on here? Pyke and Coltrane (1996) explain this finding in terms of gratitude. Women whose first husbands were unfaithful feel grateful that the second husbands are not, and repay them by not pressing too hard for more help with housework. Men who reformed their cheating ways in their second marriages may feel they deserve credit and gratitude for being such good husbands without doing more chores.

10. Thompson (1991) and Major (1993) argue that women may not think the situation is unfair because they have different values than men (e.g., they may enjoy and value childcare and housework or the appreciation they get for doing it), because they compare themselves to other women rather than their husbands, and/or because they accept their husbands' justifications and excuses for why they can't do as much domestic work as their wives.

In a random sample of dual-earner couples, only 35 percent of the women thought the distribution of labor was unfair, despite doing an average of more than two thirds of the work at home (Lennon & Rosenfield, 1994). What men do at home does matter in their wives' perception of fairness, however. Women were increasingly likely to think the distribution of labor was unfair, the smaller the proportion of traditional female chores their husbands took on (Blair & Johnson, 1992; Greenstein, 1996; John, Shelton, & Luschen, 1995; Lennon & Rosenfield, 1994; Sanchez, 1994; Sanchez & Kane, 1996). Yet even the vast majority of women who were doing 60–65 percent of the work at home did not think it was unfair. Only when women were doing 75 percent of the work did they begin to cry uncle (Lennon & Rosenfield, 1994).

11. Blair and Johnson (1992) found that employed wives were less likely to feel unfairly put upon by an unequal division of labor at home if they felt appreciated by their husbands.

12. Goode (1982) and Polatnick (1984) discuss why men resist.

13. About a quarter of the unequal men in my study indicated that they felt

guilty or uncomfortable about not doing a greater share of family work, especially when their wives laid "guilt trips" on them. Husbands with relatively more education than other men saw their wives as more burdened by the inequity in the division of household labor (DeMaris & Longmore, 1996).

14. Shelton, 1992. See Bond, Galinsky, and Swanberg (1998) for some hopeful signs that the gap between men and women may be narrowing.

15. I am not the first to notice that men use a variety of ingenious strategies to avoid domestic labor. Pat Mainardi (1993), for example, gives a searing account of her husband's attempts to escape his share of the housework. Hochschild (1989) also mentions men's strategies. Coltrane (1996) observed men's "claimed incompetence."

16. Gunter and Gunter (1991) conducted the only study I know of that examines the effect of "the need for cleanliness" on the division of household labor. Researching 139 full-time employed dual-earner couples, they discovered that men who cared more about household order did perform a greater share of domestic tasks than other men but not more than their wives. Women's need for cleanliness, however, did not affect how many household tasks they did.

17. See Gerstel and Gross (1995).

18. Remember the husband who resisted becoming a sharer rather than a helper. He did get his wife's point about who deserved to relax at the end of the day: "If she's tired and had a rough day too, I would put my foot in my mouth if I came home and said something to her like, 'I'm tired, I worked hard today.' Well, she worked hard today too. And there's times when I think about saying that and I go, 'Whoa, you better not say that because she worked hard.'"

19. It is even possible that some of the unequal women might have made adamant demands for equality earlier in their relationships, but had their bluffs called. This is, of course, highly speculative, because they don't report such occurrences. However, we know that retrospective accounts are subject to reconstruction (Schacter, 1996). It is conceivable that the equally sharing women are more likely to recall their "nonnegotiable" stances than other women because they worked.

20. Major, 1993; Thompson, 1991.

21. See Major (1988) for a discussion of why women might be motivated to justify their own exploitation.

5. Friends and Foes

1. Like everyone else, equal sharers care about what other people say and think about them. As William James (1890) observed over a century ago, "We are not only gregarious animals, liking to be in sight of our fellows, but we have an innate propensity to get ourselves noticed and noticed favorably, by our kind" (p. 293).

2. Robert Merton (1948) coined the term "self-fulfilling prophecy," which he defined as "a false definition of the situation evoking a new behavior which makes the originally false conception come true" (p. 195).

The most powerful contemporary demonstration of self-fulfilling prophecies is the social psychological experiment Robert Rosenthal and colleagues (1968) conducted to show that teachers' expectations shape students' performance. Rosenthal knowingly misinformed some elementary school teachers that several students within their classes were expected to make exceptional scholastic gains during the year. Unbeknownst to the teachers, these students were actually no different from any of the others, except that they had been randomly chosen by Rosenthal to be the targets of the teachers' positive expectations. After an academic year in the classes of these teachers, the targeted students had, in fact, made exceptional gains. They were the beneficiaries of a self-fulfilling prophecy.

The existence of self-fulfilling prophecies attests to the power of social expectations. How, we might ask, did the teachers' expectations so powerfully affect the students' performances? If we could sit in those classrooms we might see myriad ways in which teachers respond differently to students whom they expect to do well compared to those they don't. See Harris and Rosenthal (1985) for a meta-analytic summary of research on the mediators of teacher expectancy effects and Jussim (1986) for an integrative review.

Self-fulfilling prophecies have been demonstrated outside the classroom as well. Perceivers' expectations of a target's stereotypical gender behavior (Skrypnek & Snyder, 1982), popularity (Curtis & Miller, 1986), competitiveness (Kelley & Stahelski, 1970), and social skill (Snyder, Tanke, & Berscheid, 1977) all create self-fulfilling prophecies. See Snyder (1984) and Miller and Turnbull (1986) for excellent reviews of the research demonstrating self-fulfilling prophecies and the processes that underlie them.

See Jussim and Eccles (1995), however, for a revisionist review, which argues that naturally occurring self-fulfilling prophecies are not as pervasive as previously claimed. Even they concede, though, that self-fulfilling prophecies are most likely to occur in new situations when targets have uncertain self-concepts. The implications are not good for equally shared parenting. The pervasive expectations that men will not take care of infants push all but the few confident and determined men toward inequality.

3. We all rely on other people to validate and sustain our identities. William Swann Jr. (1987, 1997) and his colleagues have conducted extensive research on these self-verification processes, which demonstrate that people seek out feedback from other people that confirms their self-conceptions, even when the feedback is negative. Self-conceptions both influence and are influenced by appraisals of others (McNulty & Swann, 1994).

A long theoretical tradition within social psychology and sociology considers the self a social entity. Symbolic interactionists, beginning with Cooley (1902) and Mead (1934), have argued that self-conception develops primarily as a reflection of others' appraisals. See reviews by Shrauger and Schoeneman (1979) and Gecas and Schwalbe (1983), however, for challenges to the symbolic interactionist view of self-conception.

4. In a 1993 Gallup poll, 86 percent of Americans approved of a married woman's holding a job "in business or industry if her husband is able to support her." This represents an increase of 18 percentage points since 1975, when only 68 percent approved.

5. A Gallup poll in 1990 found that 73 percent of Americans thought that children were better off if "their mother is home and doesn't hold a job." The same year 41 percent of Americans polled disagreed with the statement "A working

mother can establish just as warm and secure a relationship with her children as a mother who does not work." There was a difference between the responses of women and men. Only 34 percent of women disagreed, whereas 48 percent of men disagreed.

6. For a more detailed account of this double standard, see Deutsch and Saxon (1998b).

7. However, see Gerson (1985) for a discussion of the criticism employed women heap on mothers who eschew paid employment to stay home with children.

8. Hochschild, 1989.

9. Some research suggests that women compensate when they make more money than their husbands by taking on additional domestic chores (Biernat & Wortman, 1991; Deutsch, Lussier, & Servis, 1993; Hochschild, 1989).

10. Women who grew up with depressed or alcoholic 1950s mothers, however, have nothing to feel guilty about in comparison to them.

11. In *The Cultural Contradictions of Motherhood* (1996), Sharon Hays shows us just how deeply entrenched and pervasive is the ideology of "intensive mothering." One of the few remaining holdouts against marketplace morality, motherhood demands unselfishness. Above all, "good mothers" put the interests of their children above their own.

12. In a much-cited study of how group members respond to dissenters (Schacter, 1951), subjects were asked to discuss what should be done about "Johnny Rocco," a juvenile delinquent who had committed a minor offense. In the group discussions that ensued, a confederate in cahoots with the experimenter advocated a punitive response, in opposition to the majority view that Johnny should be treated leniently. An analysis of communication patterns showed that comments of group members were disproportionately directed at the dissenter, at least until it was clear that he wouldn't alter his position. These findings demonstrate the pressure brought to bear on group members who dissent from the common view. Impervious to the pressure, the confederate was ultimately rejected by the group.

Kiesler (1971) explains how public commitment bolsters attitudes. Schultz, Oskamp, and Mainieri (1995) recently showed that public commitment increases people's recycling of bottles and cans.

13. Powerful conformity effects can be drastically reduced by one dissenting voice. In a classic set of experiments on conformity, subjects were more likely to conform to a unanimous majority of three than to a majority of eight with one lone dissenter (Asch, 1951).

Even when dissenters don't elicit public support for their views, however, they may very well influence opinions. People who espouse minority views are successful in changing others' opinions when they present their dissenting position confidently and consistently. Majorities and minorities appear to influence others through quite different processes. Confronted with a majority that holds an opposing view, a person experiences an interpersonal conflict, whereas confronted with an opposing minority, a person faces a cognitive conflict. Majority influence works through compliance, and its power is often limited to the public expression of agreement rather than real internalization of a new viewpoint. Conversely, minority influence works through conversion and is often more evident in the private acceptance of a new idea than in its public expression (Maass & Clark, 1984;

Moscovici, 1985; Nemeth, 1986). Minorities, like the men who dissented from a work culture that devalues family, may not always get everyone to go along or agree with them, but they get other people to think about the issue in a new way.

14. Berger and Kellner (1964) describe how the ongoing conversation between husbands and wives creates a shared understanding of the world.

15. Fischer (1982) argues that urban subcultures support nontraditional behavior, because for people's unconventional behavior to thrive, they need the support of like-minded peers. Likewise, Riley (1990) found that involved fathers had a greater proportion of friends versus local kin in their social networks than did fathers who were less involved in the daily care of their children. The friends included a high proportion of other young parents, who presumably supported the fathers' involvement.

16. Duck, 1983; Newcomb, 1961.

17. I am aware that American parents vary in how they treat bedtime, from strictly enforcing a specific time to permitting their children to go to sleep when they choose or when they "crash." Yet to my knowledge no American parent I have met has inferred that our son's eight-thirty bedtime meant that we didn't like children.

18. For more on Italian greetings, see Tim Parks's (1995) amusing description of how Italian grandparents greet their grandchildren.

6. Babies, Breastfeeding, Bonding, and Biology

1. For a highly technical description of these hormonal changes, see Yen (1990).

2. In a study comparing a matched sample of lesbian and heterosexual couples who became parents through donor insemination, the lesbians divided childcare equally, whereas the heterosexuals did not. Although, like the fathers, the nonbiological lesbian mothers had not experienced pregnancy, birth, or lactation, that did not prevent them from doing significantly more childcare than the men (Chan, Brooks, Raboy, & Patterson, 1998).

3. See Stuart-Macadam (1995) for a summary of the health benefits of breastfeeding to mother and baby, and for an impassioned plea for mothers to consider those benefits in making the choice of how to feed. A search of abstracts in the Readers' Guide turned up numerous articles that appeared in popular magazines between 1990 and 1997, which supported breastfeeding. Articles in *Ms.* (Quick, 1997), *FDA Consumer* (Williams, 1995), the *New York Times* (Brody, 1994), and *Good Housekeeping* (Eaton & Cassidy, 1991) all advocated breastfeeding because of the nutritional benefits of breast milk. The IQ boost received by breastfed babies (Glick, 1997) was another benefit reported in the popular media. Other benefits reported were stress reduction ("Off the Chest," 1996), easier loss of weight gained during pregnancy ("The Milk Diet: Breast-feeding May Take Off Pregnancy Pounds," 1994), and reduced risk of premenopausal breast cancer (Fackelmann, 1994).

Moreover, one of the best-selling books for new parents, *What to Expect in the First Year* (1996), lists "strong mother-baby relationship" as one of the benefits of breastfeeding over bottle-feeding. Although the list ostensibly balanced the pros and cons of breast and bottle, this benefit could override all others. Imagine the guilt provoked in a mother who rejects a method of feeding that promises a better relationship with her child. The title of Renee Bacher's article "Confessions of a Breast-feeding Dropout" (1994) implies that women now have to apologize if they decide not to breastfeed and "drop out."

Notwithstanding the widespread endorsement of nursing, Katherine Dettwyler (1995) shows that the popular media discourage women from breastfeeding "too long." Two popular articles she mentions (Bernstein, 1993; Conrad, 1992) give lip service to the notion that any time is the right time to wean while giving advice on how to wean that applies only to children two years old or younger. These articles subtly communicate that two years is the upper age limit on breastfeeding, despite its being commonplace to nurse for longer than two years in most of the world.

Our cultural schizophrenia about nursing was also expressed in the controversy surrounding breastfeeding in public. After a mall security guard in Florida ordered a nursing mother to cover herself up, the state of Florida, followed by seven other states, passed legislation exempting nursing from laws governing indecent exposure (Mahtesian, 1995). The need for this kind of legislation belies the blanket endorsement for nursing we sometimes hear.

Despite the ubiquitous messages, subtle and not so subtle, that good mothers choose breastfeeding, I could find no scientific evidence that breastfed babies felt more secure or had better relationships with their mothers. In fact, a study that compared the mother-infant attachments in adoptive versus biological families found no difference between the two groups, at least in the intraracial families (Singer, Brodzinsky, Ramsay, Steir, & Waters, 1985). Although this was not specifically a study about breastfeeding, the adoptive mothers could not nurse, whereas, presumably, many of the biological mothers did.

4. These figures are based on a representative sample survey that has been conducted annually by the Ross Laboratories in Columbus, Ohio, since the 1950s (Martinez & Nalezienski, 1981; Mothers' Survey, 1996).

Valerie Fildes's (1995) research shows the enormous range of breastfeeding attitudes and behaviors in different cultures, in different historical periods, and among women of different social classes. For example, a study of contemporary nursing practices among low-income mothers in Lagos, Nigeria, found that over 90 percent of the mothers breastfed for at least six months and over 70 percent for over a year, far higher proportions than corresponding percentages in the United States. Moreover, whereas in the United States longer nursing is associated with more education, the study of Nigerian mothers found an inverse relationship between how long women nursed and how much education they had (Ekanem, 1993). Quant's (1986) study of the breastfeeding style of sixty-two first-time mothers in the United States shows quite a bit of intracultural variation as well. Cross-cultural, cross-class, intracultural, and historical variability should warn us to be leery of treating breastfeeding as a purely "natural" or "instinctive" maternal behavior. Quant discusses cultural factors that may interact with the biology of breastfeeding to influence breastfeeding style, which may mediate decisions about supplementation with other foods as well as the duration of breastfeeding.

5. Husbands' views on breastfeeding have a strong effect on women's choices. In one study, 98 percent of the women whose husbands strongly endorsed breast-

feeding chose it over bottle-feeding, whereas only 27 percent of the women whose husbands were indifferent breastfed (Littman, Medendorp, & Goldfarb, 1994).

6. Working full time does seem to put a damper on breastfeeding. Although the same percentage of employed and nonemployed women (55 percent in 1987) breastfed their children in the hospital, by the time the babies were six months old, only 10 percent of full-time working women were breastfeeding, whereas the comparable figure for nonemployed women was 24 percent (Ryan & Martinez, 1989).

7. When a group of in-training pediatric house staff members were quizzed about breastfeeding, they were found to be supportive, but not knowledgeable. On average, they answered only 53 percent of the questions posed correctly (Williams & Hammer, 1995).

8. Throughout the book, unless otherwise noted, I refer to a couple's division of labor at the time I interviewed them. So, for example, the deferring equal sharers I discuss here were not equally sharing as parents of a nursing infant.

9. One study found that the mothers who exclusively breastfed spent an average of over three hours a day nursing when their infants were four weeks old (Quandt, 1986). (I swear I once spent eleven hours nursing in one day when my son was about two months old.) *Nursing Your Baby* (Pryor & Pryor, 1991), a guide for new mothers, reports that a nursing mother may produce between twenty and thirty-four ounces of milk in one day, and that a thousand calories are expended in producing thirty-four ounces of milk.

10. By the third month of life babies are awake for about ten hours a day and can have an attention span of up to forty-five minutes. Babies at this age are social creatures who need the stimulation of play and human talk (Caplan, 1993; Eisenburg, Hathaway, & Murkoff, 1996). Three-month-olds can recognize their parents and will stop crying when they see them, even before being picked up (Campos & Lamb, 1982). For anyone paying attention, three-month-olds are rewarding social partners because they can actively smile and coo (Rosenblith & Sims-Knight, 1985).

11. See Ralph and Maureen LaRossa's book, *Transition to Parenthood: How Infants Change Families* (1981), for a fascinating discussion of the relentless time demands of infant care. Infants need continuous coverage in either primary time, which involves physical care or interaction, or secondary time, in which a parent is available if needed. If one parent is primarily responsible for infant care, that parent can only get "down time," during which she or he doesn't have to pay attention at all, if the other parent takes on at least the secondary mode.

12. For many mothers, however, it is not so easy. The existence of advice books on breastfeeding, like *The Complete Book of Breast-Feeding* (Eiger & Olds, 1987), which has sold over a million copies, as well as popular articles offering advice to new nursing mothers (e.g., Benson, 1995; Morse, 1996), suggests that breastfeeding is not simply an automatic, problem-free, instinctual behavior. The Pryors, who wrote *Nursing Your Baby* (1991), tell new mothers that it takes two or three weeks to learn how to nurse and a couple of months to become expert. Books on nursing detail the numerous problems women may encounter, including the baby's difficulty in latching on, sore nipples, engorged breasts, mastitis, and leaking.

13. We cannot underestimate the importance of holding and cuddling infants. In the (1958) study that made him famous forty years ago, Harry Harlow showed that

baby rhesus monkeys, when given the choice between a wire monkey "mother" with a feeding bottle and a cuddly cloth "mother," much preferred the cuddly mother surrogate. Although they used the wire monkey for food, they spent far more time with the cloth mother surrogate, upward of 10 hours a day. When frightened, the infant monkeys rushed to the cloth mother, clutched her, and apparently used her as a source of security. Ironically, although Harlow rightly concludes that "the variable of nursing appears to be of absolutely no importance" in the development of attachment (p. 678), he and most other psychologists do not appreciate the egalitarian implications of these findings. If cuddling is the key component in the development of attachment, fathers as well as mothers can provide it. Although Harlow repeatedly refers to the cloth monkey as a surrogate "mother," there's nothing female about it. It could as readily represent a surrogate father. Nursing may necessitate mothers' holding their infants for hours every day, but fathers could also hold those infants when they weren't feeding. See the final paragraph of Harlow's article for his brief acknowledgment (perhaps tongue-in-cheek) that the results demonstrate men's ability to successfully compete with women in the rearing of infants.

14. I had good information about the fathers' roles during the breastfeeding period for approximately half of the 75-25 couples. Those couples are the base I used to determine that half of the fathers were more involved at that stage.

15. See Lorber (1994) for a discussion of how biology is used to justify gender inequality.

16. The term "bonding" came into vogue as a result of research reported in the early 1970s (Klaus, Jerauld, Kreger, McAlpine, Steffa, & Kennell, 1972), which purported to show that when mothers and infants are given extra time together immediately after birth, mothering skills and babies' development are enhanced. This research supposedly demonstrated a biologically based sensitive period for women to connect with their infants. Diane Eyer's brilliant book, *Mother-Infant Bonding: A Scientific Fiction* (1992), explores the politics and ideology behind the reasons why, despite the shaky basis for the claims made by Klaus and his colleagues, the scientific community as well as the public eagerly jumped on the bonding bandwagon. Today, though the scientific evidence for "bonding" has been thoroughly debunked, the term is current in popular parlance. The belief in the biological basis of a mother-infant bond is tenacious despite scientific disconfirmation.

17. I am using the word "attachment" here in its commonsense meaning. The field of psychology has spawned an enormous theoretical and empirical literature concerning attachment. See Jeremy Holmes's book *John Bowlby and Attachment Theory* (1993) for an excellent summary of the theorizing of the principal architect of attachment theory, and a concise review of some of the subsequent empirical work it has generated. Although Bowlby believed that attachment is "monotropic"—occurs with a single principal figure—contemporary research focuses on the infant's capacity for multiple attachments, including her attachment to her father, and the quality of those attachments (e.g., Cox, Owen, Henderson, & Margard, 1992; Goossens & van IJzendoorn, 1990; van IJzendoorn & De Wolff, 1997). As Philip Cowan (1997) points out, what we do not yet know is how the quality of mother-infant attachments and the quality of father-infant attachments combine or interact to affect children's development.

18. Coltrane (1996) mentioned a similar pattern.

19. Two meta-analyses of the quality of children's attachments to mothers and fathers show a pattern of concordance (Fox, Kimberly, & Schafer, 1991; van IJzendoorn & De Wolff, 1997), suggesting that secure attachment with a father in no way weakens a child's attachment to his or her mother. In fact, the two seem to go together.

In my study, siblings sometimes had stronger attachments to different parents. I counted families in which one child was more attached to the mother and the other to the father as examples of equal child attachment.

20. The children of 75-25 fathers may sometimes develop secure attachments to them because of the fathers' responsiveness when they are available. Although these fathers may not participate in the work of parenting, they may be emotionally attuned to their children. Fathers' emotional involvement with children in the 75-25 families varies greatly. For example, families in which mothers work part time may be classified as 75-25 because of the mothers' disproportionate shares, but may include fathers who are quite attentive to their children.

The relation between parents' behavior and the quality of children's attachments is currently being scrutinized in many studies of attachment. Mary Ainsworth, who developed the Strange Situation procedure to assess the quality of children's attachments, argued that secure attachments are developed when parents provide sensitive and responsive parenting (Ainsworth, Blehar, Waters, & Wall, 1978). This kind of parenting entails correctly interpreting infant signals, promptly responding, and maintaining an appropriate level of stimulation. Recent research (e.g., Cox, Owen, Henderson, & Margard, 1992; Rosen & Rothbaum, 1993; van IJzendoorn & De Wolff, 1997), however, has obtained conflicting results with respect to the relation between parental sensitivity and attachment. See Seifer and Schiller (1995) for a review.

21. Silverstein (1996) makes a convincing case for men's capacity to nurture, and the desirability of encouraging men to do so. She reports recent primate research, which shows that even among nonhuman primates there are no significant differences in males' and females' ability to nurture. She does, however, note that one study did find that male rhesus monkeys would only care for a strange infant if there was no adult female present. The omnipresence of mothers may inhibit men's capacity to nurture.

22. Kyle Pruett's book, *The Nurturing Father* (1987), offers a moving account of the relationships househusbands develop with young children. Likewise, Barbara Risman's (1986) study of men who became single fathers through divorce or widowerhood shows that men do develop nurturing qualities when they are thrust into a "maternal" role. Kathleen Gerson's book, *No Man's Land* (1993), also includes testimony from men who developed the ability to nurture.

23. In a recent observational study, Brenda Geiger (1996) compared parent-infant interactions in two groups of families in which mothers and fathers took dramatically different roles. When fathers took a primary role by caring for an infant more than half of the infant's waking hours, they engaged in levels of caregiving behavior similar to those of primary-care mothers. In fact, primary-care dads showed even more affection toward their babies than their female counterparts, and engaged in more synchronous interaction. Infants, in turn, exhibited more affection

toward their primary caregivers than their secondary caregivers, regardless of the caregiver's gender. When stressed, they sought out the primary caregiver for comfort or reassurance, regardless of whether the primary caregiver was the mother or the father. Primary caregiving fathers were sought even when the mothers were nursing.

24. Ironically, some contemporary feminist as well as antifeminist accounts of parenting maintain that women's essential difference from men makes them better parents. Although few today would argue that women are inherently less capable than men of becoming chemists, lawyers, doctors, or politicians, many still endorse women's special talent for nurturing. As I have already shown, a conservative position invokes the biological basis of women's superiority, through either a special "maternal instinct" harbored by women or a unique bond forged between mother and child during pregnancy, childbirth, and nursing.

Alternatively, Nancy Chodorow's (1978) view, the most widely held feminist perspective on essential gender differences, argues that women's predisposition and capacity to parent stems from asymmetrical parenting arrangements in which women mother. Because both men and women experience their earliest intimate relationship with a woman, women develop a sense of self in connection to a mother who is like them; men develop a sense of self in separation from a mother who is different from them. Given these differing senses of self, the psychological connection to others that women later seek is fulfilled by and well suited to mothering. The separation that is the hallmark of male psychology is an impediment to parenting. Although the theory is "feminist" because it implies that radical change is possible if parenting arrangements are made egalitarian, the theory itself, paradoxically, describes a dynamic in which it is almost impossible to imagine that those egalitarian parenting arrangements could be achieved. If mothering reproduces itself, as Chodorow argues it does, that reproduction seems to preclude the necessary conditions for changing men's inferior nurturing capacities. (See, however, Jackson [1989], who argues via a stochastic model that Chodorow's theory actually implies the opposite—that families will become more equal over time.) Nonetheless, in the face of both conservative views of maternal instinct and feminist views that women are more tuned in and nurturing than men because of their "relational selves," some fathers today are "mothering" and mothering well.

25. A 1993 Gallup poll reported that 65 percent of Americans believed that men and women were basically different in terms of personalities, interests, and abilities. Half of those polled who believed in these differences thought they were biologically based. Nonetheless, in 1990 (the last year in which the question was asked), 78 percent of those polled agreed with the statement "Men who stay home and care for children rather than work are just as capable as women of being good parents."

7. Career Detours

1. Two hypotheses have been developed to explain the relation between paid work and the division of domestic labor. The first hypothesis, that men and women will contribute to the unpaid work of the family to the extent that they are available and their spouses are not, goes under three different names: time availability

(Godwin, 1991), practicality (Ishii-Kuntz & Coltrane, 1992a), and demand/response (Coverman, 1985).

The second hypothesis, the "relative resources" hypothesis, exists in two different versions. The first version assumes that the division of domestic labor in the family is based on a power struggle. Economic resources, such as earnings, occupational prestige, and education, confer power within the family. That power is then used to liberate its possessor from the work of the household. Thus because in most families men earn more than women, men do less childcare because they have the power to get out of it.

The second version of the relative resources hypothesis is more benign, although the prediction is the same: the more money and education a husband has relative to his wife, the less he will participate in childcare. However, instead of depicting husband and wife as adversaries, struggling to obtain individual advantage, this version envisions the family as a team. To the extent that one spouse outearns the other it makes economic sense for the high earner to spend a greater portion of time in the paid workforce, while the low earner spends relatively more time tending the home fires. This economically wise arrangement, so the hypothesis goes, benefits the whole family. (See Coverman [1985] for a review.)

2. Women's work hours have been shown to influence men's contributions to domestic labor in numerous studies. See note 12 in Chapter 1. Men's work hours had a negative impact on their contributions to domestic work in at least two studies (Antill & Cotton, 1988; Shelton & Firestone, 1988). However, there is a limit to the effect of free time on men's willingness to shoulder household work. In a study that compared employed and unemployed men in Israel, except for a few narrow tasks, unemployed men did not do more domestic work than their employed counterparts. Although their wives were working for pay, they certainly did not take over their wives' roles at home (Shamir, 1986).

3. For mixed findings on the relative resource hypothesis, see note 11 in Chapter 1. Blumstein and Schwartz (1991) found an interaction between relative income and ideology, which might account for earlier inconsistencies in the research. They discovered that the relative income effect found for some families did not exist when couples endorsed an explicitly antiprovider ideology: that men were not exclusively responsible for breadwinning.

4. On average, men earned $19,498 more than their wives in the 75-25 group, $18,976 more in the 60-40 group, but only $6,179 more in the 50-50 group, yielding a significant statistical difference for income difference across the three groups, $F(1, 59) = 4.02, p < .05$.

5. Steil (1997) also discusses how the effects of economic resources are influenced by the gender of the person who possesses them. She found, for example, that when men earned significantly more than their wives, those men's careers were considered more important in the family. But if women earned more, the reverse was not true (Steil & Weltman, 1991).

6. Of course, it is theoretically possible that the jobs men and women could get, given potentially different professions, made it more feasible for men to work longer hours than women. In this group, however, women were as highly educated as men and had professions that were as flexible or inflexible as their husbands'.

7. Men only outwork women in terms of the relative number of hours they put

into paid work. See Bielby and Bielby (1988) for evidence that women expend more mental and physical energy on the job than men do.

8. As a social psychologist, I am well aware of the difficulty in imagining alternative historical outcomes. In a widely cited series of experimental studies, Baruch Fischhoff (1975) demonstrated the existence of the "hindsight" effect: that perceivers estimate a lower likelihood of the same event when predicting the future than when explaining the past. In other words, if we think Tammy and Thomas's inequality and Joan and Mark's equality were highly predictable from the start, we had better think twice. We are being influenced by the hindsight bias. Our predictions would probably have been different if we had been assessing their circumstances earlier in those marriages. The hindsight bias is particularly powerful because we are unaware of its effect on our judgments.

9. For two years, students in my research methods course conducted a series of studies in which real dual-earner men and women read a story about Lisa and Rob, a fictitious dual-earner couple, and evaluate them as parents. In different versions of the story, the division of labor between them is varied. We conducted the studies to determine whether women would be seen as worse mothers if they shared childcare 50-50 with their husbands. Overall, the results have been encouraging for proponents of equality. Lisa was not criticized for sharing the care of her children. In fact, Rob took the heat when he didn't pitch in. Rob was rated worse when he contributed only 25 percent of the childcare than when he contributed 50 percent, which suggests that standards for fathers are changing. (However, fathers are still not expected to be 50-50 parents. Rob was rated no worse when he contributed 40 percent of the childcare than when he contributed 50 percent.) Interestingly, when Rob contributed 25 percent of the childcare, his parenting was criticized just as much when he was depicted working fifty hours a week as when he was reading the newspaper while Lisa took care of the kids. Providing financially for the family is not sufficient for good fatherhood today.

10. Kaplan and Granrose (1993) discovered that after childbirth only two factors distinguished women who quit from women who continued to work at their jobs: unmet job expectations and support from husbands. For additional evidence that husbands' support or lack of it influences women's employment decisions, see Glass (1988).

11. U.S. Bureau of the Census, 1990.

12. A tenured faculty member could theoretically spend anywhere from ten to over ninety hours a week working. The only fixed hours are those actually inside the classroom. Time devoted to teaching preparation, research, committee meetings, and administrative work varies from person to person. Research time invested was typically negotiated in the families in my study.

Universities and prestigious colleges expect their faculties to conduct research and to publish. The number and quality of a professor's publications usually play a central role in whether that professor receives tenure after a six-year probationary period. If denied tenure, the professor loses his or her job and may have great difficulty getting a commensurate academic job. If granted tenure, the professor virtually is assured a job for life. Although expected to publish after tenure, if the professor never publishes another word, his or her job is secure, and probably his or her salary will remain relatively unaffected (although scholarly success is necessary to obtain grants and other outside perks, such as speaking engagements, that carry financial remuneration). Most faculty members want to do scholarly research, but once they have received tenure, strictly speaking their jobs do not compel them to do so.

13. Hessing, 1993.

14. Increased flexibility in men's jobs does not necessarily translate into a greater share of domestic labor. Flextime, the flexible scheduling of the start and end of the workday, is an interesting example. Mellor (1986) reported that approximately 13 percent of workers have flextime available, and a recent study of federal workers showed that men are as likely to use flextime as women (Ezra & Deckman, 1996). However, a review of studies on the effects of flextime concluded that there was no evidence that it changed the division of labor in the family (Christensen & Staines, 1990). For example, Lee (1983) showed that when fathers used flextime they did not increase their contributions to housework or childcare unless they had a "radical" egalitarian ideology.

15. Rosalind seemed to experience an increase in self-esteem when she could cut back on paid work, unlike many other women. Pietromonaco, Manis, and Markus (1987) found that the relation between employment status and self-esteem in new mothers is moderated by career orientation. Among career-oriented women, those who were employed full time had higher self-esteem than their part-time or unemployed counterparts. But if women were not career-oriented, self-esteem was not affected by employment status.

16. In *The Hearts of Men,* Ehrenreich (1983) explores the historical roots of the contemporary breakdown of the breadwinning ethic.

17. In 1996, among two-parent families with a child under a year old, 44.1 percent of the mothers were not employed; 28.2 percent of all two-parent families with children conform to the father employed, stay-at-home mother model. These data show it is common for women to take time off, but by no means universal. A majority of mothers of infants work outside the home, and an overwhelming majority of mothers in two-parent families with children of all ages are employed (CPS Publications, 1997).

18. In 1996, a third of the employed mothers of children under three years old in two-parent families were working part time (CPS Publications, 1997).

19. Interruptions in women's work histories depress their salaries, affect their job status, and partially account for the wage gap between men and women (Blau & Ferber, 1986; Corcoran & Duncan, 1979; Olson, Frieze, & Detlefson, 1990; O'Neill, 1985; Polachek, 1975; Schneer & Reitman, 1990; Stewart & Greenhalgh, 1984).

20. See Steil (1997). This deference is reflected in family migration patterns. Shihadeh (1991) found that among migrant families with children, three fourths of the women who had moved said they had followed their husbands, whereas only 4 percent of the men said they had followed their wives. Bird and Bird (1985) also documented that men's jobs had more influence than women's on the last family move. Both Bielby and Bielby (1992) and Markham and Pleck (1986) found that women were less willing than men to relocate for a good job offer if the move would hurt their spouses' careers, although egalitarian ideology attenuated this gender difference.

In the studies cited above, women's income and education did not influence the gender bias in moves or willingness to move (except in Bird and Bird's study). Likewise, in a study of two-career marriages in which one spouse was either a Ph.D.-level psychologist or biologist, couples were more likely to have moved because of the husbands' rather than the wives' careers (Wallston, Foster, & Berger, 1978). Finally, a recent study of migration patterns of male and female scientists showed that female, but not male migration was reduced by having children (Shauman & Xie, 1996). The inequity in migration patterns hurts women's careers (Morrison & Lichter, 1988; Shihadeh, 1991; Shauman & Xie, 1996; Spitze, 1986a).

21. Lewis (1991) makes a similar argument.

22. Mahoney (1995) makes a similar argument.

23. All three groups reported approximately 62 hours per week of parental time with children, $F (2, 62) = 180.11, p > .50$.

24. Equally sharing mothers spent an average of 14.4 hours per week alone with their children, as compared with 24.7 hours spent by 75-25 mothers and 21.2 hours spent by 60-40 mothers, $F (2, 62) = 9.1, p < .001$. Equally sharing fathers spent an average of 14.4 hours per week alone with children, as compared with 12.7 hours spent by 60-40 fathers and 8.8 hours alone spent by 75-25 fathers, $F (2, 62) = 4.13$, $p < .05$.

25. The equal sharers spent 33.6 hours together with their children, as compared to 30.3 hours for the 60-40 parents and 27.5 for the 75-25 parents, $F (2, 62) = 2.99, p < .06$.

8. Why Couples Don't Practice What They Preach

1. See note 13 in Chapter 1 for mixed findings on the relation between gender-role ideology and the domestic division of labor, and for studies that have failed to confirm that relation. Some of the confirming studies have shown that men's ideology influences the division of labor more than women's, which suggests that men have greater power to actualize their beliefs in the family (e.g., Antill & Cotton, 1988; Bird et al., 1984; Wright, Shire, Hwang, Dolan, & Baxter, 1992). In contrast, however, McHale and Huston (1984) found that women's ideology predicted paternal involvement in infant care more than men's did. Keep in mind that a statistically significant relation between ideology and behavior implies neither that ideology and behavior are always linked, nor that when they are, the link is necessarily causal. People may subscribe to a particular gender-role ideology simply to justify their behavior.

2. See Josephs, Markus, and Tafarodi (1992) for more general evidence that self-esteem derives from adhering to cultural norms about gender.

3. See Cowan and Cowan (1992) for a discussion of obstacles to egalitarian parenting, despite parents' egalitarian beliefs.

4. Hochschild (1989) also observed that couples seem to have a "surface ideology" and a deeper set of feelings about gender, which sometimes clash.

5. Although today's women may have been raised in families where their mothers took a traditional role at home, many of them were encouraged to achieve and aspire to professional careers. According to Susan Douglas, author of the highly acclaimed book about the media, *Where the Girls Are,* girls of the baby boom genera-

tion were told to work hard, get educated, and achieve, while at the same time they were warned that femininity required them to be "pliant, cute, sexually available, thin, blond, poreless, wrinkle-free, and deferential to men" (p. 9).

6. Peters (1997) argues, for example, that "overparenting" children is detrimental.

7. The alternating-shift couples, who will be discussed in detail in Chapter 9, are the obvious exceptions. In those families the full-time parental care is shared by the mother and the father, each providing care when the spouse is at work.

8. L. and G. Ndikumana, personal communication, 1996.

9. Coontz, 1992; Skolnick, 1991.

10. They must be watching a lot of television. A recent study of 5,000 randomly selected American households found that, on average, two- to five-year-olds spend 23 hours and 31 minutes per week watching TV (Nielsen Media Research, 1997). Other recent research shows similarly high rates of TV watching. For example, a longitudinal study of 160 children aged three to five documented approximately 19.5 hours of television watching per week (Huston, Wright, Rice, Kerkman, & St. Peters, 1990). Likewise, a study of television watching among children with rules about TV versus children without rules found that even the regulated children watched an average of over 4.5 hours of TV per day, whereas the unregulated children watched in excess of 5 hours per day (Griffore & Phenice, 1996).

I couldn't find statistics on the number of hours children at home with their mothers spend watching TV, as compared with children in daycare. However, given that children in quality center-based care watch no TV during daycare hours, I suspect children at home with their mothers, cared for by relatives, or in family-based care watch more TV overall. See note 3 in Chapter 3 for some evidence.

Of course, I am not arguing that every daycare center is good, but simply that we should not always assume that maternal care is best. Center-based providers have the advantage of not being isolated the way at-home mothers often are. It is conceivable that adult collaboration in caring for children might translate to better care. No one has done the research to assess the quality of care given by stay-at-home mothers.

11. The research on which these results are based is a multisite, multi-investigator longitudinal study of 1,364 infants born in 1991. (See NICHD Early Child Care Research Network [1997c] for a description of the sample and method.) This study was designed by some of the leading child-development experts in the country, representing both sides of the daycare debate, and we can be confident its findings are sound.

Although there were no overall negative effects of daycare on maternal attachment, poor-quality daycare, when combined with low maternal responsivity, did result in a lower likelihood of secure attachment to mothers. Also, the researchers found a surprising interaction between the child's sex and the effects of daycare. Male infants in daycare in excess of thirty hours a week were at greater risk for insecure attachments than male infants in fewer hours of daycare, whereas female infants in daycare less than ten hours a week were more likely to have insecure maternal attachments than those who received more nonmaternal care (NICHD Early Child Care Research Network, 1997c). Some of the differences may reflect that, on average, girls receive higher-quality nonmaternal care than boys in childcare homes and, to a lesser degree, in daycare centers (NICHD Early Child Care Research Network, 1997b).

The quality of daycare children receive certainly matters more than time in daycare per se. For example, although children who had spent more time in daycare showed some signs of problems at age two (as reported by mothers and caregivers), by age three no such effects were evident. However, children who had had high-quality caregivers showed fewer problems at both two and three years of age than children with less sensitive and attentive caregivers (NICHD Early Child Care Research Network, 1998). High-quality child-caregiver interaction was also associated with better cognitive and linguistic outcomes (NICHD Early Child Care Research Network, 1997a).

Caregivers gave better-quality care to infants when they were responsible for a smaller group with a lower child-to-adult ratio, in a safe, clean, and stimulating environment. Nonauthoritarian beliefs of caregivers are also associated with better care (NICHD Early Child Care Research Network, 1996). Overall, the quality of nonmaternal care found in this study was better than that described in other studies, probably for a variety of reasons, including the broad scope of the study, both in terms of type of care (in-home care, family daycare, and daycare centers) and in terms of geographic locations (NICHD Early Child Care Research Network, 1996).

12. U.S. Bureau of Labor Statistics, 1997.

13. Alison Deal and I collaboratively developed this analysis, which informed the work for her honors thesis (Deutsch & Deal, 1996).

14. Perhaps the most famous and researched theory in social psychology, cognitive dissonance theory (Festinger, 1957), explains why and illustrates how beliefs follow behavior. More directly germane to my study, both Gerson (1985) and Hertz (1987) show that the choices women make in balancing work and family color their beliefs.

15. When I compared the 75-25, 60-40, and 50-50 mothers, I found a statistically significant effect of the division of labor on gender-role attitudes relevant to parenting, $F(2, 62) = 5.02, p < .01$. Mothers who did 75 percent of the childcare had more conservative attitudes about parental roles than mothers who contributed only 60 or 50 percent of the childcare. When I compared fathers in the three groups, however, I found that gender-role attitudes differed only slightly across the three groups, $F(2, 62) = 3.06, p < .06$, and no difference between any two of the groups reached statistical significance.

16. These attempts struck me as similar to people's efforts to bolster their self-images after having failed to live up to strongly held beliefs by grabbing the next available opportunity to act in accordance with those beliefs. For example, when "feminist" students realized they had failed to solve a riddle because of their own sexist assumptions, they were subsequently more likely to judge a sex-discrimination case in the woman's favor, presumably to reemphasize their feminism (Sherman & Gorkin, 1980).

17. Self-monitoring distinguishes between individuals who act according to their beliefs and those who do not. Low self-monitors tend to choose situations that support their attitudes and subsequently experience those attitudes as salient and consequently more influential in future decisions. High self-monitors are less likely to put themselves in attitude-consistent situations, and are less likely to be influenced

in subsequent situations by the choices they've made historically (DeBono & Snyder, 1995).

18. I don't mean to suggest that the people who do practice what they preach are simply guided by their desire for congruence between beliefs and behavior. The desire to live up to one's beliefs is only one factor among others influencing how people act.

9. The Mother and Mr. Mom

Portions of this chapter originally appeared in *Sex Roles, 38,* 331–332, published by Plenum Press (Deutsch & Saxon, 1998a).

1. Eric Olin Wright and his colleagues conducted a rigorous study of the relation between class and division of domestic labor in the United States and Sweden. Despite extensive analyses searching for class effects, they were forced to conclude that very little of the variation in the division of labor across households can be explained by class (Wright, Shire, Hwang, Dolan, & Baxter, 1992). Their findings debunk the stereotype that working-class men do less work at home than their upper-middle-class counterparts.

2. Alternating work shifts is not an entirely new social phenomenon. In 1977, for example (the first year for which the relevant statistics are available), 14.4 percent of dual-earner families with preschoolers used father care while mothers worked, whereas 18.5 percent did in 1996 (Casper, 1998). But when you take into account the higher employment rate for mothers of preschool children in 1996, you can see that the increase in paternal care of young children is more dramatic. When you consider all preschool children living with married parents, in 1977 5.6 percent received primary care from their fathers some of the time, whereas by 1996, the figure had doubled to 11.3 percent (Casper, 1998; U.S. Bureau of Labor Statistics, 1989, 1998).

In my study the parents of the alternating-shift couples (predominantly working class themselves) showed a much more traditional pattern in the division of labor than their offspring. In approximately two thirds of those families, fathers worked while mothers stayed at home. Two of the forty-six alternating-shift parents reported that their own parents had followed the same pattern, reflecting the national trends. But many more of them reported fathers who were gone most of the time working at two or three jobs or who were absent for other reasons.

3. The numbers refer to both part-time and full-time workers (U.S. Bureau of Labor Statistics, May 1997).

4. In dual-earner families with children under fifteen years of age, fathers are the primary caretakers of children during mothers' work hours in 4 percent of the families in which both parents work a day shift, 14 percent of the families in which mothers work a day and fathers work a nonday shift, 21.3 percent of the families in which mothers work a nonday and fathers work a day shift, and 17.5 percent of the families in which mothers and fathers both work a nonday shift (Casper, 1997). No data are available on how many of these families intentionally choose different shifts so they can alternate childcare, but many of the alternating shifters I interviewed reported that they had done so.

5. Casper, 1998.

6. Simon, 1990.

7. I did interview six other families who were alternating work shifts but had higher-status jobs. They were excluded from the analysis both because they are unrepresentative of alternating shifters and because they cannot illuminate the gender dynamics of sharing in blue-collar families. Statistical tests confirmed that the six families excluded had significantly higher incomes, more education, and higher job statuses than the rest of the alternating shifters. This group included, for example, teachers and master's-level nurses.

8. In approximately two thirds of the alternating-shift families the mother works the evening shift while the father works the day shift; in the other third the father works evenings while the mother works days. In one family, the father works the graveyard shift. Equal sharers report that on average fathers do 50.7 percent of the morning routine tasks with children; alternating shifters report that fathers do 26.8 percent.

9. The alternating-shift fathers report doing an average of 52 percent of the bedtime routines, the equal sharers 48 percent, and the 75-25 fathers 40 percent.

10. A closer look reveals that because the division of labor depends on who has which shift, some alternating-shift dads put kids to bed more than their wives and supervise morning routine as much as their wives. On average, the dads who work the day shift do 69 percent of the putting children to bed in their families. Dads who work the evening shift contributed 47.5 percent of the supervision of children's morning routines, virtually the same as the equally sharing dads.

11. The average age of the youngest child was five in the equally sharing families and three in the alternating-shift families. (This difference was statistically significant when only the two groups were compared, $t\,(47) = 2.34, p < .05$. But the difference was only marginally significant ($p < .11$) in an analysis of variance comparing the four groups, which is reported in "How I Did the Study.") Almost all (91 percent) of the alternating-shift fathers cared for at least one child younger than six years of age, and over two thirds cared for children younger than five. Three of the fathers were caring for babies at the time I interviewed them, but many more reminisced about their baby care in years past.

Two explanations might account for the difference in the age of the youngest child in the equally sharing and alternating-shift families. First, alternating shifts is disproportionately done by families with younger children (Casper, 1997), so the sample might reflect real demographic differences between the two groups. Second, there might have been a selection bias in the way I recruited participants. The affluent participants were more likely to be recruited from daycare centers and schools, whereas the alternating shifters were more likely to be recruited through word of mouth. If the recruitment methods were confounded with the age of the child, then the difference between groups in my study might not reflect a real demographic difference.

12. Nine percent of the 75-25 couples, 17 percent of the 60-40 couples, and 3 percent of the equally sharing couples reported conflict over housework, whereas 30 percent of the alternating-shift couples reported it.

13. In 1993 there were 8.1 million families whose preschool children needed care while their mothers were at work. Over half of the families paid for that care, an average of $74 per week, or 8 percent of their family income. Of course, the

lower their income, the higher the percentage cost. For example, if the monthly family income was between $1,200 and $2,999, paid childcare constituted 12 percent of their expenditures (Casper, 1995).

14. See Hertz, 1986. Of course, in an egalitarian world subtracting daycare costs from women's incomes wouldn't make sense. Doing so implies that women are responsible for childcare, and, as Hertz points out, it lowers the worth of women's work.

15. In a representative sample of employed mothers in Detroit, when household income was controlled, mothers who believe parental care is best were less likely to use paid childcare than other mothers (Kuhlthau & Mason, 1996).

16. The relation between the cost and quality of daycare is not as clear cut as one might think. Certainly better-trained daycare providers and better staff-to-children ratios, which both increase the cost of care, contribute to a higher quality of care (Mocan, Burchinal, Morris, & Helburn, 1995). But the cost of producing high-quality care is not identical to the costs parents incur. Many childcare centers are subsidized. In a study comparing the quality of care in different types of daycare centers (public, nonprofit-independent, for-profit), public centers were found to provide the best care, which was also the most expensive to produce. But, on average, the cost to parents was lower in public centers than in for-profit chains, which, despite their high price tag, provided relatively low-quality care (J. Morris, personal communication, January 16, 1998).

When it comes to center-based care, the working-class parents might have the worst of all possible worlds. The NICHD Early Child Care Research Network (1997b) uncovered a curvilinear relationship between family income and quality of care for children who receive center-based care. Poor and affluent children get better care at daycare centers than children from moderate-income families. The working-class families' relative lack of access to subsidized daycare centers means that their children fare worse than even poor children if they use center-based care.

The relation between family income and quality for family daycare and home-based care (excluding father and grandfather care) was more straightforward. Families who could pay more for these types of care purchased better care (NICHD Early Child Care Research Network, 1997b). When different types of care were compared overall in the NICHD study, more positive caregiving was observed in in-home care than in family daycare, which, in turn, offered more positive caregiving than did centers. Fathers received higher scores in quality of caregiving than other in-home providers, such as grandparents or babysitters (NICHD Early Child Care Research Network, 1996). We can't assume from these data that fathers provide better care than the highest-quality paid daycare. But since working-class couples can't afford or don't have access to the highest-quality daycare, it seems reasonable to assume that fathers' care is the best way to maximize quality.

17. Blumberg and Coleman (1989) elaborate this argument. Thompson (1991) also observed that women feel more entitled to have help with domestic work if they see themselves as contributing to the breadwinning.

18. Mason & Lu, 1988; Wilkie, 1993. The working-class alternating shifters in my study endorsed more traditional attitudes than the predominantly upper-middle-class couples in the 50-50, 60-40, and 75-25 groups. The alternating-shift couples had the lowest mean egalitarianism scores of the four groups on each of the

five subscales of the Beere-King Sex Role Egalitarianism Scale (education, employment, marital, parental, and social-interpersonal). Moreover, this pattern was most pronounced on the marital and parental subscales, the most relevant ones. Although both men and women were more traditional than their middle-class counterparts, the alternating-shift wives had more egalitarian views than their husbands. See Deutsch and Saxon (1998) for a more detailed statistical analysis.

19. The good provider role developed with the advent of industrialization in the early nineteenth century, and linked a masculine definition of self with the ability to provide for a family (Bernard, 1981). Today, even with so many women employed, because of the link between masculinity and providing, both men and women are reluctant to see wives as providers. Only a minority of couples think that the woman has the same kind of responsibility and obligation to provide for the family as the man (Hood, 1986; Potuchek, 1992, 1997). For example, only 12 percent of the 153 couples Potuchek (1997) interviewed thought of themselves as true co-providers. See Thompson and Walker (1989) for a summary of research on the gendered nature of the provider role, and see Potuchek (1992) for a detailed analysis of the meanings employed women and men attribute to their earnings.

Cohen (1993) speculated that working-class men are especially likely to see themselves as contributing to the family by providing because their jobs do not offer the intrinsic rewards available to professional men. Moreover, two studies of blue-collar women have found that even when they feel responsible for helping their husbands provide, they view themselves as secondary providers (Rosen, 1987; Zavella, 1987).

Consistent with these past findings, among the alternating-shift couples I interviewed, 18 (78 percent) of the men and 15 (65 percent) of the women emphasized that the men are the breadwinners in their families. Only one of the men and three of the women explicitly challenged that idea. Hood's category of "ambivalent co-provider" (1983) seems to best capture the attitudes that were prevalent in my sample. Couples recognized the necessity of wives' financial contributions but were not entirely comfortable with it, especially the men.

20. Other researchers have noted that couples sometimes emphasize the relative importance of men's jobs by earmarking men's incomes for essentials and women's for "extras" (Potuchek, 1997; Thompson & Walker, 1989). (Sometimes those "extras," however, can be pretty essential.)

21. Organizing family life this way also preserves women's roles as the primary parents.

22. See Thompson and Walker (1989) for a summary of other studies of working-class couples that also show that women's needing to work for the money did not preclude their wanting to work. Lillian Rubin (1969) uncovered some similar patterns in her study of working-class families. Although women derived status from having husbands who could earn enough so that they didn't need paid work, even in the 1960s the women who were forced to work outside the home for financial reasons discovered that they liked having paid employment.

23. In two other families, either the husband or the wife reported fighting over this issue, but the spouse in each case denied there had been a conflict.

24. Komter, 1989.

25. Garey (1995) also observed that hospital nurses who work the night shift

construct themselves as "at-home" mothers because they are home during the day, even though many are home sleeping.

26. Coltrane, 1996; Gerson, 1993.

27. In her (1993) analysis of the gendered nature of giving "care" in a family, Thompson says that "men are more likely to display care when there is a clear need for care, no one else is around to provide care, and the recipient is dependent" (p. 564). These are exactly the circumstances of the alternating-shift fathers. Their children need care, their wives are at work, and their children are dependent on them.

28. See Hammond and Mahoney (1983) for an example of how another nontraditional group, female coal-miners, maintains a traditional feminine identity.

29. As the division of labor changes at home, "doing gender" in these blue-collar families is shifting from the enactment of different male and female behaviors to the construction of gendered meanings for what are often the same behaviors (Ferree, 1990; West & Zimmerman, 1987). As others have argued and these families show, family is often the locus of the creation of gender (Osmond & Thorne, 1993).

30. Likewise, a study of the families of male Air Force security guards who worked off-shifts showed that although the husbands took care of their children when their wives were employed, they had not changed their ideas that mothers were ultimately responsible for child care (Hertz & Charlton, 1989).

31. Lein's (1979) intensive study of twenty-five dual-earner households in the 1970s found a similar result among a broader income group.

32. In several articles, Myra Marx Ferree (1980, 1983, 1984a, 1984b) has argued that the traditionalism of working-class women has been exaggerated. She has taken to task middle-class feminists who assume that working-class women would rather be home as housewives than out in the paid labor force. In fact, she showed that when middle-class and working-class employed women and housewives were compared, the working-class housewives were the least satisfied group (1984b).

10. Constructing Identities as Parents and Professionals

1. See Stewart (1982) for a discussion of life changes as an impetus to changes in identity. In my discussion of identity in this chapter, I am assuming that an individual has multiple selves or identities that vary in importance. These identities both give meaning to and regulate behavior. My assumptions are similar to those made by both sociologists who study identity (e.g., Burke & Reitzes, 1991; McCall, 1987; Nuttbrock & Freudiger, 1991; Stryker, 1968, 1987; Stryker & Serpe, 1994) and psychologists who study the self (see Markus, 1987, for an excellent review).

2. See Garey (1995) for a discussion of how mothers construct themselves as the kind of mothers they want to be out of what they do as mothers. Also, see Miller (1996) for a description of how new mothers negotiate their identities in the transition back to careers.

3. My use of the word "professional" in this chapter is not meant to limit the implications of my analysis to people with careers in professions like law, medicine, and college teaching. Here, "professional" refers to a person who derives a sense of identity from work, and experiences (or expects to experience) mastery and accomplishment at his or her job.

4. In a study of the transition to parenthood in seventy-two couples, new parents were asked to divide a pie into wedges that represented the relative importance of different parts of their selves. Women saw themselves more as mothers than as workers, whereas men saw themselves more as workers than as fathers (Cowan & Cowan, 1992; Cowan, Cowan, Heming, & Miller, 1991).

Bielby and Bielby (1989) also found that men were somewhat more likely to identify with work roles, whereas women were more likely to identify with family roles. Moreover, they showed (with 1970s data) that women's family and work identities were at odds, whereas men's were not. For men, commitment to dual roles did not create a conflict, presumably because the meaning of fatherhood for men is not as tied to spending time with and taking responsibility for children as it is for women. Although I don't have comparable data for my participants, I suspect that equal sharers would show a very different pattern. Equally sharing mothers probably feel less conflict between parenting and work identities than other women, whereas equally sharing fathers probably feel more conflict than other men.

5. The split in the nature of gendered identities is a product of nineteenth-century industrialization and the ideology of separate spheres. Presumably pioneer women and colonial mothers had productive work at home besides childrearing, which informed their identities.

6. These enriched identities enhance self-esteem. In Cowan and Cowan's (1992) transition to parenthood study, women who invested more of themselves in parenting (and presumably less in work) relative to other women had lower self-esteem; fathers who invested themselves more in parenting than other men had higher self-esteem.

7. Equally sharing women earn $36,547 a year, on average, compared to $27,787 and $27,708 for the 75-25 and 60-40 women. These differences do not quite reach statistical significance ($p < .13$), but might with a larger sample.

8. Ehrensaft (1987) reported a distinction between "doing" and "being" among a group of nontraditional parents she studied in the 1970s. Mothers "were" parents, whereas even highly participant fathers "did" parenting. In contrast, the equally sharing fathers in my study *were* parents every bit as much as their wives. They incorporated parenting into the center of their identities.

9. For example, people maintain their self-esteem by disinvesting in domains in which they have been outperformed by someone close (Tesser, 1988). Likewise, stigmatized groups maintain their self-esteem by devaluing domains in which their group does poorly (Crocker & Major, 1989). Stryker (1987) argued that the higher the role-specific self-esteem is, the more salient the identity based on that role.

10. The discouraging effect of wives' competence in parenting is consistent with self-evaluation maintenance theory, which asserts that when people who are close outperform us, their excellence threatens our self-esteem if the performance dimensions are important to us, but enhances self-esteem if the dimensions are not relevant, through reflected appraisal (pride) (Tesser, 1988). Thus relationships in which people excel in different areas work better, and people will avoid performing on dimensions of excellence of their friends, siblings, and spouses. For example, a study of marital partners showed that they avoided tasks and activities in which one partner outperformed the other in a domain the inferior partner

thought was important (Beach, Tesser, Mendolia, Anderson, Crelia, Whitaker, & Fincham, 1996). This dynamic poses a dilemma for equally shared parenting, in which both parents need to invest in being good parents. If the mother is clearly the superior parent, self-evaluation maintenance theory predicts that the father would avoid parenting.

11. The equal sharers' disappointments with their own fathers paralleled the disappointment of men in the other groups. About half of the men in the 50-50, 60-40, and 75-25 groups depicted their own fathers as unavailable or worse while they were growing up. Among the alternating-shift fathers, three quarters gave negative reports.

12. In a classic article, Nancy Felipe Russo (1976) described the "motherhood mandate," which prescribes that the goal of all women's lives should be to have children (at least two) and to raise them well. Implicit was the notion that the good mother is the exclusive and irreplaceable caretaker of her children. Despite the changes of the last three decades, the motherhood mandate is still very much with us (Phoenix & Woollett, 1991; Thurer, 1994).

But the ideals of an exclusive maternal-child bond, as well as those of responsive and sensitive mothering, are culturally and historically bound (Hays, 1996; Thurer, 1994). Although today the ideal of maternal exclusivity is quite powerful in the dominant white middle-class culture in the United States, that ideal is rejected by poor and working-class African American mothers (Blum & Deussen, 1996), who value "other-mothers" of their children, often kin of the biological mother (Greene, 1990). Welles-Nystrom, New, and Richman's (1994) comparison of motherhood ideals and maternal behavior in the United States, Sweden, and Italy shows significant cross-cultural variation even among middle-class Western countries.

13. No one has written more eloquently about the anguish mothers experience trying to fulfill the requirements of "the institution of motherhood" than Adrienne Rich in *Of Woman Born*. Rich raised her children in the 1950s. Sharon Thurer (1994) argues that standards for ideal mothering have become even more exacting since then, subjecting mothers, who feel compelled to fulfill them, to self-doubts, guilt, and a profound sense of inadequacy.

14. Ruth and Rhona's experiences conform to a pattern of maternal self-definitional processes described by Hartrick (1997): "nonreflective doing" (simply falling into socially prescribed roles), "living in the shadows" (coming to acknowledge their discontent with conventional roles), and "reclaiming and discovery" (rejecting conventional roles to come to a more authentic way of living).

15. Almost 40 percent of the equally sharing mothers expressed guilt about something during their interviews. That percentage, though high, was lower than the percentage of the mothers who expressed guilt in the other groups (57 percent, 56 percent, and 68 percent for the 75-25, 60-40, and alternating-shift mothers, respectively). Although the differences between the groups are not statistically significant, at least they suggest that equally sharing mothers do not have to bear an extra burden of guilt.

16. Motherhood entails a moral transformation of the self. Women judge themselves as having become better human beings by virtue of loving and nurturing their children unselfishly (McMahon, 1995). The women who successfully trans-

formed motherhood in my study maintained its moral claims, deeming themselves good mothers because they possessed the right feelings toward their children.

11. Equality Works

1. Crittenden, 1995.

2. Hochschild, 1989.

3. The imagined internal monologues I include in this section are not actual quotations but constructions based on my analysis of the fears about equality that women express.

4. I have borrowed this phrase from Karl Marx, who wrote in the *Communist Manifesto:* "Workers of the world unite. You have nothing to lose but your chains, and a world to gain."

5. Laura Servis interviewed the ten- and eleven-year-old children of my participants as part of her honors thesis and discovered that children had higher self-esteem when their fathers contributed a greater proportion of parental attentiveness, nurturance, and discipline, and when the children felt closer to their fathers (Deutsch, Servis, & Payne, 1998).

6. Equal sharing also teaches children an ideology of gender equality, particularly with respect to adult rights and roles. But egalitarian families notwithstanding, children may adopt stereotypical ideas about boys and girls that reflect the gendered world outside their homes (Risman & Myers, 1997).

7. See Susan Moller Okin's wonderful book, *Justice, Gender, and the Family,* for a passionate and compelling argument that equally shared parenting is imperative if we are to create just families and a just democracy.

8. Suitor (1991) found that women were more satisfied with their marriages if they were satisfied with the division of labor. Dissatisfaction with the division was greatest when there were preschool and school-age kids at home, when the burden was greatest on women.

9. Pepper Schwartz (1994) argues that shared parenting facilitates the deep friendship which is at the core of the best marriages.

10. Men also accrue mental health benefits from being involved in fatherhood (Barnett & Rivers, 1996).

11. Papanek (1973) describes the peculiar American institution of the "two-person career."

12. Fowlkes (1987) argues that a conventional career is only feasible for men because it relies on the support of wives. She shows that the wives of physicians and academics play an important role in ensuring their husbands' success by freeing them from the constraints of family life, as well as by giving them outright help and support in their work.

13. Bem (1993) argues that our social institutions promote three "lenses of gender" that bolster sexual inequality: gender polarization, androcentrism, and biological essentialism. Equally sharing parents, as "gender nonconformists," challenge all three, and promote the transformation of careers and families into social institutions that hinder rather than foster inequality.

14. See LaRossa (1988, p. 454) for a description of the "technically present but functionally absent father."

15. Fathers in the equally sharing families did 18 percent of the clothes-buying and 34 percent of the arranging of play dates.

16. Equally sharing fathers certainly did more managing than fathers in the 60-40 or 75-25 couples. In fact, on average, the equal sharers did about 40 percent of the managing in their families.

17. Arlie Hochschild's eye-opening analysis in *Time Bind* (1997) shows how employers with ostensibly family-friendly policies subtly and not-so-subtly discourage employees from taking advantage of those policies.

18. In an important analysis of the Family and Medical Leave Act, Gerstel and McGonagle (1998) show that people who need leaves the most are often not in a position to take them. Blacks, for example, need leaves more than whites, but take them less frequently. Married white women in affluent families take the greatest advantage of family leaves.

How I Did the Study

1. Because of the nature of the recruitment procedures, it is difficult to calculate the response rates from daycare centers, schools, and recommendations, or from our random sample. A total of 419 couples either answered our initial inquiries or were recommended by other participants. All were contacted by my research assistants or me and asked to participate in a 15-minute telephone interview assessing the division of childcare responsibilities in their families. Of the 419 couples contacted, only 14 (3%) declined to participate. An additional 25 (6%) were ineligible, and interviews with 6 couples had to be discarded because only one spouse was contacted. Thus these procedures yielded 374 participating couples, 90% of those who showed some initial interest.

In the random telephone survey, 639 couples were reached by phone, but 484 of those reached were ineligible to participate (76%) and 90 (14%) refused to participate. In 10 couples only one spouse completed the telephone interview. Thus the random sampling procedure yielded 55 participating couples for the telephone interview.

2. Five of the wives interviewed by phone were Asian American, 4 African American, 6 Latino, and 1 Eurasian. One of the husbands was Native American, 1 Asian American, 6 African American, 6 Latino, and 1 Eurasian.

3. Two independent coders rated occupational prestige on the Hollingshead (1975) scale and attained an inter-rater reliability of $r = .93$.

4. The lists of characteristics served as an ice-breaker during the interviews and have not yet been analyzed further; King and King, 1990; Spanier, 1976.

5. I will not explain here all the elaborate decision rules we applied to determine whether a change in a husband's and/or wife's report of the division of labor was large enough to merit reclassification. More detailed information about the classification system is available from me.

6. The very stringent quantitative criteria meant that 9 cases were excluded from the equally sharing group in statistical analyses because although either a husband or wife reported equality during both interviews, the other spouse reported that the husband was contributing more than half. In 6 out of the 9 cases, the mean estimates for husbands' contributions did not exceed 55%, and in one of those

cases it was only 51%. Although I did not include them in statistical analyses, I did use them as examples of equal sharers in elaborating the qualitative analysis.

7. Note that some participants were not included in the 60-40 or 75-25 groups for subsequent statistical analyses even though both agreed that the division was unequal. I included these clearly unequal couples in qualitative analyses if the level of inequality was unimportant to the issue I was considering.

8. Analyses of variance and Chi square analyses were used to test differences on the demographic variables, except for income differences, which were assessed with k-sample median tests. Unless otherwise noted, all p's $< .001$.

9. Based on fertility rates for different age groups as a function of family income reported by the U.S. Bureau of the Census (1997), maternal age for first births is lower in working-class families than in upper-middle-class families. Thus it is not surprising that the alternating-shift couples were younger than couples in the other groups.

10. My approach is best described by the 10 principles and practices synthesized in Tesch's (1990) qualitative analysis of the advice given by the major proponents of qualitative research.

11. The Ethnograph (Seidel, Kjolseth, & Seymour, 1988) allows one to print out the answers all participants gave to a particular question, and even to sort them according to different groups of participants. It also allows one to print out information participants gave related to a theme, but only after the themes have been categorized, coded, and marked by the researcher.

12. I used the guidelines set out by Clifft (1986) in his discussion of how to disguise the case material of psychiatric patients. Although my study did not use a clinical sample, I believe the same ethical issues apply.

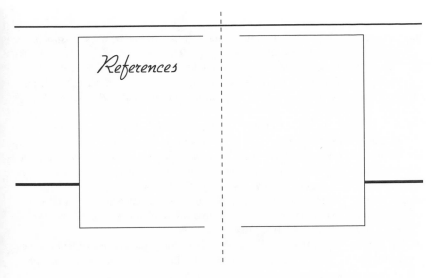

Ainsworth, M. D. S., Blehar, M. C., Waters, E., & Wall, S. (1978). *Patterns of attachment: A psychological study of the strange situation.* Hillsdale, NJ: Lawrence Erlbaum Associates.

Almeida, D. M., Maggs, J. L., & Galambos, N. L. (1993). Wives' employment hours and spousal participation in family work. *Journal of Family Psychology, 7,* 233–244.

Anderson, W. T., Golden, L. L., Umesh, U. N., & Weeks, W. A. (1992). Timestyles: Role factor influences on the convergence and divergence of couples' complementary and substitute activity patterns. *Psychology & Marketing, 9,* 101–122.

Antill, J. K., & Cotton, S. (1988). Factors affecting the division of labor in households. *Sex Roles, 18,* 531–553.

Asch, S. E. (1951). Effects of group pressure upon the modification and distortion of judgments. In H. Guetzkow (ed.), *Groups, leadership, and men* (pp. 177–190). Pittsburgh: Carnegie Press.

Aytac, I. (1990). Sharing household tasks in the United States and Sweden: A reassessment of Kohn's theory. *Sociological Spectrum, 10,* 357–371.

Bacher, R. (1994). Confessions of a breast-feeding dropout. *Redbook, 184,* p. 71.

Barker, K. (1993). Changing assumptions and contingent solutions: The costs and benefits of women working full- and part-time. *Sex Roles, 28,* 47–71.

Barnett, R. C., & Baruch, G. K. (1987). Determinants of fathers' participation in family work. *Journal of Marriage and the Family, 49,* 29–40.

Barnett, R. C., & Rivers, C. (1996). *She works he works: How two-income families are happier, healthier, and better-off.* San Francisco: Harper.

Baruch, G. K., & Barnett, R. C. (1981). Fathers' participation in the care of their preschool children. *Sex Roles, 7,* 1043–1055.

—— (1986). Consequences of fathers' participation in family work: Parents' role strain and well-being. *Journal of Personality and Social Psychology, 51,* 983–992.

Baxter, J. (1988). The sexual division of labour in Australian families. *Australian Journal of Sex, Marriage, and Family, 9,* 87–93.

Beach, S. R. H., Tesser, A., Mendolia, M., Anderson, P., Crelia, R., Whitaker, D., & Fincham, F. D. (1996). Self-evaluation maintenance in marriage: Toward a performance ecology of the marital relationship. *Journal of Family Psychology, 10,* 379–396.

Beckett, J. O., & Smith, A. D. (1981). Work and family roles: Egalitarian marriage in Black and White families. *Social Service Review, 55,* 314–325.

Beckman, L. J., & Houser, B. B. (1979). The more you have, the more you do: The relationship between wife's employment, sex-role attitudes, and household behaviors. *Psychology of Women Quarterly, 4,* 160–174.

Belsky, J. (1985). Exploring individual differences in marital change across the transition to parenthood: The role of violated expectations. *Journal of Marriage and the Family, 47,* 1037–1044.

Belsky, J., Lang, M., & Huston, T. L. (1986). Sex typing and division of labor as determinants of marital change across the transition to parenthood. *Journal of Personality and Social Psychology, 50,* 517–522.

Bem, S. L. (1993). *Lenses of gender: Transforming the debate on sexual inequality.* New Haven: Yale University Press.

Benin, M. H., & Agostinelli, J. (1988). Husbands' and wives' satisfaction with the division of labor. *Journal of Marriage and the Family, 50,* 349–361.

Benson, J. R. (1995). Nursing made easy. *Parents, 70,* 22–23.

Berardo, D. H., Shehan, C. L., & Leslie, G. R. (1987). A residue of tradition: Jobs, careers, and spouses' time in housework. *Journal of Marriage and the Family, 49,* 381–390.

Berger, P., & Kellner, H. (1964). Marriage and the construction of reality: An exercise in the microsociology of knowledge. *Diogenes, 46,* 1–23.

Berger, P. L., & Luckmann, T. (1967). *The social construction of reality: A treatise in the sociology of knowledge.* Garden City, NY: Anchor Books.

Berheide, C. W. (1984). Women's work in the home: Seems like old times. *Marriage and Family Review, 7,* 37–55.

Berk, S. F. (1985). *The gender factory: The apportionment of work in American households.* New York: Plenum Press.

Bernard, J. (1981). The good provider role: Its rise and fall. *American Psychologist, 36,* 1–12.

Bernstein, L. (1993). Weaning. *Parents, 68,* 94–96.

Bertram, B. (1978). *Pride of lions.* New York: Charles Scribner's Sons.

Bielby, D. D., & Bielby, W. T. (1988). She works hard for the money: Household responsibilities and the allocation of work effort. *American Journal of Sociology, 93,* 1031–1059.

Bielby, W. T., & Bielby, D. D. (1989). Family ties: Balancing commitments to work and family in dual earner households. *American Sociological Review, 54,* 776–789.

——— (1992). I will follow him: Family ties, gender-role beliefs, and reluctance to relocate for a better job. *American Journal of Sociology, 97,* 1241–1267.

Biernat, M., & Wortman, C. B. (1991). Sharing of home responsibilities between professionally employed women and their husbands. *Journal of Personality and Social Psychology, 60,* 844–860.

Bird, G. A., & Bird, G. W. (1985). Determinants of mobility in two-earner families: Does the wife's income count? *Journal of Marriage and the Family, 47,* 753–758.

Bird, G. A., Bird, G. W., & Scruggs, M. (1984). Determinants of family task sharing: A study of husbands and wives. *Journal of Marriage and the Family, 46,* 345–356.

Blain, J. (1994). Discourses of agency and domestic labor: Family discourse and gendered practice in dual-earner families. *Journal of Family Issues, 15,* 515–549.

Blair, S. L., & Johnson, M. P. (1992). Wives' perceptions of the fairness of the division of household labor: The intersection of housework and ideology. *Journal of Marriage and the Family, 54,* 570–581.

Blair, S. L., & Lichter, D. T. (1991). Measuring the division of household labor: Gender segregation of housework among American couples. *Journal of Family Issues, 12,* 91–113.

Blau, F. D., & Ferber, M. A. (1986). *The economics of women, men, and work.* Englewood Cliffs, NJ: Prentice Hall.

Blood, R. O., & Wolfe, D. M. (1960). *Husbands and wives: The dynamics of married living.* New York: Free Press.

Blum, L. M., & Deussen, T. (1996). Negotiating independent motherhood: Working-class African American women talk about marriage and motherhood. *Gender and Society, 10,* 199–211.

Blumberg, R. L., & Coleman, M. T. (1989). A theoretical look at the gender balance of power in the American couple. *Journal of Family Issues, 10,* 225–250.

Blumstein, P., & Schwartz, P. (1991). Money and ideology: Their impact on power and the division of household labor. In R. L. Blumberg (ed.), *Gender, family, and economy: The triple overlap* (pp. 261–288). Beverly Hills: Sage Publications.

Bond, J. T., Galinsky, E., & Swanberg, J. E. (1998). *The 1997 National study of changing work force.* New York: Families and Work Institute.

Brayfield, A. A. (1992). Employment resources and housework in Canada. *Journal of Marriage and the Family, 54,* 19–30.

Brody, J. E. (1994, April 6). With all the reasons to breastfeed, too few do so. *New York Times,* p. C11.

Bureau of Labor Statistics. (1994). *Employment and Earnings Characteristics of Families: Fourth Quarter 1993* (USDL 94–33). Washington, DC: U.S. Department of Labor, Bureau of Labor Statistics.

Burke, P. J., & Reitzes, D. C. (1991). An identity theory approach to commitment. *Social Psychology Quarterly, 54,* 239–251.

Calasanti, T. M., & Bailey, C. A. (1991). Gender inequality and the division of household labor in the United States and Sweden: A socialist-feminist approach. *Social Problems, 38,* 34–53.

Campos, J. J., & Lamb, M. E. (1982). *Development in infancy: An introduction.* New York: Random House.

Caplan, T. (1993). *The first twelve months of life.* New York: Putnam Publishing Group.

Carlson, B. E. (1981). Preschoolers' sex-role identity, father-role perceptions, and paternal family participation. *Journal of Family Issues, 2,* 238–255.

———— (1984). The father's contribution to child care: Effects on children's perceptions of parental roles. *American Journal of Orthopsychiatry, 54,* 123–136.

Casper, L. M. (1995). What does it cost to mind our preschoolers? (Current Population Reports: Household Economic Studies P70–52). Washington, DC: U.S. Census Bureau.

———— (1997). My daddy takes care of me! Fathers as care providers (Current Population Reports: Household Economic Studies P70–59, table 5). Washington, DC: U.S. Census Bureau.

———— (1998). Who's minding our preschoolers? (Fall 1994 update; Current Population Reports: Household Economic Studies, detailed tables for P70–62, PPL-81). Washington, DC: U.S. Census Bureau. On-line: http://www.census.gov/population/www/soc demo/child care.htm.

Chan, R. W., Brooks, R. C., Raboy, B., & Patterson, C. (1998). Division of labor among lesbian and heterosexual parents: Associations with children's adjustment. *Journal of Family Psychology, 12,* 402–419.

Charles, M., & Hopflinger, F. (1992). Gender, culture and the division of household labor: A replication of U.S. studies for the case of Switzerland. *Journal of Comparative Family Studies, 23,* 375–387.

Chira, S. (1994, October 9). One who left and doesn't look back. *New York Times,* sec. 3, p. 6.

Chodorow, N. (1978). *The reproduction of mothering: Psychoanalysis and the sociology of gender.* Berkeley: University of California Press.

Christensen, K. (1988). Women's labor force attachment: Rise of contingent work. In *Flexible workstyles: A look at contingent labor* (pp. 76–82). Washington, DC: U.S. Department of Labor, Women's Bureau.

Christensen, K. E., & Staines, G. L. (1990). Flextime: A viable solution to the work/family conflict? *Journal of Social Issues, 11,* 455–476.

Clifft, M. A. (1986). Writing about psychiatric patients: Guidelines for disguising case material. *Bulletin of the Menninger Clinic, 50,* 511–524.

Cohen, T. F. (1993). What do fathers provide? Reconsidering the economic and nurturant dimensions of men as parents. In J. C. Hood (ed.), *Men, work, and family* (pp. 1–22). Newbury Park: Sage Publications.

Coltrane, S. (1988). Father-child relationships and the status of women: A cross-cultural study. *American Journal of Sociology, 93,* 1060–1095.

———— (1989). Household labor and the routine production of gender. *Social Problems, 36,* 473–490.

———— (1996). *Family man: Fatherhood, housework, and gender equity.* New York: Oxford University Press.

Coltrane, S., & Ishii-Kuntz, M. (1992). Men's housework: A life course perspective. *Journal of Marriage and the Family, 54,* 43–57.

Conrad, E. (1992). When to wean. *Working Mother, 15,* p. 46.

Cooley, C. H. (1902). *Human nature and the social order.* New York: Charles Scribner's Sons.

Coontz, S. (1992). *The way we never were: American families and the nostalgia trap.* New York: Basic Books.

Corcoran, M., & Duncan, G. J. (1979). Work history, labor force attachment, and earnings differences between the races and sexes. *Journal of Human Resources, 14,* 3–20.

Coverman, S. (1983). Gender, domestic labor time, and wage inequality. *American Sociological Review, 48,* 623–637.

———— (1985). Explaining husbands' participation in domestic labor. *The Sociological Quarterly, 26,* 81–97.

Cowan, C. P., & Cowan, P. A. (1992). *When partners become parents: The big life change for couples.* New York: Basic Books.

Cowan, C. P., Cowan, P. A., Heming, G., & Miller, N. B. (1991). Becoming a family: Marriage, parenting, and child development. In P. A. Cowan and M. Hetherington (eds.), *Family transitions* (pp. 79–109). Hillsdale, NJ: Lawrence Erlbaum Associates.

Cowan, P. A. (1997). Beyond meta-analysis: A plea for a family systems view of attachment. *Child Development, 68,* 601–603.

Cox, M. J., Owen, M. T., Henderson, V. K., & Margard, N. A. (1992). Prediction of infant-father and infant-mother attachment. *Developmental Psychology, 28,* 474–483.

CPS Publications (1997). *Employment characteristics of families: 1996.* On-line: http://www.bls.census.gov/cps/pub/famee_0697.htm.

Crittenden, D. (1995, August 22). Yes, motherhood lowers pay. *New York Times,* p. A15.

Crocker, J., & Major, B. (1989). Social stigma and self-esteem: The self-protective properties of stigma. *Psychological Review, 96,* 608–630.

Crosby, F. J. (1991). *Juggling: The unexpected advantages of balancing career and home for women and their families.* New York: Free Press.

Crouter, A. C., Perry-Jenkins, M., Huston, T. L., & McHale, S. M. (1987). Processes underlying father involvement in dual-earner and single-earner families. *Developmental Psychology, 23,* 431–440.

Curtis, R. C., & Miller, K. (1986). Believing another likes or dislikes you: Behaviors making the beliefs come true. *Journal of Personality and Social Psychology, 51,* 284–290.

Davis, M. R. (1982). *The impact of organizations on family life.* New York: Praeger Publishers.

Davis, R. F., & Sanik, M. M. (1991). Fathers' participation in infant-care. *Journal of Consumer Studies and Home Economics, 15,* 45–55.

Day, R. D., & Mackey, W. C. (1989). An alternate standard for evaluating American fathers. *Journal of Family Issues, 10,* 401–408.

DeBono, K. G., & Snyder, M. (1995). Acting on one's attitudes: The role of a history of choosing situations. *Personality and Social Psychology Bulletin, 21,* 629–636.

DeFrain, H. (1979). Androgynous parents tell who they are and what they need. *The Family Coordinator, 28,* 237–243.

DeMaris, A., & Longmore, M. A. (1996). Ideology, power, and equity: Testing competing explanations for the perceptions of fairness in household labor. *Social Forces, 74,* 1043–1071.

DeMeis, D. K., & Perkins, H. W. (1996). "Supermoms" of the nineties: Homemaker and employed mothers' performance and perception of the motherhood role. *Journal of Family Issues, 17,* 776–792.

Demo, D. H., & Acock, A. C. (1993). Family diversity and the division of domestic labor: How much have things really changed? *Family Relations, 42,* 323–331.

Dettwyler, K. A. (1995). A time to wean: The hominid blueprint for the natural age of weaning in modern human populations. In P. Stuart-Macadam and K. A. Dettwyler (eds.), *Breastfeeding: Biocultural perspectives* (pp. 39–73). New York: Aldine de Gruyter.

Deutsch, F. M., & Deal, A. (1996, August). Managing contradictions between beliefs about gender equality and the reality of inequality at home. Paper presented at the twenty-sixth International Congress of Psychology, Montreal, Canada.

Deutsch, F. M., Lussier, J. B., & Servis, L. J. (1993). Husbands at home: Predictors of paternal participation in childcare and housework. *Journal of Personality and Social Psychology, 65,* 1154–1166.

Deutsch, F. M., & Saxon, S. E. (1998a). Traditional ideologies, nontraditional lives. *Sex Roles, 38,* 331–362.

—— (1998b). The double standard of praise and criticism for mothers and fathers. *Psychology of Women Quarterly, 22,* 665–683.

Deutsch, F. M., Servis, L. J., & Payne, J. D. (1998). Paternal participation in childcare and its effects on children's self-esteem. Manuscript submitted for publication.

Douglas, S. (1995). *Where the girls are.* New York: Random House.

Douthitt, R. A. (1989). The division of labor within the home: Have gender roles changed? *Sex Roles, 20,* 693–704.

Duck, S. (1983). *Friends, for life: The psychology of close relationships.* New York: St. Martin's Press.

Dyer, E. D. (1963). Parenthood as crisis: A re-study. *Marriage and Family Living, 25,* 196–201.

Eaton, A. P., & Cassidy, A. (1991). Breast-feeding your baby. *Good Housekeeping, 213,* 162.

Ehrenreich, B. (1981). Stop ironing the diapers. In Ehrenreich, *The worst years of our lives: Irreverent notes from a decade of greed* (pp. 145–149). New York: Pantheon Books.

—— (1983). *The hearts of men: American dreams and the flight from commitment.* Garden City, NY: Anchor Press/Doubleday.

Ehrensaft, D. (1987). *Parenting together: Men and women sharing the care of their children.* New York: Free Press.

Eiger, M. S., & Olds, S. W. (1987). *The complete book of breastfeeding.* New York: Bantam.

Eisenburg, A., Murkoff, H., & Hathaway, S. E. (1996). *What to expect in the first year.* New York: Workman Publishing.

Ekanem, E. E. (1993). The epidemiology of breastfeeding cessation in sub-urban Lagos, Nigeria. *Early Child Development and Care, 84,* 111–116.

Ephron, N. (1983). *Heartburn.* New York: Alfred A. Knopf.

Eyer, D. E. (1992). *Mother-infant bonding: A scientific fiction.* New Haven: Yale University Press.

Ezra, M., & Deckman, M. (1996). Balancing work and family responsibilities: Flextime and child care in the federal government. *Public Administration Review, 56,* 174–179.

Fackelmann, K. (1994). Nursing protects moms from breast cancer. *Science News, 145,* 38.

Farkas, G. (1976). Education, wage rates, and the division of labor between husband and wife. *Journal of Marriage and the Family, 38,* 473–483.

Ferree, M. M. (1976). Working class jobs: Housework and paid work as sources of satisfaction. *Social Problems, 23,* 431–441.

—— (1980). Working class feminism: A consideration of the consequences of employment. *The Sociological Quarterly, 21,* 173–184.

—— (1983). The women's movement in the working class. *Sex Roles, 9,* 493–505.

—— (1984a). The view from below: Women's employment and gender equality in working class families. In B. Hess & M. Sussman (eds.), *Women and the family: Two decades of change* (pp. 57–75). New York: Haworth Press.

—— (1984b). Class, housework, and happiness: Women's work and life satisfaction. *Sex Roles, 11,* 1057–1074.

—— (1990). Beyond separate spheres: Feminism and family research. *Journal of Marriage and the Family, 52,* 866–884.

—— (1991). The gender division of labor in two-earner marriages: Dimensions of variability and change. *Journal of Family Issues, 12,* 158–180.

Festinger, L. (1957). *A theory of cognitive dissonance.* Palo Alto: Stanford University Press.

Fildes, V. (1995). The culture and biology of breastfeeding: An historical review of western Europe. In P. Stuart-Macadam and K. A. Dettwyler (eds.), *Breastfeeding: Biocultural perspectives* (pp. 101–126). New York: Aldine de Gruyter.

Fischer, C. S. (1982). *To dwell among friends: Personal networks in town and city.* Chicago: University of Chicago Press.

Fischhoff, B. (1975). Hindsight is not equal to foresight: The effect of outcome knowledge on judgment under uncertainty. *Journal of Experimental Psychology: Human Perception and Performance, 1,* 288–299.

Fish, L. S., New, R. S., & Van Cleave, N. J. (1992). Shared parenting in dual-income families. *American Journal of Orthopsychiatry, 62,* 83–92.

Fowlkes, M. R. (1987). The myth of merit and male professional careers: The roles of wives. In N. Gerstel & H. E. Gross (eds.), *Families and work* (pp. 347–360). Philadelphia: Temple University Press.

Fox, K. D., & Nickols, S. Y. (1983). The time crunch. *Journal of Family Issues, 4,* 61–82.

Fox, N. A., Kimmerly, N. L., & Schafer, W. D. (1991). Attachment to mother/attachment to father: A meta-analysis. *Child Development, 62,* 210–225.

Frankenhaeuser, M., Lundberg, U., & Mardberg, B. (1990). *The total workload of men and women as related to occupational level and number and age of children* (Report No. 726). Stockholm: Stockholm University.

Friedan, B. (1963). *The feminine mystique.* New York: W. W. Norton.

Gallup poll: Public opinion, the (1990). Wilmington, DE: Scholarly Resources.

—— (1993). Wilmington, DE: Scholarly Resources.

Garey, A. I. (1995). Constructing motherhood on the night shift: "Working mothers" as "stay-at-home moms." *Qualitative Sociology, 18,* 415–437.

Gecas, V., & Schwalbe, M. L. (1983). Beyond the looking-glass self: Social structure and efficacy-based self-esteem. *Social Psychology Quarterly, 46,* 77–88.

Geerken, M., & Gove, W. R. (1983). *At home and at work: The family's allocation of labor.* Beverly Hills: Sage Publications.

Geiger, B. (1996). *Fathers as primary caregivers.* Westport, CT: Greenwood Press.

Gerson, K. (1985). *Hard choices: How women decide about work, career, and motherhood.* Berkeley: University of California Press.

——— (1993). *No man's land: Men's changing commitments to family and work.* New York: Basic Books.

Gerstel, N., & Gross, H. (1984). *Commuter marriage: A study of work and family.* New York: Guilford Press.

——— (1995). Gender and families in the United States: The reality of economic dependence. In J. Freeman (ed.), *Women: A feminist perspective* (pp. 92–127). Mountainview, CA: Mayfield.

Gerstel, N., & McGonagle, K. (1998, June). Taking time off: Job leaves, the family and medical leave act, and gender. Paper presented at the Institute for Women's Policy Research Fifth Women's Conference, Washington, DC.

Glass, B. L. (1988). A rational choice model of wives' employment decisions. *Sociological Spectrum, 8,* 35–48.

Glass, J., & Fujimoto, T. (1994). Housework, paid work, and depression among husbands and wives. *Journal of Health and Social Behavior, 35,* 179–191.

Glick, D. (1997, May). Rooting for intelligence. *Newsweek* (special issue), 32.

Godwin, D. D. (1991). Spouses' time allocation to household work: A review and critique. *Lifestyles: Family and Economic Issues, 12,* 253–294.

Goode, W. J. (1982). Why men resist. In B. Thorne & M. Yalom (eds.), *Rethinking the family* (pp. 287–310). Boston: Northeastern University Press.

Goossens, F. A., & van IJzendoorn, M. H. (1990). Quality of infants' attachments to professional caregivers: Relation to infant-parent attachment and day-care characteristics. *Child Development, 61,* 832–837.

Greene, B. (1990). Sturdy bridges: The role of African-American mothers in the socialization of African-American children. In E. Cole and J. P. Knowles (eds.), *Motherhood: A feminist perspective* (pp. 205–225). New York: Haworth Press.

Greenstein, T. N. (1996). Gender ideology and perceptions of the fairness of the division of household labor: Effects on marital quality. *Social Forces, 74,* 1029–1041.

Griffore, R. J., & Phenice, L. A. (1996). Rules and television viewing. *Psychological Reports, 78,* 814.

Gronseth, E. (1978). Work sharing: A Norwegian example. In R. Rapoport, R. N. Rapoport, and J. M. Bumstead (eds.), *Working couples* (pp. 108–121). New York: Harper & Row.

Gunter, B. G., & Gunter, N. C. (1990). Domestic division of labor among working couples: Does androgyny make a difference? *Psychology of Women Quarterly, 14,* 355–370.

——— (1991). Inequities in household labor: Sex role orientation and the need for cleanliness and responsibility as predictors. *Journal of Social Behavior and Personality, 6,* 559–572.

Haas, L. (1981). Domestic role sharing in Sweden. *Journal of Marriage and the Family, 43,* 957–967.

——— (1982a). Determinants of role-sharing behavior: A study of egalitarian couples. *Sex Roles, 8,* 747–760.

——— (1982b). Parental sharing of childcare tasks in Sweden. *Journal of Family Issues, 3,* 389–412.

—— (1992). *Equal parenthood and social policy: A study of parental leave in Sweden.* Albany: State University of New York Press.

—— (1993). Nurturing fathers and working mothers. In J. C. Hood (ed.), *Men, work, and family* (pp. 238–261). Newbury Park, CA: Sage Publications.

Hammond, J. A., & Mahoney, C. W. (1983). Reward-cost balancing among women coalminers. *Sex Roles, 9,* 17–29.

Harlow, H. F. (1958). The nature of love. *American Psychologist, 13,* 678–685.

Harris, M. J., & Rosenthal, R. (1985). Mediation of interpersonal expectancy effects: 31 meta-analyses. *Psychological Bulletin, 97,* 363–386.

Hartrick, G. A. (1997). Women who are mothers: The experience of defining self. *Health Care for Women International, 18,* 263–277.

Hays, S. (1996). *The cultural contradictions of motherhood.* New Haven: Yale University Press.

Hersch, J., & Stratton, L. S. (1994). Housework, wages, and the division of housework time for employed spouses. *The American Economic Review, 84,* 120–125.

Hertz, R. (1986). *More equal than others: Men and women in dual-career marriages.* Berkeley: University of California Press.

—— (1987). Three careers: His, hers, and theirs. In N. Gerstel & H. E. Gross (eds.), *Families and work* (pp. 408–421). Philadelphia: Temple University Press.

Hertz, R., & Charlton, J. (1989). Making family under a shiftwork schedule: Air force security guards and their wives. *Social Problems, 36,* 491–507.

Hessing, M. (1993). Mothers' management of their combined workloads: Clerical work and household needs. *Canadian Review of Sociology and Anthropology, 30,* 37–63.

Hewlett, B. S. (1991). *Intimate fathers: The nature and context of Aka pygmy paternal infant care.* Ann Arbor: University of Michigan Press.

Hill, M. S. (1985). Patterns of time use. In F. T. Juster & F. P. Stafford (eds.), *Time, goods, and well-being* (pp. 133–176). University of Michigan: Survey Research Center, Institute for Social Research.

Hiller, D. V. (1984). Power dependence and division of family work. *Sex Roles, 10,* 1003–1019.

Hiller, D. V., & Philliber, W. W. (1986). The division of labor in contemporary marriage: Expectations, perceptions, and performance. *Social Problems, 33,* 191–201.

Hobbs, D. F. (1965). Parenthood as crisis: A third study. *Journal of Marriage and the Family, 27,* 367–372.

Hobbs, D. F., & Cole, S. P. (1976). Transition to parenthood: A decade replication. *Journal of Marriage and the Family, 38,* 723–731.

Hochschild, A. (with A. Machung) (1989). *The second shift.* New York: Avon Books.

Hochschild, A. (1997). *The time bind: When work becomes home and home becomes work.* New York: Metropolitan Books.

Hollingshead, A. B. (1975). *Four factor index of social status.* New Haven: Yale University Press.

Holmes, J. (1993). *John Bowlby and attachment theory.* London: Routledge.

Hood, J. C. (1983). *Becoming a two-job family.* New York: Praeger.

———— (1986). The provider role: Its meaning and measurement. *Journal of Marriage and the Family, 48,* 349–359.

Hossain, Z., & Roopnarine, J. L. (1993). Division of household labor and child care in dual-earner African-American families with infants. *Sex Roles, 29,* 571–583.

Huber, J., & Spitze, G. (1981). Wives' employment, household behaviors, and sex-role attitudes. *Social Forces, 60,* 150–169.

Huston, A. C., Wright, J. C., Rice, M. L., Kerkman, D., & St. Peters, M. (1990). Development of television viewing patterns in early childhood: A longitudinal investigation. *Developmental Psychology, 26,* 409–420.

Ishii-Kuntz, M., & Coltrane, S. (1992a). Predicting the sharing of household labor: Are parenting and housework distinct? *Sociological Perspectives, 35,* 629–647.

———— (1992b). Remarriage, stepparenting, and household labor. *Journal of Family Issues, 13,* 215–232.

Izraeli, D. N. (1994). Money matters: Spousal incomes and family/work relations among physician couples in Israel. *The Sociological Quarterly, 35,* 69–84.

Jackson, R. M. (1989). The reproduction of parenting. *American Sociological Review, 54,* 215–232.

Jacobs, D. L. (1994, October 9). Back from the mommy track. *New York Times,* sec. 3, pp. 1, 6–7.

James, W. (1890). *Principles of Psychology,* vol. 1. New York: Dover Publications.

John, D., Shelton, B. A., & Luschen, K. (1995). Race, ethnicity, gender, and perceptions of fairness. *Journal of Family Issues, 16,* 357–379.

Jones, C. L., & Heermann, J. A. (1992). Parental division of infant care: Contextual influences and infant characteristics. *Nursing Research, 41,* 228–234.

Jones, J. (1985). *Labor of love, labor of sorrow: Black women, work, and the family from slavery to the present.* New York: Basic Books.

Josephs, R. A., Markus, H. R., & Tafarodi, R. W. (1992). Gender and self-esteem. *Journal of Personality and Social Psychology, 63,* 391–402.

Jussim, L. (1986). Self-fulfilling prophecies: A theoretical and integrative review. *Psychological Review, 93,* 429–445.

Jussim, L., & Eccles, J. (1995). Naturally occurring interpersonal expectancies. In N. Eisenberg (ed.), *Review of personality and social psychology, vol. 15: Social development* (pp. 74–108). Thousand Oaks, CA: Sage Publications.

Kamo, Y. (1988). Determinants of household division of labor: Resources, power, and ideology. *Journal of Family Issues, 9,* 177–200.

Kaplan, E., & Granrose, C. S. (1993). Factors influencing women's decision to leave an organization following childbirth. *Employee Responsibilities and Rights Journal, 6,* 45–54.

Kelley, H. H., & Stahelski, A. J. (1970). Errors in perception of intentions in a mixed-motive game. *Journal of Experimental Social Psychology, 6,* 379–400.

Kessler, R. C., & McRae, J. A. (1981). Trends in the relationship between sex and psychological distress: 1957–1976. *American Sociological Review, 46,* 443–452.

———— (1982). The effect of wives' employment on the mental health of married men and women. *American Sociological Review, 47,* 216–227.

Kiesler, C. A. (1971). *The psychology of commitment.* Orlando: Academic Press.

Kim, K. C., Kim, H. C., & Hurh, W. M. (1979). Division of household tasks in Korean immigrant families in the United States. *International Journal of Sociology of the Family, 9,* 161–175.

King, L. A., & King, D. W. (1990). Abbreviated measures of sex-role egalitarian attitudes. *Sex Roles, 23,* 659–673.

Klaus, M. H., Jerauld, P., Kreger, N. C., McAlpine, W., Steffa, M., & Kennell, J. H. (1972). Maternal attachment: Importance of the first postpartum days. *New England Journal of Medicine, 286,* 460–463.

Klein, S. (1995, December 17). 2 clocks for one working woman. *New York Times,* sec. 3, p. 14.

Klemesrud, J. (1981, May 7). Conflicts of women with jobs. *New York Times,* pp. C1, C6–7.

——— (1983, January 19). Mothers who shift back from jobs to homemaking. *New York Times,* pp. C1, C10.

Komter, A. (1989). Hidden power in marriage. *Gender and Society, 3,* 187–216.

Kuhlthau, K., & Mason, K. O. (1996). Market child care versus care by relatives: Choices made by employed and nonemployed mothers. *Journal of Family Issues, 17,* 561–578.

LaRossa, R. (1977). *Conflict and power in marriage: Expecting the first child.* Beverly Hills: Sage Publications.

——— (1988). Fatherhood and social change. *Family Relations, 37,* 451–457.

LaRossa, R., & LaRossa, M. M. (1981). *Transition to parenthood: How infants change families.* Beverly Hills: Sage Publications.

Larson, R. W., Richards, M. H., & Perry-Jenkins, M. (1994). Divergent worlds: The daily emotional experience of mothers and fathers in the domestic and public spheres. *Journal of Personality and Social Psychology, 67,* 1034–1046.

Lee, R. A. (1983). Flexitime and conjugal roles. *Journal of Occupational Behavior, 4,* 297–315.

Leete-Guy, L., & Schor, J. B. (1992). *The great American time squeeze: Trends in work and leisure, 1969–1989.* Washington, DC: Economic Policy Institute.

Lein, L. (1979). Male participation in home life: Impact of social supports and breadwinner responsibility on the allocation of tasks. *The Family Coordinator, 28,* 489–495.

LeMasters, E. E. (1957). Parenthood as crisis. *Marriage and Family Living, 19,* 352–355.

Lennon, M. C. (1994). Women, work, and well-being: The importance of work conditions. *Journal of Health and Social Behavior, 35,* 235–247.

Lennon, M. C., & Rosenfield, S. (1994). Relative fairness and the division of housework: The importance of options. *American Journal of Sociology, 100,* 506–531.

Levant, R. F., Slattery, S. C., & Loiselle, J. E. (1987). Fathers' involvement in housework and child care with school-aged daughters. *Family Relations, 36,* 152–157.

Lewis, S. (1991). Motherhood and employment: The impact of social and organizational values. In A. Phoenix, A. Woollett, & E. Lloyd (eds.), *Motherhood: Meanings, practices, and ideologies* (pp. 195–215). London: Sage Publications.

Littman, H., Medendorp, S. V., & Goldfarb, J. (1994). The decision to breastfeed: The importance of father's approval. *Clinical Pediatrics, 33,* 214–219.

Loose, C. (1993, September 6). The price of going legal with child care. *Washington Post*, pp. A1, A8.

Lorber, J. (1994). *Paradoxes of gender*. New Haven: Yale University Press.

Maass, A., & Clark, R. D. (1984). The hidden impact of minorities: Fifteen years of minority influence research. *Psychological Bulletin, 95*, 428–450.

Mackie, M. (1983). The domestication of self: Gender comparisons of self-imagery and self-esteem. *Social Psychology Quarterly, 46*, 343–350.

Mahony, R. (1995). *Kidding ourselves: Breadwinning, babies, and bargaining power*. New York: Basic Books.

Mahtesian, C. (1995). The politics of nature's nurture. *Governing, 8*, 54.

Mainardi, P. (1993). The politics of housework. In A. M. Jaggar & P. S. Rothenburg (eds.), *Feminist frameworks: Alternative theoretical accounts of the relations between women and men* (pp. 19–23). New York: McGraw-Hill.

Major, B. (1988). Women and entitlement. *Women and Therapy, 6*, 3–19.

——— (1993). Gender, entitlement, and the distribution of family labor. *Journal of Social Issues, 49*, 141–159.

Marciano, T. D. (1986). Why are men unhappy in patriarchy? *Marriage and Family Review, 9*, 17–30.

Maret, E., & Finlay, B. (1984). The distribution of household labor among women in dual-earner families. *Journal of Marriage and the Family, 46*, 357–364.

Markham, W. T., & Pleck, H. (1986). Sex and willingness to move for occupational advancement: Some national sample results. *The Sociological Quarterly, 27*, 121–143.

Markus, H. (1987). The dynamic self-concept: A social psychological perspective. *Annual Review of Psychology, 38*, 299–337.

Martinez, G. A., & Nalezienski, J. P. (1981). 1980 update: The recent trend in breast-feeding. *Pediatrics, 67*, 260–263.

Marx, K. (1950). *Communist manifesto*. Chicago: Regency.

Mason, K. O., & Lu, Y. (1988). Attitudes toward women's familial roles: Changes in the United States, 1977–1985. *Gender and Society, 2*, 39–57.

McAllister, I. (1990). Gender and the household division of labor: Employment and earnings variations in Australia. *Work and Occupations, 17*, 79–99.

McCall, G. J. (1987). The structure, content, and dynamics of self: Continuities in the study of role identities. In K. Yardley & T. Honess (eds.), *Self and identity: Psychosocial perspectives* (pp. 133–145). Chichester, NY: John Wiley & Sons.

McDermid, S. M., Huston, T. L., & McHale, S. M. (1990). Changes in marriage associated with the transition to parenthood: Individual differences as a function of sex-role attitudes and changes in the division of household labor. *Journal of the American Family, 52*, 475–486.

McHale, S. M., & Crouter, A. C. (1992). You can't always get what you want: Incongruence between sex-role attitudes and family work roles and its implications for marriage. *Journal of Marriage and the Family, 54*, 537–547.

McHale, S. M., & Huston, T. L. (1984). Men and women as parents: Sex role orientations, employment, and parental roles with infants. *Child Development, 55*, 1349–1361.

McMahon, M. (1995). *Engendering motherhood: Identity and self-transformation in women's lives*. New York: Guilford Press.

McNulty, S. E., & Swann, W. B. (1994). Identity negotiation in roommate relationships: The self as architect and consequence of social reality. *Journal of Personality and Social Psychology, 67,* 1012–1023.

Mead, G. H. (1934). *Mind, self, and society from the standpoint of a social behaviorist.* Chicago: University of Chicago Press.

Meissner, M., Humphreys, E. W., Meis, S. M., & Scheu, W. J. (1975). No exit for wives: Sexual division of labour and the culmination of household demands. *Canadian Review of Sociology and Anthropology, 12,* 424–439.

Mellor, E. F. (1986). Shift work and flexitime: How prevalent are they? *Monthly Labor Review, 109,* 14–21.

Merton, R. K. (1948). The self-fulfilling prophecy. *Antioch Review, 8,* 193–210.

Miles, M. B., & Huberman, A. M. (1984). *Qualitative data analysis: A sourcebook of new methods.* Beverly Hills: Sage Publications.

Milk Diet, the: Breastfeeding May Take off Pregnancy Pounds (1994). *Prevention, 46,* 22.

Miller, D. T., & Turnbull, W. (1986). Expectancies in interpersonal processes. *Annual Review of Psychology, 37,* 233–256.

Miller, S. (1996). Questioning, resisting, acquiescing, balancing: New mothers' career reentry strategies. *Health Care for Women International, 17,* 109–131.

Mocan, H. N., Burchinal, M., Morris, J. R., & Helburn, S. W. (1995). Models of quality in center child care. In S. Helburn (ed.), *Cost, quality, and child outcomes in child care centers: Technical report* (pp. 279–304). Denver: Economics Department, University of Colorado at Denver, Center for Research in Economic and Social Policy.

Model, S. (1981). Housework by husbands: Determinants and implications. *Journal of Family Issues, 2,* 225–237.

Morrison, D. R., & Lichter, D. T. (1988). Family migration and female employment: The problem of underemployment among migrant married women. *Journal of Marriage and the Family, 50,* 161–172.

Morse, M. B. (1996). Nursing know-how. *Parents, 71,* 60–62.

Moscovici, S. (1985). Social influence and conformity. In G. Lindzey & E. Aronson (eds.), *Handbook of social psychology* (vol. 2, pp. 347–412). New York: Random House.

Moss, P., Bolland, G., Foxman, R., & Owen, C. (1987). The division of household work during the transition to parenthood. *Journal of Reproductive and Infant Psychology, 5,* 71–86.

Mothers' Survey (1996). Columbus: Abbott Laboratories, Ross Products Division.

Nelson, E. N. (1977). Women's work—housework alienation. *Humboldt Journal of Social Relations, 5,* 90–117.

Nemeth, C. J. (1986). Differential contributions of majority and minority influence. *Psychological Review, 93,* 23–32.

Newcomb, T. M. (1961). *The acquaintance process.* New York: Holt, Rinehart, and Winston.

NICHD Early Child Care Research Network (1996). Characteristics of infant child care: Factors contributing to positive caregiving. *Early Childhood Research Quarterly, 11,* 269–306.

——— (1997a, April). Cognitive and language performance over the first three years of life: Results from the NICHD Study of Early Child Care. Paper presented at the Society for Research in Child Development, Washington, DC.

——— (1997b). Familial factors associated with the characteristics of nonmaternal care for infants. *Journal of Marriage and the Family, 59,* 389–408.

——— (1997c). Infant child care and attachment security: Results of the NICHD Study of Early Child Care. *Child Development, 68,* 860–879.

——— (1998). Early child care and self-control, compliance, and problem behavior at 24 and 36 months. *Child Development, 69,* 1145–1170.

Nickols, S. Y., & Metzen, E. J. (1982). Impact of wife's employment upon husband's housework. *Journal of Family Issues, 3,* 199–216.

Nicola, J. S., & Hawkes, G. R. (1985). Marital satisfaction of dual-career couples: Does sharing increase happiness? *Journal of Social Behavior and Personality, 1,* 47–60.

Nielsen Media Research (1997, October). *American Audience Demographics, 1,* 11.

Nock, S. L., & Kingston, P. W. (1989). The division of leisure and work. *Social Science Quarterly, 70,* 24–39.

Nuttbrock, L., & Freudiger, P. (1991). Identity salience and motherhood: A test of Stryker's theory. *Social Psychology Quarterly, 54,* 146–157.

Off the Chest (1996). *Psychology Today, 29,* 15.

Okin, S. M. (1989). *Justice, gender, and the family.* New York: Basic Books.

Olson, J. E., Frieze, I. H., & Detlefsen, E. G. (1990). Having it all? Combining work and family in a male and a female profession. *Sex Roles, 23,* 515–533.

O'Neill, J. (1985). The trend in the male-female wage gap in the U.S. *Journal of Labor Economics, 3,* S91–S116.

Osmond, M. W., & Thorne, B. (1993). Feminist theories: The social construction of gender in families and society. In P. G. Boss, W. J. Doherty, R. LaRossa, W. R. Shumm, & S. K. Steinmetz (eds.), *Sourcebook of family theories and methods: A contextual approach* (pp. 591–623). New York: Plenum Press.

Papanek, H. (1973). Men, women, and work: Reflections on the two-person career. In J. Huber (ed.), *Changing women in a changing society* (pp. 90–110). Chicago: University of Chicago Press.

Parks, T. (1995). *An Italian education: The further adventures of an expatriate in Verona.* New York: Grove Press.

Perrucci, C. C., Potter, H. R., & Rhoads, D. L. (1978). Determinants of male family-role performance. *Psychology of Women Quarterly, 3,* 53–66.

Perry-Jenkins, M. (1988). Future directions for research on dual-earner families: A young professional's perspective. *Family Relations, 37,* 226–228.

Perry-Jenkins, M., & Crouter, A. C. (1990). Men's provider-role attitudes: Implications for household work and marital satisfaction. *Journal of Family Issues, 11,* 136–156.

Perry-Jenkins, M., Seery, B., & Crouter, A. C. (1992). Linkages between women's provider-role attitudes, psychological well-being, and family relationships. *Psychology of Women Quarterly, 16,* 311–329.

Peters, J. K. (1997). *When mothers work: Loving our children without sacrificing ourselves.* Reading, MA: Addison-Wesley.

Peterson, R. R., & Gerson, K. (1992). Determinants of responsibility for child care arrangements among dual-earner couples. *Journal of Marriage and the Family, 54*, 527–536.

Phoenix, A., & Woollett, A. (1991). Motherhood: Social construction, politics, and psychology. In A. Phoenix, A. Woollett, & E. Lloyd (eds.), *Motherhood: Meanings, practices, and ideologies* (pp. 13–27). Newbury Park, CA: Sage Publications.

Pietromonaco, P. R., Manis, J., & Markus, H. (1987). The relationship of employment to self-perception and well-being in women: A cognitive analysis. *Sex Roles, 17*, 467–477.

Piotrkowski, C. S., & Repetti, R. L. (1984). Dual-earner families. *Marriage and Family Review, 7*, 99–124.

Pleck, J. H. (1979). Men's family work: Three perspectives and some new data. *The Family Coordinator, 28*, 481–488.

Polachek, S. W. (1975). Discontinuous labor force participation and its effect on women's market earnings. In C. B. Lloyd (ed.), *Sex, discrimination, and the division of labor* (pp. 90–124). New York: Columbia University Press.

Polatnick, M. R. (1984). Why men don't rear children: A power analysis. In J. Trebilcot (ed.), *Mothering: Essays in feminist theory* (pp. 21–40). Totowa, NJ: Rowman & Allanheld.

Poloma, M. M., & Garland, T. N. (1971). The married professional woman: A study in the tolerance of domestication. *Journal of Marriage and the Family, 33*, 531–540.

Potuchek, J. L. (1992). Employed wives' orientations to breadwinning: A gender theory analysis. *Journal of Marriage and the Family, 54*, 548–558.

——— (1997). *Who supports the family? Gender and breadwinning in dual-earner marriages.* Stanford: Stanford University Press.

Presser, H. B. (1988). Shift work and child care among young dual-earner American parents. *Journal of Marriage and the Family, 50*, 133–148.

Pruett, K. D. (1987). *The nurturing father: Journey toward the complete man.* New York: Warner Books.

Pryor, K., & Pryor, G. (1991). *Nursing your baby.* New York: Pocket Books.

PsycINFO (1995). On-line: American Psychological Association.

Pyke, K., & Coltrane, S. (1996). Entitlement, obligation, and gratitude in family work. *Journal of Family Issues, 17*, 60–82.

Quandt, S. A. (1986). Patterns of variation in breast-feeding behaviors. *Social Science and Medicine, 23*, 445–453.

Quick, B. (1997). Breast milk: It does a body good. *Ms., 7*, 32–35.

Rachlin, V. C. (1987). Fair vs. equal role relations in dual-career and dual-earner families: Implications for family interventions. *Family Relations, 36*, 187–192.

Radin, N. (1981). Childrearing fathers in intact families, I: Some antecedents and consequences. *Merrill-Palmer Quarterly, 27*, 489–544.

——— (1982). Primary caregiving and role-sharing fathers. In M. E. Lamb (ed.), *Nontraditional families: Parenting and child development* (pp. 173–204). Hillsdale, NJ: Lawrence Erlbaum Associates.

Radin, N., & Goldsmith, R. (1985). Caregiving fathers of preschoolers: Four years later. *Merrill-Palmer Quarterly, 31*, 375–383.

Radin, N., & Harold-Goldsmith, R. (1989). The involvement of selected unemployed and employed men with their children. *Child Development, 60,* 454–459.

Radin, N., & Sagi, A. (1982). Childrearing fathers in intact families, II: Israel and the USA. *Merrill-Palmer Quarterly, 28,* 111–136.

Reiss, D. (1981). *The family's construction of reality.* Cambridge: Harvard University Press.

Rexroat, C., & Shehan, C. (1987). The family life cycle and spouses' time in housework. *Journal of Marriage and the Family, 49,* 737–750.

Rich, A. (1986). *Of woman born: Motherhood as an experience and institution.* New York: W. W. Norton.

Richardson, B. L. (1988, April 20). Professional women do go home again. *New York Times,* pp. C1, C10.

Riley, D. (1990). Network influences on father involvement in childrearing. In M. Cochran, M. Larner, D. Riley, L. Gunnarsson, & C. R. Henderson (eds.), *Extending families: The social networks of parents and their children* (pp. 131–153). Cambridge: Cambridge University Press.

Rimer, S. (1988, September 23). Sequencers: Putting careers on hold. *New York Times,* p. A21.

Risman, B. J. (1986). Can men "mother"? Life as a single father. *Family Relations, 35,* 95–102.

Risman, B. J., & Johnson-Sumerford, D. (1998). Doing it fairly: A study of postgender marriages. *Journal of Marriage and the Family, 60,* 23–40.

Risman, B. J., & Myers, K. (1997). As the twig is bent: Children reared in feminist households. *Qualitative Sociology, 20,* 229–252.

Robinson, J. P., Andreyenkov, V. G., & Patrushev, V. D. (1989). *The rhythm of everyday life: How Soviet and American citizens use time.* Boulder: Westview Press.

Roby, P. A. (1975). Shared parenting: Perspectives from other nations. *School Review, 83,* 415–431.

Rosen, E. I. (1987). *Bitter choices: Blue-collar women in and out of work.* Chicago: University of Chicago Press.

Rosen, K. S., & Rothbaum, F. (1993). Quality of parental caregiving and security of attachment. *Developmental Psychology, 29,* 358–367.

Rosenblith, J. F., & Sims-Knight, J. E. (1985). *In the beginning: Development in the first two years of life.* Monterey, CA: Brooks/Cole Publishing Co.

Rosenfield, S. (1989). The effects of women's employment: Personal control and sex differences in mental health. *Journal of Health and Social Behavior, 30,* 77–91.

Rosenthal, R., & Jacobson, L. (1968). *Pygmalion in the classroom: Teacher expectation and pupils' intellectual development.* New York: Holt, Rinehart, & Winston.

Ross, C. E. (1987). The division of labor at home. *Social Forces, 65,* 816–833.

Ross, C. E., Mirowsky, J., & Huber, J. (1983). Dividing work, sharing work, and in-between: Marriage patterns and depression. *American Sociological Review, 48,* 809–823.

Rossi, A. (1965). Barriers to the career choice of engineering, medicine, or science among American women. In J. A. Mattfeld & C. G. Van Aken (eds.), *Women and the scientific professions: The M.I.T. symposium on American women in science and engineering* (pp. 51–127). Cambridge: MIT Press.

Rubin, L. B. (1969). *Worlds of pain: Life in the working-class family*. New York: Basic Books.

Ruble, D. N., Fleming, A. S., Hackel, L. S., & Stangor, C. (1988). Changes in the marital relationship during the transition to first time motherhood: Effects of violated expectations concerning division of household labor. *Journal of Personality and Social Psychology, 55*, 78–87.

Russell, C. S. (1974). Transition to parenthood: Problems and gratifications. *Journal of Marriage and the Family, 36*, 294–302.

Russell, G. (1982a). Highly participant Australian fathers: Some preliminary findings. *Merrill-Palmer Quarterly, 28*, 137–156.

—— (1982b). Shared-caregiving families: An Australian study. In M. E. Lamb (ed.), *Nontraditional families: Parenting and child development* (pp. 139–171). Hillsdale, NJ: Lawrence Erlbaum Associates.

—— (1989). Work/family patterns and couple relationships in shared caregiving families. *Social Behaviour, 4*, 265–283.

Russo, N. F. (1976). The motherhood mandate. *Journal of Social Issues, 32*, 143–153.

Ryan, A. S., & Martinez, G. A. (1989). Breast-feeding and the working mother: A profile. *Pediatrics, 83*, 524–531.

Safilios-Rothschild, C. (1976). A macro- and micro-examination of family power and love: An exchange model. *Journal of Marriage and the Family, 38*, 355–362.

Sagi, A. (1982). Antecedents and consequences of various degrees of paternal involvement in child rearing: The Israeli project. In M. E. Lamb (ed.), *Nontraditional families: Parenting and child development* (pp. 205–232). Hillsdale, NJ: Lawrence Erlbaum Associates.

Sanchez, L. (1993). Women's power and the gendered division of domestic labor in the Third World. *Gender and Society, 7*, 434–459.

—— (1994). Gender, labor allocations, and the psychology of entitlement within the home. *Social Forces, 73*, 533–553.

Sanchez, L., & Kane, E. W. (1996). Women's and men's constructions of perceptions of housework fairness. *Journal of Family Issues, 17*, 358–387.

Sanik, M. M. (1990). Parents' time use: A 1967–1986 comparison. *Lifestyles: Family and Economic Issues, 11*, 299–316.

Schacter, D. L. (1996). *Searching for memory: The brain, the mind, and the past*. New York: Basic Books.

Schacter, S. (1951). Deviation, rejection, and communication. *Journal of Abnormal and Social Psychology, 46*, 190–207.

Schneer, J. A., & Reitman, F. (1990). Effects of employment gaps on the careers of M.B.A.'s: More damaging for men than for women? *The Academy of Management Journal, 23*, 391–406.

Schor, J. B. (1991). *The overworked American: The unexpected decline of leisure*. New York: Basic Books.

Schultz, P. W., Oskamp, S., & Mainieri, T. (1995). Who recycles and when? A review of personal and situational factors. *Journal of Environmental Psychology, 15,* 105–121.

Schwartz, F. N. (1989). Management women and the new facts of life. *Harvard Businesss Review, January–February,* 65–75.

Schwartz, P. (1994). *Love between equals: How peer marriage really works.* New York: Free Press.

Seccombe, K. (1986). The effects of occupational conditions upon the division of household labor: An application of Kohn's theory. *Journal of Marriage and the Family, 48,* 839–848.

Seidel, J., Kjolseth, R., & Seymour, E. (1988). The Ethnograph (version 3.0). Computer software. Corvallis, OR: Qualis Research Associates.

Seifer, R., & Schiller, M. (1995). The role of parenting sensitivity, infant temperament, and dyadic interaction in attachment theory and assessment. In E. Waters, B. E. Vaughn, G. Posada, & K. Kondo-Ikemura (eds.), *Caregiving, cultural, and cognitive perspectives on secure-base behavior and working models: New growing points of attachment theory and research.* (Monographs of the Society for Research in Child Development, 60) (pp. 146–174). Chicago: Society for Research in Child Development.

Shamir, B. (1986). Unemployment and household division of labor. *Journal of Marriage and the Family, 48,* 195–206.

Shauman, K. A., & Xie, Y. (1996). Geographic mobility of scientists: Sex differences and family constraints. *Demography, 33,* 455–468.

Shelton, B. A. (1990). The distribution of household tasks: Does wife's employment status make a difference? *Journal of Family Issues, 11,* 115–135.

——— (1992). *Women, men, and time: Gender differences in paid work, housework, and leisure.* Westport, CT: Greenwood Press.

Shelton, B. A., & Firestone, J. (1988). Time constraints on men and women: Linking household labor to paid labor. *Sociology and Social Research, 72,* 102–105.

Shelton, B. A., & John, D. (1993). Ethnicity, race, and difference: A comparison of White, Black, and Hispanic men's household labor time. In J. Hood (ed.), *Men, work, and family* (pp. 131–150). Newbury Park, CA: Sage Publications.

Sherman, S. J., & Gorkin, L. (1980). Attitude bolstering when behavior is inconsistent with central attitudes. *Journal of Experimental Social Psychology, 16,* 388–403.

Shihadeh, E. S. (1991). The prevalence of husband-centered migration: Employment consequences for married mothers. *Journal of Marriage and the Family, 53,* 432–444.

Shrauger, J. S., & Schoeneman, T. J. (1979). Symbolic interactionist view of self-concept: Through the looking glass darkly. *Psychological Bulletin, 86,* 549–573.

Silverman, A. B. (1987, March 22). A study of working mothers. *New York Times,* sec. 11WC, p. 1.

Silverstein, L. B. (1996). Fathering is a feminist issue. *Psychology of Women Quarterly, 20,* 3–37.

Simon, B. L. (1990). Impact of shift work on individuals and families. *Families in Society: The Journal of Contemporary Human Services, 71,* 342–348.

Singer, L. M., Brodzinsky, D. M., Ramsay, D., Steir, M., & Waters, E. (1985).

Mother-infant attachment in adoptive families. *Child Development, 56,* 1543–1551.

Singer, M. (1996, February 26 & March 4). Mom overboard! *New Yorker,* 65–74.

Skolnick, A. S. (1991). *Embattled paradise: The American family in an age of uncertainty.* New York: Basic Books.

Skrypnek, B. J., & Snyder, M. (1982). On the self-perpetuating nature of stereotypes about men and women. *Journal of Experimental Social Psychology, 18,* 277–291.

Smith, V. (1983). The circular trap: Women and part-time work. *Berkeley Journal of Sociology, 28,* 1–17.

Snyder, M. (1984). When belief creates reality. In L. Berkowitz (ed.), *Advances in experimental social psychology,* vol. 18 (pp. 247–305). Orlando: Academic Press.

Snyder, M., Tanke, E. D., & Berscheid, E. (1977). Social perception and interpersonal behavior: On the self-fulfilling nature of social stereotypes. *Journal of Personality and Social Psychology, 35,* 656–666.

Spanier, G. B. (1976). Measuring dyadic adjustment: New scales for assessing the quality of marriage and similar dyads. *Journal of Marriage and the Family, 38,* 15–28.

Spitze, G. (1986a). Family migration largely unresponsive to wife's employment (across age groups). *Sociology and Social Research, 70,* 231–234.

———— (1986b). The division of task responsibility in U.S. households: Longitudinal adjustments to change. *Social Forces, 64,* 689–701.

Statham, A., Vaughan, S., & Houseknecht, S. K. (1987). The professional involvement of highly educated women: The impact of the family. *The Sociological Quarterly, 28,* 119–133.

Steil, J. (1997). *Marital equality: Its relationship to the well-being of husbands and wives.* Thousand Oaks, CA: Sage Publications.

Steil, J. M., & Turetsky, B. A. (1987a). Marital influence levels and symptomatology among wives. In F. Crosby (ed.), *Spouse, parent, worker: On gender and multiple roles* (pp. 74–89). New Haven: Yale University Press.

———— (1987b). Is equal better? The relationship between marital equality and psychological symptomatology. In S. Oskamp (ed.), *Family processes and problems: Social psychological aspects* (pp. 73–97). Newbury Park, CA: Sage Publications.

Steil, J. M., & Weltman, K. (1991). Marital inequality: The importance of resources, personal attributes, and social norms on career valuing and domestic influence. *Sex Roles, 24,* 161–179.

Stewart, A. J. (1982). The course of individual adaptation to life changes. *Journal of Personality and Social Psychology, 42,* 1100–1113.

Stewart, M. B., & Greenhalgh, C. A. (1984). Work history and the occupational attainment of women. *Economic Journal, 94,* 493–519.

Stryker, S. (1968). Identity salience and role performance: The relevance of symbolic interaction theory for family research. *Journal of Marriage and the Family, 30,* 558–565.

———— (1987). Identity theory: Developments and extensions. In K. Yardley & T.

Honess (eds.), *Self and identity: Psychosocial perspectives* (pp. 89–103). New York: John Wiley & Sons.

Stryker, S., & Serpe, R. T. (1994). Identity salience and psychological centrality: Equivalent, overlapping, or complementary concepts? *Social Psychology Quarterly, 57,* 16–35.

Stuart-Macadam, P. (1995). Biocultural perspectives on breastfeeding. In P. Stuart-Macadam and K. A. Dettwyler (eds.), *Breastfeeding: Biocultural perspectives* (pp. 1–37). New York: Aldine de Gruyter.

Suitor, J. J. (1991). Marital quality and satisfaction with the division of household labor across the family life cycle. *Journal of Marriage and the Family, 53,* 221–230.

Swann, W. B. (1987). Identity negotiation: Where two roads meet. *Journal of Personality and Social Psychology, 53,* 1038–1051.

—— (1997). The trouble with change: Self-verification and allegiance to the self. *Psychological Science, 8,* 177–180.

Tavecchio, L. W. C., van IJzendoorn, M. H., Goossens, F. A., & Vergeer, M. M. (1984). The division of labor in Dutch families with preschool children. *Journal of Marriage and the Family, 46,* 231–242.

Tesch, R. (1990). *Qualitative research: Analysis types and software tools.* New York: Falmer Press.

Tesser, A. (1988). Toward a self-evaluation maintenance model of social behavior. *Advances in Experimental Social Psychology, 21,* 181–227.

Thompson, L. (1991). Family work: Women's sense of fairness. *Journal of Family Issues, 12,* 181–196.

—— (1993). Conceptualizing gender in marriage: The case of marital care. *Journal of Marriage and the Family, 55,* 557–569.

Thompson, L., & Walker, A. J. (1989). Gender in families: Women and men in marriage, work, and parenthood. *Journal of Marriage and the Family, 51,* 845–871.

Thurer, S. (1994). *The myths of motherhood: How culture reinvents the good mother.* Boston: Houghton Mifflin.

U.S. Bureau of Labor Statistics (1989). *Handbook of labor statistics* (table 57). Washington, DC: U.S. Government Printing Office.

—— (1997). Current Population Survey, table 6 of 1997 news release. On-line: http://www.bls.gov/news.release/famee.t0c.htm.

—— (1997, May). *Workers on flexible and shift schedules* (Current Population Survey, unpublished data). Washington, DC.

U.S. Bureau of the Census (1990). The 1990 Census. Washington, DC: U.S. Government Printing Office.

—— (1993). *Money income of households, families, and persons in the United States: 1992* (Current Population Reports, series P-60, no. 184). Washington, DC: U.S. Government Printing Office.

—— (1995). *Statistical Abstract of the United States, 115th edition* (p. 481, table 746). Washington, DC: U.S. Government Printing Office.

—— (1997). *Statistical Abstract of the United States, 117th edition* (p. 81, table 103). Washington, DC: U.S. Government Printing Office.

Van IJzendoorn, M. H., & De Wolff, M. S. (1997). In search of the absent father—

meta-analyses of infant-father attachment: A rejoinder to our discussants. *Child Development, 68,* 604–609.

Waller, W. (1951). *The family: A dynamic interpretation.* New York: Dryden Press.

Wallston, B. S., Foster, M., & Berger, M. (1978). I will follow him: Myth, reality, or forced choice—job-seeking experiences of dual-career couples. *Psychology of Women Quarterly, 3,* 9–21.

Welles-Nystrom, B., New, R., & Richman, A. (1994). The "Good Mother": A comparative study of Swedish, Italian, and American maternal behavior and goals. *Scandinavian Journal of Caring Sciences, 8,* 81–86.

West, C., & Zimmerman, H. (1987). Doing gender. *Gender and Society, 1,* 125–151.

Wilkie, J. R. (1993). Changes in U.S. men's attitudes toward the family provider role, 1972–1989. *Gender and Society, 7,* 261–279.

Williams, E. L., & Hammer, L. D. (1995). Breastfeeding attitudes and knowledge of pediatricians-in-training. *American Journal of Preventive Medicine, 11,* 26–33.

Williams, R. D. (1995). Breast-feeding: Best bet for babies. *FDA Consumer, 29,* 19–23.

Wilson, M. N., Tolson, T. F., Hinton, I. D., & Kiernan, M. (1990). Flexibility and sharing of childcare duties in Black families. *Sex Roles, 22,* 409–425.

Wright, E. O., Shire, K., Hwang, S., Dolan, M., & Baxter, J. (1992). Non-effects of class on the gender division of labor in the home: A comparative study of Sweden and the United States. *Gender and Society, 6,* 252–282.

Yao, E. L. (1987). Variables for household division of labor as revealed by Chinese women in Taiwan. *International Journal of Sociology of the Family, 17,* 67–86.

Yen, S. S. C. (1990). Clinical endocrinology of reproduction. In E-E. Baulieu & P. A. Kelly (eds.), *Hormones: From molecules to disease* (pp. 445–481). New York: Chapman and Hall.

Yogev, S. (1981). Do professional women have egalitarian marital relationships? *Journal of Marriage and the Family, 43,* 865–871.

Young, M., & Willmott, P. (1973). *The symmetrical family.* New York: Pantheon.

Yu, L. C., Wang, M. Q., Kaltreider, L., & Chien, Y. Y. (1993). The impact of family migration and family life cycle on the employment status of married, college-educated women. *Work and Occupations, 20,* 233–246.

Zavella, P. (1987). *Women's work and Chicano families: Cannery workers of the Santa Clara Valley.* Ithaca: Cornell University Press.

Zick, C. D., & McCullough, J. L. (1991). Trends in married couples' time use: Evidence from 1977–78 and 1987–88. *Sex Roles, 24,* 459–487.

Acknowledgments

No one has ever had more help writing a book. Although other authors may claim out of politeness that they couldn't have done it without the help, I'm not kidding. It is one of the hardest things I have ever done. Words seem woefully inadequate to express my enormous gratitude to all the people who have helped me.

First, I want to thank the three hundred men and women I interviewed for the study. I wish I could acknowledge each of you by name and include your photographs in the book. Interviewing you was one of the most profoundly enriching experiences of my life. I learned what I needed to write this book, but I also learned a lot more from you about parenting, love, generosity, and hospitality. Special thanks to the mother who got my car out when it was stuck in the mud, to the father who met me at the bottom of the steep hill near his house so I wouldn't have to drive up, and to all of you who fed me.

The National Science Foundation supported the research with grant #BSN-9108826. Mount Holyoke supported it in the early stages with a faculty grant award.

Many people helped me along the way in my career, even before this book was a gleam in my eye, enabling me to get to the point of writing it. There's a special place in my heart for Shirley Weitz, who asked me to write a book review for *Sex Roles* when I was just starting out, giving me that first all-important publication; for Peter Hwang, who typed my Ph.D. dissertation in the old days before word-processing; for Diane Ruble, who invited me to work with her during my pre-tenure sabbatical, giving my career a critical boost at a key moment; and for Janice Steil, who has been a steadfast friend and encouraging colleague since graduate school, stimulating me with thought-provoking conversation, and always making me feel smarter than I felt before talking to her.

I am fortunate to teach at the oldest women's college in the country, Mount Holyoke College, which has an abundance of bright, eager students interested in why women are still doing a majority of the work at home. Kristen Bannish, Jill Cholette, Emily Crooks, Bianca Erickson, Alison Deal, Kristen Deshaies, Natasha Domina, Randy Dorman, Christine Greipp, Tara Kirkpatrick, Sharon Kaufman, Elizabeth Knaplund, Kim Kretzer, Jen Lozy, Jean Martin, Dante Payne, Gale Pearce, Lauren Peterson, Mia Robinson, Josipa Roksa, Laura Servis, Amy Strano, Jean Talbot, Phyllis Wentworth, Candace White, and Lynn Wolfson worked in my lab as research assistants or research students. Laurie Shannon and Deb Donnelly also worked in the lab. They all contributed in myriad ways: coding data, interviewing participants by phone, finding journal articles, analyzing transcripts, conducting statistical analyses, locating obscure information, reading drafts of book chapters and related articles, and asking the important questions. Their energy, enthusiasm, and curiosity made it a lot more fun to do the research and to write the book. Alison Deal, Natasha Domina, Gale Pearce, and Laura Servis, also wrote honors theses based on data from my study that shaped my thinking on the topics they studied. Susan Trumbetta developed the telephone interview. Josipa Roksa's meticulous work in ferreting out errors and helping me put the final manuscript together was extraordinary.

One of the best decisions I've ever made was to hire Susan Saxon as my professional research assistant for the NSF project. She did an outstanding job of assisting me in every aspect of the research. She managed the innumerable details of keeping the ESP (equally shared parenting) lab running, all the while inspiring the students to perform at the very highest level. Her excellent interpersonal and intellectual skills added immeasurably to the quality of the research, and helped me keep my sanity in the process.

Bryan Goodwin, reference librarian at Mount Holyoke, dazzled me with his wizardry in obtaining all the obscure information I needed, doing so graciously without ever complaining about my endless requests. Candace Schuller, assistant director of career counseling, cleverly came up with comparable careers I could use to disguise my participants. Cindy Legare, the superwoman of computers, calmly and expertly dealt with every software and hardware problem along the way. Joan Dwight transcribed approximately six hundred hours of audiotapes. Starting at six in the morning every day for several months, she worked in my office before her real job started. Her cheerful demeanor when I arrived, after she had already been typing for several hours, was even more astonishing than her hundred-words-a-minute typing speed. Nancy Clemente of Harvard University Press copyedited the manuscript. Her skilled, scrupulous work saved me from embarassing lapses in grammar and saved the reader from reading eight words when one would suffice.

I was shameless in asking friends and colleagues to read the book and give me comments. I always wished they would just say the book was great as it was and leave it at that, but I'm grateful now that they respected me enough to tell the truth. I probably should have taken more of their suggestions.

Barbara Burns, Faye Crosby, Karen Hollis, Judy Kroll, Paula Matthews, Maureen Perry-Jenkins, Gail Robinson, Susan Rosen, Jenny Spencer, Juliet Schor, Bob Shilkret, and Liz Tobin all read parts of the book and gave advice, suggestions, criticisms, and encouragement. Jenny Spencer told me how to fix the original introduction, which no one had liked. Karen Hollis provided boundless sympathy and spent hours on end fussing with me over awkward phrasing. Who but my "most valuable colleague" and good friend, Karen, would be willing to discuss one particularly troublesome sentence for two hours? Barbara Burns cheered me on throughout the work, buoying up my flagging spirits and insisting we celebrate each small achievement along the way.

Robert Zussman read my first and misguided draft of the entire manuscript and helped immensely by telling me what I was trying to say. Mark Breibart, Sheryl White, Robert Moyer, and Lynn Rice read a later version. All of them gave me detailed, insightful, and useful comments. I am honored by and extremely thankful for their effort and care.

Naomi Gerstel and Ed Royce, two of my favorite sociologists, gave me indispensable guidance. I am deeply touched by the extraordinary amount of time they took away from their own work to help me with mine. Both read the first complete draft of the manuscript and spent countless hours discussing it with me. I lost track of how many revisions of chapters I have since asked Ed to read, but I have not forgotten that he always did so quickly and graciously. His insightful suggestions, delivered with the utmost gentleness and tact, aided me enormously.

From Naomi, I have learned and unlearned more about "the family" than from anyone else. In addition to her helpful comments on the first and later drafts of the book, my work has benefited over many years from her keen, unconventional intellect. She never fails to raise the provocative question that makes me think more deeply about an issue. Moreover, her excellent book, *Commuter Marriage,* beautifully illustrated the advantages of qualitative research and encouraged me to use it in my own work. Naomi's enthusiastic endorsement of my penultimate draft gave me the confidence to keep going. As grateful as I am for her intellectual help, I am even more grateful for her loving friendship.

I spared a few of my oldest and closest friends my requests for comments because I was afraid I couldn't be objective about them. Nevertheless, the love and support of Virginia Brabender, Cindy Cohen, Beth Hay, and Hedda Orkin throughout our many years of friendship have sustained me in profound ways. I couldn't have written the book without their faith in me and their tolerance for my preoccupation with this project.

When I count my lucky stars, three shine especially brightly: Janet Crosby, Jennie McDonald, and Elizabeth Knoll. Janet Crosby, administrative assistant of the Psychology and Education Department at Mount Holyoke, performed innumerable tasks associated with the project with consummate professionalism and skill. Her unflappable temperament, empathy, and great wisdom helped me weather the inevitable ups and downs of this process. Jennie McDonald, world's greatest literary agent, showed me how to speak to people's hearts as well as their minds without compromising the complexity of ideas. She guided me and protected my ego through the ins and outs of book publishing. I often wish I could have her as my agent in life, not just in publishing. Elizabeth Knoll, my brilliant, witty, and compassionate editor at Harvard University Press, lavished attention on the book. Her astute comments on draft after draft, patient answers to my continual questions, and good-natured humor in the face of my worries have been priceless gifts. Her own elegant writing (even in email messages) tempted me to plagiarize and inspired me to write better myself. Getting to know her has been one of the great unexpected bonuses of writing this book.

It takes a husband to support a wife's career (see Chapter 7), and I have just such a husband. Jerry Epstein has supported me in so many ways that it would take another book to tell them all. From the time he sent me a telegram telling me to "knock 'em dead" when I interviewed for a tenure-track position in my department at Mount Holyoke, to his writing a song for the same department when I became chair fifteen years later, he has done more to help me than anyone could reasonably expect. He read every word in the book many times, and dropped everything when I needed some quick feedback. Virtually all of our long car trips while I wrote the book were devoted to discussions of it. He helped me clarify arguments, come up with chapter titles, and tone the book down when I got carried away.

People often asked me while I worked on the book, "So, does your husband share parenting equally?" Yes, he does. However, he doesn't need my thanks for that. The joy of knowing our unique, sweet, humorous, lovable Eli as well as I do is more than enough reward for his parenting. He does need and deserve my thanks, though, for his willingness to shoulder more than his share of the drudge work of the household while I wrote this book. I can't say he never complained, but, despite knowing I would never pay him back, he did it anyway. For that act of love, and for loving me even after knowing the worst, I am more grateful than he knows. Finally, Jerry gets the credit for thinking up what I believe is a brilliant title: *Halving It All*.

Last, but far from least, I thank my wonderful child, Eli Epstein-Deutsch. He spurred me on when I got discouraged with the sweet refrain, "Mom, it is going to be a bestseller!" For his love, faith in me, and for his mere existence, I am thankful every day. I feel like the luckiest person on earth because I got to be his mother.

Index

Academic achievement, 221
Adoption, 114, 219
Adult-to-child ratio, 44
Alternating-responsibility households, 2, 19, 24, 30, 76
Alternating-shift households, 7, 93; careers/employment choices, 134–135; dual-earner households as, 169–171, 186–189; unequal parenting in, 171–173; gender roles in, 172–173, 193–194; financial circumstances and, 173–174, 176–177, 180, 182, 184–186, 187–189, 194; daycare choices and, 174–178; shared values and time together, 176–178; change and resistance to change, 178–183; father/child relationship in, 182, 230; men as breadwinner/provider, 184–186; mother as primary parent, 190–193; egalitarian ideals and, 194
Ambition: differences in, 45, 47, 57–58, 68–69, 69; compromise of, 101, 202–205; egalitarian ideals and, 154–155; of women, 155, 196–199, 221–222; identity issues and, 213–214, 216
Ambivalence, 13, 224; in fight for equality, 70, 72, 73, 101, 224; of men, 92; toward careers/employment choices, 131; about traditional family structure, 144, 154, 163
Anger, 13, 21, 23–24; over unequal parent-

ing, 54–55, 57, 66–68, 81–82; at self, 70–71; job-related, 180

Babysitters, 34, 50, 144, 159. See also Daycare
Barry and Rosemary, 100–101, 196, 198, 200, 204–205, 235
Beere-King Sex Role Egalitarianism Scale, 243
Ben and Judy (husband's lack of support for wife's career), 135–138, 155–156
Benita and Clifford, 163–164
Bernice and Kyle, 102–103, 105, 111, 119; professional life identity issues and, 198–200
Beverly and Dennis, 45, 46
Bias. See Gender inequality: bias as
Biology, 107; as factor in parenting abilities, 108, 115, 118–119, 121–125, 234; gender stereotypes and, 122, 124
Blame. See Criticism
Bonding. See Father/child relationship; Mother/child relationship
Breadwinner/provider, 104, 184–186; women as, 3, 96–97, 98, 134, 136, 185, 188, 219; men as, 10–11, 27, 29, 32, 36, 71, 91, 104, 132, 138, 144, 145, 155, 163–164, 193, 212; gender roles and, 181–182; in alternating-shift households, 184–186. See also Careers/employment choices; Labor, workforce

husband/wife relationship affected by,
56, 229; changes in, 72, 84, 113, 123,
145–148, 158, 167; unchanging standards and, 78; strategies of resistance,
84; social pressures and, 106–107, 162,
224; breastfeeding and, 115–118; myth
of women's superiority and, 122–125;
careers/employment choices, 129–132,
134; job-related factors, 142–145, 148,
149, 151; as practical choice, 149, 167;
in alternating-shift households, 171–
173; move toward, from equal parenting, 212, 219–222. *See also* Egalitarian
ideals, failure of; Explanation of un-

equal parenting; Supermom and
slacker syndrome; Traditional families

Victims, women as, 48

Wage rates, 185. *See also* Equal wages
Women's movement. *See* Feminism/femi-
nist ideology
Workplace: flexibility, 63, 126, 135, 141–
142, 161, 196, 204, 224, 233, 236; double
standard at, 87–89, 100–101; sex discrimination in, 148. *See also* Ca-
reers/employment choices; Professional
life